WITHDRAWN

D1179430

Sustainable Development in Mineral Economies

Sustainable Development in Mineral Economies

Richard M. Auty and Raymond F. Mikesell

CLARENDON PRESS · OXFORD
1998

Oxford University Press, Great Clarendon Street, Oxford OX2 6DP
Oxford New York
Athens Auckland Bangkok Bogota Buenos Aires Calcutta
Cape Town Chennai Dar es Salaam Delhi Florence Hong Kong Istanbul
Karachi Kuala Lumpur Madrid Melbourne Mexico City Mumbai
Nairobi Paris São Paolo Singapore Taipei Tokyo Toronto Warsaw
and associated companies in Berlin Ibadan

Oxford is a registered trade mark of Oxford University Press

Published in the United States
by Oxford University Press Inc., New York

British Library Cataloguing in Publication Data
Data available

Library of Congress Cataloging-in-Publication Data
Auty, R. M. (Richard M.)
Sustainable development in mineral economies / Richard M. Auty and
Raymond F. Mikesell.
p.   cm.
Includes bibliographical references and index.
1. Mineral industries—Developing countries.   2. Mineral
industries—Environmental aspects.   3. Sustainable development.
I. Mikesell, Raymond Frech.   II. Title.
HD9506.D452A948   1998
338.2'09172'4—dc21   98–8568
ISBN 0–19–829487–5

1 3 5 7 9 10 8 6 4 2

Typeset in 10/12pt Times
by Graphicraft Limited, Hong Kong
Printed in Great Britain
on acid-free paper by
Biddles Ltd, Guildford and King's Lynn

Acknowledgements

We gratefully acknowledge a grant for $10,000 from Rio Tinto to cover the field-work for the pilot study of Jamaica and Chile in 1994 out of which this project grew. We are also grateful to the Centre for Resource Studies at Queen's University in Kingston, Ontario, for providing $4,500 to fund the collection of data in Colombia and Peru. In addition, we are pleased to acknowledge our debt to the many people in government, academia, and the mining industry within the nine countries in our study who helped us by the provision of data and insights. However, the views expressed in the book are those of the authors who bear full responsibility for them.

Contents

List of Figures

List of Tables

Part I

Overview

1   Aims and Structure of the Book

Basic Concepts

How do we justify another contribution to the prodigious literature on sustainable development? First, the mineral economies comprise around one-fifth of the developing countries and they face special problems in achieving sustainable development and they have as a whole been less successful than resource-poor countries. Second, there is a need for a better understanding of the problems faced by the mineral economies as a basis for policy decisions required to overcome them. The term 'sustainable development' is often used ambiguously to identify a particular social, economic, or ideological objective. We shall refrain from presenting yet another general concept of sustainable development (for the diversity of approaches compare, for example, Atkinson *et al.* (1997), Nordhaus (1992), Norgaard (1994), and WRI (1992)), but use an interpretation that reflects the principal concern of this study, which is: How can a country's mineral resources best be employed for achieving and maintaining the maximum rate of economic growth consistent with the country's social objectives? The degree to which this objective is realized becomes our general measure of sustainability.

Our concept of sustainable development requires that the contribution to economic development be maintained, both during periods of temporary reduction in mineral exports and over the long run when mineral-producing capacity declines relative to the size of the overall economy. What is required is not the sustainability of the mineral production that initially generates growth, but the maintenance of economic and social conditions for sustaining that growth. As is shown in Chapter 6, many of the mineral-exporting countries reviewed in this study have not realized the full potential of their mineral resources for achieving and maintaining growth. The capacity for a mineral-driven country to achieve any particular rate of growth differs with the kind and amounts of minerals produced and with the world markets for them. But the sustainability of the contribution of the mineral sector to growth depends upon how the economies adjust to fluctuations in product prices and to other factors affecting export revenues in the relatively short run, and upon the structural adjustments in the economy required to sustain growth over the longer run when mineral exports will inevitably constitute a relatively smaller portion of the economy. These two aspects of sustainability are closely interrelated and both types of adjustment are analysed in this study, together with case studies illustrating successful and unsuccessful adjustment.

Many of the mineral-exporting countries reviewed in this study have not realized the full potential of their mineral resources for achieving and maintaining growth.

An important purpose of this study, therefore, is to explore the reasons why many mineral-exporting countries have not realized this potential. The capacity for a mineral-driven economy to achieve any particular rate of growth differs with the kinds and amounts of minerals produced and with the world markets for them. But the sustainability of the contribution of the mineral sector to growth depends on the macro-policies adopted for dealing with distortions caused by fluctuating export revenues, as well as on structural changes in the mineral industry itself.

The unique contribution of a country's mineral sector to economic growth is found in the mineral rents, or the revenues produced by the mineral sector after deducting all costs associated with the discovery and production of minerals. Since mineral reserves are depleted in the process of production, an important element in sustainability is for the country to save and reinvest a sufficient portion of the mineral rents to compensate for the loss of net income from the depleted mineral resources. This means that after a mineral reserve is exhausted, reinvested mineral rents will be sufficient to yield a net revenue equal to that produced by the depleted reserves. This requires that the rents be invested productively so that the equivalent net income will be realized. However, sustainability also requires that economic distortions created by the production and marketing of the minerals be avoided or mitigated so that sustainability is not impaired by their impacts on other sectors of the economy. The policies required for dealing with these distortions constitute a major portion of this study.

Measuring the contribution of the mineral sector to sustainability presents difficult analytical problems. The contribution to growth will be much larger for a country with substantial mineral reserves relative to its size than for a country with only modest reserves. Rather than trying to measure the contribution of the mineral sector for individual countries with varying mineral potential, the overall sustainability of a country's development is evaluated. In doing so, this study does not adopt rigid criteria in terms of either the overall growth rate or variations in the growth rate over given periods. Rather, the average growth rates of mineral-exporting countries are compared with those of non-mineral developing countries. Changes in growth rates and in the social conditions that accompany fluctuations in mineral revenues reflect the ability of a country to avoid or mitigate the economic impacts of externally generated disturbances such as price and exchange rate shocks. The broad development experience of the mineral-exporting countries is considered, including the realization of recognized social objectives, such as the elimination of poverty and equality of opportunity. As will be shown, social development also plays a role in economic sustainability.

Measuring sustainable output

Assessing the degree to which sustainability is actually achieved by a country requires the application of environmental and natural resource accounting (EARA). EARA differs from the traditional system of national accounts (SNA) by deducting the depletion of natural resource stocks and damage to the natural resource base from the national product as calculated by the SNA. This gives the environmental domestic product (EDP), which should be used for measuring sustainability because it excludes output representing natural capital depletion and deterioration in the quality of the environment. Application of EARA is important for countries that obtain a major portion of their income from natural resources because the depletion of these resources may boost the income of the present generation at the expense of the next. This applies to mineral-producing countries as well as those countries heavily dependent on forest products or on products that deplete soil productivity. But whereas forests and soil can be managed as renewable resources, the finite 'once-for-all' nature of mineral exploitation renders environmental accounting especially critical. This study reviews analytical work on EARA done by the United Nations, the World Bank, and private research organizations (Harrison 1992; Hartwick and Hageman 1992), and discusses some case studies applying EARA to mineral economies.

The EDP of the mining sector provides an indication of the degree to which that sector is conforming with sustainable development. For example, if a country is depleting its mineral resource capital without a compensating increment in savings and investment, it may be engaging in net capital consumption. Winter-Nelson (1995) presents evidence from sub-Saharan Africa that countries with relatively closed economies tended to maintain growth solely by resource extraction. A key index in this regard is the genuine saving rate which is measured as gross savings, minus depletion of produced capital, minus depletion of natural capital, minus net foreign saving (Hamilton and O'Connor 1994; Pearce *et al.* 1996).

EARA may also show how a nation can promote or restore the growth rate by determining how alternative investment projects would affect the growth of EDP. By taking account of mineral resource depletion and environmental degradation, a project is likely to show a lower value and priority than would be the case if it were valued in accordance with the SNA. We review several case studies in which EARA is applied to developing countries.

The mineral cycle

Mineral-driven development proceeds in stages, beginning with the discovery and development of a major mineral reserve, followed by further discoveries and output expansion until the mature stage is reached, when the mineral potential of the country is being exploited and mineral output has nearly peaked or levelled off. Provided mineral reserves are ample, the country may continue to expand output for a time, or the depletion of reserves may cause a gradual decline in mineral output. In the youthful stage, mineral exports may constitute a relatively large portion of total exports and make a substantial contribution to the rate of economic growth, but this contribution will not be sustained for two reasons. One is that the initial *growth* in mineral output cannot be sustained. Second, as the non-mineral sectors of the economy grow, mineral production will represent a declining share of total national output. Sustainable development is indicated by the behaviour of the economy over the course of these stages. The absence of sustainable development would be indicated by a sharp decline in the economic growth rate or even a negative growth rate in the later stages. Non-sustainability might also be indicated by the failure of the growth rate to recover to its long-term trend following a sharp decline in mineral revenue.

One material indicator of sustainable development is the ratio of investment to gross domestic product (GDP). A rising ratio would indicate that mineral rents were being invested in the economy so that the growth rate should continue as the relative contribution to growth of the mineral sector declines. Maintaining this growth rate may also require a stable or improving incremental-capital/output ratio (ICOR), which means that the investments are being made in productive projects rather than, say, largely in social projects that yield low economic returns. These measures could be supplemented by determining whether the basic sectors (manufacturing, agriculture, and infrastructure) are growing in accordance with norms based on the development experience of successful economies.

The onset of early maturity requires policies to accelerate economic diversification in order to generate additional foreign exchange and also to diversify tax sources. This book examines a range of responses to the onset of maturity in order to show not only the appropriate policies, but also how those policies should be adapted to individual countries because of differences in their per capita income, the structure of their economy, their natural resource endowment, and the nature of their political system. Policies for improved economic and environmental performance have limited utility if they are developed without regard to a country's implementation capacity, as constrained by the nature of the political state (Lal and Myint 1996).

The 'resource curse' hypothesis

We provide data showing that hard-mineral exporters as a group have had the lowest rate of growth among the developing countries over the 1970–93 period. This finding is in line with the statistical finding that resource-abundant countries generally have had lower rates of growth than resource-poor countries over the past three decades. This finding has been called the 'resource curse' hypothesis. We examine some of the explanations for this hypothesis as applied to mineral economies. Our theoretical analysis provides the basis for a set of conclusions and recommendations on the policies that promote sustainable development for mineral economies in adjusting for temporary shortfalls in mineral exports, and in making structural adjustments for long-term sustainability. The case studies show that mineral economies with a relatively good growth performance over the 1970–93 period have followed the policies for promoting sustainability derived from our theoretical analysis. Those countries that have not adopted these policies have had less satisfactory growth and general sustainability performance.

Social sustainability

In recent years, there has emerged in the literature considerable interest in the conditions for social sustainability, that is, for alleviating conflicts between key groups who experience economic, environmental, and social disruption from resource exploitation. For example, Killick (1995) has drawn attention to the changing role of institutions in facilitating economic adjustment through the early, middle, and late stages of the industrial transition. Elsewhere, Koo and Perkins (1995) report on an interdisciplinary symposium on social capability in which scholars attempt to define and measure what social capability comprises. (See also the World Bank 1997.) As shown in later chapters of this book, major mining companies are increasingly commissioning 'social audits' as well as environmental ones in order to sustain their projects.

Outline of the Study

Part II of this book examines the literature pertaining to the contribution of natural resources to economic growth; disturbances to the economy resulting from operations of a dominant mineral-exporting sector; macroeconomic policies for dealing with economic distortions; measuring mineral reserve depletion; and the role of natural resource degradation and protection in sustainable development

Chapter 2 reviews natural resources in neoclassical growth models and explores the relationship between trade theory and economic growth. Attention is given to the paradoxical association between natural resource abundance and relatively poor economic growth performance.

Chapter 3 examines the macro-policy requirements for sustained mineral-driven development. It explores the role of exogenous factors with reference to trends in world mineral prices and export revenues, and to capital flows. The contributions of monetary and fiscal policies in minimizing external shocks are assessed and the case is made for the establishment of a mineral revenue stabilization fund. Finally, the nature of mineral rents and their effective taxation is reviewed.

Chapter 4 focuses on accounting for mineral asset depletion. The case for conserving mineral resources is reviewed and dismissed. It is shown how discounting the benefit stream can affect the distribution of the mineral revenue stream between income and saving and, therefore, between present and future generations. The various methods of dealing with mineral depletion in the national accounts are evaluated and reasons are presented for selecting the user-cost approach associated with El-Serafy. Also discussed is the need to reduce dependence on mineral exports during the mature stage of the mineral-driven cycle.

Chapter 5 turns to the environmental degradation which mining causes. The principal categories of environmental impacts are described and a distinction is made between the reversible damage to environmental assets and permanent damage, including global damage (which, however, is excluded from the present study, given its focus on national economies). Consideration is also given to the consequences of mining for recreational and cultural damage. Finally, an important distinction is made between private and social externalities.

Part III reviews the experience of the mineral-driven economies over the 1970–93 period. Chapter 6 presents an overview of the macro-performance of the mineral economies, noting the generally disappointing growth rate compared with the resource-deficient countries. But a handful of mineral economies is identified, notably Indonesia, Botswana, and post-1982 Chile, which have performed far better than the mean. We first attempt to account for the differences in performance among the countries with reference to their preconditions in the early 1970s, and to the scale and direction of their external shocks. Neither of these conditions is highly correlated with performance. Economic policies emerge as the dominant factor explaining the divergence in economic growth rates, and the type of political State affects the capacity of governments to pursue coherent policies for sustainable development. A distinction is made between those political States which pursue an autonomous development strategy for maximizing long-term social welfare and those which do not. The former have been relatively rare in the developing countries. The mineral economies are more likely to be factional States whose capacity to pursue a coherent economic policy is impaired by the political need to use mineral rents for winning political support.

Chapter 7 focuses on the four most successful countries in the sample, namely Indonesia, Botswana, Chile, and Papua New Guinea. It begins by tracing the highly successful Indonesian transition through all three stages in the mineral-driven cycle (youth, early maturity, and late maturity). Then the growth record of Botswana is reviewed during its youthful stage, characterized by a large and stable rent stream and a political consensus in favour of prudent rent absorption. By contrast, PNG experienced during its youthful stage a more feeble and more erratic rent stream and had a highly factional political State, which created acute tensions over the distribution of rents. Finally, unlike PNG, Botswana, or Indonesia, the Chilean economy had accumulated severe distortions over many years before reforms of the Pinochet regime established Chile as the best-performing economy in Latin America. The Chilean experience suggests that reform should proceed in a careful sequence from stabilization to trade and financial reform.

In Chapter 8 we show that the four less successful mineral economies failed to adjust to the distortions created in the early-mature phase of the mineral-driven cycle. This thesis is illustrated by the gyrations of policy in Peru which led to heavy state controls in the late 1980s, followed by the 'big bang' reforms of the Fujimori government. In contrast, the smaller mid-income mineral economies of Trinidad and Tobago and Jamaica were reluctant reformers: they experienced prolonged falls in per capita income and had yet to establish sustained rapid economic growth by the mid-1990s. Namibia also experienced a prolonged period of economic decline and stagnation. These findings underline the importance of adopting orthodox economic policies and of reducing micro-level distortions.

Chapter 9 explores the changing structure of the economy. It contrasts the greater diversification opportunities of the larger, better-endowed countries (Indonesia, Chile, and Peru) with the more limited options of the smaller, resource-constrained countries (Jamaica, Trinidad and Tobago, PNG, Botswana, and Namibia).

Part IV reassesses the conclusions based on conventional accounting in Part III, in light of three additional sets of sustainability criteria: compensating for the depletion of mineral assets; internalizing environmental degradation costs; and building socio-political sustainability. Chapter 10 establishes the sensitivity of the SNA to two measures of mineral asset depletion, namely the net income approach and the user-cost approach. Throughout the chapter, the substantial differences in depletion estimates yielded by the net income and user-cost depletion coefficients are noted and the policy implications drawn.

Chapter 11 examines three elements of environmental degradation, namely mine-site despoliation; water pollution from ore concentration and refining and atmospheric impacts of copper smelting. The implications of differences in environmental absorptive capacity for mine-site rehabilitation are contrasted between densely settled Jamaica and the Atacama desert of Chile. Contrasts in coping with water pollution are provided by Chile (whose mitigation efforts may have enhanced farm productivity for non-leaf crops), and by the mountainous, high-rainfall regions of New Guinea, where problems with tailings storage have led to large-scale riverine dumping. Finally, the costs of abating atmospheric pollution are analysed, contrasting the experiences of older state-owned refineries, which must invest in back-fitting expensive abatement equipment, with that of the multinational mining companies, which tend to upgrade their abatement technology under pressure from international lending agencies and shareholders.

Chapter 12 reviews the increasingly important problems which arise from socio-political stress. The size of mines and their revenues in relation to the local economy create tensions, such as conflicts between the mines and landowners, and with the traditional social order of the local communities, which are often located in remote regions of the country. These conflicts also frequently strain relations between the local and the national governments. The role of social audits, which compare the revenue flows and social costs between the national government and the local communities is evaluated as an emerging solution to these problems.

Part V, the concluding part of the book, presents the policy implications. Chapter 13 summarizes the principal findings and policy implications of the research. Chapter 14 applies the policy lessons derived from the empirical analysis to Colombia, a country which can be described as a nascent mineral economy in the early 1990s with the expansion of mineral production led by the oil sector. The oil sector of Colombia is unlikely to reach a size, relative to the non-mineral economy, as large as that of the mining sectors of rent-rich Indonesia, Trinidad and Tobago, or Botswana.

Part II

Requirements for Sustainable Mineral-Driven Development

2 Economic Theory, Natural Resources, and Economic Growth

This chapter reviews the role of natural resources in theories of economic development and considers the degree to which scarcity of natural resources constitutes a limitation on growth. This is followed by a discussion of theories that regard primary commodity export-led growth as incompatible with broadly based and sustained development. The chapter then examines some of the conditions created by primary commodity exports that may impede sustainability, with special reference to the 'Dutch disease'. (Chapter 3 discusses the policies that mineral-exporting countries should adopt in order to avoid the symptoms of the Dutch disease and other factors that impair sustainability.) Finally, Chapter 2 examines the finding that resource-abundant countries have lower economic growth than resource-scarce developing countries, a phenomenon which has been called the 'resource curse'.

Role of Natural Resources in Neoclassical Growth Models

Throughout the history of economic thought, natural resources have been variously viewed, but generally as less important than capital and labour. Some have regarded natural resources as being available in unlimited supply, while others regarded them as a potential constraint on production. In the early part of the nineteenth century, classical economists were concerned with natural resources, particularly land, as constituting a limit to growth in per capita output. Their pessimism earned economics the attribution of the 'dismal science'. By Alfred Marshall's time most economists believed that Western society could overcome the Malthusian population trap and the law of diminishing returns, so that perpetual economic and social progress is highly probable, if not assured. This optimism was supported by the development of new territories for agricultural production, the continued discovery of mineral reserves, and the rapid technological advances for extracting and refining lower ore grades.

By the end of the nineteenth century, conventional economists believed that increased capital and technological progress would prevent natural resources from ever becoming a constraint on world growth. However, this optimism was questioned by the conservation movement which developed during the late nineteenth and early twentieth centuries. The conservationists, most of whom were not professional economists, adopted the position that the rapidly expanding consumption of natural resources by the current generation would reduce the productive capability of future generations. However, instead of developing a programme for reallocating natural resources that would achieve intergenerational equity, conservationists simply advocated 'conservation' and 'wise use' (Barnett and Morse 1963: 67).

The first comprehensive theoretical analysis of world scarcity of natural resources and its impact on growth was undertaken by Barnett and Morse (1963), who provided a rigorous analysis of historical scarcity models, together with an empirical analysis of natural resource depletion. They examined historical resource costs to determine whether the trend had been upward or downward, including the unit costs of agricultural products, minerals, forests, and commercial fishing. They calculated an index of natural resource product costs, which they found declined between 1870 and the late 1950s, thus negating the scarcity hypothesis as applied to this period. It appeared that much of this decline was due to technological advance and institutional change. Regarding the question of whether continually expanding output in the future against a fixed resource base will result in rising costs for natural resource inputs, or even limiting output growth, the authors took the optimistic position that 'the heritage of knowledge, equipment, and economic institutions that the industrial nations are able to transmit to future generations is sufficient . . . to avoid quantitative diminishing returns' (ibid. 250). This became the prevailing view among conventional economists.

In response to the emerging interest in the economic growth of developing countries following World War II, a number of growth models were formulated based on production functions, such as the Cobb–Douglas (Douglas 1934: 131) and the Harrod–Domar functions (Harrod 1939; Domar 1946). Natural resources played almost no role in these models, but became the basis for formulating post-World War II national economic plans and foreign assistance programmes for achieving those plans.[1] Assuming constant returns to scale and fixed technology, capital was the engine of growth, while technological advances served to increase the productivity of capital by lowering the capital/output ratio. The growth models showed how constraints on domestic investment kept developing-country income at low levels, and how foreign investment, technical assistance, and government planning and policy reforms might remove these constraints (Rosenstein-Rodan 1943; Lewis 1952; Nelson 1956: 894–908; Rostow 1956; Liebenstein 1957; Nurkse 1957). Natural resource constraints on growth were ignored since countries could purchase resource-based products in the world market with revenue from exports of labour-intensive products.

Despite the widely held view that world supplies of natural resources would not be a limit to world growth, the rapid increases in non-fuel mineral and petroleum prices in the early-1970s, together with the publication of the report of the Club of Rome entitled *Limits to Growth* (Meadows *et al.* 1972), led the professional economic community to take account of the threat of natural resource scarcity as a constraint on growth. The Meadows report emphasized the scarcity of minerals and arable land as limiting growth in the intermediate term, and pointed to the long-term consequences of the degradation of life-supporting environmental assets. Although the report met with considerable criticism, the consequences of the exhaustion of

[1] For a review of early post-World War II development models, see Mikesell (1968: ch. 2).

natural resources on intergenerational equity began to be addressed by mainstream economists (Solow 1974; Hartwick 1977; Stiglitz 1979). Solow (1974) argued that technological advance can prevent a decline in the marginal product of capital by enhancing capital productivity, and set forth the conditions for a constant level of per capita consumption through all time, given a finite amount of natural resources. He adopted a Cobb-Douglas production function which is homogeneous in the degree $1-h$.

$$Q = F(K, L)R^h,$$

where K is capital, L is labour, and R is an exhaustible resource. Solow pointed out that if the elasticity of substitution between an exhaustible resource and other factors exceeds unity, the resource is not indispensable to production.[2] If less than unity, the average product of the resource is bounded and only a finite amount of output can ever be produced from the finite pool of the resource. In the absence of technical progress, the only way a positive flow of consumption can be maintained is by accumulating capital fast enough to drive K/L towards infinity, as R/L drops towards zero—but this is not feasible. Solow suggests that continued technological progress will be necessary for a positive consumption flow to be maintainable (Solow 1974: 36). With unlimited technological progress and an elasticity of substitution between natural resources and labour- and capital-intensive goods no less than unity, a finite pool of resources can support a continual flow of consumption with additions to the stock of reproducible capital (ibid. 41).

Joseph Stiglitz (1979: 123–37) presented a model showing the conditions under which, with capital accumulation and technological change, per capita consumption can grow indefinitely with a fixed stock of exhaustible resources. In this article, Stiglitz also stated that stocks of natural goods are "like capital goods". The conditions under which technical change make sustained per capita consumption possible require a positive rate of resource-augmenting technical progress, which rate should be at least equal to the rate of decline in the natural resource input. Stiglitz (ibid.) stated

if the resource pessimists are correct that we are going to be facing a serious resource problem in the immediate future, they must convincingly show that (1) within each sector the elasticity of substitution is low and the demand elasticities are also low so that as resources become scarcer, we do not, or cannot, substitute less resource-intensive commodities for more resource-intensive commodities; (2) the prospects of adapting tastes to economic circumstances are poor; and (3) the prospects are bleak for technical changes that would enable us to better use what resources we have.

---

[2] The elasticity of substitution gives the percentage change in the input ratio (say, natural resources to capital), which would be engendered by a percentage change in the relative price of capital to natural resources. If a 1% change in relative price does not give rise to a change in factor inputs, the elasticity of substitution is zero. If we discontinue using the factor whose price has risen, the elasticity is infinite. The central case where a 1% change in factor price gives rise to a 1% change in factor inputs is the Cobb-Douglas production function. If the elasticity of substitution between natural resources and capital and/or labour is constant, then a sustained constant per capita consumption is feasible (1) if the elasticity is greater than unity; or (2) if the elasticity is unity; and (3) if the share of capital exceeds that of natural resources.

The concept of substitution with which Solow and Stiglitz were concerned has to do with technological advances that make it possible to substitute produced goods for natural resource inputs, so that the marginal productivity of capital is maintained and growth can continue as natural resources are depleted. This problem has to do with the technical conditions limiting substitution in a world production function. The problem does not apply to national economies since there is a wide range of goods and services which can be produced with their factor endowments. No individual country faces limited growth because of technical limitations on production since they have access to world technology appropriate for the goods and services they are best equipped to produce.

This study of the mineral sector uses substitutability for individual countries in a somewhat different sense. It has to do with the country's ability to channel net revenues from mineral production into economic sectors in a way that will provide a continuous flow of true income equal to that produced by the mineral sector. This kind of substitutability concerns the transfer of income from the minerals sector to other productive sectors, and the avoidance of changes in domestic and foreign demand, which may reduce the output of certain sectors. Substitution is greatly influenced by changes in exchange rates, and by fiscal and monetary policies that affect different sectors of the economy. As is shown in Chapter 3, a sharp increase in mineral exports may give rise to conditions that depress some economic sectors and prevent other sectors from expanding.

Most economists are optimistic regarding the outlook of supplies for natural resource inputs and in the substitutability of capital and technology for resources. The more abundant the supplies of natural resources, the less will growth need to depend on substitution. The supplies of natural resource inputs are not fixed, but respond to increases in demand. Prices of natural resources reflect the costs of labour and capital required to produce them. However, the prices also reflect the degree of scarcity of the resource, which determines the rent earned by the owners of the resources. Prices of natural resource inputs are equal to their marginal products in alternative employments, and in equilibrium, the marginal products should be equal in all economic sectors (Chenery and Strout 1956). In the modern world economy, supplies of natural resources may affect world growth, but the growth of individual national economies is not limited by supplies of tradeable natural resources for the domestic economy since these resources can be acquired in international markets. Therefore, the relationship between the tradeable natural resources of a country and its growth is basically concerned with production for sale in world markets, of which domestic demand is a part. For this reason, analysing the growth of mineral-producing economies is closely associated with international trade theory.

Trade Theories and Growth

Trade theory seeks to explain why a country has a competitive advantage in producing and exporting certain commodities while importing others. However, trade in natural resource products has never been well integrated with traditional trade theory. Neoclassical trade theory was based on the factor proportion theorem of comparative advantage formulated by Ohlin (1967) with further refinements by Samuelson (1948). Relative factor proportions between two regions (or countries) determine the commodities in which each region will specialize. Factor endowments of labour, capital, and land are assumed to be fixed in the basic Heckscher–Ohlin–Samuelson (H–O–S) theorem. There are serious difficulties in treating natural resources that produce tradeable goods as a fixed factor of production. Supplies of natural resources are continually changing because of new discoveries and depletion from extraction. Moreover, the amount of resources produced depends upon the amount of labour and capital that goes into their discovery and development.

Special trade theories have been formulated for explaining growth, but such trade theories are usually in conflict with the H–O–S comparative cost theorem because of the assumption of fixed factor supplies (Chenery 1961). The quantity and quality of all factors of production change substantially over time, in part as a result of the production process itself. What is important is the relative scarcity or abundance of particular skills and experience, and not of the quantity of labour alone. Also, economies of scale are not only important for many economic sectors, but their significance for different-sized markets depends upon a number of dynamic factors, such as the market environment at the time production is initiated. To make comparative advantage consistent with growth theory based on trade, it is necessary to allow for changes in the quality and quantity of factors of production over time, and to take account of internal and external economies of scale. Therefore, the commodities to be exported will not be determined by a simple ranking procedure based on relative factor availability. Often overlooked in the comparative advantage theorem are the intangible benefits coming from trade in the form of new products and improved technology. The conflicts between trade theories for explaining growth and the traditional comparative cost theorem all apply to natural resources when they are regarded as a factor of production. It should be noted that despite these difficulties, modern trade theorists, such as Leamer (1987) and Findlay (1995), find the H–O–S to models have considerable explanatory power.

Prior to the present century, primary commodities dominated world trade and there were very few cases in which countries began to develop without the strong support of primary commodity exports. Economic historians generally emphasized the critical role of expanding primary commodity exports in the development of Western-oriented countries during the nineteenth century—the USA, Canada, and Australia (North 1963). However, since most primary exporting countries failed to achieve satisfactory growth during the twentieth century, it is important to understand why many resource-rich countries have not developed, and how natural resources have contributed to the growth of others. For the most part, it is necessary to show how and under what conditions primary commodity exports transmit growth to the rest of the economy.

Following World War II, there arose a controversy among development economists with respect to the contribution of primary commodity exports to growth.

Mainstream economists accepted the H–O–S comparative advantage doctrine, and argued that primary commodity exports are the only way that countries in the early stages of development can generate the foreign exchange necessary to pay for essential imports and to service external debt. Also, an expansion of trade attracts foreign investment and the transfer of modern technology. Growth is maximized by maintaining free internal and external markets for goods, and by allocating capital in free capital markets.

An opposing school favoured planning and non-market allocation of resources achieved through a variety of controls and government incentives for domestic investment, prices, and foreign trade. This approach, which tended to dominate development theory during the 1950–80 period, was characterized by the formulation of a number of development models for achieving growth. These included 'balanced growth' models designed to assure congruent expansion of the various sectors of the economy, such as infrastructure, manufacturing, agriculture, and other natural resource industries. Most of these models advocated reduced dependence on primary commodity exports and favoured heavy investment in manufactures and infrastructure financed by capital imports. The most popular approach among the officials of developing countries was put forward by Raul Prebisch in his capacity as Secretary-General of the United Nations Conference on Trade and Development (UNCTAD) in a report entitled *Towards a New Trade Policy for Development* (1964).[3] This Report advanced the thesis that slow growth in primary exports is an inevitable result of the increasing use of synthetics, smaller raw material content of finished products, low elasticity of demand for raw materials, and agricultural protectionism, plus modern agricultural techniques in the industrial countries. Prebisch also projected a downward trend in the terms of trade for primary commodities in relation to manufactured goods imported by the developing countries. He argued that any increase in productivity in primary commodity production tends to be shifted to the industrialized countries, while productivity increases in industrial countries result in wage increases rather than in decreases in the prices of manufactures. Therefore, developing countries must move into manufacturing to supply their domestic markets. Finally, heavy dependence on primary commodity exports rendered developing countries vulnerable to the fluctuating world prices for these commodities. It should be mentioned that several mainstream economists supported the position of Prebisch on fluctuating primary commodity prices. For example, the British economist, Cairncross (1962: 213) stated that 'The prices of primary products are notoriously volatile and the damaging effects of this volatility on the economies of exporting countries are beyond question.' However, most mainstream economists rejected Prebisch's denigration of primary commodity exports on both empirical and theoretical grounds.

Several studies appeared during the 1960s that contradicted the hypothesis that instability of export prices of primary commodities constituted a significant obstacle

---

[3] For a discussion of the UNCTAD conference of 1964 and criticisms of the Prebisch report, see Friedeberg (1969).

to growth (Coppock 1962; Macbean 1966; Michaely 1962). MacBean found that short-term export instability was not an important constraint on development, and that there was not a strong relationship between domestic variables and export fluctuations. One reason is the relatively low level of the foreign trade multiplier in most developing countries. Another is that there is a substantial lag in the reaction of domestic variables to an initial change in export income. Macbean (1966: ch. 15) found a fairly high correlation between import instability and export fluctuations, but that instability of investment is only weakly related to fluctuations in exports. An examination of a dozen underdeveloped countries that experienced export instability during the 1946–58 period found the explanation to be specific local causes rather than in world market factors. Variations in supplies of exports appear to have been more important than fluctuations in demand (Macbean 1966: 34).

Kindleberger (1956) and Morgan (1959) did not find a clear empirical case for Prebisch's declining terms of trade argument. Although Kindleberger found that 'European long-run terms of trade favoured the developed against the undeveloped countries,' this finding does not necessarily apply to the terms of trade of developing countries with the rest of the world (Morgan 1959: 296). Kindleberger argued that developing countries are less able to shift their resources in response to changes in prices than developed countries. Presumably this inherent difficulty would exist regardless of the composition of the exports. Kindleberger also pointed to the difficulty in identifying long-term shifts in the terms of trade between primary and manufactured commodities. One reason for the decline in primary commodity prices has been lower transportation costs, which costs are more important for primary goods than for manufactures. Another factor is that price data do not reflect improvements in the quality of manufactures, while the quality of primary products for specific grades does not change. Actually, there have been a number of periods during which the terms of trade of primary producing countries improved. During the 1928–55 period, export prices of primary producing countries rose 97 per cent, while the increase in the unit value of industrial-country exports was 80 per cent. Balassa (1964: 4) pointed out that one of the fastest growing markets for developing-country primary exports is other developing countries rather than industrial countries, and that this was likely to continue long into the future.

The position that exports are an 'engine of growth' had the support of some development economists throughout the post-World War II period. Maizels (1968: 6) made foreign exchange availability an effective constraint on growth, and projected probable economic growth rates for countries on the basis of export projections. His recommendations for promoting growth included increasing exports of traditional commodities, together with diversification of exports. He strongly favoured expanding trade among developing countries and expanding exports to centrally planned countries. Maizels was somewhat pessimistic about exports of important agricultural commodities, such as cocoa and sugar, the demand for which is relatively inelastic with respect to both price and income. Hence, the expansion of exportable supplies may lead to sharp price declines and reduced export earnings. He was more optimistic regarding mineral exports (ibid. ch. 9).

The basic argument of conventional economists against both the Prebisch thesis and the development planners, who favoured balanced growth or other growth patterns achieved by government controls over trade, prices, and the allocation of capital, is that governments misallocate resources and impair both domestic and foreign investment. Governments should confine their economic activities to fiscal, monetary, and exchange rate policies, for stabilizing domestic prices and preventing balance of payments disequilibrium. This argument gained strong support from the phenomenal growth of the East Asian newly industrialized countries (NICs), which have followed relatively liberal economic policies. Yet the governments of these countries have by no means refrained from intervening in foreign trade and investment.

Modern Trade Theory and the Role of Natural Resources

Modern trade theory has overcome some of the shortcomings of neoclassical growth models and of the static H–O–S theorem for explaining the contribution of natural resources to output and to the composition of trade. Modern trade theory is also an advance over the simple export-led growth theories because it analyses the interactions between particular export sectors and other sectors of the economy. In place of the traditional two-sector model, Leamer (1987) regards natural resources as independent factors producing intermediate products. Comparative advantage depends not simply on the relative scarcities of labour and capital, but is directly influenced by the relative abundance of natural resources. The inclusion of natural resources brings about the possibility of many different paths of development (ibid.). In the two-factor model, countries may produce either labour-intensive manufactures or capital-intensive manufactures, depending upon the labour capital ratio. Land and other natural resources play no role in the outcome. Introducing land as another factor explains why a country scarce in land will develop a manufacturing sector at a much lower level of capital per person than a country with more abundant land. In fact, countries with very abundant natural resources may never turn to manufacturing at all.

The discovery of minerals in a country tends to increase returns to capital, which may be accompanied by capital accumulation. Capital accumulation favours more capital-intensive products, such as aluminum and steel, and lowers the demand for labour. However, the mineral country may not be able to produce capital-intensive products at prices competitive with imports. Hence, these industries are sometimes established with the aid of import restrictions, with the result that all domestic production is hampered by high-cost inputs. Labour-intensive manufactures may also require import restrictions and subsidies to compete with imports. These developments cannot be explained by a model that omits natural resources.

In contrast to the traditional two-sector trade models, Leamer (1987, 1995) uses a model with a number of economic sectors or categories of economic activity. All sectors produce either tradeable or non-tradeable goods. The tradeable category includes manufacturing, agriculture, minerals, and leading primary exporting industries as distinct sectors; non-tradeables include construction, transportation, and services. Labour-intensive, capital-intensive, and resource-intensive commodities may exist within both tradeable and non-tradeable categories. In an open economy, the prices of tradeables are determined by international markets, while prices of non-tradeables are determined by domestic demand and supply. Hence, determining comparative advantage in multifactor and multisector models requires much more than the relative abundance or scarcity of the factors. It requires an analysis of prices in domestic and world markets, changes in world demand for natural resource products, shifts in resources among sectors, movements in real exchange rates, and rates of capital accumulation induced by resource movements.

Dynamic factors, such as timing the introduction of a new product and economies of scale, also play a role in explaining why a country has a competitive advantage in a particular product. Increasing returns to scale for certain production technologies helps to explain why initial producers, usually industrial countries, are able to maintain or even increase their lead over other countries (Roemer 1996). Instead of static comparative advantage determined by the relative abundance of capital and labour, Leamer (1995) analyses the composition of trade in terms of development paths, and natural resources play a role in determining these paths. International trade itself affects growth, since R&D is transmitted from industrial countries to developing countries through trade. These innovations to trade and growth theory are applied in this study when discussing the role of mineral exports in sustainable growth.

Special Problems Created by Primary Exports

Mainstream economists reject the doctrine of Prebisch and other spokesmen for developing countries which advocates a rapid reduction of dependence on primary commodity exports by means of import-substituting trade controls and other direct governmental action. They believe that free trade and competitive domestic markets will maximize economic growth. Support for this position faces two obstacles. First, there is empirical evidence that the most successful developing countries are resource-poor, and that most resource-rich countries averaged relatively slow growth or stagnation during the past three decades. Second, countries enjoying export booms, such as the petroleum-producing countries experienced in the 1970s, often undergo a decline in their manufacturing industries and sometimes in agriculture as well. Instead of promoting growth, the export boom is followed by declining output. This problem has come to be called the 'Dutch disease'—a name derived from the Dutch experience following the discovery of natural gas in Holland in the late-1950s. The symptoms of the disease are recession in manufacturing and commercial agriculture, inflation, and, in some cases, a transfer of resources out of the natural-resource booming industry itself, especially after the collapse of the boom. The first phenomenon relates to the long-term path of development while the second has to do with the short-term effects of an export boom. However, in analysing the first phenomenon, some economists have associated the slow growth of resource-rich countries with the Dutch disease. In this review, the Dutch disease phenomenon arising from an export boom is dealt with first and the long-term growth problem is addressed later.

The Dutch disease

Although there is evidence of the Dutch disease phenomenon going back to the nine-teenth century, a formal analysis developed by Corden and Neary (1982), has become a standard model in the literature.[4] Their three-sector model provides for (1) a boom-ing sector, such as oil or other primary product exporting industry, (2) a sector of other tradeables, which would include both manufacturing and agriculture, and (3) non-tradeables. The booming sector could be agricultural products, but since this review is mainly interested in the role of mineral exports, it is assumed that the booming sector is some mineral export. The rapid expansion of the booming sec-tor may occur as a result of an increase in the world price of the mineral, a major resource discovery, or development of a prior discovery, or some cost-reducing techno-logical innovation which increases resource rents.

The booming sector has three separate effects: a spending effect, a relative price effect, and a resource movement effect. Spending the increased export revenues increases the demand for both tradeables and non-tradeables, but spending on trade-ables fails to raise their domestic prices because in an open economy their prices are determined in international markets. Therefore, any excess demand is met by imports. Unless the increase in foreign exchange income is sterilized, there will be an appreciation of the currency, which reduces the domestic prices of exports and of imports competing with domestic output. A currency appreciation will also reduce the rents of the booming sector, but it may not be sufficient to reduce that sector's output.

The domestic prices of the non-tradeables will rise with the increase in demand, and these prices will not be affected by either the currency appreciation or com-petitive imports. Hence, there is a rise in the prices of non-tradeables relative to the prices of tradeables, with a consequent shift of resources from tradeables to non-tradeables, and a reduction in exports and increase in imports. The movement of resources between sectors will also affect capital accumulation. If the non-tradeables sector is relatively labour-intensive while the tradeables sector is capital-intensive, the movement in favour of the non-tradeables sector will tend to raise wages and lower returns to capital, thereby reducing capital accumulation. These adjustments following an export boom summarize the classic model of the Dutch disease. But whether they give rise to harmful symptoms and impede growth depends largely on governmental monetary, fiscal, and foreign exchange policies.

---

[4] Although the Dutch disease concept is usually attributed to Corden, the principle was recognized much earlier. According to Gelb *et al.* (1988: 21), John Cairns first recognized the effects of the 1851 gold discoveries in Australia on other sectors of the economy.

Exchange rate appreciation

In analysing the role of exchange rate appreciation following an export boom, a distinction should be made between the *nominal* exchange rate and the *real* exchange rate. The enhanced inflow of foreign exchange will initially tend to raise the nominal exchange value of the domestic currency. However, if there is a sharp increase in domestic demand accompanied by inflation, the increased demand for foreign exchange may offset the initial nominal exchange rate appreciation so that the nominal exchange rate may not appreciate and may even depreciate. There may, nevertheless, be a *real* exchange rate appreciation indicated by an increase in the prices of non-tradeables relative to those for tradeables. According to this defini-tion, the real exchange rate (RER) may be expressed as follows:

$$RER = \frac{\text{price index of tradeable goods}}{\text{price index of non-tradeable goods}}.$$

A decline in RER indicates a real exchange rate appreciation, which has the effect of increasing the domestic costs of producing tradeable goods and reducing the country's international competitiveness. Most developing countries control their exchange rates either by restricting the sale of foreign exchange or by intervention in the market. In either case, developing countries tend to prevent their nominal exchange rates from depreciating in line with inflation, so that their exchange rates may be overvalued. Exchange controls may also be used to prevent an appreci-ation of the nominal exchange rate by requiring recipients of foreign exchange income to sell their foreign exchange receipts to the government. For these reasons, changes in the nominal exchange rate may not play a direct role in the Dutch dis-ease phenomenon.[5]

Another way of defining RER is the purchasing power parity (PPP) approach. PPP is equal to the nominal exchange rate, E, multiplied by the ratio of the foreign price level, P^*, to the domestic price level, P. Thus, PPP $= EP^*/P$. Edwards (1989: 6) points out that the two definitions of RER will yield different values, and argues that PPP fails "to capture changes in the relative incentives guiding resource alloca-tion across tradeable and non-tradeable sectors". Harberger (1986: 392–4) rejects the measure of the real exchange rate favoured by Edwards in favour of a form of PPP, on the grounds that it does not reveal the effects of differential movements of tradeable prices. For example, the effects on RER of a world oil boom will differ from the effects of an increase in the real costs of producing a particular class of goods, such as metallic minerals. Harberger prefers to define RER as E/P_d, where P_d is the general level of domestic prices. However, this is an oversimplified

---

[5] Edwards (1986: ch. 7) shows that in the Colombian experience a rise in coffee prices typically results in a balance of payments surplus and the accumulation of international reserves. If the increase in reserves is not sterilized, the monetary base will increase and an excess supply of money will cause inflation. Thus, the increase in the price level will be one of the mechanisms through which real appreciation takes place. He also shows that the short-run monetary effects of commodity booms have also taken place in Indonesia and Kenya.

definition. Harberger (ibid. 406) suggests that in designing empirical work aimed at explaining movements in *RER*,

an ideal list of explanatory variables would include: net capital inflow spent on tradeable goods; net capital inflow spent on non-tradeables goods; the world price level of a country's exports; the world price level of its competitive exports; the world price of its non-competitive imports; the average strength of tariffs and other restrictions inhibiting import demand; and the average strength of export taxes (subsidies) and other policies inhibiting (or promoting) export supplies.

Such an index would be very difficult to apply.

The PPP approach greatly complicates the problem of measuring RER because it must take into account the rise in domestic prices relative to the rise in prices in other countries with which the country is in competition. These countries will differ for each tradeable product. There is also a problem in selecting the nominal exchange rate to be used in Harberger's formula, E/P_d. For one thing, there is unlikely to be an equilibrium rate at any time in the recent past and the controlled rate will differ from the shadow equilibrium rate. Also, the same rate may not be used for all transactions, as in the case of multiple exchange rates. *E* should be a multi-lateral trade-weighted rate, with the weights determined by the country's trade with a number of countries whose exchange rates make up the composite rate. The multi-lateral trade-weighted value of, say, the Chilean peso, may differ radically from the dollar value of the Chilean peso. For example, there is a tendency to measure the appreciation of the US dollar between 1990 and the end of 1994 in terms of the dollar value of the yen, which declined nearly 50 per cent over the period. However, during the same period the multilateral trade-weighted value of the US dollar changed hardly at all. Rugoff (1996: 665) questions the usefulness of PPP as a measure of real exchange rates because of the wide and long-lasting deviations between real exchange rate changes and changes in PPP. He suggests this divergence is due to the existence of substantial trading barriers between domestic markets, which are in themselves more integrated than international goods markets. It may be concluded, therefore, that measuring RER by the ratio of the price index of tradeables to the price index of non-tradeables is the more satisfactory method.

A decline in RER (or exchange rate appreciation) may also occur as a result of an increase in capital imports. Capital imports may be induced by the prosperity of a booming natural resource export sector. An example is to be found in Chile where large net capital inflows over the 1975–82 period were accompanied by real exchange rate appreciation. Real exchange rate appreciation arising from an appreciation of the nominal exchange rate can be modified or prevented by central bank intervention in the exchange market, or by preventing an increase in foreign exchange income from affecting the foreign exchange market. If the government is the recipient of the foreign exchange income, it can simply hold the foreign exchange in the central bank or use it to buy imports not normally purchased. When the central bank purchases foreign exchange in the exchange market with domestic currency, the intervention may be 'sterilized' or 'unsterilized'. In the former case, the central bank prevents the intervention from increasing commercial bank reserves and the money supply. Thus, the central bank may borrow the domestic currency from the banking system so that there is no net increase in bank reserves. Sterilized intervention also avoids real exchange rate appreciation by preventing inflation, as well as by preventing a rise in the nominal exchange rate.

Central bank intervention is warranted when there is a sharp increase in foreign exchange income which is believed to be temporary. A permanent increase in export income should be permitted to gradually increase the exchange value of the domestic currency since, otherwise, the country will continue to have a current account surplus, which must either take the form of a net capital outflow or an accumulation of foreign exchange reserves (which is a form of capital outflow). Real exchange appreciation will induce a larger volume of imports and perhaps slow the rate of increase in exports by the tradeable sector. Properly managed, an export boom need not cause unemployment and overcapacity in the manufacturing sector, but there would be a slowdown of the rate of growth of that sector relative to the rate of growth in the non-tradeable sector. Such an adjustment will also require careful monetary management to prevent either inflation or recession.

Currently, the government of Chile is faced with an adjustment problem arising from its booming copper sector, as well as from an expansion of agricultural and lumber exports. Nominal exchange rate appreciation is being retarded, but this has had the effect of making Chile a net capital exporter with substantial investments in Argentina and other Latin American countries. This has disturbed some Chilean economists who believe that, as a developing country, Chile should be a net capital importer. In order for Chile to be a net capital importer, the foreign exchange value of the Chilean peso should rise, either by allowing the nominal exchange rate to increase, or by expanding the money supply. Monetary policy should be guided by the objective of avoiding inflation. Hence, Chile is faced with two contradictory economic objectives: restoring its position as a net capital importer versus improving its international competitive position.[6]

When does an export boom lead to symptoms of a 'disease'?

There is a tendency to confuse adjustments required by an export boom with the *symptoms* of the Dutch disease. Symptoms to be avoided are unemployment, impaired growth, and inflation (which is likely to lead to the other two symptoms). Whether there are harmful consequences from an export boom depends on the sustainability of the export revenue, and on the nature and rapidity of the adjustment process. To prevent a sudden decline in the relative prices of tradeables, with a consequent increase in unemployment and loss of productivity, the adjustment process should be gradual. A permanent expansion of export income will require reallocating resources among economic sectors to avoid a continuing current account

---

[6] We discussed this issue with Rolf Luders, former Chilean Minister of Economy and currently Professor of Economics at the Catholic University in Santiago, Chile.

surplus. The adjustment should take the form of a slower rate of growth in the tradeable sector, a gradual increase in imports, and a relative expansion of the non-tradeables sector. As Neary and van Wijnberger (1986: 40–1) point out, some deindustrialization may be a symptom of the economy's adjustment to equilibrium rather than a symptom of a disease.

A common approach to avoiding the harmful symptoms of the Dutch disease is to impose import restrictions on those tradeables most seriously impacted by real exchange appreciation. This further increases production costs in the tradeable sectors and makes them less competitive in international markets. It also interferes with the process of adjustment to a new equilibrium, which requires that some tradeable sectors grow more rapidly than others—as determined by their relative competitive advantage in world markets. Price distortions created by trade restrictions have been shown to impede growth in both resource-rich and resource-poor countries.

Natural Resource Abundance and Long-Term Growth

Recent studies provide rather convincing evidence that on the average, natural resource-rich countries had slower growth during the 1970–92 period than countries with less abundant resources; and that the countries with highest growth rates during this period were relatively resource-poor. This phenomenon has been called the 'resource curse'. Over the period 1980–92 the average annual per capita GDP growth rate of twenty-four developing country mineral exporters was negative, and only five of these countries (Indonesia, Colombia, Chile, Oman, and Botswana) had positive rates of growth (Table 2.1). For all developing countries, the average rate of growth in per capita GDP for this period was 0.9 per cent.

Sachs and Warner (1995a) found a negative relationship between growth rates and the ratio of natural resource exports to GDP for eighty developing countries during the 1971–89 period. The poor performers include such oil-rich countries as Mexico, Nigeria, and Venezuela. Over this same period, the star performers among the developing countries—Korea, Taiwan, Hong Kong, and Singapore—were resource-poor. The authors found this result to remain significant in cross-country growth regressions after controlling for a large number of additional variables, including initial GDP, trade policies, investment rates, and trade volatility. The authors found no simple explanation for this relationship between resource abundance and growth, nor did they conclude that countries should subsidize or protect non-resource sectors as a strategy for growth. Any single explanation for this finding, such as terms-of-trade volatility, must be shown to be both uniquely characteristic of the resource-rich countries and have a high negative correlation with growth. The simple fact of being a resource-abundant country alone is not a satisfactory answer. The major explanations put forth for this phenomenon are next briefly reviewed.

One explanation for the resource curse is the Prebisch terms-of-trade hypothesis which holds that over the long term, prices of primary commodities decline relative to prices of manufactures. However, the evidence that this has existed is very

Table 2.1 Exports of fuels, minerals, and metals, per capita GNP, and average annual growth, 1980–1992

	Share of exports (%)	Per capita GNP (in 1992 dollars)	Average annual growth (%)
Sierra Leone	34	160	−1.4
Niger	86	280	−4.3
Nigeria	96	320	−0.4
Togo	45	390	−1.8
Mauritania	84	530	−0.8
Indonesia	38	670	4.0
Zambia	98	753	n/a
Bolivia	66	680	−1.5
Papua New Guinea	52	950	0.0
Peru	49	950	−2.8
Congo	92	1,030	−0.8
Ecuador	45	1,070	−0.3
Jordan	34	1,120	−5.4
Colombia	29	1,330	1.4
Algeria	97	1,840	−0.5
Iran	90	2,200	−1.4
Chile	47	2,730	3.7
Venezuela	86	2,910	−0.8
Mexico	34	3,470	−0.2
Trinidad and Tobago	64	3,940	−2.6
Gabon	89	4,450	−3.7
Oman	94	6,480	4.1
Saudi Arabia	99	7,510	−3.3
Botswana	n/a	2,790	6.1

Note: To these we may add Zaire with a high proportion of mineral exports, but low per capita income and growth.

Source: World Bank (1994*a*).

weak. In addition, there is no significant correlation between long-run declining real export prices and economic growth of the exporting countries. Cost reduction to increase productivity has enabled some countries, such as Chile, to maintain resource rents in the face of declining real mineral prices.

Another explanation is that resource-rich countries have relatively high terms of trade *volatility* and this has more factual basis than the Prebisch terms-of-trade argument. Over the period 1960–93, the standard deviation in annual percentage price changes for forty-nine primary commodities was 26.4 per cent, while the standard deviation in the World Bank primary commodity price index was half that percentage. The terms-of-trade volatility of the regions with the highest primary export shares—Latin America, sub-Saharan Africa, Middle East, and North Africa—was two to three times that of industrial countries over the 1970–92 period. (Westley (1995) defines the terms-of-trade volatility as the standard deviation of the percentage growth rate of the terms of trade.) However, the theoretical basis for a causal relationship between terms-of-trade volatility and growth is exceedingly weak. Movements in terms of trade do not cause sharp movements in domestic economic conditions. Hence, these price movements are not directly transmitted to the domestic economy. In addition, governments can adopt policies to reduce or eliminate the effects of changes in the terms of trade on the domestic economy.

Hirschman (1958) finds that resource industries have lower linkage effects than manufactures, and suggests that growth may be transmitted to the rest of the economy more effectively by manufacturing.[7] However, his analysis does not explain how manufacturing gets started, or why parallel development occurs in some countries but not in others. For example, in the nineteenth century, farmers who exported grain and livestock to other regions and abroad provided the entrepreneurship and the capital for industrial development in their regional urban centres, so that the growth of primary commodity exports promoted rather than discouraged manufacturing development. There was a similar symbiotic relationship between mining and industrial development in the American West, and these same conditions were also present in Canada.

A third explanation for the resource curse is that the primary resource sector attracts capital, skilled labour, and entrepreneurs from the manufacturing sector, which is thereby doomed to slow growth. In the pre-Civil War US South, investment in cotton production through developing new lands and acquiring slaves was reported to be so profitable that other forms of investment could not compete for capital. But much of this can be explained by the organization of the cotton plantations and the failure to create urban centres in cotton-growing areas. Most of the essential manufactured goods required by the plantation were produced inefficiently on the plantations themselves. In the North, small farmers bought their manufactures and delivered their farm output for processing in the urban centres, where production could take place with better technology and economies of scale. Moreover, such activities provided a profitable outlet for the capital accumulated by the farmers. The difference between development in the North and South occurred because of the existence of slavery and the political dominance of the white plantation owners, rather than from the fact that one region was more resource-abundant than the other (Auty 1995a: 215–19).

A fourth explanation is that the primary export sector keeps the value of the currency so high that other tradeables sectors cannot compete internationally. A large export surplus for one sector requires an import surplus in other sectors to avoid a continuous current account surplus. However, this does not require a lower rate of growth in the entire manufacturing sector or in agriculture. With the dominant

---

[7] Hirschman (1958) gives the average degree of interdependence through backward linkage (purchases from other economic sectors) in Italy, Japan, and the USA for metal mining and petroleum at 21% and 15% respectively, as contrasted with 56% for iron and steel and 67% for textiles.

primary sector fuelling domestic demand, imports of some tradeables will rise and this can occur without an overall slowdown in the growth of production by the tradeables sectors. The number of tradeables sectors is very large, and so are the possibilities for achieving international competitive advantage by economies of scale and adopting appropriate technology. Not all tradeables sectors need to develop and some can have large import surpluses. A large primary sector can affect the pattern of growth among the other tradeables sectors, but does not condemn these sectors to slow overall growth. Moreover, the primary export sector can provide the capital for the growth of other tradeables sectors. In the Canadian West, growth was impelled by a series of resource industries, starting with the fur trade and followed by mining and oil. Conceivably, the ratio of manufacturing to resource production might have been higher in the absence of western Canada's rich natural endowment, but growth would surely have been slower.

Finally, Matsuyama (1992) argues that manufacturing is favourable to growth because it is characterized by learning by doing, which is external to the enterprise but internal to the manufacturing sector as a whole. This has some relevance for Matsuyama's two-sector model of agriculture and manufacturing. However, the US and Canadian mining industries have been at least as innovative in developing and applying new technology for increasing productivity in both discovery and extraction, as have most manufacturing sectors. Learning by doing is certainly a common characteristic of the mineral industries. Furthermore, the argument that the mining industry lures skilled labour and entrepreneurs away from manufacturing overlooks the symbiotic relationship among the sectors, which has made possible the rapid parallel growth of both.

There seems to be no convincing reason why natural resource abundance should in itself condemn countries to relatively low growth. By following the right policies, natural resources should be a boon and not a curse. There may, of course, be special difficulties for countries heavily dependent upon natural resource exports to follow the right policies. However, it is policies (along with basic social conditions and cultural history) and not resource composition that determines growth. This position is supported by Sachs and Warner (1995b: 23) who found that all developing countries following a reasonable set of political and economic policies between 1970 and 1989 achieved annual per capita growth of 2 per cent or greater.

Welfare versus growth

Although the 1974–8 and 1979–81 oil export booms did not contribute to the growth of many oil-rich countries, they did increase consumption substantially and, therefore, welfare. If the capital value of the depleting resource continues to decline, consumption is not sustainable and it can only be sustainable if a portion of the output is invested in other sectors. But a nation with a hundred-year supply of a mineral reserve may well decide that its welfare is better served by a high level of consumption for the next century. Given the uncertainty regarding future technology during the next century and the unknown tenure of a habitable planet, a high level of consumption decision might be a rational one.

Summary

Most economists reject the view that world growth will be limited by a shortage of natural resources. They believe that man-made capital can substitute for natural resources and that this process will be accompanied by continual technological advances. Some environmental economists dispute this optimistic position. In any case, limited world tradeable resources will not impair the growth of mineral-exporting countries, since they would benefit from the rise in mineral prices. However, technological advances and the substitution of capital for natural resources may prevent a substantial increase in mineral prices.

In this chapter we reviewed the treatment of natural resources in growth and international trade theories, and showed that conventional growth and trade theories have tended to neglect the role of natural resources. Neither the capital-oriented growth models nor the comparative advantage trade theory takes account of the dynamic impacts of natural resource industries on both the growth and the composition of trade. Economists have formulated special theories on the relationship between primary commodity exports and growth, but these theories are not integrated with general growth or comparative advantage theories. They fail to show how resource exports transmit growth to the various sectors of the economy.

Despite the strategic role of primary commodity exports in initiating growth and in financing development during the early nineteenth century, the contributions of the natural resource industries came under assault from three sources following World War II. One was the Prebisch hypothesis according to which natural resource-induced growth tends to stagnate because of the declining terms of trade and low elasticities of demand for resource products. The second source was the failure of a high proportion of countries with large export shares of resource-intensive goods to grow as fast as the relatively resource-poor developing countries. The Prebisch position favouring government controls and subsidies for promoting manufacturing at the expense of the raw material industries was largely negated by the success of countries that adopted free enterprise and competitive markets. This success applied to both resource-rich and resource-poor countries. The third source of assault is based on reliable statistical findings that countries with a high ratio of resource-intensive exports to total exports have grown more slowly than have the resource-poor countries. But there is no explanation for this phenomenon that would involve a causal relationship between resource endowment and slow growth.

In order to determine the conditions for sustainable development, it is necessary to examine the impact of trade on intersectoral price relationships, and the effects of relative price changes on different economic sectors under alternative economy policies. An export boom tends to increase the foreign exchange value of the domestic currency, which, in turn, will have the effect of reducing the prices of tradeables relative to non-tradeables. This constitutes an appreciation of the real rate of exchange, which is measured by the ratio of the price index of tradeables to the price index of non-tradeables. A sharp appreciation of RRE would increase production costs relative to domestic prices in the manufacturing and other tradeable sectors, and give rise to what has been called the 'Dutch disease'. The policies required in order to avoid the symptoms of the Dutch disease are discussed in Chapter 3.

3 Macro-Requirements for Sustained Mineral-Driven Development

This chapter deals with the macroeconomic conditions necessary for sustained development, with particular reference to mineral-exporting countries. The fundamental condition for sustained growth in a mineral-exporting country is that the contribution of mineral exports to growth must be maintained over time, regardless of the capacity of the country to maintain its mineral production. This contribution includes not simply the current volume of mineral exports, but the investment of a sufficient portion of the mineral revenues to maintain the rate of growth induced by the initial mineral exports. As countries grow, mineral exports are likely to constitute a smaller proportion of GDP, even if mineral production is maintained or increased. Hence, the original stimulus to GDP from mineral exports is likely to decline. Also, the domestic demand for minerals will grow, thereby reducing minerals available for export. If the rate of national savings as a percentage of GDP is maintained or enhanced, the rate of growth of GDP will be maintained provided there is a proper allocation of national savings into productive investment.

The first part of this chapter discusses macroeconomic policies that minimize or avoid the adverse effects of external disturbances, or of changes in internal structure, on sustainable development. We then turn to the function of government in managing the distribution and use of mineral rents created by the production and marketing of mineral resources. In order to maintain the conditions for sustained growth, governments must adopt appropriate policies for dealing with disturbances and for managing mineral rents. The conditions include: maintaining the overall volume of investment required for growth by channelling the proper portion of mineral rents into productive investment; preventing price distortions arising from inflation and real exchange rate changes that reduce incentives for production and investment in the tradeables sectors; avoiding large and prolonged fiscal deficits while maintaining government expenditure for essential social services and productivity without impairing foreign and domestic investment; maximizing resource rents available to the domestic economy; and managing external debt in a manner consistent with sustainable growth.

External and Internal Disturbances

The disturbances addressed in the following paragraphs are: fluctuations in export revenues caused by changes in world prices; changes in exchange rates accompanying fluctuations in export revenues; large capital imports or exports; and internal structural changes. These disturbances in turn give rise to a number of conditions incompatible with sustained growth. They are (1) sharp fluctuations in government expenditures, which affect both economic welfare and the level of investment in human and physical capital required for sustained growth; (2) price distortions that affect production and investment in the tradeables sectors of the economy in favour of non-tradeables; (3) deterioration of the balance of payments that results in a substantial loss of foreign exchange reserves and/or an increase in foreign indebtedness; and (4) reduced mineral exports which may result from depletion of mineral reserves, failure to explore and develop new mineral reserves, or reduced competitiveness of the mineral industry in world markets.

Fluctuations in export revenue

Minerals are more subject to world price fluctuations than are manufactures or services. Individual minerals, such as copper and petroleum, display different patterns of fluctuation in time and degree, in part because of differences in their sensitivity to world business conditions and in part because of differences in market structure. Most mineral markets have some degree of oligopoly and the degree of producer control over prices varies over time. Petroleum prices have at times been subject to substantial control by the Organization of Oil Exporting Countries (OPEC) cartel, as was the case during the early 1970s. For several decades after World War II, US copper prices were controlled by the producers' price system, while the London Metal Exchange (LME) governed prices in the rest of the world (Mikesell 1979). Today the world market for copper is integrated and competitive. Copper has substitutes for a number of uses, but since substitution requires changes in technology, short-term price elasticity of demand is low. The same is true of most non-fuel minerals, with the result that fluctuations in world demand contribute to substantial price instability.

When declining prices regularly recover to previous levels within a period of, say, two or three years, their economic impact can be mediated by a stabilization programme combined with appropriate monetary and fiscal policies. Export diversification can also stabilize export income, provided the individual exports follow inverse price patterns. Minerals are also subject to long-term trends in real prices. For example, real metal prices declined by nearly 10 per cent between 1970 and 1992 (IMF 1994). The real price for all the major minerals—copper, tin, nickel, aluminium, lead, zinc, and iron ore—followed a similar downward path during this period. Real prices for petroleum and coal declined steadily between 1980 and 1994. A long-run decline in world prices may not impair profits in the mining industry if costs are reduced commensurately. Over the past three decades mining costs have declined sharply due to technological developments and better management, but much of the reduction has been in labour costs. Reduced demand for labour and other domestic inputs can have an adverse impact on the economy, even if mining profits are maintained.

Changes in *import* prices also generate macro-effects on the economy. Some economists use the concept of 'terms-of-trade shock', which represents the impact of combined changes in export and import prices. Thus, if a sharp decline in export prices is accompanied by a rise in import prices, say, as a consequence of an increase in the price of petroleum, the terms-of-trade shock is much greater than with a decline in export prices alone. However, the macroeconomic effects of an increase in import prices differ from the effects of a decrease in export prices. A rise in import prices will shift expenditures to domestic products, while a decline in export prices may reduce the demand for domestic goods as a result of the decline in export revenue. However, increases in essential imports such as food and energy, for which demand is highly inelastic, may increase foreign exchange expenditures at the expense of intermediate and capital goods essential for domestic production. Unless accompanied by a decline in production, a fall in mineral export prices may have little impact on wages; the major impact is likely to be on the resource rent (the difference between export revenues and full production costs). A decline in profits may have a long-term effect on investment in the extractive industry, but little immediate effect on mine operations.

Fluctuating export prices usually have their greatest impact on government revenue since government revenue from the minerals industry tends to be a substantial portion of total government revenue in mineral economies. How the government allocates increases in its revenue from export booms and adjusts its expenditures to a sharp decline in export revenue has a major impact on all sectors of the economy. During periods of export boom governments frequently increase expenditures for social programmes that tend to increase consumption, and there is strong political pressure to maintain these programmes when export revenues decline. The result is likely to be fiscal deficits financed by credit creation, or current account deficits financed by foreign borrowing. The government may also launch large infrastructure investment programmes during periods of export boom, and it is difficult to curtail expenditures for these projects once they are committed. When fiscal expenditures are maintained by borrowing directly from the public, savings are transferred to the government at the expense of private investments. Fiscal deficits also tend to raise interest rates unless accompanied by some form of credit creation. Credit creation (money expansion) will, over time, increase nominal interest rates as a result of inflationary expectations. Inflation will encourage capital flight and a deterioration of the balance of payments, which will promote further capital flight. Maintaining current expenditures by foreign borrowing creates fewer internal problems, but increasing foreign debt may have adverse effects on the balance of payments. Policies for dealing with fluctuations in government revenue are explored later in this chapter.

Changes in foreign exchange rates

As discussed in Chapter 2, export booms generate a surge of foreign exchange income that if uncontrolled may distort domestic prices by appreciating the foreign exchange value of the currency. Prices of tradeables in competition with imports, as well as prices of exports sold in competitive world markets, tend to decline with currency appreciation. Prices of non-tradeables may rise with the increase in income generated by the export boom. This disparity in sectoral relations reduces incentives to produce and invest in the tradeables sectors on which long-run sustainability must depend. Some countries have sought to deal with the problem by increasing tariffs and other import restrictions, but such actions create further price distortions and impair exports by increasing the costs of domestically produced inputs. A temporary increase in the real exchange rate as a consequence of a surge in raw material exports is a form of market failure, since it changes the relationship between domestic costs, including labour and world market prices. Domestic producers of tradeable goods are faced with lower prices in terms of their own currency for both imports and goods competing with their exports in foreign markets. Reducing production and investment in the tradeables sectors and over-stimulating the non-tradeables sectors, reduces growth, and is likely to lead to a current account deficit following the export boom. Even though the foreign value of the domestic currency may decline following the export boom, it may take several years before the appropriate relationship between tradeables and non-tradeables can be re-established, and, meanwhile, growth is impaired. A sharp decline in the exchange rate may also generate inflation and further price distortions unless prevented by appropriate monetary and fiscal policies. For these reasons, macroeconomic management must include a foreign exchange rate policy closely integrated with monetary and fiscal policies.

Capital imports and exports

Mineral-rich countries may experience substantial increases in foreign direct investment. This may occur because of large mineral discoveries or as a result of a change in the foreign investment climate. Since it requires several years for companies to explore, negotiate mining agreements, and develop new mines, capital imports for mining investment create fewer macro-problems than capital imports taking the form of portfolio investments in bonds and stocks. In the latter case, the principal 'foreign' investors are often citizens of the country who are repatriating their capital in response to higher interest rates or other favourable conditions in domestic markets.

A surge in capital imports may give rise to Dutch disease symptoms similar to those experienced with a sudden increase in export income. However, if the government requires that the domestic currency needed by a foreign mining firm to pay for wages, materials, and property be acquired directly from the central bank rather than purchased on the foreign exchange market, currency appreciation can be avoided and the government can hold the foreign exchange until a time when foreign exchange revenues may be lower.

A sudden withdrawal of foreign direct investment capital is unlikely to occur in the mining industry. Foreign firms will withdraw capital when their mineral reserves are exhausted, or sell their properties to the government or domestic buyers. In the latter case, payments to foreigners are usually made over a period of years. Withdrawal of portfolio capital can be triggered by a variety of domestic or international events, and mineral-exporting countries are no more vulnerable to such withdrawals than other developing countries. Capital flight, such as that occurring in Mexico in 1994, is owing in part to the recent tendency of developing countries to remove controls on capital movements, and in part owing to a globalized capital market in which investors find opportunities for speculative returns in developing countries, but are quick to sell the investments on hearing reports of financial problems.

Mineral-exporting countries tend to be heavy foreign borrowers, especially if their mineral industry is state owned. Foreign investors are usually responsible for their own foreign indebtedness, but in the case of joint ventures, the obligations may be shared by the government. The higher the ratio of debt service to current foreign exchange income, the more vulnerable a country is to balance of payments difficulties or default. Default can dry up sources of foreign capital, including foreign direct investment. Foreign direct investment usually does not give rise to debt service problems since payments to foreign owners are a function of earnings, which depends upon the exports of an enterprise. When governments nationalize a mining or petroleum industry by buying out foreign-owned firms, they convert foreign direct investments into national debt obligations.

Many state mineral enterprises have borrowed heavily from the World Bank and regional development banks, as well as from foreign private financial sources. In some cases, high export revenues have promoted increased foreign borrowing because higher earnings raise the country's borrowing capacity. External indebtedness increases a country's vulnerability to default from a decline in export revenue since the debt service payments do not decline with a decline in export earnings. Much of the low growth and reduced level of investment of many developing countries during the 1980s was due to large payments on debt obligations. Mineral-exporting countries appear to be especially vulnerable to debt crises, in part because of past nationalizations, and in part because of the instability of export revenues. Default on external obligations reduces foreign investment and promotes capital flight.

Governments frequently borrow from the IMF or other sources during periods of export revenue shortfall. They plan to repay short- or intermediate-term credits when export revenues rise by an amount equal to the borrowings plus interest. Very often the export earnings are not fully restored so that the debt tends to be rolled over and interest payments accumulate as additional debt. Much of the current borrowing by developing countries from both the IMF and the World Bank is simply a roll-over of past debts (Kenen 1994). Such borrowing does not generate income and the interest payments impair sustainability.

Internal structural changes

In addition to macro-changes resulting from external forces, mineral economies are vulnerable to structural changes that create macro-imbalance. They may exhaust their mineral reserves, or domestic demand for minerals may rise to the point where there is no export surplus. Mineral economies often fail to undertake exploration and new mineral development sufficient to exploit their full mineral reserve potential, or even offset depletion of existing mines and petroleum fields. This is especially the case with countries that nationalize their mining industries and close investment to foreign firms. There may also be a lack of incentives and financing for private domestic mining firms. Unless mineral production expands in line with the demand for imports that accompanies growth, nations heavily dependent on mineral exports for foreign exchange must find alternative exports. Unless new investment is financed by an inflow of capital, there must be an increase in domestic savings and investment directed to the export market.

An important structural change in the world mineral industries is increased productivity and decreased costs. Therefore, mineral industries in individual countries must continually improve productivity and lower costs if they are to remain competitive in world markets. Where costs are high relative to world costs, production and investment in the mineral industry is likely to decline. Policies for dealing with these structural changes in the mineral industries are discussed in Chapter 4.

Policies for Dealing with Distortions Resulting from External Disturbances

The major impacts of the external disturbances to the economies of mineral-exporting countries discussed above are (1) sudden increases or decreases in government domestic expenditures; (2) exchange rate appreciation or depreciation, which affects the relationship between tradeables and non-tradeables; and (3) balance of payments deterioration. The policies for dealing with these impacts are discussed in the following paragraphs.

Government expenditures

While short-run fluctuations in export revenues from mineral exports cannot be avoided, a combination of appropriate monetary and fiscal policies and the establishment of a mineral reserve stabilization fund (MRSF) can modify the effects of these external disturbances in a manner that will avoid impairment to long-run sustainability.

Governments can avoid sharp reductions in expenditures by accumulating funds in periods of rising income, and using these funds to maintain expenditures when revenue declines. However, because the pattern of export revenue is uncertain, accumulated funds may be exhausted, and the government will need to find new sources of funds in order to avoid sharply reducing social programmes, or curtailing important investment activity essential for growth. Governments of industrial countries are generally able to offset temporary reductions in tax revenue by issuing securities for purchase by domestic and foreign investors; developing countries usually lack well-developed securities markets, and risk premiums are often high, ranging from

3 to 15 per cent over US Treasury bonds.[1] Poor domestic capital markets lead investors to channel their savings abroad while governments resort to credit creation, which may generate inflation. Maintaining an efficient domestic securities market for government borrowing requires a low level of inflation, which in turn requires credit restraint. Credit restraint will tend to raise nominal interest rates, but inflation inevitably results in a rise in interest rates at least equal to the rate of inflation. Government revenue can be supplemented temporarily with foreign borrowing, say, from the IMF, but borrowing for current government expenditures should be limited to amounts essential for a transition to lower government expenditures. Except in short-term emergencies, foreign borrowing should be for the purpose of increasing productive investment that will yield income well above the annual debt service payments.

Foreign exchange rate policy

Foreign exchange rate policy should aim at preventing a temporary rise in export income from appreciating the real exchange rate to a degree that domestic prices of tradeables decline relative to non-tradeables. As noted in Chapter 2, real exchange rate appreciation may result from price inflation as well as from an increase in the nominal value of the domestic currency. Thus an export boom may create a certain amount of inflation while at the same time increasing the nominal exchange rate, with the result that there is a substantial appreciation of the real exchange rate. Foreign exchange policy may also be used to avoid a substantial decline in the real exchange rate during periods of low export income.

There are several types of foreign exchange systems, each of which has advantages and disadvantages. In the absence of any exchange controls, the government will sell foreign exchange derived from export taxes or from state mining companies in the foreign exchange market, and mining companies will also sell their foreign exchange revenues from exports on the foreign exchange market. In periods of export boom, sales of foreign exchange will result in an appreciation of the domestic currency. The central bank could prevent this appreciation by buying foreign exchange in the market with domestic currency and in this way maintain a fixed exchange rate, or allow some movement in the rate to correct for inflation. An alternative system is for the central bank to acquire all foreign exchange proceeds from both government and private sources and allocate the foreign exchange to importers and others that require exchange at a controlled rate.

There are advantages and disadvantages to controlling exchange rates as contrasted with allowing the rates to move freely with the demand for and supply of foreign exchange. Fixed exchange rates provide stability for import prices, and prevent a sharp rise in export revenue from decreasing the domestic currency prices of tradeables. Fixed rates also avoid the depreciation often accompanying a decline in export

---

[1] Before the December 1994 devaluation of Mexican currency, the country's risk premium reflected in bond prices was roughly 3% over US Treasury bond rate of the same maturity. There was a spread of 7% for Argentina and about 13% for Venezuela (Gavin *et al*. 1996: 1)

income. A freely floating exchange rate system may avoid an overvalued currency and subsequent large devaluations forced by speculative capital flight and sharp decreases in foreign exchange reserves. On the other hand, a freely floating rate system may result in real exchange appreciation in periods of export boom. There is a tendency for countries to maintain fixed exchange rates long after the currency is substantially overvalued, because devaluation is often delayed for political reasons.

Under a freely floating exchange rate system, a decline in export revenue will cause the currency to depreciate. While depreciation will tend to reduce import demand, it will do little to expand mineral exports in the short and intermediate run. In fact, the short-term effect of exchange rate depreciation may worsen the current account balance due to the J-curve phenomenon.[2] Also, exchange rate depreciation will contribute to inflation. In general, efficient macroeconomic policy is promoted by a fixed but adjustable exchange rate under the control of a politically independent central bank. Whatever the exchange rate system, changes in rates must be closely integrated with monetary and fiscal policies if the changes are to have the intended effects. For example, exchange rate depreciation not accompanied by sufficient monetary restraint may result in inflation, which nullifies the effect of the nominal depreciation on the relationship between domestic and foreign prices.

Balance of payments management

The immediate effect of a sharp decline in export revenue is likely to be a current account deficit (excess of current payments for goods and services, including debt service, over current receipts from exports, services, and income from foreign investment). Since it requires time, perhaps one to two years, to adjust the current account by reducing payments without economic and social disruption and by expanding export earnings, it is desirable to finance the current account deficit by drawing on reserves, or if necessary, by borrowing from the IMF or other low-cost sources. The larger a country's foreign exchange reserves the more efficiently it can adjust a current account deficit. However, reserve losses and short-term borrowing, if not accompanied by well-publicized policies for restoring equilibrium, may well trigger capital flight and discourage foreign capital inflow. As was noted in the preceding section of this chapter, although exchange depreciation may be warranted, it usually requires a couple of years before depreciation can be effective in improving the current account balance. Because of the volatility of world mineral markets, mineral-exporting countries should plan in advance for sharp reductions in export revenue, including a determination of which expenditures should have priority and

---

[2] According to the J-curve principle, the immediate effect of currency depreciation will be to worsen the current account balance, followed by a gradual improvement after a year or two. The reason is that despite an increase in domestic prices of imports following depreciation, consumers will be slow to shift their purchases from imports to domestic substitutes, while exporters will for a time maintain the domestic currency prices of their exports. Foreigners will also be slow to increase their purchases in response to the lower foreign currency prices in the depreciating country (Krugman 1991: ch. 2).

which should be cut; what incentives to provide in order to induce new sources of exports; and how a temporary deficit would be financed.

A Mineral Reserve Stabilization Fund (MRSF)

Perhaps the most important instrument for macro-management for mineral-exporting countries for dealing with volatile export revenue is the MRSF. Several countries have established an MRSF, including Botswana, Chile, and Papua New Guinea. The MRSF can serve several functions:

- stabilizing foreign exchange expenditures;
- stabilizing government domestic expenditures;
- allocating mineral rents between consumption and investment expenditures; and
- preventing real exchange rate appreciation or depreciation.

Payments made into an MRSF may be all of the mineral rents accruing to the government, or payments may be limited to increases in mineral rents, according to a formula designed to capture windfalls. Stabilizing expenditure of mineral rents may involve alternately accumulating and disbursing funds as rents rise and decline around a historical average. However, uncertainties concerning export prices and other factors affecting the future course of export revenues may lead to the exhaustion of funds following a long period of historically low receipts. It might be better to have at least a minimum percentage of revenue paid into the fund each year, with a rising percentage paid in as revenues increase. Net withdrawals could be permitted for limited periods in years of exceptionally low revenue. Maximum accumulation might be determined by the amount required for, say, ten years of annual withdrawals without exhausting the fund. In any case, the arrangements for accumulations and withdrawals should be made by specialists, with no interference from political interests and in accordance with the designated purposes of an MRSF.

Since payments to the MRSF take the form of foreign exchange, it would be desirable to have the MRSF operated by the central bank, which might chair an advisory committee consisting of economic, financial, and commodity specialists. Payments into the fund could include both taxes on private extraction firms and transfers to the fund by government enterprises. In order to stabilize the availability of foreign exchange derived from mineral exports, a portion of the annual receipts should be invested abroad. These foreign exchange funds should be available for maintaining foreign exchange expenditures in periods of sharp declines in receipts, but not used as continuous supplements to foreign exchange income. When the government transfers foreign exchange to the MRSF, it should receive a counterpart credit in domestic currency at the central bank. It would also be desirable for the MRSF to have control over the release of the domestic currency credits in the fund.

The MRSF could sterilize a portion of the domestic currency credits and not make them available for government expenditure. In order to stabilize government expenditures, the portion of the annual credits in the fund that would be sterilized could be increased as export revenues paid into the fund rose; while in periods of exceptionally low export revenues, none of the annual accumulations would be sterilized and additional amounts of domestic currency would be withdrawn from the fund.

Should windfalls of private mining companies also be paid into an MRSF? The government could tax the windfalls of private mining firms by a special excess profits tax. However, this might discourage investment in mining since the windfalls make up for losses in periods of low prices. A recent IMF Working Paper concludes that privately retained windfalls from export booms are unlikely to be inflationary when accompanied by appropriate monetary policies and that, therefore, the taxation of private windfalls is not justified (Collier and Gunning 1996).

The MRSF could allocate mineral rents paid into the fund between consumption and investment in a manner designed to invest a sufficient portion of the rents to maintain the capital value of the exhausting mineral reserves. This function is discussed in the following chapter. The MRSF could also prevent a surge in export revenues from appreciating the foreign exchange value of the currency in a way that would produce symptoms of the Dutch disease. Foreign exchange payments into the fund, as contrasted with sales in the foreign exchange market, would help to prevent an appreciation of the domestic currency. The MRSF could also mitigate depreciation of the domestic currency when there is a sharp reduction in foreign exchange income. In these and other ways the MRSF could mitigate the destabilizing effects of fluctuating export revenue and facilitate macro-management to avoid distortions in the economy that impede growth.

Managing Mineral Rents

Mineral rents

Revenue from the sale of minerals may be divided into resource rent and payments for labour and capital required for discovery and extraction. Resource rent is defined as the market value of the mineral, minus all costs of production—including the minimum return on capital necessary to induce the investment. If production costs absorb all the revenue, there is no rent. The total rent generated by a mine (or petroleum field) is the present value of the net proceeds (after deducting all costs) over the entire life of the mine.[3] The present value of the least profitable mine that could ever be in production would be zero, and would not generate rent (Garnaut and Clunies-Ross 1983: 4). Such a mineral deposit is regarded as marginal, while deposits with richer ores or those less expensive to develop will generate rent. Assuming a competitive market in which mining firms compete for mining rights,[4]

[3] Although this discussion of rents is oriented to mining, all natural resource production may provide resource rents; parallel types of taxation involving similar problems can be applied to petroleum. Thus, petroleum taxes can be levied on the basis of a royalty for each barrel or on the basis of an *ad valorem* tax on the value output, and there can be various types of income or profits taxes or joint ventures.

[4] As the governments of most developing countries own all of the subsoil minerals, foreign investors must negotiate mining contracts with the government.

the price paid for the rights should reflect the capitalized value of the rent after adjustment for risk. Different firms competing for mineral rights will have different perceptions of risk, even where they may be more or less in agreement on production costs.

How the mineral rents are distributed and used (absorbed in the economy) determines in large measure the contribution of the mineral industry to the development of the economy. The government obtains mineral rents from taxing private mineral firms or from the profits of state enterprises. Mineral rent not taken by the government accrues to the private owners of the minerals as income in excess of their costs, including the return on their capital necessary to make the investment after allowing for risk. It is even possible for labour or landowners to obtain a portion of the mineral rent by being able to charge more than the competitive wage or price. The government is also responsible for how its share of the mineral rent is used (or absorbed). This may take the form of investment in the economy, increased reserves or consumption. Non-governmental recipients may use the rent for domestic investment, consumption or for capital exports that make no contribution to the economy. However, governmental policies can influence how the rent is used.

Resource rent is the unique contribution of a mineral resource to a nation's economy. Since the labour and capital required to produce the minerals could be used to produce goods in non-resource industries equivalent in value to their full production costs, resource rent is the surplus over cost attributable to the resource alone. Since in most developing countries the government owns the minerals in the subsoil, the objective of the government should be to maximize its resource rents from mineral production. Such an objective is difficult to achieve with precision because the investor must be compensated for full production costs—including the various risks associated with exploring and developing a mine—none of which can be known with certainty.

Mineral rents fluctuate by a greater percentage than total export earnings since they constitute the residual after mining costs, just as net profits fluctuate more than total revenue for any industry. Therefore, if the tax system is designed to capture a portion of mineral rents, government revenue will be quite sensitive to fluctuations in mineral revenues. Governments can adopt a tax system for the mineral industry designed to stabilize tax receipts, or one designed to maximize the government's share of mineral rents without impairing production and future investment in the industry.

Taxing mineral income

Taxation in mining and petroleum is complicated by the existence of multiple government objectives, which include maximizing the government's share of the revenue, maximizing mineral rents, stabilizing tax revenue, and making the mineral industry attractive to investors. These objectives are not wholly compatible with one another. For example, maximizing the government's share of the revenue may not be compatible with maximizing the mineral rents, with stabilizing government revenue, or with attracting new investment.

There are several types of taxation, each of which differs in its ability to maximize government revenue. The most common are: a royalty on each unit of output; an *ad valorem* tax on the value of the output; a proportional income tax, which may be higher than the normal income tax rate; a progressive profits tax (PPT); and an equity-sharing arrangement. In the usual equity-sharing arrangement, the government is permitted to acquire a portion of the equity at cost, after the investor has assumed the risks of exploration and initial development. Several types of taxation may be combined so that, for example, there may be both a royalty and a PPT, or equity sharing and a progressive tax on the investor's share of the profits. None of the tax arrangements noted above fully maximizes both the resource rent and the government's share of the rent. A royalty or *ad valorem* tax represents an additional cost per unit of output, and the mining firm will produce only to the point at which marginal revenue is equal to marginal cost, including the tax. This will mean that production is less than that required to maximize rent. However, a royalty will provide greater stability of government revenue than some form of profits tax.

Mine operators have an incentive to mine the highest ore grades first and bypass lower grades or delay their extraction, with a consequent increase in cost and lower output. The net present value (NPV) of early returns is higher and maximizing early returns involves less risk to the mining firm. A royalty or export tax raises the minimum profitable cut-off grade, with the result that some ore that would have been mined in the absence of an output-based tax will be left in the ground and probably never mined. For a tax to be consistent with maximizing rent, it should be neutral with respect to the mining firm's decision regarding how much to produce and how to adjust output over time (Garnaut and Clunies-Ross 1983: ch. 7). A PPT is more neutral with respect to production than a royalty or export tax, but it could affect decisions on the time-pattern of the cash flow (Beals 1980: ch. 2). Because risk increases over time, the more profitable ore may be extracted first, even though there will be some additional cost for recovering the lower grade ore at a later stage. Under a PPT, a mining firm's extraction plan may call for mining the richest and most accessible ore in the early period, leaving ore in the ground in locations where it might never be economically mined. As Garnaut and Clunies-Ross (1983) point out, PPT will yield different tax receipts from two projects with the same maximum NPV if they have different patterns of cash flow. For this and other reasons, Garnaut and Clunies Ross favour a 'resource rent tax' (RRT), which taxes the positive NPV for the life of the project at a constant discount rate. A 100 per cent RRT would tax the entire mineral rent, but this is unlikely to be acceptable to the investor. There are some problems in applying an RRT on an annual basis, especially since net cash flows are unlikely to be constant over the life of the mine. Nevertheless, the RRT comes the closest to tax neutrality and is based on the calculation of maximum resource rent. Both the rate of discount and the share of the resource rent are subject to bargaining between mining companies and the government. Garnaut and Clunies-Ross (1983) have proposed a methodology for applying an RRT, but there are no examples of a pure RRT in use.

Countries often insist on acquiring a share of the equity in a mining investment, either for domestic political reasons, or to increase governmental control over the enterprise. In many cases, equity sharing not only increases the government's financial risk, but it may pay a higher price for control than necessary. Without any ownership, the government has the power to require companies to take actions or adopt policies on matters in which the government has a special national interest. This applies especially to labour conditions, the environment, and company purchases of domestic inputs. Owning a share of the equity in a mining enterprise also means that the government shares the investment risk.

Tax regimes differ with respect to the risk imposed on the investor. Risk determines the investor's risk-adjusted rate of discount, and this rate will be affected by the tax regime. If the investor is required to pay a high tax before receiving any net return, he will demand a higher rate of return. An up-front fee paid by the mining firm for the right to explore and develop a mine imposes the greatest risk, since the tax is paid whether or not there is any net revenue. A royalty limits taxes to actual output, while a PPT applies only when the project yields annual net revenue. An RRT has an advantage over a PPT because taxes are paid only if the NPV over the life of the project is positive. Under a PPT, if a mine were highly profitable in one year and incurred a loss the next year, the firm would pay a high marginal tax the first year, but this high tax would not be offset by a loss in the poor year. The RRT avoids this problem by taxing the NPV of the project at a single rate.

The government is subject to a greater risk in the case of a PPT or RRT than in the case of a royalty, while it assumes no risk under up-front payments. The government also accepts risk with an equity-sharing arrangement since, unless the project is profitable, it receives no revenue. Hence, there is a trade-off for the government between risk and revenue, and its choice of a tax regime should depend, in part at least, on its degree of risk aversion.

The method of tax administration will affect revenues and risk, and each type of tax regime presents special administrative problems. Taxes or tax equivalents can be negotiated, subjected to competitive bidding, or fixed by legislation. When there are several competing firms interested in investing, auctioning the mining rights may be the best way to obtain maximum revenue. If all the bids are regarded as too low, the government can consider exploring and developing the area with a state enterprise, but this will subject the government to all of the risk. State enterprises have a poor record of efficiency even though they can contract out both exploration and mine operation with an international resource company.

The more complex the tax regime the more difficult it is to use the auction method for negotiating mining contracts. Fixed up-front fees and royalties are more suited to competitive bidding than are income taxes, since the latter involve complex provisions for calculating costs and annual capital deductions. PPT and RRT arrangements are more difficult to submit to competitive bidding. Tax stability is promoted by legislation applying to all mining firms, but there are two major drawbacks. First, the provisions in the legislation may not attract any mining firms or they may give up too much of the potential resource rent. Second, provisions in a mining contract often need to be tailored to the particular circumstances of the project, or to the requirements of the potential investor. Most mining agreements are negotiated under a framework of legislation that permits some negotiating flexibility. Flexibility is particularly important for complex equity-sharing arrangements. Whatever the provisions, government negotiators must be fully informed about mining contracts in other countries in order to negotiate agreements that approach the realization of maximum revenue from a project.

Private ownership of subsoil resources

In the case of countries whose subsoil minerals are privately owned, resource rents are usually divided between the government and the legal owners. If the government were to tax away all the rents, private entities might not be willing to buy or hold mineral resources. Since governments normally tax all sources of income, there is no reason some of the output attributed to natural resources should not be taxed. Moreover, there are persuasive arguments for society to claim a portion of natural resource rents. Natural resources, in contrast to assets produced by capital and labour, represent an endowment to society—a form of capital inherited by mankind. Because of mankind's dependence on natural resources, there is an element of the 'commons' in all natural resources. This means that the way they are used and the distribution of the services they provide affect social welfare, not simply private welfare. Unlike man-made assets, natural resources cannot be duplicated or their volume expanded. Moreover, as will be discussed in Chapter 4, it can be argued that the capital value of natural resources should be maintained for the benefit of future generations. These arguments suggest that mineral rents should be subject to special taxes that reflect society's right to a share of the contribution of natural resources to output, but what that share should be, if any, has long been subject to dispute. The 'single tax', which was put forward more than a century ago by Henry George and has many adherents today, provides that all capital gains from holding land and other natural resources should be fully taxed by the government (Young 1916). Since the capital gains on mineral resources are the capitalized value of the resource rents (which were zero when the resources were in unlimited supply), the single tax would capture all mineral rents. However, there are many costs involved in discovering and holding mineral resources, including risk. Taxing all the mineral rents of privately owned resources would discourage investment in mineral exploration and development.

Since concentrating, smelting, and refining minerals constitute production with capital and labour, the question arises whether taxing income derived from mineral processing should be at a normal corporate tax rate. Most governments tax the profits of mining companies regardless of the source of earnings. However, a higher than normal tax may discourage companies from processing ores and encourage shipping them abroad. This might be avoided by treating ore mining as a separate project for the purpose of taxing mineral rents.

Should governments maximize their share of the mineral rents?

Aside from providing the private investors with a sufficient share of the mineral revenue to induce them to invest, should the government seek to maximize its share of mineral rents? An argument can be made that private investors will allocate more of their net income to productive investment than will the government, and therefore governments should not levy a tax on mineral rents greater than, say, the normal income tax. In dealing with this question, it is necessary to distinguish between foreign investors who are unlikely to have a preference for investing in the host country as against investing in other countries, and domestic private investors who are more likely to invest in their own country. In a competitive mining industry, it is likely that private mining firms would invest in mining or other productive industries a larger share of the mineral rents than would the government. Moreover, the private rents are likely to be capitalized and accrue as capital gains, which are more likely to be saved. However, the mineral rents might go to a few oligopolists or royal families who would not save and invest them. As will be discussed in later chapters, mineral rents may influence the policies of governments in ways that affect social development and social sustainability. It is not possible to answer the question posed above because of a number of social and economic factors which will differ among mineral-exporting countries. There is also the issue of whether some portion of the rents from natural resources should not accrue to society.

Conclusions

Macroeconomic conditions for sustained growth in mineral-exporting countries are affected by a number of external and internal developments, including fluctuations in world prices of mineral exports and basic imports; changes in exchange rates; capital imports and exports; and structural changes affecting a country's capacity to produce minerals. The impacts of these developments can be mitigated by appropriate monetary, foreign exchange, and fiscal policies, and by establishing an MRSF designed to stabilize both foreign exchange and government domestic currency expenditures. Mineral rents are the unique contribution of a nation's natural resources to national output. How these rents are shared involves complex social and economic issues which are considered later in this book. The way mineral rents are consumed or invested has important consequences for sustainable development.

4 Mineral Asset Depletion and Sustainability

This chapter deals with how the depletion of national mineral reserves may affect sustainability and how sustainability can be maintained with depleting mineral assets. One approach is to conserve the mineral assets, which for mineral-exporting countries means delaying mineral development and export growth. Another approach, which is favoured here, is to permit mineral development as determined by competitive market conditions, while preventing mineral depletion from resulting in national capital consumption. The conventional arguments for conservation are reviewed before dealing with the conceptual and analytical problems in measuring the value of mineral depletion and its importance for environmental and resource accounting (EARA). The chapter concludes with a discussion of the role which managing a nation's mineral industry plays in promoting sustainable development.

Mineral asset depletion affects the sustainability of the world economy as well as that of individual mineral-producing countries. However, the depletion of world mineral resources may benefit mineral-producing countries that have ample reserves, since reduced world supplies should raise mineral prices. We shall consider how the interests of the mineral producers can be reconciled with global sustainability.

Arguments for Conserving Mineral Resources

Conservationists concerned with world sustainability have argued for reducing the rate of exploitation of mineral wealth in order to provide for the needs of future generations. The Club of Rome (Meadows *et al.* 1972) advocated conserving mineral resources by limiting the GDP growth of the industrial countries. Their argument was supported by erroneous predictions of mineral scarcity based on annual production/mineral reserve ratios existing in 1970. Their predictions of severe shortages of important minerals by the year 2000 resulted in a loss of their credibility; applying the same flawed methodology today is likely to yield equally erroneous predictions. Although no effort has been made to promote global mineral policies based on the warnings of the Club of Rome, mineral producers or their governments have sometimes advocated conservation of national mineral reserves. Such policies to restrict exports to conserve national mineral reserves have been implemented in Australia and Venezuela for iron ore, in Canada for uranium, and in the Netherlands for natural gas (Radetzki 1992: 43). Governments have also deferred negotiations with foreign investors desiring to develop the country's minerals on the grounds they lacked the institutional framework to negotiate agreements and monitor mining operations. In some instances, development was delayed until it could be undertaken by state enterprises (ibid. 47–9).

Deferral of mineral development has been advocated on the grounds that the output of a new large mining project would depress mineral prices. Prior to its development in 1991, some Chilean officials recommended that Chile's Escondida copper mine be deferred on the grounds that, given the inelastic world demand for copper, Escondida's annual output of 1.2 million tonnes would reduce world copper prices and thereby reduce Chile's export earnings (Radetzki 1992: 50–2). Countering this argument, it was pointed out that constructing the low-cost Escondida mine may have discouraged other potential projects and reduced the output of higher-cost mines elsewhere in the world. Had the Chilean government deferred construction of Escondida, the foreign investors might have backed away from the project and invested in copper production elsewhere.

Cartels and iternational commodity agreements (ICAs)

Collusive agreements among producers to control prices by restricting output have taken the form of cartels sponsored by governments, and of ICAs, which have been sanctioned by United Nations agencies (Radetzki 1990: 127–8). The OPEC cartel was the most successful in terms of controlling prices, which rose severalfold from the mid-1970s to the early 1980s. However, OPEC's ability to maintain prices virtually vanished in the late 1980s and early 1990s, and real petroleum prices declined to the levels of the early 1970s. Although OPEC still has considerable potential power, its portion of the total fuel market has declined significantly. The spectacular increase in prices in the early 1980s undoubtedly encouraged new sources of petroleum production outside OPEC, an expansion of the market for substitutes, and energy conservation.

A second example of producer collusion occurred in 1974–5, when Jamaica increased production levies and export taxes in order to raise the price of bauxite, and persuaded several other producers, including Suriname, the Dominican Republic, and Guinea, to adopt similar measures. Although Jamaica's action doubled the price of bauxite imported into the USA, the Caribbean bauxite producers lost some of their share of the market to Australia and Brazil. There were also cartel efforts in phosphate rock and uranium, which achieved only temporary success in raising prices, but had the effect of reducing demand in favour of substitutes or encouraging other sources of supply.

ICAs differ from cartels in that they are designed to stabilize prices rather than to maximize monopoly profits. In some cases, ICAs have been supported by consumer and producer countries, since commodity price stability has been regarded as beneficial to both. However, prices are often set at unsupportable levels, and the welfare of both producers and consumers is impaired. The principal ICA in non-fuel minerals was the International Tin Agreement (ITA), which provided for a buffer stock plus export quotas for member countries. The buffer stock manager purchased tin between 1982 and 1985 in an effort to defend a price higher than the equilibrium level. By October 1985 the manager's resources for defending the agreed price were exhausted, and the world price of tin plummeted. It is conceivable that a well-managed buffer stock could reduce world price fluctuations, but export quotas have never been successful due to smuggling and outright cheating by member governments. Also, political interests often dictate a price which is unsustainable, with the result that prices eventually decline by more than they would have in the absence of an ICA.

Reducing dependence on mineral exports

Mineral-exporting countries have sometimes deferred the development of their minerals in order to avoid heavy dependence on a single industry that is subject to price instability. Deferral has taken the form of discouraging foreign and domestic investment in mining through discriminatory taxation, or of delaying negotiation of mining agreements with potential investors. Such a policy could reduce the rate of growth of GDP since restricting investment in one industry would not ordinarily increase investment in other industries. Even if a way could be found to redirect investment from the industry yielding the highest returns to another industry, the government might be paying too high a price for diversification. Mineral industries are likely to yield higher returns than other industries because they produce rents in addition to returns on invested capital.

All investment decisions involve risk, and the price uncertainty of minerals is simply another factor that should go into determining the probable return on investment of a mining project. Moreover, as was noted in Chapter 3, there are ways of moderating the risk of price uncertainty. Over the long-term, expanding mineral output does not necessarily increase a country's dependence on a single industry, because a portion of the rents generated should go into other industries and thereby promote diversification. As mineral-producing countries grow, they do not simply expand production of minerals: growth is accompanied by an expansion of all industries and by a reduction in the relative importance of the mineral industry in total output.

We conclude that deferring output of minerals is not a sound policy for either individual producing countries or for a group of countries acting collectively. Such a policy usually stimulates an increase in world supply from other sources and also may encourage the development of substitutes for the mineral. But should not the global community take action to reduce current consumption of minerals in order to meet the needs of future generations? Such a policy involves complex issues, such as the uncertainty of world mineral resources and the requirements of future generations with economic structures different from those of today. The world reserves of virtually all minerals are larger today than they were a generation ago, despite the substantial increase in the output of minerals. This is due to advances in mining technology and development of substitutes for natural resources. Therefore, we think that the present generation should continue to meet its requirements for mineral resources, but should also save and invest an amount that will assure an expanding flow of total output in the future.

Minerals left in the ground do not benefit future generations nearly as much as high levels of investment in factories, infrastructure, exploration, technical research, and education. The efficient use of natural resources can contribute far more to sustainable development than *pro forma* conservation. However, in order for the present generation to assure comparable opportunities for future generations, it must pass on an overall economic base capable of maintaining or increasing future per capita output. The capital value of the mineral endowment, not the reserves of particular minerals, should be preserved for future generations.

Optimum Mineral Output and the 'Hotelling Rule' (HR)

Is there an optimum level of world output for a mineral at any point in time? Such an optimum was suggested by the mineral economist, Harold Hotelling. According to the Hotelling Rule (Hotelling 1931), the operation of competitive markets will automatically reduce the output of a mineral as it becomes scarce, so that the reserves of any mineral will deplete slowly and never be completely exhausted. Hotelling assumed that the relative price of a depleting mineral will rise with increasing scarcity, so that the increase in price will tend to promote conservation. According to the HR, the rate of depletion of a uniform finite resource will be governed by the relationship between the rate of increase in the price of the mineral and the rate of interest. Mining firms have the option of producing a mineral and selling the output, or holding the mineral in the ground and realizing a capital gain from the increase in its value due to increasing scarcity. Whenever the annual income from producing the mineral and holding the proceeds at the current rate of interest is less than the capital gain from holding the mineral in the ground for an additional year, it will pay to delay production. The capital gain (Hotelling rent) will depend upon the rate of increase in the price of the mineral, which will rise at a rate determined by demand and supply. According to the HR, extraction ceases when the rate of increase in the price of the mineral is greater than the current rate of interest. In the absence of a substitute for the mineral resource, the last units of the resource might never be mined since without production the price would rise to a level at which there would be no demand. If there is an available substitute, the price of the substitute sets a limit on the increase in the price of the resource, since the remaining stock of the resource cannot be sold at a price higher than the price of the substitute.

For all producers as a group operating in a competitive market, HR provides the optimum path for mineral production. The exhaustion of mineral reserves will be delayed until substitutes can be found for either the mineral or for the products using the mineral. However, due to market failure, the price of the mineral may not rise as the reserves are depleted. It has, therefore, been suggested that some form of collective action is desirable in order to assure optimal production of the resource. This argument for collaboration is rejected by Radetzki (1992: 40) because of the unreliability of the HR. Since discoveries are continually being made, the ultimate quantity of a mineral reserve cannot be known. Also, the quality of mineral reserves varies widely. Deposits that are not economical to produce today, may, as a result of technical advances in mining and metallurgy, become economic in the future. In the late nineteenth century, copper with a grade of less than 6 per cent could not be profitably extracted; and iron ore deposits were of little value if the ore had to be transported from distant places such as Brazil. Today, ore containing less than 0.5 per cent copper can be profitably extracted, and reduced shipping costs have made it possible to transport ore thousands of miles to steel mills. Finally, long-term price trends in metals and fuels bear little relation to scarcity based on estimated output/reserve ratios. There can be no assurance that real prices of metals and fuels will be higher in 2020 than they are in 1997.

Reliance on the operation of HR would not promote intergenerational equity nor provide a model for promoting sustainability in mineral-exporting countries. Lower output at higher prices would prevent a sudden exhaustion of a mineral, but would not provide future generations with the natural resources required for maintaining total output. Also, supply conditions in individual countries do not conform to world conditions of relative mineral scarcity. Therefore, the operation of HR would not result in an optimum production path for achieving national sustainability, nor would its operation assure global sustainability.

In the Hotelling model, resource rent is defined as the difference between the market price of a mineral and the marginal cost of extraction, including the cost of development and discovery. Resource rent multiplied by the quantity of the mineral extracted equals depletion. Hotelling's concept of depletion as being equal to resource rent became the basis for one of the concepts of depletion discussed in the following section. However, Hotelling's model assumes a continual increase in both scarcity and extraction costs, which has not occurred for most minerals due to both technological improvements that reduce costs and new discoveries of reserves.

Accounting for the Capital Depletion of a Mineral Resource

As was discussed in Chapter 2, sustainability of the contribution of a mineral industry to growth under conditions of finite mineral resources, depends upon saving and investing a sufficient portion of the mineral revenue to compensate for the loss of output from the depletion of the resource. Therefore, a major problem in determining the conditions for sustainability is how to define depletion and what its relationship is to resource rent, the unique contribution of the natural resource to output. This section discusses depletion as an element in EARA, which recognizes the specific contribution of natural resources to national output. It begins with the traditional concept of gross domestic product (GDP) and shows how the environmental accounting measure of the national product, called the environmental domestic product (EDP), is derived.

GDP is defined by the US Department of Commerce as equal to the sum of personal consumption expenditures (C), gross private domestic investment (I_d), government expenditures (G), and net exports ($X\text{–}M$), expressed symbolically as:

$$GDP = C + I_d + G + (X - M).$$

Net domestic product (NDP) is defined as GDP less consumption of fixed assets (CFA) produced in the economy, plus minor adjustments, so we may write:

$NDP = GDP - CFA$ + minor adjustments.

There have been a number of criticisms of GDP and NDP as defined above. For example, GDP is faulted for not including the services of housewives and volunteers or of the amenity services provided by wilderness areas. However, we lack data on most of these services. Economists concerned with environmental accounting have objected to the failure of NDP to take account of the depletion of natural resources by commercial extraction; the deterioration of the quality of natural resources resulting from human activities; and the amount society spends on protecting and restoring the natural resource base. It is argued that capital consumption should not be restricted to consumption of fixed assets (CFA) produced in the economy, but should include depletion of natural resources (RD), the deterioration of the quality of natural resources (DQR), and expenditures for protecting or restoring natural resources from damage by human activities (PR). The rationale for deducting PR from NDP is that such expenditures make no contribution to either consumption or net investment. However, to the degree that PR restores damage to the environment, DQR is reduced. Since there are virtually no data on DQR and only partial data on PR, one definition of the environmental domestic product (EDP*1*) as a corrected substitute for NDP is:

$EDP1 = GDP - CFA - RD$ − minor adjustments.

However, a fully corrected definition of EDP is:

$EDP2 = GDP - CFA - RD - DQR - PR$ − minor adjustments.

This chapter is concerned with RD, specifically as it relates to the depletion of mineral resources. DQR and PR are dealt with in Chapter 5.

Deducting mineral depletion in calculating EDP1 is related to sustainability in two ways. First, sustainability of income from mineral production requires that the capital value of the mineral stock before extraction is maintained after the minerals are exhausted. Second, mineral depletion should not be included in income available for consumption. Sustainability of mineral income requires that natural resources are treated as capital with a capital-depletion element that is not to be consumed; man-made capital can substitute for resource assets; and capital depletion is saved so that the accumulated savings can provide an infinite stream of income equal to that provided by the resource before depletion. The first condition has its roots in traditional economics and was stated by Hicks (1946) in his concept of true income—income that excludes capital depletion. The second and third conditions can be traced to Solow (1974) as described in Chapter 2 of this book. All three principles were formalized by Hartwick (1977, 1978). A key element in this analysis is the valuation of depletion.

US Department of Commerce definition

One method of accounting for mineral depletion is to multiply annual physical extraction by the current price of the mineral. This method greatly overstates depletion since the value of the mineral being produced reflects all extraction costs, including labour, capital, and materials. The following method of valuing depletion was published by the US Department of Commerce (1994):

1. Calculate gross rent as total annual revenue produced by the mine less current operating expenditures (those associated with extracting the mineral from the deposit).
2. Resource rent is obtained by subtracting from gross rent both annual depreciation of man-made capital and a normal return to the capital invested in the mine. (The normal return is usually the average real rate of return on corporate bonds.)
3. Per unit rent of the resource equals resource rent divided by the physical quantity extracted.
4. Depletion is resource rent per unit times the quantity of the resource extracted during the year. If there are additions to reserves, they are valued at rent-per-unit times the physical quantity, and subtracted from depletion.

Resource rent in the Department of Commerce definition above, differs from Hotelling's concept of rent mainly because he defines rent as the difference between the market price of a mineral and the marginal cost of extraction, while in the former definition, resource rent is the difference between price and average cost of production. This could make a difference in extraction costs charged between the periods for which rent is calculated, but producers are likely to be more sensitive to marginal costs in their decisions on output.

The net price approach

Repetto *et al.*'s (1989) 'net price' approach to depletion is similar to that of Hotelling, except that resource rent or 'net price' is defined as the current market price minus *average* extraction costs, including an estimated normal profit on the capital investment. Resource depletion is the net reduction in the stock of the natural resource (extraction minus increase in estimated reserves) times the 'net price'. This enables Repetto to use current profits in excess of the normal return on the capital investment as a measure of the appreciation of the mineral stock. However, if marginal extraction costs are rising, profits will be higher than Hotelling rent (or depletion), since Hotelling depletion is the profit on the marginal tonne. The existence of different qualities of mineral reserves in a mine results in a rise in extraction costs as lower quality reserves are extracted, thereby reducing the rents on marginal tonnes. Therefore, Hartwick and Hageman (1993: 233) state that by using *average* extraction costs for measuring rent, Repetto's method overestimates depletion as measured by HR. In practice, Repetto estimates depletion by subtracting the estimated 'normal' return on capital investment from data on the current profits of mineral companies. However, it is not always clear whether this method yields pure resource rent or includes an allowance for risk on capital investment.

The present-value method

An alternative method for calculating the value of annual depletion is to determine the reduction in the present value of the expected net revenue (after deducting all extraction costs) between two periods (Hartwick and Hageman 1993: 214–16). This method requires selecting an appropriate discount rate, and making assumptions regarding future mineral prices and extraction costs to arrive at the expected present value for each period. It is also necessary to determine the optimum path of exploitation since the optimum path is usually not constant annual production.

It can be argued that the present-value method of calculating depletion provides a better measure of the change in capital value of the mineral asset than simply calculating Hotelling rent or Repetto's 'net price'. However, Hartwick and Hageman (1993: 215) show that given the same assumptions, depletion computed by the present-value method should be equal to Hotelling rent times the amount extracted. In both cases, resource rent reflects the intertemporal scarcity of the exhaustible resource. However, since the present-value method is based on assumptions regarding future mineral prices and extraction costs, it seems likely to yield quite different estimates of depletion than the Hotelling or Repetto methods, which are based on current prices and extraction costs.

According to the methods for computing depletion described above, an addition to reserves between the two periods increases the capital value of the reserves, thus offsetting extraction. The quantity of mineral resources designated as reserves (ore that can be economically mined) may also rise with the price of the mineral. Hence, the capital value of the mineral reserves of a country may increase despite the fact that there is ongoing extraction, and there could actually be an increase in capital value between the periods. This is not the case with El Serafy's (1989) user-cost method.

El Serafy's user-cost method for calculating mineral depletion

El Serafy (1989) rejects the Hotelling, Repetto, and the present-value methods outlined above. His method is not based on measuring depletion by determining the depreciation of mineral reserve assets between two periods. Instead, he divides the net receipts from mineral extraction into capital consumption representing the amount earned at the expense of eroding the value of the asset, and net receipts available for consumption. The latter represents 'true income' and is based on the Hicksian (1946) notion that true income is a level of consumption that can be sustained indefinitely. El Serafy calls the capital consumption component 'user cost' after Keynes (1936: ch. 6), who used the term to indicate the loss in value of a capital good during use. El Serafy defines annual revenue, R, from producing a resource as physical output times price minus extraction costs. R consists of two components: an income component, X, and a capital depletion component, $R - X$, or user cost. X is that portion of R that constitutes income to the holder of the mineral deposit, while $R - X$ is that portion which must be saved and reinvested each year to accumulate at compound interest a fund sufficient to yield X per year in perpetuity. $R - X$ is the present value of R, which we may express as $R/(1 + r)^n$, where r is the rate of interest and n the life of the mineral reserve. Thus, we may write

$$X = R - R(1 + r)^n.$$

Now the present value of R per year at r years is

$$\frac{1}{R\left(1 - \frac{(1 + r)^n}{r}\right)} = \frac{R}{R - (1 + r)^n} = \frac{X}{r}.$$

Xr will provide a perpetual annual income of X when the mineral reserve is depleted, so that the capital value of the net income from the mineral deposit is maintained for all time.

To provide a numerical example, assume R is \$250,000 per year, the life of the mine is twenty years, and the interest rate is 10 per cent. Using the above formula, the present value of R per year for twenty years is \$2,130,000, $R - X$ or $R/(1 + r)^2$ is \$37,000, and annual income, X, is \$213,000. When saved and compounded at 10 per cent over twenty years, $R - X$ also equals \$2,130,000 and provides a perpetual income of \$213,000. The longer the life of the mineral reserve, the smaller the proportion of R that needs to be saved for depletion (see Table 10.3). This proportion declines rapidly with the life of the reserves, n. If n is fifty years and the other variables are the same as in the above example, annual depletion, $R - X$, is only \$2,125, or 1 per cent of R as contrasted with 15 per cent when n is twenty years. If the life of the reserve is 100 years, the amount that needs to be saved annually and reinvested is less than \$100.

The proportion of R that needs to be saved to maintain a perpetual income is also sensitive to the rate of interest (see Table 10.3). Assuming R is \$250,000 per year, the life of the mine is twenty years and the discount rate is 5 per cent, the amount that needs to be saved annually is \$94,250, and the annual income, X, is \$155,750. This compares with the \$37,000 that needs to be saved per year at a discount rate of 10 per cent in order to maintain a perpetual income of \$213,000 per year. Thus, more needs to be saved at the 5 per cent discount and the income to be maintained in perpetuity is less than that for a 10 per cent discount rate. These examples show the sensitivity of El Serafy's depletion formula for both the interest rate and the life of the mine.

In El Serafy's formulation, X is the net income to the owner of the natural resource (or to the economy) which is attributable to the resource, and it is this income that should be perpetuated after the resource has been depleted. For a given level of R, $R - X$ (or depletion) will be smaller and X will be larger, the longer the life of the mine. As the life of the mine increases, the depletion fund grows larger and can, therefore, provide a higher annual return following depletion of the mine. For the world mining industry, the discovery of additional reserves may tend to increase output and to reduce the market price of the product. However, the market price would not be substantially affected in the case of an individual mine. El Serafy handles new discoveries and increases in reserves simply by increasing n and assuming the same annual output and value of R. These assumptions are unlikely to be the case for the world mining industry.

There is a contrived identity in El Serafy's approach whereby the amount of depletion is determined by the amount necessary to create a fund to provide an annual return in perpetuity, while that annual return is determined as the difference between annual revenue and annual depletion. Logically, this is correct. Given constant annual revenue and the expected life of the mine, annual depletion is determined mathematically as the amount necessary to create a depletion fund sufficient to yield an annual income net of depletion in perpetuity. One could argue that X is too large or too small, but a change in X must not destroy the identity.

One of the consequences of El Serafy's method of dealing with new discoveries is that, unlike the capital depreciation method, depletion can never become negative. Nevertheless, a period of continual discoveries in excess of current depletion may reduce annual depletion to a minuscule level. As a consequence, the portion of R that constitutes capital consumption declines and the portion that constitutes true income rises. Even though new discoveries or technological advances may increase reserves by more than annual output, an increase in the capital value of the reserves is not recognized. Nevertheless, the user-cost method is consistent with the position of Hicks (1946: ch. 13), Solow (1974), and others, that sustainability requires maintaining the true income generated by the natural resource asset and not the capital value of the asset.

El Serafy's user-cost method has been regarded as an important contribution by leading environmental economists (Hartwick and Hageman 1993). It has been applied in a case study of the PNG mining industry (Bartelmus *et al.* 1992: 115). Since neither sales revenues nor extraction costs were available for individual mines, shareholder profits were used as a proxy for net revenue, R (sales revenue minus extraction costs). Stockholders, profits may overstate R since they include the return on invested capital and not simply the contribution of the resource to output. Presumably, depreciation of plant and structures would be deducted to arrive at stockholders' profits, but whether depletion of mineral reserves was also deducted depends upon the method of accounting used by the mining companies. The same study also applied the Repetto depreciation method to the PNG mining industry. The change in mineral reserves between the two periods times the 'net price' reflects depletion (ibid. 115–17). Bartelmus *et al.* found user cost to be substantially lower than depletion estimated by Repetto's 'net price' method over the 1985–90 period (except for 1988 when there was a substantial increase in mineral reserves due to new discoveries). A study by Young and Seroa da Motta (1995) showed that when applying user cost and the Repetto net price method to Brazilian mineral extraction data, there were wide differences in depreciation estimates and in sustainable income generated by natural resources. One reason for these results is that the user-cost method splits resource rent into 'true income' and user-cost, while under the net price method depletion includes the entire resource rent.

Hartwick and Hageman (1993) argue that the Hotelling rent, the present value, and the user-cost methods will, under certain rigorous assumptions, yield similar estimates of depletion, but most empirical studies applying the net price and user-cost methods have found wide differences in results. Much depends upon the pattern of changes in resource income and upon the amount and timing of new discoveries. When new discoveries exceed extraction, the two approaches diverge since depletion becomes negative under the present value method, while user-cost is always positive.

Which method should be used?

Which method should be applied for estimating depletion for the purpose of determining the portion of gross mineral revenues that should be saved to assure sustainability of a country's net mineral income? It should be one that provides ample savings in the event of future adverse conditions affecting revenue from the mineral reserves. El Serafy (1989) argues, with some justification, that under both the Repetto and the present-value methods, all of the resource rent constitutes depletion, so that there is no income for the owners of the mineral reserves beyond a return for their capital investment in developing the mine. On the other hand, depletion under the El Serafy user-cost method might be too small in the case of a country with very large mineral reserves, say, providing for fifty years or more of current output before exhaustion. In such cases a sharp reduction in world demand might lower net revenue with the result that savings would be insufficient to maintain the earlier revenue. One way of dealing with this problem would be to place a limit on the volume of reserves to be used for calculating depletion under the user-cost method, say, twenty years, supply at the current level of production. Another problem can arise from the choice of interest rate. As was shown in the numerical example above, the lower the interest rate used in calculating the annual amount of depletion, the higher the rate of depletion will be. Interest rates are likely to fluctuate over the life of the mineral reserves, but the higher the amount of annual depletion, the more likely the total amount saved and invested will be sufficient to provide a perpetual income equal to the net rent produced by the depleting reserves. Therefore, the selection of a relatively low interest rate will help to assure sufficient savings over the life of the mineral reserve. Finally, under the user-cost method, R could be adjusted by a probability coefficient to reflect the uncertainty of revenue over time. With these adjustments the user-cost method might be the preferred method for estimating depletion. It has the advantage of being easier to calculate, and is theoretically more closely related to the Hicksian concept of true income that can sustain consumption indefinitely. In Chapter 10 we provide estimates of mineral reserve depletion for several countries using alternative methods of calculating depletion.

Substituting for Mineral Assets

A criticism of the capital depletion and user-cost models described above is that the elasticity of substitution of produced goods for natural resources may not be sufficiently high for output to be maintained after the exhaustion of the natural resource. This criticism applies more to a world production function than to that for individual countries since the latter can always import the natural resource products and thereby avoid having to substitute man-made goods for natural resources. However, an increasing world scarcity of natural resources would increase the cost of natural resource products and thereby reduce the productivity of capital. Much depends upon the rate of technological progress, which in recent years has brought forth substitutes for nearly all scarce minerals, at lower costs than for the minerals. It should also be said that simply preventing consumption of natural resource capital will not by itself guarantee the maintenance of the net income produced by the resources. All aspects of the economy are integrated and there must be sufficient saving to maintain all sectors, including infrastructure, manufacturing, agriculture, research, and human capital formation.

Saving depletion and sustainability

Mineral revenues vary annually and may rise to a maximum level and then decline, so that the contribution of the mineral reserves to net income is not stable and saving the capital value of depletion does not provide for the maintenance of net income during an earlier period of higher revenue. In a recent paper by Vincent *et al.* (1995), the authors found that depletion allowances for Indonesian oil production during the 1971–84 period were significantly lower than Indonesia needed to invest in order to maintain consumption, after taking account of capital losses in periods of falling prices. If we define sustainability of the mining industry as maintaining the highest annual contribution to national income ever provided by the mining industry, sustainability is impossible unless the maximum revenue is sustained over a number of years. David Stern (1994: 11) suggests that mining income should be regarded as sustainable, 'if cumulative mining induces a permanent annual increase in income per capita that is as great as the highest annual mining income per capita ever achieved.' Stern uses a long-run mining income multiplier to calculate the increase in permanent per capita annual income induced by mining in a particular year. The long-run multiplier is a function of total mineral reserves, population growth, total GDP, future mineral prices, and rates of extraction. This requires a long-run projection of the entire economy. Stern's long-run multiplier is subject to the same uncertainties as the constant long-term mineral revenue assumed in the user-cost method.

How important is mineral depletion among the conditions for sustainability of mineral exporting countries? Many mineral-rich countries have mineral reserves that would support current or growing output for many decades. Sustained or even growing output is not a guarantee or even the most essential condition for sustainable development. As a country develops, its economic structure must change, with manufacturing, services, and agriculture (for countries with large land areas) constituting relatively larger shares of total output. The country will also be absorbing a larger amount of its own mineral output, so that mineral exports will be a smaller share of total exports. A country with large potential reserves may fail to develop and exploit its potential because it loses its competitive position in world markets and may not attract foreign capital for development. The general development policies a country follows are likely to be much more important for sustainable development than a 100-year supply of mineral reserves. Even if a country avoids consuming its natural resource capital, the way it invests capital depletion may not be consistent with sustainable development.

Managing the Mineral Industry

Sustainability is also promoted by managing the mineral industry itself for achieving the most effective use of mineral resources. Most mineral-exporting countries have neither fully explored nor developed more than a fraction of their potential resources. In some cases, new mineral reserves are not being identified as fast as reserves are depleted in current production. The best way to sustain the contribution of mineral exports to national output is continuous exploration and investment. This is true even though, over time, the mineral sector's contribution to growth will decline for two reasons. First, there are natural limits on the rate of discovery and development of new mineral reserves, and second, as overall growth continues, other sectors of the economy will normally expand at a greater rate so that the mineral sector will constitute a declining proportion of total output. For some countries, domestic demand for minerals will begin absorbing a larger and larger share of total mineral output, even though mineral output continues to expand.

Mineral management includes the exploration of mineral reserves, mineral strategies for maximizing rents, environmental standards and controls, marketing the mineral products, and financial incentives, such as the tax system discussed in Chapter 3. Exploration may be undertaken either by the government or by private domestic of foreign enterprise. While private exploration has proved to be more efficient than government exploration, private exploration can be promoted by financial incentives, liberal procedures for acquiring exploration rights and mineral concessions, and geological surveys made available by the government to prospective investors. Where there is little private interest in exploring certain areas, the government itself should provide incentives under the initial exploration and auction mining concessions for the areas explored. Although in many countries the constitution provides that minerals in the subsoil be owned by the government, the government should forgo state mining operations in favour of private enterprise. Moreover, foreign enterprises should be permitted to compete on an equal basis with domestic enterprises in exploring and developing mineral reserves.

Mining development in many countries, especially in Latin America, lagged during the 1960s and 1970s because of nationalization of foreign enterprises, restrictions on private sector access to land for mineral exploration and development, and favouring state mineral enterprises, to the detriment of private investors. Over the past decade, several countries have changed their mineral policies by liberalizing foreign investment in minerals and providing better management for the domestic private mining industry. Reforms have been initiated by Argentina, Bolivia, Ecuador, Mexico, and Peru, and many state mining enterprises have been privatized, especially in Mexico and Peru. Chile, which began reform well ahead of other countries, has attracted several billion dollars in private investment in mining (World Bank 1996*a*).

Mineral policy reform is also needed in such fields as taxation, security of title, the right of judicial appeal for alleged contract violations, the ability to transfer and mortgage concessions, and other aspects of the legal framework applying to minerals. Tax regimes need to be overhauled with a view both to maximizing government revenues and promoting the efficient development of mineral resources. Exchange controls that impede imports of goods and services required by mines and the transfer of after-tax profits should be eliminated. Environmental controls should be applied to all mineral operations, whether private or government, and should be based on social benefit-cost criteria. Labour regulations for health and safety should apply to all firms, as should also regulations pertaining to remuneration, hours, and worker tenure. In order to mitigate the popular objection to the domination of mining by foreign firms, an effort should be made to encourage local medium and small mines by removing obstacles to obtaining mining rights, and providing technical assistance and opportunities for various forms of financing, including access to foreign capital.

For many mineral countries there is a need to restructure the system of mineral management by enhancing the role of public institutions such as the ministry of mines and the geologic survey. This often requires upgrading personnel, and giving these institutions adequate authority and budget to implement mineral laws. Laws that deal with environmental and social impacts of the mineral industry are often unenforced. Mineral laws are often administered by several government departments that do not work together and their operations are not integrated for realizing the country's long-run mineral objectives. Several World Bank loans have been made for upgrading government mining institutions (World Bank 1996*b*: 137).

Conclusions

Sustainability in mineral-producing countries does not require delaying mineral extraction below the optimum output for maximizing the net returns from producing the resource. Natural resources represent an endowment of the people of a nation, and most developing countries own the minerals in the subsoil. The government should obtain its share of the resource rents through a system of taxation that does not impair the total amount of rent being generated. Sustainability requires that the *net* income from the revenue attributable solely to the resource (excluding natural resource capital depletion) be sustained after the resource is exhausted. This requires saving the annual depletion in order to accumulate a capital fund, which by the time the resource is exhausted, will be sufficient to provide a level of annual income equal to the net income generated by the depleted resource. Of the four methods of estimating natural resource depletion or capital consumption—Hotelling rent, net price, the present-value method, and user-cost—the net price and user-cost methods are the easiest to apply and the ones mainly used. Their application is illustrated in case studies for determining the EDP of mineral countries in Chapter 10. As indicators of how much mineral revenue should be saved to sustain net income following exhaustion of a mineral, both methods are vulnerable to long-term increases in future mineral prices, and probability coefficients should be applied to reflect the uncertainty of future mineral income. In any case, saving and reinvesting the proper amount of mineral revenue to allow for depletion does not guarantee sustainable development of the economies. National sustainability depends upon how the mineral rents are allocated, how their allocation affects sectoral prices, and the macroeconomic policies pursued by the government.

Sustainability of the minerals sector's contribution to economic growth is promoted by managing the industry to achieve the most efficient use of the country's mineral resources. This means continuous exploration and investment in new projects by attracting foreign and domestic capital, establishing a system of taxation that will maximize mineral rents, and creating a system of management that will both encourage the optimal growth of the industry and regulate its impact on the environment and on the welfare of the workers.

5 Environmental Issues

Environmental damage and sustainability are closely related, but they are not the same. Environmental damage may impair the sustainability of output and impede the transfer to future generations of the non-renewable resources required for production and for human enjoyment. However, following the best environmental practices will not guarantee sustainability nor will the failure to adopt certain environmental practices prevent the achievement of sustainability. This chapter identifies the principal types of impacts of mineral industries on the environment and describes how these impacts affect output and social welfare. It also reviews the measures that mitigate environmental harm, and analyses the relationship between the social costs of avoiding or mitigating environmental damage and the social benefits derived from doing so. The concern is, therefore, with the economics of environmental damage and not simply with its existence and alternative ways of avoiding it.

Social Benefits and Costs

Mineral extraction and processing create a number of environmental problems at the local, national, and international levels. Extraction changes the primordial state of the earth, but whether it does environmental damage depends on how it affects the services provided by the environment disturbed. To justify measures to prevent or mitigate the impairment of these services, an evaluation of the loss of services in relation to the social benefits from extraction or to the social cost of avoiding the impairment of services should be made. A rigid rule that mining companies must restore a mined area to exactly the way it was before extraction, might not be in accord with the principle of maximizing the difference between social benefits and social costs. Mining and concentrating have adverse impacts on groundwater and adjacent streams, but the degree to which these impacts should be mitigated depends on a comparison of the social benefits and costs involved.

Private and social costs are often confused in analysing environmental issues. Private costs affect the balance sheet of individuals and firms; social costs are borne by other members of society. It is sometimes argued that so long as a private firm pays the cost of environmental protection, no social cost is involved. This is not true since private costs tend to be added to the price of the products or are reflected in social costs. Social costs have different impacts on different social classes and different groups of consumers. In general, environmental costs should be borne in the first instance by the producers responsible for the environmental damage, or by the consumers who may be responsible for damage. The rationale for this position is that the producer is best able to minimize the cost of preventing or minimizing environmental damage. Although the producer is likely to pass on environmental costs to the consumer, the consumer will minimize his cost by conserving on the use of the products or using alternative products, and consumers are best able to make these decisions for maximizing their welfare. Special welfare problems arise when the benefits of environmental change are borne by a large group of consumers, such as power users, while the environmental damage is borne by a small group adversely affected, say, by the loss of a scenic canyon which might be dammed to generate power at a lower cost than power from other sources. It may be that the social cost of impairing the natural beauty of the canyon is very small in terms of the number of people affected, while the social cost of not generating the power is quite large. A related problem has to do with whether the social cost of the environmental damage to the canyon is limited to that experienced by the present generation or should include the costs borne by generations to come. These cases often involve complex social welfare issues that cannot be resolved on the basis of rigid rules.

In valuing environmental costs and benefits, a monetary measure is used in this study. Monetary costs and benefits are not necessarily market prices, but monetary values may be imputed for non-market benefits or costs estimating how much money people are willing to pay for them or to accept in exchange for doing without them. Some environmentalists object to monetary valuations, but when it is necessary to compare environmental benefits with environmental costs, there is no other means of making the comparisons. Therefore, at times the monetary value of a scenic canyon or wilderness area must be estimated, or in some cases estimates must be made of the value of human suffering or even loss of life.

In analysing the impacts of environmental damage, a distinction should be made between the effects on the global environment and those mainly on the national economy. The contribution of a mine to global warming may have a measurable impact on global output, but little or no effect on national output. In measuring the social costs of mining operations at the national level, global costs should not be included for purposes of comparing national social costs with national social benefits. Measures for dealing with global impacts require international agreements on how the global social costs should be distributed among nations and therefore added to national costs.

There are local environmental costs, such as air and water pollution, that fall on residents near the mine, which, when properly valued, are small either in comparison to the national benefits of a mine, or in comparison to national costs of avoiding the environmental damage. Neither the environmental costs nor the benefits of mineral production are equitably distributed within a nation. Frequently, environmental costs fall mainly on indigenous people living in mountains or jungles where mines or oil wells are located, while the benefits go mainly to those in urban centres. These situations create difficult problems in comparing environmental costs with the benefits of avoiding environmental damage. Medical costs for treating lung disease are very low for villages served only by a first aid station and a shaman, as compared with medical costs in a city with modern health facilities. As usually estimated, the monetary value of life for indigenous people with low life expectancy and low real incomes is only a fraction of the value of life for residents of the modern economic sector.

Social welfare has a cultural content that is not uniform among regions with differing patterns of living and social values. For the natives on the Island of Bougainville, sustainability was maintaining traditional village life, and they were willing to shut down the Bougainville copper mine at the expense of employment opportunities and higher monetary income (see Chapters 11 and 12). The benefits of the mine to Papua New Guinea were allegedly being won at the cost of destroying a unique island culture. National income accounting does not recognize regional differences in social values.

Internalizing environmental damage

Some environmentalists condemn all activity that impairs the services of environmental assets. Carried to the extreme, this leads to the disapproval of virtually all mineral extraction, since some impairment of environmental services is almost inevitable. The position taken here is that environmental costs should be treated in much the same way as any other production cost. Most environmental damage resulting from mineral production is borne by society, and is not included in the cost and revenue accounts of individual firms. Social benefit and cost accounting requires that all social costs be internalized by the producer, either by a tax on the producer or by the producer's absorbing the cost of avoiding the damage. In either case, the cost is usually added to the price of the product. This is the well-known 'polluter pays' principle, which requires that the producer, and ultimately the consumer, bear the social cost of externalities.

One problem with this principle is that when social costs are compensated by the producer through payment of pollution taxes, the payments may not go to the members of society who actually bear the costs. Society is not a homogeneous group of people, and what we call social benefits and costs are distributed very unequally. This is a welfare problem that economists have struggled with but not solved. Pareto optimality requires that every decision affecting production must benefit some members of society without causing harm to any other member. Pareto's rule can only be applied through a scheme in which those who benefit devote some of their gains to compensating the losers. However, strict application of this principle is not possible.

Complete internalization of all social costs could never be achieved, in part because we do not always know the social costs of certain activities or the exact causal relationship between specific activities and the environmental harm. Virtually all producers and consumers are responsible for some social costs, so that environmental policy should concentrate on the most important and measurable costs. Internalization of environmental costs will help to maximize the net social product by reducing disparities between costs and prices, which results in a more efficient allocation of resources. Internalizing the degradation of environmental assets provides a means of either avoiding the degradation or of compensating future generations for the loss of environmental capital. In these ways environmental policy can contribute to sustainability.

As was discussed in Chapter 4, a more accurate estimate of sustainable income, EDP2, should be calculated by deducting from GDP natural resource depletion (RD), the deterioration to the quality of natural resources caused by production (DQR), and the expenditures undertaken for prevention or restoration of environmental damage (PR). In the long run, income or output is not sustainable unless damage to environmental capital is either restored or an amount of other productive capital equal to the damage is substituted for the capital value of the damage. To the extent that all environmental costs are deducted in calculating sustainable income, the measure of national output will be closer to that required for measuring sustainable development.

Categories of Environmental Impacts

Each of the several stages in the mining process—exploring, extracting, moving ore, concentrating, smelting, and refining—is responsible for specific environmental hazards (see Figure 5.1). Extraction and, to a lesser extent, exploration are responsible for extensive land degradation, ecosystem disruption, and soil and water pollution from accumulated waste. Before the present century, most mining was underground and relatively high-grade ores were extracted. Today mining removes large amounts of material from the surface, leaving open pits and mountains of waste, as the actual mineral recovered is only a small percentage of the material moved. Surface mines produce eight times as much waste per tonne of ore as underground mines. The average grade of copper produced in the USA is less than 1 per cent; the average grade of lead and nickel is 2.5 per cent; the average grade of tin is 1 per cent; and the average grade for gold is 0.0003 per cent (Warhurst 1994*a*: 20). Mine excavating and overburden dumping destroys the habitat of flora and fauna; drainage from the dumps may clog streams or react with rainwater to produce acidic drainage, resulting in degradation of both surface and groundwater.

Concentrating and smelting processes leave tailings soaked with sulphuric acid and other chemicals that can pollute water supplies and the soil, while smelters are among the most potent air polluters and can cause acid rain hundreds of miles from the site. Rivers are sometimes dammed to create tailings ponds with a consequent loss of fish and plant life in the river. Ore may be leached instead of concentrated so that the metals are extracted in a solution through electro-winning. Hydrometallurgical (leaching) methods are used for gold, uranium, and aluminum, and to some extent copper, zinc, and nickel ores. This process may also cause damage to water and soil if the liquids are not fully confined. The use of mercury and cyanide in the process to extract gold from ore can also cause serious environmental problems.

The environmental impacts from mineral production are discussed below under the following four major categories of damage: air, water, and soil pollution causing

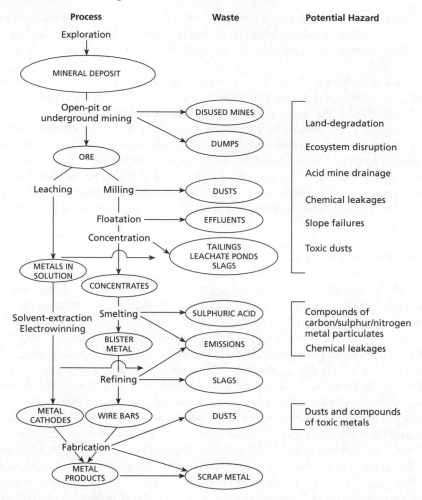

Figure 5.1 The mining process and the environment: processes, waste, and potential hazards are interrelated

Source: Warhurst (1994a).

damage to health and property; permanent or long-term damage to rivers, watersheds, and soil; recreational and cultural damage; and transnational and global damage. The main purpose of the analysis is to identify the economic basis for public policy in dealing with environmental damage.

Pollution

As is the case with most industries, extracting, transporting, and processing minerals may give rise to air emissions that are toxic to humans, crops, and animals; discharges into waterbodies that affect the health of humans, fish, and animals, and impair the various uses for rivers and lakes; and discharges of toxic materials into the soil and groundwater. The damage can be dealt with either by placing specific limits on the amount of harmful emissions or by assessing fees on emissions above a certain level. Since monetary incentives are usually more efficient and more adjustable than mandating specific performance, control through fees is generally preferred. Regardless of the method used, the regulators should aim at a level of pollution abatement that equalizes the marginal cost of abatement with the marginal benefit of reducing pollution. Any quantitative limit on emissions requires justification in terms of the amount of damage that would occur if the limit is exceeded. As a rule, limiting harmful emissions is subject to increasing marginal cost while, beyond a certain level, reducing emissions tends to provide smaller additional benefits in terms of damage to health and property. Fees on emissions should be designed to equalize the marginal costs of abatement with the marginal benefits. Government regulators can draw on a large number of empirical studies relating levels of emissions to impacts on health and damage to property.

Many health impacts from industrial pollution occur after long periods of time, e.g. twenty years or more in the case of cancer. Such damage does not cease with the elimination of pollution. If social costs were discounted, estimates of future damage would be quite small. The preferred practice is to assess the social costs without regard to the time they occur.

Permanent damage to environmental assets

Permanent or long-term damage to environmental assets differs from pollution that can be abated at different levels in accordance with its temporary impact on health and property. In the former case, damage is not reversible except over long periods of time, and the damage impairs the services of an environmental asset rather than simply imposing harm directly on humans or property. This type of environmental damage may not immediately affect the services of environmental assets, but may do so gradually over time. For example, small amounts of toxins discharged into rivers may not affect fish or other wildlife immediately, but may do so as the toxins accumulate. The accumulation of toxins in fish may not only reduce the fish stock, but cause illness in those who eat them. Increased sedimentation of a river caused by mining may in time affect downstream uses of the river, such as irrigation and navigation. Acid rain caused by smelters will over time damage lakes. Similarly, mining operations will impair watersheds and the quality of groundwater over a period of years.

If the social cost of the damage occurs well into the future, its present value may be very small relative to the cost of avoiding it. This problem can be handled by charging the estimated future damage to current production costs. The total value of the reduction in the services of the damaged environmental asset might be divided by the expected life of the project to arrive at the annual cost, which could be internalized through an annual tax. For example, suppose that despite the installation of all known protective devices, a mine is expected to damage a river by $10 million over the twenty-year life of the mine. The total revenue from the tax, accumulated with interest, could approximate the value of the damage to be assessed by an annual tax. The government could then allocate the proceeds from the tax to compensate those affected by the damage.

Mines have a limited operating life and frequently the major damage occurs after they are closed. The damage is not simply an unsightly hole in the ground that may create an unwanted lake polluted with toxic chemicals. The greatest harm usually comes from the waste dumps, the run-off from which continues to pollute water and soil many years after the mine is closed. One approach would be to charge mine restoration costs as current production costs each year over the life of the mine.

Recreational and cultural damage

There are many examples of mines and oilfields spoiling beautiful landscapes and recreational qualities through extracting and processing activities; through support facilities (such as tailings ponds, highways, and railroads), and from an influx of workers. When there are two conflicting uses for a resource, one commercial and the other recreational/aesthetic, the standard approach is to compare the present value of the social benefits from the two uses. For the commercial use, the social benefit is the net revenue or rent; for the recreational use, the social benefit is the imputed value of the recreational services. One way of estimating the benefits from a recreational site is to use the travel cost method in which the value of a visit is based on the travel cost, plus a shadow price for the travel time. Another method is interviewing visitors to determine the maximum entrance fee they would be willing to pay, or what they would be willing to accept as a reward for not visiting the area. The value of a recreational site derived by one of these methods could be supplemented by estimating option value (the value individuals attach to the option of visiting the place), and existence value (the value individuals attach to the existence of, say, the Grand Canyon, even though they may be unable ever to visit the place).

Elaborate models have been developed for applying these and other methodologies to recreational sites threatened by commercial development (Freeman 1993: ch. 13). In a pioneering case study, Krutilla and Fisher (1975: ch. 7) compared the net present value of the revenue from a potential mineral development with the present value of the recreational benefits for the White Cloud Peaks area located in the Sawtooth Mountain range of Idaho. There are several mining claims on this magnificent area enjoyed by hikers and fishermen. In 1969, American Smelting and Refining Company (ASARCO) applied for a permit to build an access road into two proposed open-pit molybdenum mines. In addition, ASARCO planned a 400-ft high dam to create a reservoir to serve as a settling pond for tailings disposal. Krutilla and Fisher calculated the present value of the wilderness recreation benefits of the White Cloud area, using willingness to pay estimates for an expected number of initial annual visitor days.[1] Starting with the initial year's benefits from

---

[1] No survey was conducted for the White Cloud Recreation Area, but Krutilla and Fisher used a willingness-to-pay cost of $10 per day based on a survey of a similar area (1975: 168).

the White Cloud recreation area of $46,000, the present value of the benefits was calculated using alternative assumptions for three variables, namely the rate of interest, the projected rate of growth in the number of visitor days, and the annual rate of increase in willingness to pay (based on income elasticity of demand for amenity services, increasing scarcity of similar services, and other factors (Krutilla and Fisher 1975: 128–30)). Assuming 7, 10, and 4 per cent, respectively, for the three variables, the authors arrived at a range of $3.4 million to $4.9 million for the present value of the benefits, but if the interest rate variable increases to 10 per cent, the value range declines to one of $1.6 million to $1.8 million (ibid. 169).

The limited data available for evaluating the present value of the social benefits of the proposed molybdenum mine/mill operation made it impossible for the authors to estimate a comparable present value for the benefits of the mineral resource. However, certain factors tended to reduce the value of the mineral project. First, the mineral content of the ore indicated a marginal deposit with a high waste/metal ratio. Second, the existence of excess capacity in the industry suggested that development and mining operations would not take place for a number of years in the future. Assuming development costs of $100 million and a 14 per cent rate of return (ASARCO's risk-adjusted rate), and that operations would not begin for thirty years, the net present value of the stream of deferred income, discounted at 10 per cent, would be only $2.3 million. The impact of the mining complex on the recreational value of the area was regarded as complete and irreversible, but recreation could continue prior to development. There was some justification for using a higher rate of discount for the benefits from development than for those of recreational use because of the greater risk and uncertainty for the former. The authors concluded that 'the decision to establish the White Cloud Peaks as part of the protected Sawtooth National Recreation Area reflects sound economic judgment' (Krutilla and Fisher 1975: 185).

The cultural values of indigenous people are among the most difficult to measure because they do not pertain to a specific use of an environmental asset to which we can assign a monetary value. These values differ from the costs of damage to health and property. People can be compensated for the loss of their land and given opportunities for employment as a substitute for their traditional occupations. Yet, they may feel a deep sense of loss of their culture. How can a value be put on the loss of traditional village life when it is replaced by employees earning wages several times the market value of their traditional income? What are the rights of a group of people not integrated with the economy and culture of the larger nation? The traditional practice of the last century has been to confiscate the land and put the natives on a reservation. In recognition of the international human rights codes adopted by the United Nations and other international organizations, the modern way is to negotiate agreements that protect the culture to the maximum extent possible and compensate for economic costs. National governments have an obligation to promote and become a party to such agreements.

Failure to reach satisfactory agreements can mean failure for the mineral enterprise, as in the case of the Bougainville mine in PNG; or to international condemnation of and discrimination against the resource firm, as in the case of Shell Oil in

Nigeria. The cost to the resource company should be whatever is needed to satisfy the indigenous population within the framework of international guidelines established by the United Nations, the World Bank, and other international agencies. The rights of indigenous peoples are now strongly supported by local non-governmental organizations (NGOs) and by international NGOs which have a growing influence on multinational corporations.

Global and transnational damage

Mineral industries are responsible for global damage, mainly deforestation and the emission of greenhouse gases. The social costs are mainly world costs, rather than national or local costs. There are also cases of transnational damage arising from river and groundwater pollution, air pollution, and acid rain, which destroy the amenity services of lakes. The regulation of global and transnational damage requires international agreements or treaties between adjoining countries. Controls over transnational pollution exist within the EU and in North America, but there is little effective worldwide cooperation in the area of global damage.

One approach would be to recognize global damage as a social cost of production, which must be internalized either by prevention or by taxation to generate revenue that can be used to reduce global damage from other sources. For example, a colloquium of World Bank representatives, scientists, and economists, meeting in 1995 agreed that a shadow price of $10 to $20 per ton of carbon emissions is a reasonable estimate of potential damage from climate change (World Bank 1996c). The proceeds of a carbon tax could go into an international fund to be used for a variety of global environmental projects, such as reforestation. Mineral industries are responsible for only a fraction of total global damage, and any international programme for minerals should be part of a comprehensive programme covering all industries.

Valuing Non-Market Services

It has been noted that some forms of environmental degradation result in the loss of non-marketed environmental services. The major methods used to measure the value of these non-marketed services are travel costs, hedonic values, effects on productivity, and contingent valuation. The first three are regarded as indirect techniques, while the fourth is considered a direct approach (Kopp and Smith 1993: ch. 7). In contingent valuation, individuals are asked to value an environmental service in terms of what they would be willing to pay for it or accept for not having the experience, say, of fishing or hiking in an area. The hedonic model measures the change in the value of a house, or some other property resulting from environmental damage, such as pollution of a nearby river. The productivity method involves the services of the environmental asset as a factor of production. Therefore, the impairment of the environmental services affects the output.

Kopp and Smith (1993) provide a case study of valuing the services of a river impaired by damage from mine tailings. The tailings continued to be released into the Eagle River in Colorado after the mine closed, but the damage at issue was a five-mile section of the river. To support the suit brought against the owners of the mine, the plaintiff conducted two household mail surveys, one for residents of Eagle County and the other for the entire State. The county survey collected information for use in three methods for measuring components of damage:

1. How many days each respondent would spend in fishing and water-based recreation activities if the five-mile section of the river were restored to its pre-mine condition?
2. How much each respondent would be willing to pay annually for ten years to clean up this section of the Eagle River?
3. If the respondent was a homeowner, what was the purchase price of the home and the purchase date. (Here the purpose was to discover any decrease in the value of the home as a result of the mine.)

The state-wide survey estimated the value of restoring the Eagle River to baseline conditions from the value of similar sites in Colorado. The analyst for the defendant (Gulf-Western Industries) developed a travel cost recreation demand model, according to which it was assumed that when there is damage to the river's ability to support fishing, recreationists would go to the next best alternative—the river above the mine site—travelling a maximum of five miles further each way. By contrast, the plaintiff's analysis highlighted the uniqueness of the Eagle River site and estimated both use and non-use values. Not surprisingly, the value of the site determined by the plaintiff was several times the value calculated by the defendant.

Non-use values are independent of people's present use of resources. They arise from a variety of motives, including a desire to bequeath certain environmental resources to future generations; a sense of stewardship or responsibility for preserving certain features of natural resources (existence value); and the desire to preserve the option of future use by the individual (option value). The irreversibility of damage to a unique scenic source or ecological system is a key component of non-use value—what is destroyed can never exist again. Collective non-use values for a well-known area may be quite large, even larger than what the people who actually visit the area would be willing to pay. Conservationists often raise large sums to preserve areas, even though the donors never expect to visit the sites. In the case of well-known gems, such as the Grand Canyon and Yellowstone, many millions of dollars could be raised by private contributions from those who never expect to visit the areas in the future.

The Social Rate of Discount

In comparing social benefits with social costs involving different time-periods, present or (discounted) values are used. Present values are also used in comparing the social benefits to be derived from alternative uses of a natural resource. Because of the sensitivity of present value to the rate of interest, it is important to consider the selection of the discount rate. In valuing the social benefits and costs to future generations resulting from actions taken by the present generation, it is often argued that intergenerational equity requires that future benefits and costs not be discounted, or that a lower rate of discount be used. This argument is rejected. It would not be possible to make rational comparisons of values without regard for time, and any positive rate of discount will reduce the value of benefits 100 years from now to near zero. It is frequently argued that the proper rate of discount should reflect the preference of society for present goods over future goods. However, time preference not only differs enormously among individuals, but appears to vary substantially over time, as reflected in market rates of interest. From 1970 to 1995, real rates of interest on US government securities varied from negative rates to over 5 per cent, and there was an even greater variation in real returns on common stocks.

For decades economists have debated the proper basis for determining the social rate of discount when evaluating public projects, or for comparing public with private projects. Fisher (1907) argued that the market rate of interest on riskless securities expresses collective private time preference and that this should be the basis for the social rate of discount. Knight (1931: 176–212) argued that collective time preference has little or nothing to do with determining the rate of interest, which he believed is determined by the productivity of capital—the ratio of the increment of net output per annum to the amount of capital goods employed. Arrow (1966) proposed a 'natural rate of interest' equal to the marginal rate of substitution between present and future consumption, plus the rate of change in the marginal utility of consumption times the rate of change in consumption.[2] This concept of the rate of discount defies objective measurement, however conceptually attractive it may be.

The most reliable basis for the social rate of discount is the marginal rate of return on private capital in competitive equilibrium markets. This rate measures what capital could earn under equilibrium conditions. It is the social opportunity cost of capital invested in public projects. However, since virtually all private investment involves some risk, a premium rate of return is required to induce the investment. The question arises as to whether a premium for risk should be included in the social rate of discount used for evaluating public projects. Government investments are by no means riskless. If a government invests in a power project, it is subject to most of the risks faced by a private utility. Therefore, should not the government apply the rate of discount necessary to attract a private utility to the project? The risks involved in establishing a wilderness or recreation area are less than those faced by a mining company, but there are risks in estimating the demand for the amenity services, and risks from natural disasters of various kinds. This suggests that in determining the present value of the benefits from a wilderness area, a proper discount rate might be, say, 7 per cent, as contrasted with, say, 14 per cent for determining the present value of the net return from a mine. Where there are private projects

[2] For a brief history of economists' views on the social rate of discount, see Mikesell (1977: ch. 1).

comparable to the public projects being evaluated, the rate for determining the present value of the public project should be equal to the rate of return necessary to induce a private investment in a similar project.

Arrow argues that since the government undertakes a very large number of projects, each of which has an expected flow of net benefits, the actual return from the whole group should be approximately the weighted average of the expected returns from individual projects. Hence, the expected returns from each project should be discounted at the riskless rate (Arrow 1966). Arrow's position is rejected by Baumol (1968: 797) who argues that, if the average rate of return in the private sector is 8 per cent, of which 3 per cent is the necessary payment for risk, a shift of investment from the private sector to the public sector where the rate of return is only 5 per cent would constitute an inefficient distribution of investment resources.

The difference between these approaches hinges in part on whether risk should be regarded as a social cost. Yet, if a risk premium is necessary to induce private investment, should not the premium be included in the social cost of the investment? A related question has to do with the distortion created by the corporate income tax which is applied to private investment, but not to public investment. Aside from the question of the desirability of the corporate income tax, it would appear that neutrality between the private and the government sectors requires applying the corporate tax rate to public projects. Otherwise, there is discrimination in the allocation of capital in favour of public investment.

Discounting should be used for comparing present values of yields from alternative uses of resources and for comparing social benefits with social costs occurring within the same time-frame. Present value should also be used for comparing public expenditures for environmental purposes with the social returns on these expenditures. However, in determining the long-run social cost of current damage to the environment, the present value of environmental harm that occurs far into the future should not be used because this would put a very low value on the welfare of future generations. In comparing the cost of avoiding environmental damage with the value of the future harm caused by the damage, it might be assumed that all the environmental harm occurs at the same time as the damage. Another approach, somewhat less favourable to future generations, would be to assume that the total environmental harm was spread equally over a number of years in the future, and compare the cost of avoiding the damage with the present value of the annual cost of the harm. If annual payments for the environmental harm were accumulated with interest, the resulting fund might be sufficient to compensate those affected by the future environmental harm.

Environmental Controls

Environmental regulations applying to the mineral industries may be included in mining laws, in mining and petroleum agreements between the government and the producing firms, or in general environmental laws applying to all industries. Because of the special environmental hazards associated with mineral industries and because the operations are often in remote areas, there is an advantage in having special environmental legislation and regulations for the extractive industries. Mining agreements covering operations in particular areas provide a means of tailoring environmental regulations to the special conditions of the project and to the mining area. There are four general categories of environmental regulations: those that specify the technology and equipment; those that provide for fixed limits on emissions or for maintaining specified ambient standards; those that provide economic incentives to limit emissions as opposed to setting fixed amounts; and those that require the restoration of damaged assets. There may be some combination of the four. For example, the regulations may require a particular kind of mining or concentrating process, while limiting discharges into water or air, or imposing a fee for discharges. In some cases, the required technology may reduce the likelihood of large accidental discharges that would do extensive damage.

There are important advantages in using economic incentives as contrasted to other methods. First, the producer is usually better able to determine the least-cost methodology for achieving a given abatement objective. Second, different mines and different operations within mines have quite different costs for pollution abatement, and it is economical to encourage the largest amount of abatement in operations in which the abatement cost is lowest. The use of emissions fees promotes this objective since producers will tend to abate up to the point at which the marginal abatement cost is equal to the fee, and the fees can be set at levels that achieve the overall abatement objective of the government. Alternatively, tradeable emission permits can be auctioned with much the same result, while at the same time providing the government with full control over the total amount of emissions.

The introduction of new equipment, together with better worker training, provides the most economical means of reducing pollution in mining operations. End-of-pipe technology and reduced output during certain periods are more costly. New mining and processing technology tends to be more productive in terms of both environmental efficiency and reducing per unit costs. For example, new concentrators and roasting plants are totally computerized, which makes possible accurate monitoring of emissions and control of pressure and heat for ore-feeds of variable composition and pollution content. The same technology that conserves energy and improves efficiency of concentrators and smelters also helps to reduce pollution (Warhurst 1994b: 142–3).

The close relationship between improved technology, managerial competence, and worker training on the one hand, and environmental performance on the other, has implications for environmental regulations. Environmental regulations are often based on old technology and do not encourage investment in new technology. Emissions fees and tradeable permits for specific amounts of pollutants provide strong economic incentives to invest in modern technology, while at the same time allowing total emissions to be tailored to the desired ambient results. Fees and tradeable permits also provide a mechanism for adjusting abatement costs to the social benefits of improved environmental conditions (Milliman and Prince 1989: 247–8; Warhurst 1994b: 165–6).

A major environmental problem created by mining is the accumulation of mining wastes, which may be hazardous and are generally environmentally undesirable. The US Resource Conservation and Recovery Act (RCRA) provides for comprehensive regulating and monitoring of waste accumulation, and sets standards for waste treatment and eventual disposal. However, the RCRA and subsequent amendments could not deal with the thousands of potentially hazardous sites where waste had already been accumulated. This problem is dealt with by the Comprehensive Environmental Response Compensation and Liability Act (CERCLA) of 1980, which makes those responsible for the waste pay for remediation in accordance with the polluter-pays principle. CERCLA (or the Superfund Act) has proved to be inefficient and costly, and has made only a small dent in cleaning up old hazardous waste sites that have accumulated over many decades. In its implementation, it has also violated the polluter-pays principle by requiring remediation by firms that bought the properties from those originally responsible for the pollution and have gone out of business. In reviewing the activities of the Superfund, Tilton (1994) has suggested that the government take over responsibility for cleaning up the sites, rather than incur litigation and other costs of finding those originally responsible for the waste. But what about future cases, where mines are closed but the owners fail to provide funds for waste disposal because they are bankrupt, or avoid taking action through litigation, which may last for years? In such cases, the costs of adequate waste disposal would not become part of the production costs passed on to consumers. One remedy, which Tilton does not deal with, is to require every mine to pay an annual fee into a government clean-up fund to be used after the mine has closed. This provides a means of internalizing the disposal cost during the active life of the mine.

Mining laws frequently require filling in the open pits created by surface mining, or neutralizing the potential damage from tailings after the mine and processing operation has been shut down. Restoration may require considerable time during which the services of the damaged environmental asset are impaired. One of the best-known cases of damage to an environmental asset is the EXXON Valdez oil spill in Alaska. Assessments were made of the cost of restoration, of the loss of commercial production, such as fisheries, and the loss of the non-market services such as enjoyment of birds destroyed by the oil. There are cases where full restoration is impossible. Fish may never return to a bay damaged by oil spills or to a lake polluted by acid rain. In such cases, the present value of the loss of environmental services from the damaged environmental asset may be used for assessing fines instead of restoration cost. Where the cost of restoration is substantially higher than the social costs of not restoring, restoration would be a misallocation of resources from a social point of view. It has been suggested that this is the case with a full clean-up of some Superfund sites.

Mining Agreements

Modern agreements between mining companies and governments often go into considerable detail on environmental issues. However, unless a comprehensive environmental assessment study has been undertaken, the agreement may lack specific commitments. Vague agreements often lead to disputes after operations begin. A comprehensive environmental assessment for a large mine may cost many millions of dollars, and companies are reluctant to undertake such assessment during the exploration period prior to obtaining a licence to proceed with the mine. The government could undertake the studies prior to the negotiation of a final agreement, but governments often lack the funds to do so.

The need for a comprehensive agreement based on intensive environmental assessment is well illustrated by the experience with the Ok Tedi mine in PNG. A 1976 concession agreement between the PNG government and an international consortium consisting of Broken Hill Pty. (BHP) of Australia, AMOCO Minerals of the US, and a group of German companies, provided for further exploration and submission to the government of a development proposal. Under the agreement, the consortium undertook to prepare an environmental impact study with a maximum budget of only $200,000. The consortium argued that it could not undertake exhaustive environmental work before the mining licence was granted. Actual mine construction did not begin until February 1981 when an agreement was reached on the development proposal, the financing plan, and the marketing arrangements. However, many of the environmental problems were not foreseen and, therefore, not addressed in the development plan. During construction, serious environmental problems arose and dealing with them gave rise to disputes between the consortium and the government which, are discussed in Chapter 11.

Arguments against rigorous environmental regulation

The following arguments have been made against rigorous environmental regulations by governments of mineral-exporting countries. First, the needs of developing countries for revenue from mineral exports are so great that any impairment of these revenues caused by environmental regulations is likely to result in a net loss of economic welfare; second, strict environmental regulations discourage investment in extractive industries, because the costs impair competitiveness; and third, most mining and petroleum exploitation in developing countries occurs in mountainous and desert regions where the social costs of pollution and other environmental damage are negligible.

Recent studies have challenged all three arguments (Eggert 1994; Warhurst 1994b; Jaffe et al. 1995). The first argument has been challenged on two grounds. The social costs of polluted air and water caused by the mines are often undervalued, if they are valued at all. Moreover, much of the mineral revenue goes to support urban centres and commercial agriculture at the expense of peasant farmers. Second, there is considerable evidence that measures taken for environmental protection also increase productivity, so that export revenue and environmental protection are complementary. Warhurst (1994a: 11) points out that new technologies, such as hydro-metallurgical processes, that either mitigate or treat pollution, offer prospects of higher value added and the enhanced potential for producing by-products. For example, prior to building the Los Broches mine in Chile, EXXON planned to use a conventional open-pit copper mine, with the large tonnages of over-burden and low-grade ore to be piled in dumps. There was a danger that acidic mine drainage from the dumps would flow into the Mantaro River, which is the source of Santiago's drinking water. The government threatened to impose financial penalties for water treatment costs. This threat led the company to use a bacterial leaching technology which produced additional copper from the waste and solved the problem of acid drainage (ibid. 75). Comprehensive impact assessments done prior to formulating plans for exploration and development will often reveal strategies to protect the environment without extensive increases in costs (ibid. 13).

Regarding the second objection to strict regulation, there is relatively little evidence to support the hypothesis that environmental regulations have a significant adverse effect on competitiveness. 'Studies attempting to measure the effects of environmental regulations on net exports, overall trade flows, and plant-location decisions have produced estimates that are either small, statistically insignificant, or not robust to tests of model specifications' (Jaffe *et al.* 1995: 157–8). A survey by Eggert (1994) found that lax environmental regulations have not been a significant factor in investment decisions by mining firms. Investors are more interested in stability and clarity than in comparing the content of regulations among countries.

Finally, regarding the third argument, when populations in developing countries move into the deserts and mountains where mines are often located, social costs of environmental degradation increase. In addition, more is being learned about the effects of pollution of underground water sources in mountains on more heavily inhabited areas. Therefore, the argument that mining in these areas has no significant environmental effect has less validity.

Mining company environmental practices

A distinction may be made among the environmental practices of three types of mining companies in developing countries: multinationals (MNCs), state-owned enterprises (SOEs), and small and medium locally owned mines. Mining MNCs have a better environmental record than SOE or private small and medium mines. Environmental legislation and regulations may apply to all categories of mines, but compliance is likely to be much greater in the case of the MNCs. In the case of SOE mines where the State is both the regulator and the regulated, as the financial interests of the State often prevail over the environment. Mine regulation is often left to local administrators that have a vested interest in local mining. What is needed are strong NGOs and national legislation, together with an independent judicial system willing to oppose state administrators—all of whom are rare in developing countries. But, although foreign investors have a far better environmental record than do state enterprises in the extraction industries, not all foreign enterprises are environmentally conscious. This is shown by Southern Peru Copper Corporation (see Chapter 11).

In some developing countries, state mining and petroleum companies are beginning to realize their responsibility for the environment. Like those of most other developing countries, Chile's environmental policies in mining changed from little concern for environmental impacts in the 1970s to the adoption of laws and standards in the 1990s that approach those of industrial countries (Lagos 1994). Chile's mines are located almost entirely in the northern desert and in the high-altitude Andes region. Nevertheless, Chilean communities have suffered from uncontrolled sulphur dioxide emissions from smelters that cause destruction of orchards and olive groves, as well as health hazards, and from river and bay pollution. Despite a constitutional provision that every citizen 'has the right to live in an environment free of contamination' (Art. 19 of 1980 constitution), a number of suits by workers and citizens against both CODELCO (the state mining enterprise) and private mining companies have been unsuccessful.

Prior to the mid-1980s at least, the attitude of the government was that the development of the mining industry was too important to be impeded in any way by environmental concerns. A precedent for Chilean environmental law was set in 1988 when citizens won a case against CODELCO involving a tailings pond at the El Salvador mine (for a long period tailings were dumped into the Salado River). Following the election of President Patricio Aylwyn in 1990, a number of environmental actions were taken including the formulation of a national environmental policy, basic research on environmental impacts, and creation of institutional structures which include a National Environmental Commission. A decree issued in January 1992 regulated emissions of sulphur dioxide and arsenic particles, and ordered sulphur emissions reduced threefold by the end of the decade.

A number of shortcomings in Chilean environmental administration remain. Small- and medium-sized mines are often subject to provincial rather than to national regulations; the former tend to be lax and often favour business interests. The implementation of environmental laws depends largely on NGOs who protest violations and, if possible, take legal action. Legal action is frequently impaired by the lack of an honest and efficient court system that will uphold the law rather than side with business interests or with a state enterprise. By contrast, MNC mines have few local constituents and are under pressure to maintain the goodwill of the community in which they operate.

International Development Assistance Agencies and Environmental Standards in Mining

International development banks, such as the World Bank Group, the Inter-American Development Bank (IADB), and the Asian Development Bank have in the past provided substantial financing for new mining projects. Except for IFC financing, most of the loans were made to state-owned mining enterprises. The availability of public international capital on very generous terms encouraged the nationalization of the mining industry in many developing countries. Nationalization and an unfavourable investment climate contributed to a decline in foreign private investment in mining during the early post-World War II period, while world demand for metals rose rapidly. Because of fears of a worldwide shortage of major minerals during the mid-1970s, the World Bank's executive directors adopted a policy of encouraging non-fuel minerals production. Between June 1978 and June 1982 Bank and IDA loans for mining totalled $558 million; while the IFC made loans and equity investments in private mining and processing projects totalling about $287 million. The IADB made loans to the Chilean government's CODELCO and to Peru's state mining enterprise, CENTROMIN.

Since the mid-1980s, two changes have taken place in the policies of development financing agencies regarding mining projects. First, they have encouraged private investment in mining and have made relatively few loans to SOE mines. Currently, the principal agency for financing new mining projects is the IFC, which promotes both domestic and foreign investments by providing loans, minority equity capital, and loan guarantees. Some IFC assistance has helped to finance the privatization of former state-owned natural resource enterprises. In 1995, 10 per cent of all IFC assistance went to mining and non-ferrous metal projects (IFC 1995).

The second change has been the increasing attention of development lending agencies to the environmental impacts of projects they finance. Beginning in the late 1970s, the World Bank required borrowers to prepare an environmental assessment for each project, and to include in loan agreements provision for moderating or eliminating environmental impacts. However, governments were often lax in carrying out the requirements of the loan agreements. In some cases, governments sponsored environmentally harmful projects that were closely associated with the projects financed by the development assistance agency. For example, in 1982 the World Bank loaned the Brazilian state enterprise, Companhia Valle do Rio Doce (CVRD), $304 million to construct an iron mine at Carajas, an 890-km railroad, and a deepwater port, with the total project valued at $3.6 billion. Although the Bank accepted responsibility for requiring measures to protect the environment within the project area, the railroad and collateral CVRD projects resulted in a large migration into the area and the creation of environmentally destructive industries, such as charcoal-fired metallurgy projects fuelled by charcoal derived from native forests (Mikesell and Williams 1992: 237). Therefore, critics accused the Bank of promoting the deforestation of the Amazon region.

Environmental guidelines have been established for mining projects assisted by the World Bank and the IFC (World Bank 1995c). The guidelines identify the environmental consequences of mining, and outline control methods and technology. They also specify standards for air and water pollution, for land reclamation, and for the run-off from mining operations. In addition, the guidelines cover the treatment of natives who may be displaced by the mining operations, including provision for resettlement (World Bank 1988a). In recent years, the World Bank has increased its surveillance of the direct and indirect environmental impacts of the project it finances. As for the IMF, although it would not normally be involved in microeconomic environmental policies, it could make sure that the macroeconomic programmes it supports with loans to member countries are consistent with well-formulated environmental strategies (IMF 1996).

International environmental standards for projects assisted by development agencies have influenced the environmental laws and regulations of governments and the environmental practices of foreign private investors (Mikesell 1987). Governments want their regulations to conform to international environmental standards in order to comply with the guidelines of development assistance agencies. Foreign investors realize that over time, host governments are likely to insist on international environmental standards. Therefore, foreign investors tend to adopt standards required by the government of their home country, even though these standards are usually more rigorous than those currently imposed by the host country. They anticipate that sooner or later international standards will be applied locally. Also, there is a growing demand in the USA and other Western countries, for multinational companies to follow sound environmental practices, and this demand is reflected in US government policy.

Conclusions

Mineral industries create a number of environmental problems that need to be addressed as a part of the social cost of mineral production. These social costs range from air, water, and soil pollution to disturbing the economic and cultural lives of indigenous people. The general rule is that environmental costs should be borne by the mineral firms creating the damage rather than being absorbed by government or borne by members of society who are victims of pollution and other natural asset degradation. However, account must be taken of the relationship between the social cost of mitigating or avoiding environmental damage and the social benefits realized by marginal reductions, such as incremental improvements in air and water quality. Expenditures for environmental protection by mineral firms are not simply private costs, but become social costs when passed on to consumers, including other producers, in the form of higher prices for their products.

Social welfare is maximized by equating marginal social costs to marginal social benefits. Achieving this result requires informed environmental control by government agencies in setting and enforcing environmental standards. In general, the use of economic incentives, such as fees, on the emission of pollutants are more efficient than fixed emission requirements, or requirements for using specific technologies. A comparison of social benefits with social costs is also involved in determining alternative uses of land which can provide either social benefits by producing minerals, or by providing amenities to those enjoying undisturbed natural areas. For purposes of deciding on the alternative uses for public lands, the social values generated by the alternative uses should be compared.

Environmental damage created by the extractive industries should be internalized on a current basis, even in cases where the effects of damage are long delayed. This principle is analogous to that of saving the value of mineral depletion in order to preserve the capital value of the mineral asset. Treating long-term environmental damage as a current cost over the life of a project avoids the intergenerational equity problem that would arise if the social costs of long-run environmental damage were discounted. There are important long-run advantages to governments in enforcing well-formulated environmental guidelines, and there is little evidence that nations gain a competitive advantage by maintaining lax environmental standards.

Part III

The Macro Preconditions for Sustainability

6 The Mineral Economies' Economic Performance, 1970–1993

This chapter begins by comparing the economic performance of the mineral economies with that of other developing countries with different natural resource endowments. It focuses on the 1970–93 period which was characterized by sharp fluctuations in both oil and metal prices (Borenzstein *et al.* 1994). Figure 6.1 shows the sharp real increase in oil prices through the 1970s and the subsequent collapse, and traces the movement of metals and minerals prices from boom to prolonged decline. These sharp changes in real prices impacted on the mineral revenue streams to provide a stern test of the mineral economies' ability to respond in ways that did not impair their achievement of sustainable development.

The second section of the chapter subjects nine mineral economies to more detailed analysis. It examines the degree to which their economic performance over the 1970–93 period is explained by each of three sets of factors, namely (1) the socio-economic preconditions, (2) the magnitude of the external shocks, and (3) the political economy. It might be expected that the most successful countries would be those with favourable preconditions, positive external shocks, and a political economy capable of pursuing policies which maximize long-term social welfare. But such a conclusion assumes that the three sets of factors have relatively similar importance, an assumption which this chapter assesses and rejects.

Resource Endowment and Economic Growth, 1970–93

An UNCTAD database covering more than one hundred developing countries provides a useful starting point. It allows the period associated with the price shocks to be set initially in a somewhat longer time perspective because it covers per capita GDP growth for the period 1960–90. Figure 6.2 plots each country's per capita GDP growth over that period against its dependence on mineral exports 1988–90. The countries are subdivided in terms of their resource dependence into four groups, two of which are mineral economies. More specifically, the groups are, ore exporters, oil exporters, soft commodity exporters, and exporters of manufactured goods. The latter group comprises the resource-poor countries.

The resource-poor countries recorded the fastest rates of per capita GDP growth during 1960–90. Among the three groups of resource-rich countries (the primary product exporters), the oil exporters outperformed the other two, with the hard-mineral exporters displaying marginally the lowest rate of per capita economic growth. This is a surprising outcome for the hard-mineral exporters because, like the oil exporters, their additional foreign exchange revenues should boost their import

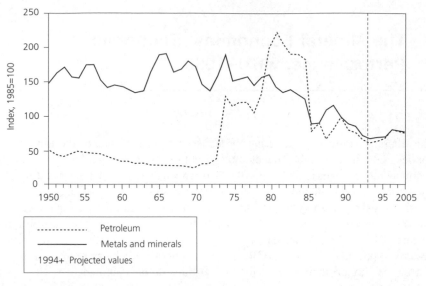

Figure 6.1 Hydrocarbon and copper price trends, 1960–93
Source: World Bank (1994*e*).

capacity *vis-à-vis* non-mineral economies, while the additional profits and tax revenues should boost the investment rate (Sachs and Warner 1995*a*).

The fact that resource-deficient countries have outperformed the resource-rich ones, appears to be a robust finding. A similar conclusion is reached if a different categorization of resource endowments is adopted. For example, the developing countries may be reclassified according to their agricultural potential and domestic market size (reflecting, respectively, the importance of agriculture in low-income countries and the scope for eventual industrialization afforded by domestic demand). The classification criteria comprise each country's per capita cropland in 1970 (WRI 1994), as a measure of agricultural potential and its 1970 aggregate GDP (World Bank 1995*a*), as a measure of its domestic market size. The classification produces four categories (Table 6.1) of which by far the largest (the small, resource-rich category), can be further subdivided by differentiating according to each country's reliance on exports of ore, oil, and soft commodities.[1] The data give adequate coverage for eighty-five countries over the period 1960–90.

[1] Some potential overlap appears in the classification e.g. the market-size criterion results in the inclusion in the two large-country categories of the six largest mineral economies (four oil exporters: Indonesia, Egypt, Nigeria, and Venezuela; and two ore exporters: Chile and South Africa). No attempt is made at reclassification, however, and there are two reasons for this. First, evidence is presented in Chapters 7 and 8 that the smaller mineral economies differ from the larger ones in having more difficulty in adapting to declining mineral production. Second, the ranking of the six groups in terms of per capita GDP growth is not affected by such a reclassification which merely changes the average growth rate by 0.1–0.2%, except for the large *resource-rich* category. In the latter case, the exclusion of the four large mineral economies raises the mean per capita GDP growth rate, but by just 0.6%, to 2.2% per annum. This change is too small to affect the overall ranking.

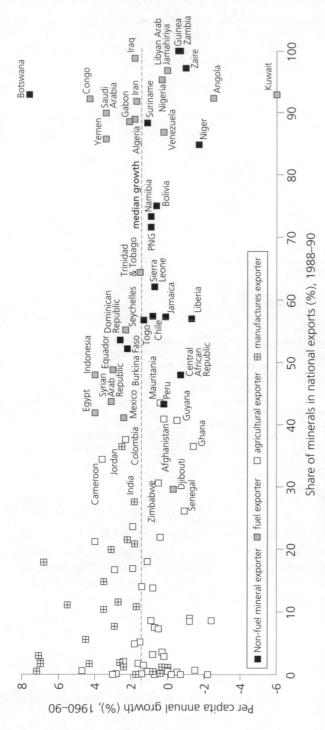

Figure 6.2 Economic growth and mineral dependency (106 developing countries)

Source: UNCTAD Secretariat.

Table 6.1 Characteristics of six natural resource categories

Resource endowment category	No. of countries	PCGDP growth 1960–90 (% yr)	1970 X PCGDP	1970 GDP ($bn)	Cropland (ha/hd)
Resource-poor					
Large	7	3.5	196	21.048	0.15
Small	13	2.5	343	1.937	0.16
Resource-rich					
Large	10	1.6	574	22.988	0.56
Small					
Non-mineral	31	1.1	250	1.406	0.57
Hard mineral	16	0.8	304	1.227	0.66
Oil exporter	8	1.7	831	2.011	0.44
All countries	85	1.6	362	5.666	0.48

Notes:
1. Resource-rich = 1970 cropland/head > 0.29 ha.
2. Market-rich = 1970 GDP > $6.99 bn.
3. The seven large, resource-deficient countries comprise: Bangladesh, China, Colombia, Egypt, Indonesia, Philippines, and S. Korea.
4. The thirteen small, resource-deficient countries comprise: El Salvador, Haiti, Hong Kong, Jordan, Kenya, Mauritania, Mauritius, Nepal, Singapore, Somalia, Sri Lanka, Taiwan, and Tanzania.
5. The ten large, resource-rich countries comprise: Argentina, Brazil, Chile, India, Mexico, Nigeria, Pakistan, S. Africa, Turkey, and Venezuela.
6. The thirty-one small, resource-rich, non-mineral economies are: Benin, Burundi, Cameroon, Chad, Costa Rica, Cote d'Ivoire, Ethiopia, Fiji, Gambia, Ghana, Guatemala, Guyana, Honduras, Lesotho, Madagascar, Malawi, Malaysia, Mali, Morocco, Nicaragua, Panama, Paraguay, Rwanda, Senegal, Sudan, Swaziland, Thailand, Tunisia, Uganda, Uruguay, Zimbabwe.
7. The sixteen hard mineral exporters comprise: Bolivia, Botswana, Burkino Faso, Central African Republic, Dominican Republic, Jamaica, Liberia, Namibia, Niger, PNG, Peru, Sierra Leone, Suriname, Togo, Zaire, and Zambia.
8. The eight oil exporters comprise: Algeria, Congo, Ecuador, Gabon, Kuwait, Saudi Arabia, Syria, and Trinidad and Tobago.
Source: Auty (1997*b*).

Table 6.1 shows that the average rate of per capita GDP growth during 1960–90 for the eighty-five developing countries is 1.6 per cent. Both sets of resource-poor countries outperform the average, with the large resource-poor countries' per capita GDP growing 1 per cent per annum faster than the small resource-poor group. Among the resource-rich countries, the oil exporters grew slightly faster than the all-country average, but only fractionally so. The remaining resource-rich countries grew at or below the mean, albeit only marginally so in the case of the large resource-rich group. The small, resource-rich group of countries recorded the most disappointing per capita GDP growth. Moreover, the average per capita GDP growth rate for the slowest-growing group, the ore exporters, halves to 0.35 per cent per annum with the removal of one outlier country, Botswana (whose per capita GDP growth was 7.6 per cent 1960–93).

Table 6.2 Changing per capita GDP growth, 1970–93: six natural resource categories

	1970–3	1974–9	1980–5	1986–93	1970–93
Resource-poor					
Large	3.4	4.6	3.0	3.6	3.7
Small	2.6	3.1	0.8	2.1	2.1
Resource-rich					
Large	0.0	−0.1	0.1	0.0	0.0
Small					
Non-mineral	2.2	1.6	−0.4	0.2	0.7
Ore-exporter	1.9	0.5	−1.5	−0.6	−0.2
Oil-exporter	5.5	2.4	−1.4	−0.9	0.8
All countries	2.6	2.0	−0.2	0.7	1.1

Source: See Table 6.1.

Table 6.2 uses the same classification to provide a more detailed breakdown of the changes in growth rates over the more recent period of price shocks and their aftermath, 1970–93. It shows an overall developing country trend of decelerating growth through the 1970s, followed by contraction in the early 1980s and then some recovery. The resource-poor countries maintained positive growth throughout, but neither the ore exporters nor the oil exporters, as a group, were able to sustain growth beyond the 1970s' boom period.

Chapters 2 to 5 suggest that, within a soundly managed economy, policies to harness the mineral resource to advantage require adjustment to each of the three main stages of the mineral cycle (youth, early maturity, and late maturity). The required policy shifts would be relatively easy to pursue, as Davis (1995) argues, if the stages of the cycle occurred smoothly and predictably (and governments functioned as maximizers of welfare). But, as the 1970–90 price swings indicate and other studies have shown (Gelb and Associates 1988; Auty 1993), the transition may be anything but smooth. Rather, the reality has been one in which countries may find themselves moving abruptly through the entire mineral-driven sequence, locked in a particular stage, or undergoing some regression. Moreover, many governments stray far from the ideal of social welfare maximization (Lal and Myint 1996).

The data presented above reveal two clear findings. First, whichever classification or time-period is used, the resource-poor groups of countries achieved superior growth rates to the resource-rich countries. Second, as a group, neither the oil exporters nor the ore exporters were able to sustain growth when their booms faded in the early 1980s and late 1970s, respectively.

The Sample of Nine Mineral Economies

In order to examine the conditions required for sustainable mineral-driven development in depth, as well as the obstacles to effective policy implementation, nine

Table 6.3 Stages in mineral-led cycle: nine countries in late 1980s

	Youthful		Early-mature		Late-mature	
	Start	End	Start	End	Start	End
Oil exporters	Columbia		Trinidad and Tobago			Indonesia
Copper exporters	PNG		Chile		Peru	
Other hard minerals	Botswana		Jamaica		Namibia	

countries are selected for detailed analysis. The nine countries cover three sets of minerals (oil, copper, and other hard minerals), and also each stage in the mineral-driven cycle (Table 6.3). But the youthful oil exporter, Colombia, warrants different and separate treatment from the other eight countries. This is because it had yet to fully qualify as a mineral economy in the mid-1990s, having embarked on a rapid expansion of mineral exports much later than the other eight. Discussion of Colombia is therefore reserved to Chapter 14 in which the lessons distilled from the other eight countries are applied.

Turning to the eight full-fledged mineral economies, Table 6.4 compares their economic performance with that of the developing countries as a whole. It uses GDP growth as an index of economic performance, rather than per capita GDP growth. This is because the World Bank (1995*a*) database used throughout the remainder of this study does not provide a mean *per capita* GDP figure for the developing countries as a whole. The eight mineral economies selected span a wide range of performances, but the sample is biased towards the better performers. For example, the average GDP growth rate of the sample countries 1970–93 is 4 per cent per annum compared with the developing country average of 3.8 per cent (Table 6.4). This bias is desirable, however, given the fact that one of the objectives of the present study is to explain how the performance of the mineral economies may be improved.

The sample includes two countries with an outstanding GDP growth record (Botswana and Indonesia); two with growth rates close to the developing country mean (Chile and PNG); and four with below-average rates (Jamaica, Peru, Trinidad and Tobago, and Namibia). The composition of the sample countries means that each class of mineral and each stage in the cycle contains at least one successful country as well as at least one less successful country (Table 6.4). Attention next turns to an examination of the extent to which the observed differences in GDP growth are accounted for by the more immutable factors, namely the socio-economic preconditions and the nature and degree of external shocks, as opposed to the political economy, a factor over which countries can exercise control through the policies they adopt.

The socio-economic preconditions include initial per capita GDP, income distribution, literacy rate, the rate of population growth, basic economic structure, and the political regime—conditions which cannot be changed by economic policies except over a considerable period of time. The economic shocks include substantial

Table 6.4 GDP growth, investment rate, and investment efficiency, eight countries, 1970–93

	1970–3	1974–9	1980–5	1986–93	1970–93
GDP growth (% /yr)					
Botswana	19.3	11.9	10.9	8.3	11.7
Chile	1.5	3.2	2.3	7.1	4.0
Indonesia	7.4	7.1	5.5	6.3	6.5
Jamaica	6.7	−2.2	−0.8	2.5	1.2
Namibia	1.0	1.0	−0.8	3.5	1.4
PNG	7.3	1.6	0.8	5.7	3.7
Peru	4.8	3.5	0.9	0.1	1.9
Trinidad and Tobago	3.2	6.6	0.1	−1.5	1.7
All developing countries	6.4	5.1	2.7	2.3	3.8
Investment (% GDP)					
Botswana	48.1	38.9	34.8	25.5	34.9
Chile	15.4	19.5	17.2	24.5	19.9
Indonesia	19.2	23.5	27.4	30.4	26.1
Jamaica	30.6	19.1	21.3	26.7	24.1
Namibia	n/a	n/a	22.1	14.2	n/a
PNG	31.9	20.6	26.8	23.3	24.9
Peru	17.2	21.9	26.7	19.4	21.5
Trinidad and Tobago	29.3	26.6	26.6	16.7	23.7
All developing countries	n/a	n/a	24.9	26.1	n/a
Incramental capital output ratios					
Botswana	2.5	3.3	3.2	3.1	3.0
Chile	10.2	6.1	7.5	3.5	5.0
Indonesia	2.6	3.3	5.0	4.8	4.0
Jamaica	4.6	−[a]	−[a]	10.7	20.1
Namibia	n/a	n/a	−[a]	4.1	n/a
PNG	4.4	12.9	33.5	4.1	6.7
Peru	3.6	6.3	29.7	194.0	11.3
Trinidad and Tobago	9.2	4.9	264.0	−[a]	13.9
All developing countries	n/a	n/a	9.2	11.3	n/a

[a] Statistic negative.

Sources: World Bank (1995a) except Hartman (1986) for Namibia, 1970–9; Central Statistical Office (1994) for Botswana, financial years 1986–7 to 1993–4.

increases or decreases in world prices of major mineral exports and of essential imports, and structural changes in the domestic or world production of the major mineral exports. The political economy factor refers to the conditions which can be more readily affected by government policies such as the rate of economic diversification, trade policies, the ratio of domestic investment to GDP, and fiscal policies (Table 6.4).

The Early 1970s' Socio-Economic Preconditions

The most favourable socio-economic preconditions prevailed in Indonesia and Botswana, despite the fact that they were the two poorest countries in 1970 (Table 6.4). The least favourable conditions were exhibited by Chile and Namibia. The four least favoured countries were mid-income mineral economies in the mature stage of their cycles. But passage into the mature stage of the cycle does not inevitably dictate a weak performance. For example, Indonesia was widely perceived to be well into its mature stage in the early 1970s, and yet its subsequent performance was outstanding. A corollary is that a favourable economic climate in the youthful stage of the cycle does not guarantee high growth, as Jamaica shows only too well.

Four dynamic economies

In the early 1970s, Indonesia was recovering from dislocations which followed the ousting of President Sukarno in the mid-1960s. The new government enjoyed high political autonomy and possessed several other favourable preconditions, which offset the social discontent that might have been expected to arise out of the country's very low per capita income, life expectancy, and literacy rates (Table 6.4). These advantages included a relatively egalitarian income distribution and the scope to boost rural incomes (a majority of the population lived in the countryside) through the rapid diffusion of green revolution techniques.

The Indonesian economy was also enjoying robust economic growth with a relatively high rate of investment for a low-income country and the capacity to use investment productively, as indicated by an ICOR of 2.6 in 1970–3 (Table 6.4). Furthermore, the perceived maturity of the Indonesian hydrocarbon province was already directing attention towards economic diversification. The government was responding through a combination of modest economic liberalization and the application of green revolution techniques aimed at rice self-sufficiency.

The second dynamic economy, Botswana, was experiencing rapid economic growth and high levels of investment on the eve of the oil shocks, as a consequence of the construction of its first major mine and copper-nickel smelter at Phikwe (Table 6.4). The government of Botswana benefited from the homogeneity of its cattle-herding society which supported cautious policies and reduced the government's need to distort policy in order to assemble a viable political coalition. The Botswana people elected governments which were remarkably conservative by the standards of sub-Saharan Africa both in terms of macroeconomic management and micro-level interventions.

Although the PNG government also displayed macroeconomic caution as it moved towards independence from Australia, its government had less autonomy than those of either Indonesia or Botswana. This is because PNG was a democracy which lacked the advantage of cultural homogeneity. A variety of regionally isolated groups looked to the political system to provide local largesse, much in line with the clientelistic model of Kurer (1996). PNG experienced political tensions which were soon to be exacerbated by the expansion of the mining sector. But in the early 1970s,

PNG like Botswana, enjoyed rapid economic growth, partly due to the construction of the Panguna mine whose investment exceeded the country's total GDP in size, and partly due to the high level of economic aid from Australia.

Finally, Jamaica experienced rapid economic growth driven by mineral expansion as a result of the construction of new alumina refining capacity. But the socio-economic preconditions for continued growth in the 1970s were less certain. The preceding two decades of rapid mineral-driven growth had been associated with heightened income inequality: for example, the income share of the poorest two-fifths of the population shrank from 7.7 per cent of the total income to a mere 5.5 per cent (Ambursley 1983). The deterioration in Jamaican social conditions was reflected in the country's shift towards a polarized democracy, as one party embraced radical change. The election of 1972, replaced a conservative government by a more radical one. The new government planned to redistribute wealth from foreign and private hands towards domestic (often state) control (Auty 1993).

Four problematic economies

The four slower-growing mineral economies in the sample (Peru, Trinidad and Tobago, Chile, and Namibia) were all in the mature stage of their mineral-driven cycle in 1970, and shared with Indonesia a need to diversify their economies. But compared with Indonesia, the four mature mineral economies had relatively high per capita incomes (Table 6.4). However, other preconditions were less favourable. Severely distorted economies (see Chapter 9) hampered the expansion of labour-intensive agriculture and also of manufacturing. Meanwhile, consistent with Sachs and Warner (1995*a*), the weakened competitiveness of the non-mining tradeables sectors had triggered policies of trade protection in Peru, Chile, and Trinidad and Tobago.

The governments of Peru, Trinidad and Tobago, and Chile were reacting to political polarization in ways which hampered the effective use of economic resources. In sharp contrast to Indonesia, the legacy of rent-driven growth in Peru's mature mineral economy was one of a highly skewed income distribution (Table 6.5) with a strong bias against the Amerindian peasantry in the Andes. An authoritarian government had begun responding in 1968 to social polarization. It redistributed land, and mineral and capital assets, but the transfer was to less productive uses and on a scale which sapped the dynamism of a hitherto advantageously diversified primary sector (Lago 1991; Thorp 1991). Private investment declined in response to the nationalization of most major mines, the redistribution of estate land to cooperatives, and the expansion of state-owned industry.

The erstwhile cautious macroeconomic policy of Trinidad and Tobago was undermined following an attempted coup in 1970. The coup severely rattled a government that had appeared invulnerable due to its monopoly of the black majority vote in an ethnically divided state. The coup prompted the government of Trinidad and Tobago to be more accommodating to demands for state ownership and other measures which adversely affected resource-use efficiency. In addition, plans to reform inefficient and heavily subsidized sectors such as sugar and import-substitution

Table 6.5 Preconditions in nine mineral economies

	Botswana	Chile	Columbia	Indonesia	Jamaica	Namibia	PNG	Peru	Trinidad and Tobago
Resource endowment									
Land area (km²)	566	749	1,039	1,812	11	823	453	1,280	5
Population 1970 (millions)	0.6	9.5	21.4	120.3	1.9	0.8	2.4	13.2	1.0
Cropland/capita (ha)	2.24	0.47	0.26	0.19	0.14	0.90	0.59	0.28	0.13
GDP 1970 ($bn)	0.083	8.426	7.199	9.657	1.405	0.435	0.646	7.234	0.822
Main-mineral	Diamond	Copper	Oil	Oil	Bauxite	Diamond	Copper	Copper	Oil
Socio-political									
GDP/head 1970 ($US)	120	830	340	80	720	560	270	520	760
Literacy (%)	41.0	89.0	80.8	56.6	96.1	n/a	32.1	72.5	92.2
Income inequality ratio	15.0	11.7	15.1	7.9	n/a	n/a	n/a	32.1	17.6
Life expectancy (yr)	52	62	61	48	68	48	47	54	65
Population growth (%)	3.5	1.8	2.4	2.4	1.4	2.6	2.4	2.8	1.0
Rural population (%)	91.6	24.8	42.8	82.9	58.5	81.4	90.2	42.6	37.0
Political regime	FDC	FDP	FDC	ABB	FDP	FOPL	FOC	FOPO	FDP
Economic									
Trade stance	O	C	PC	O	PC		PC	C	PC
GDP/ha growth 1970–3 (%)	15.9	-0.3	4.4	5.0	5.3		4.9	2.0	2.2
GDI 1970–3 (% GDP)	48.1	15.4	19.0	19.2	30.6		31.9	17.2	29.3
Debt 1971–3 (% GDP)	54.0	33.0	32.6	47.3	64.0		54.0	14.7	12.0
Exports 1970–3 (% GDP)	73.4	11.6	14.2	15.9	35.4		27.2	13.9	42.8
Agriculture 1970 (% GDP)	33.1	6.6	25.1	44.9	6.6		37.2	18.7	5.2
Manufacturing 1970 (% GDP)	5.8	24.8	20.7	10.3	15.7		5.5	19.8	25.6

Notes: ABB = Autocratic, Benevolent, Bureaucracy; FDC = Factional, Democratic, Consensual; FDP = Factional, Democratic, Polarized; FOC = Factional, Oligopolistic, Plantocracy; FOP = Factional, Oligopolistic, Populist; Trade: O = open; C = closed; PC = partly closed.

Sources: World Bank (1995a); WRI (1994).

manufacturing, were postponed following modest discoveries of natural gas (Gelb and Associates 1988).

The political situation was more tense in Chile where in 1970 a left-leaning president had been elected with only 36 per cent of the vote. The election occurred in the context of a trend since the 1930s in which, far from diversifying its economy, Chile had increased its reliance on mining as a result of successful efforts to internalize a greater fraction of the copper revenues (Auty 1993). In 1971 the new government nationalized most mining activity and also engineered an unsustainable expansion of the economy. An initial boost to real wages led to inflation, a sharp fall in the rate of investment, and the cessation of economic growth (Sachs 1989). The ensuing socio-economic turmoil culminated in the murder of the president in 1973 and the establishment of an authoritarian regime whose metamorphosis into a champion of effective economic reform was not then widely foreseen.

But the greatest social polarization among the sample countries existed in Namibia which was administered by South Africa until 1990 as the UN Trust territory of South West Africa (World Bank 1994b). This status helps to account for the dearth of statistical information prior to 1980. Apartheid marginalized the black majority on the northern border of the country while a small white minority managed the government, mines, and ranches. The education of the black majority was neglected and their numbers outstripped the meagre subsistence-carrying capacity of their homelands. The neglect was intensified by the maturation of the mining sector: the economic growth rate slowed from 6.1 per cent during 1958–70 to only 1.0 per cent in 1970–80 as diamond production decelerated (Hartman 1986). Given the territory's 2.6 per cent population growth, per capita GDP contracted by 1.6 per cent per annum through the 1970s.

Summarizing the preconditions: during the early 1970s all three youthful mineral economies (Botswana, Jamaica, and PNG) were experiencing rapid economic growth whereas among the mature mineral economies, only Indonesia was doing well. The strong economic prospects of Indonesia and Botswana were reinforced by propitious socio-political conditions. But this was less so for Jamaica and PNG, where the capacity of their governments to implement effective policies was weakened by political pressure for wealth redistribution. Finally, the four flagging countries were all mature mineral economies (Chile, Namibia, Peru, and Trinidad and Tobago) which harboured unfavourable socio-political conditions on the eve of the price shocks.

The Differential Impact of the External Shocks

Borensztein *et al.* (1994) confirm the increased price volatility during the 1970s and 1980s compared with the previous two post-war decades. They also suggest that permanent price shifts account for far less of the variance in mineral prices (30 per cent) than is the case for the soft commodities, a finding which strengthens the argument for the governments of mineral economies to deploy a MRSF. Finally, they

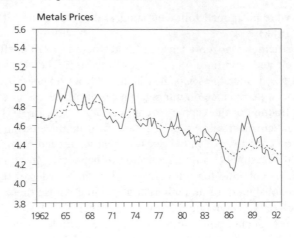

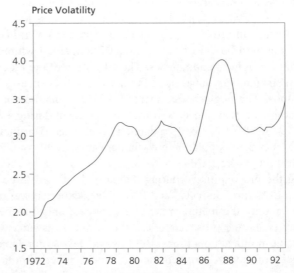

Figure 6.3 Metal prices, 1960–92 and price volatility, 1972–92
Source: Borensztein et al. (1994).

confirm the tendency for metals prices to experience a long-term decline through
1969–92 (Figure 6.3).

   The trends in the terms of trade for each of the eight mineral economies over the
period 1970–93 are summarized in Table 6.6. In addition, the table shows the magnitude of the economic shocks associated with the 1973 and 1979 oil price rises.
The shocks are measured as a ratio of GDP by calculating, after Sachs (1985), the
share of imports in GDP and then multiplying that figure by the terms-of-trade shift.
All countries faced adverse trends at some time, but conditions were unusually severe
for PNG and Chile, the two least diversified copper exporters. They were most

Table 6.6 Terms of trade trends and external price shocks: eight countries, 1970–1993

	Botswana	Chile	Indonesia	Jamaica	Namibia	PNG	Peru	Trinidad
Terms of trade (% change)								
1974–7 over 1970–3	−29.3	−31.5	132.0	30.8	n/a	−8.7[a]	−1.9	44.9
1979–82 over 1975–8	−7.2	−18.2	46.0	−21.6	n/a	−3.9	−15.0	26.3
1990–3 over 1979–82	56.6	−5.9	−38.1	−6.8	−14.8	−23.2	−19.0	−34.3
Oil shocks (% GDP)								
1974–7 over 1970–3	−24.9	−8.2	27.3	11.9	n/a	−4.2	−0.4	22.0
1979–82 over 1975–8	−6.5	−5.6	10.3	−11.7	n/a	−2.4	−3.6	12.1

[a] 1973 only.

Source: World Bank (1995*a*).

favourable for the two oil exporters, Indonesia and Trinidad and Tobago, provided they could take advantage of the mineral booms and also prudently manage the adjustment to the downswings. Elsewhere, the diamond exporters, Botswana and Namibia, also experienced moderately favourable external conditions as, initially, did Jamaica.

Gelb and Associates (1988) provide a more sophisticated measure of the scale of the impact of the oil shocks on the two oil exporters. They exclude non-oil commodity price changes and take changes in hydrocarbon export *volumes* into account. The resulting index is expressed as a share of non-mining GDP. By this measure, the Indonesian oil windfalls were the equivalent of an additional 15 per cent of non-mining GDP annually in 1974–8 and 23 per cent in 1979–81; while those of Trinidad and Tobago were significantly higher at 39 per cent and 35 per cent, respectively. However, during the 1980s both countries had to cope with an oil-price downswing which intensified sharply in 1986 (Table 6.6). Indonesia demonstrates that the price swings could be efficiently managed, whereas Trinidad and Tobago shows that things could also go very wrong (Table 6.4).

Among the three non-copper hard-mineral economies, Botswana experienced a marked improvement in its terms of trade through the 1980s following a sizeable deterioration in the previous decade. (However, even during the late 1970s, rapidly expanding diamond production meant that volume effects more than offset adverse trends in export prices.) More specifically, although the revenues from Botswana's large base-metals mine proved disappointing, a rapid expansion of diamond production (which conferred very large rents) more than compensated. The continued vigorous expansion of diamond production through the 1980s gave Botswana the most favourable external conditions of the sample countries at that time. Like Indonesia, therefore, the trade trends reinforced favourable preconditions for Botswana.

Although terms-of-trade data are not available for Namibia in the 1970s, the initial adverse effects of higher oil prices were offset by the start-up of a uranium mine which brought rising volumes and prices until the early 1980s. Then, as Table 6.6 shows, the trade effects turned negative, a trend that was amplified by falling mineral output and the country's difficult internal conditions. Jamaica, also experienced improved terms of trade in the immediate aftermath of the first oil shock (which arose out of favourable trends in both bauxite and sugar prices), but thereafter, external conditions deteriorated sharply, with adverse effects on economic growth.

Finally, the terms of trade of the three major copper producers underwent a prolonged and sizeable deterioration, especially those of the least diversified producers, Chile and PNG (Figure 6.1). The copper price was widely expected to recover in the late 1970s but instead prices deteriorated through the 1980s. In the case of Peru, however, the adverse impact of the protracted copper price decline was at first offset by that country's more diversified exports (which included oil).

Summarizing, three sets of external conditions can be recognized. First, Botswana experienced the most favourable trade price trends over the period studied and the oil exporters Indonesia and Trinidad and Tobago also enjoyed lengthy upswings. This implies that the external trends would reinforce the favourable preconditions of Botswana and Indonesia, and offset the pre-shock difficulties of Trinidad and Tobago. Second, at the other extreme, the most consistently unfavourable external environment was faced by the two countries most dependent on copper, Chile and PNG. This might be expected to reinforce the adverse Chilean preconditions and weaken the initially better prospects for PNG. Third, the less dire external conditions of Peru, Namibia, and Jamaica might be expected to offset the adverse preconditions of the first two countries and reinforce the Jamaican strengths. In fact, within each category at least one country (and five in total) performed contrary to the expectations set by the socio-economic preconditions and trade shocks thereby underlining the critical role of policy.

Role of Policy

Combining the differences in the propitiousness of the socio-economic preconditions with variations in the severity of the external environment in the period 1973–93, suggests that Botswana and Indonesia would perform well. Trinidad and Tobago might be expected to perform at, or even above, the average, given the lengthy positive shock which it enjoyed prior to the downturn in oil prices and its bias towards cautious macro-management. A more average performance, one slightly worse than Trinidad and Tobago, might have been expected of Peru and Jamaica, given the socio-economic preconditions and modest initial trade shocks in the mid-1970s. The adverse socio-economic preconditions and predominantly negative shocks of Chile and PNG might be expected to result in the worst performance. Namibia also faced an unfavourable combination of preconditions and deteriorating external shocks.

However, only three countries performed in line with these projections. Table 6.4 shows that Botswana and Indonesia performed in line with their more propitious circumstances and that Namibia also responded in line with that country's adverse circumstances. But Chile improved significantly on expectations and PNG also responded slightly better. Among the remaining countries, both Jamaica and Peru fared little better than Namibia, despite their advantages, while Trinidad and Tobago significantly underperformed. These three underperforming countries and Namibia were all in the mature stage of the mineral cycle by the mid-1970s (Jamaica having quickly propelled itself there through overestimating the scale of its rents in 1974). However, Chile shows (along with Indonesia) that maturity need not constrain economic performance if appropriate polices are adopted.

The fact that the actual performances often fail to reflect the preconditions and shocks, underlines the important role of economic policy and also the problems which many governments have in sustaining appropriate policies. Orthodox economics has tended to assume that governments will pursue policies which are economically 'rational' in the sense of maximizing long-run social welfare. For example, Findlay (1990) argues that a common view of political economy is that of the State as an agency which provides public goods and offsets externalities and similar market failures by corrective taxes and subsidies. The State may also engage in income redistribution in line with some ethical norm of social justice. Orthodox economics also assumes

Table 6.7 Typology of political states

Autonomy	Character	Variants	Examples
	Benevolent------(	Monarchy	
(		Bureaucratic	Indonesia
(			Chile 1975–90
Autonomous---(			
(			
(	Predatory---------(	Authoritarian	
		Bureaucratic	Peru 1968–78
	Democratic------(	Consensual	Botswana
			Jamaica post-1988
			Namibia post-1990
(		Polarizing	Jamaica 1972–1988
(			PNG, Trinidad and
(			Tobago
Fractional------------(			
(			
(	Oligopolistic------(	Plantocracy	Namibia pre-1990
		Populist	Peru post-1978

Source: Lal (1955).

that the state bureaucracy will be effective and that it possesses both the necessary technical capability *and* the insulation from political pressures which might deflect it from the pursuit of welfare-maximizing economic policies.

Such assumptions have proved idealistic, as this study well illustrates. All too often, a national welfare-enhancing economic policy may conflict with the rationale of politics which may seek to maximize the power of a particular individual, interest group, or coalition (Bates 1988; Bates and Krueger 1993). But an important exception is identified by Leftwich (1995) as the 'developmental State'. Such a State shares many characteristics with the benevolent autonomous State, a sub-category from a typology of political States devised by Lal (1995). That typology sheds useful insight into the reasons why some governments succeed and others do not, and it is summarized below.

Types of political State

Lal (1995) identifies two basic parameters in his typology of developing-country States. The two basic parameters are the autonomy of the State and the aims of the State (Table 6.7). The autonomous State is able to formulate and achieve its own

Table 6.8 GDP growth and political state: twenty-five sample countries

State type	Resource endowment		PCGDP growth 1960–90 (%/yr)
	Deficient	Rich	
Autonomous			
Benevolent	3	1	5.4
Predatory	1	3	2.2
PCGDP growth (%)	5.9	1.7	3.8
Factional			
Democratic	3	5	2.2
Oligopolist	3	6	0.7
PCGDP growth (%)	1.8	1.2	1.4
Autonomous and factional			
Autonomous states	4	4	3.8
Factional states	6	11	1.4
All states	10	15	2.2
PCGDP growth (%)	3.5	1.3	2.2

Notes:
1. Five small resource-deficient countries = El Salvador, Kenya, Mauritius, Sri Lanka, Taiwan.
2. Five large resource-deficient countries = China, Colombia, Indonesia, Pakistan, South Korea.
3. Five large resource-rich countries = Argentina, Brazil, India, Nigeria, and South Africa.
4. Five small resource-rich mineral economies = Namibia, PNG, Peru, Saudi Arabia, and Trinidad and Tobago.
5. Five small resource-rich non-mineral economes = Costa Rica, Guyana, Malaysia, Sudan, and Zimbabwe.

Source: Auty (1997*b*).

objectives, a situation which enhances prospects for the coherence and consistency of economic policy. The autonomous State is distinguished from the factional State whose autonomy is constrained by the need to appease political groups that are often diverse in their demands.

Turning to the second criterion—the aims of the State—Lal distinguishes within the autonomous group between platonic (or benevolent) and predatory States. Within the first subgroup, the *benevolent* autonomous State seeks to maximize long-run social welfare and to rapidly build up high levels of administrative capability. In contrast, the *predatory* autonomous State focuses on a narrower range of goals which reflect a greater concern for the immediate survival of the government.

The factional State also comprises two subgroups on the basis of their aims, namely the oligopolistic State and the democratic State. Table 6.8 shows the relationship between the type of State, resource endowment, and rate of GNP growth 1970–93 for a sample of twenty-five developing countries. It suggests that the autonomous State has a superior performance, largely due to the success of the benevolent States which, however, tend to be associated with deficient natural resource endowments.

The GDP growth rates of the factious States are lower, more so in the case of the oligopolistic subgroup than of the democratic subgroup.

The developmental State occurs with most frequency in the resource-constrained States of East Asia and has been far less common in Latin America and sub-Saharan Africa. Elsewhere, Auty (1997*b*) speculates on the reasons for this association. He suggests that as the population/cropland ratio in developing countries nears 0.1 ha, the economic hardship generates political strains which increase the probability of a political crisis which realigns government interests with peasant interests *and*, as a result, places more stress on resource efficiency rather than on rent distribution. The pursuit of rational welfare-maximizing economic policies then mitigates the pressure on developmental States for democracy, at least initially. The economic success enhances the longevity of the regime and captures the benefits of policy consistency, creating a virtuous circle. Developmental States also rapidly build up high levels of administrative capability which tend to be insulated from corrupting political pressures (Ranis and Mahmood 1992). However, Botswana, which is a consensual democracy, also qualifies as a developmental State and this indicates that the link with the resource endowment is more of a probabilistic one, rather than a deterministic one.

The evidence suggests that the political State in resource-rich countries like the mineral economies, is more likely to be a factional one which may be democratic or oligopolistic (Table 6.7). A key characteristic of the factional State is the need to capture resource rents and/or create rents (through state intervention, as with import substitution) in order to sustain power. This process usually occurs at the expense of the overall efficiency of resource use and can quickly depress growth within the economy (Gelb *et al*. 1991). One variant of the factional State, the *polarized* democracy, sees political parties vie for political support with radically different policies. This results in sharp changes in policy at elections and a loss in policy consistency. But the factional State may be oligopolistic (in which entrenched élite groups may manipulate token democracies). Factional oligopolies may take the form of either a plantocracy (of landed interests) or a populist bureaucracy. An oligopolistic State is likely to have a strongly skewed income distribution with adverse implications for skill acquisition, small-scale business formation, social cohesion, and political stability (Fajnzylber 1995).

Applying this classification to the nine mineral economies analysed in this book (Table 6.9), the governments of all four of the most successful countries (Indonesia, Botswana, post-1975 Chile, and Colombia) have exhibited high levels of autonomy which they have effectively deployed to enhance social welfare. But whereas the governments of Indonesia and Chile 1975–89 clearly fit into Lal's first category in Table 6.7, Botswana and Colombia are exceptional. Post-independence Botswana functioned as a 'consensual' democracy, a select subgroup, with broad national agreement on policy objectives. Nevertheless, Botswana is classed as a 'developmental State' by the political scientist Leftwich (1995), although his list of developmental States is dominated by autonomous States. Colombia also evolved into a consensual democracy when the two leading political parties agreed in 1958 to set up an orderly exchange of power in response to a prolonged period of internal violence.

Table 6.9 Political systems and economic performance: nine countries, 1970–1993

	Botswana	Chile	Colombia	Indonesia	Jamaica	Namibia	PNG	Peru	Trinidad and Tobago
Type of State[a]	FOC	ABB	FDC	ABB	FDP/C	FOPL	FOPL	FOPO	FDP/C
PC GNP 1970 ($US)	120	830	340	80	720	560[b]	270	520	760
PC GNP 1993 ($US)	2,790	3,170	1,400	740	1,440	1,820	1,130	1,490	3,830
PC GNP PPP 1994 (% US)[c]	20.1	34.4	20.6	13.9	13.1	16.7	10.4	13.9	33.5
GDP growth 1970–93 (% yr)	11.7	4.0	4.5	6.5	1.2	1.4	3.7	1.9	1.7
ICOR 1970–93	3.0	5.0	4.8	4.0	20.1	n/a[d]	6.7	11.3	13.9
Income ratio (top 1/5/low 1/5)	16.4	18.3	15.5	4.9	8.1	n/a	n/a	10.5	12.0
Infant mortality 1993 (per 1,000)	42	16	36	56	14	59	67	63	18[e]

Notes: [a] ABB = Autonomous benevolent bureaucracy; FDC = Factional consensual democracy; FDP = Factional polarized democracy; FOPO = Factional oligopoly, populist; FOPU = Factional oligopoly, plantocracy.
[b] Hartman (1986).
[c] World Bank (1996e).
[d] If investment assumed at 20% of GDP, the ICOR = 14.3.
[e] World Bank (1994b) for expenditure, not income.

Sources: World Bank (1995a).

Colombia became noted for macro-policies which were unusually cautious in the context of Latin America and allowed the country to avoid a severe debt crisis in the 1980s (Hughes 1988).

The less successful governments all functioned in types of non-consensual factional State. Jamaica, Trinidad and Tobago, and PNG functioned as polarizing democracies, although a consensual democracy eventually emerged in the two Caribbean countries in the 1980s. Consensual democracies displaced oligopolistic States in both Peru and Namibia in 1990. The governments of non-consensual factional States must divert resources to maintain political support in a manner that can severely depress the efficiency of resource use without resolving social tensions. All of the non-consensual factional States in this study displayed high levels of (inefficient) state intervention which contributed to the distortion of their economies and proved difficult to reform.

Conclusions

The mineral economies as a group have tended to underperform since the 1960s compared with other developing countries, and especially compared to the resource-deficient developing countries. But variations in the economic performance of individual mineral economies show that their underperformance is by no means inevitable. The variations reflect differences in the socio-economic preconditions, the scale of price shocks, and, most importantly, the capacity of the State to pursue effective policies.

The three most successful countries (Botswana, Indonesia, and post-1975 Chile) had governments which combined high autonomy with prudent macro-management and a commitment to welfare-maximization. The States which performed less well were all factional States whose internal divisions constrained government action and/or emphasized redistributive objectives at the expense of the efficient use of resources.

Of the three most successfully performing countries, Chile holds the best record for laying the foundations for sustainability by increasing the strength of its manufacturing and agriculture sectors and by socio-political improvement. Indonesia has improved its manufacturing sector, but there remain socio-political problems which could weaken sustainability. Botswana's sustainable development is less certain because of the limited scope of diversification, a problem it shares with the three other small mid-income mineral economies (Jamaica, Trinidad and Tobago, and Namibia). Chapters 7 and 8 examine in more detail the relationship between macroeconomic policy and economic performance, including the foundations for sustainable development, of the eight mineral economies. Chapter 9 focuses upon the micro-level, and compares the evolving production structure of the sample countries. It seeks to determine their progress with, and their prospects for, diversification away from mineral dependence.

7 Successful Macro-Management over the Mineral-Driven Cycle

The focus in Chapters 7 and 8 is upon macroeconomic management, using conventional national accounting. A prerequisite for mineral-driven sustainable development is the reduction of economic distortions created by external shocks or by mistaken policies, by means of the effective pursuit of macro-policy. Within a soundly managed economy, policies to deploy the mineral revenue to advantage need to be adjusted to each stage of the mineral-driven cycle (youth, early maturity, and late maturity). In particular, investment and growth must be sustained beyond the youthful stage of the cycle. This chapter focuses on the policy adjustments of the four most successful countries in the sample to the youthful stage and onset of maturity. Late maturity, which calls primarily for the intensification of the measures adopted during the second stage, is the principal focus of Chapter 8.

The youthful stage sees the rapid expansion of the mining sector, growth in government revenues, and an accelerated inflow of foreign exchange. The mineral revenue stream is unlikely to be smooth because of the cyclical nature of mineral prices. This fluctuating revenue stream, in addition to complicating macro-management, also blurs recognition of long-term trends in mineral prices and of exactly where a country is in its mineral-driven cycle. Consequently, prudent macro-policies for the youthful stage of the mineral-driven cycle need (1) to accumulate and sterilize the financial reserves in an MRSF; (2) slow the real appreciation in the exchange rate; and (3) gradually expand the absorptive capacity of the economy for the increased revenue. The MRSF acts as a buffer on government spending and also as a brake on the long-term adjustment of the real exchange rate. Therefore, it helps to prevent changes in the structure of the economy that impair sustainability.

Although in theory an MRSF may yield a suboptimal employment of resources compared with recourse to futures markets (Varangis *et al.* 1995), the practical difficulty of forecasting revenue flows and of resisting political pressure for rapid absorption justify the creation of an MRSF. In effect, an MRSF biases the rate of domestic oil rent absorption towards caution, a stance which this and other studies (Gelb and Associates 1988; Hill 1991) find to be far less damaging than the more common government response of over-optimism. Provided that clear rules are established concerning revenue sterilization (for instance, by giving responsibility for the MRSF to a high-autonomy central bank), a MRSF restricts the extent to which governments can deploy public spending to shore up political support in a way which is at odds with the requirements for sustainable development.

The second stage of the mineral-driven cycle, early maturity, is marked by a sustained relative or absolute slowdown in mining expansion, although the mineral sector is still exerting a major economic influence. Policies during this stage need to encourage diversification into alternative sources of taxation and foreign exchange, while still managing cyclical fluctuations in mineral revenues caused by mineral price swings and output fluctuations. In order to smooth adjustment to the deceleration in mineral rents while new tax sources are extended, some drawdown of the MRSF is likely to occur, along with depreciation of the real exchange rate. The objective of these measures is to avoid inflationary fiscal deficits and the overrapid build-up of foreign debt, while maintaining or boosting the share of investment in GDP which, in the more successful countries, has exceeded 25 per cent.

The historical evidence suggests that directly productive investment to diversify the economy is best achieved by the private sector (with subsidies, if any, being minimal) rather than, as was fashionable in the 1970s, by the public sector. Only if there are strong externalities, as with education and infrastructure, can a clear case be made for public investment and even then support for such public investment is not unequivocal (World Bank 1994*a*). Government intervention to force the pace of industrialization via an active industrial policy is even less likely to prove efficient. This is because, despite the apparent success of competitive industrial policies in countries like Korea and Taiwan, such policies are unlikely to prove beneficial elsewhere. The rents conferred on infant industries invariably lead to 'policy capture' by which groups (workers, executives, and nationalistic technocrats) that benefit from state intervention build a coalition which effectively blocks withdrawal of the rents (Auty 1995*b*). This retards industrial 'maturation' and imposes increasingly onerous costs on the primary sector whose relative size declines during economic development.

The undesirability of state-forced change is also shown by the mineral economies' preoccupation in the 1970s for 'adding value' to natural resources prior to export through resource-based industry (RBI). For example, the oil exporters' RBI strategies often, in effect, substituted low-rent gas-based exports for high-rent oil exports (Auty 1990). Such an RBI strategy only makes sense if the opportunity cost of natural gas is low or if the savings on raw material freight costs arising from weight loss during processing can offset not only the mineral economy's likely higher costs of capital, but also the higher freight rates on semi-finished/fabricated exports compared with bulk-shipped unprocessed goods.

The rest of this chapter focuses on the four more successful countries in our sample. The next section, deals with Indonesia, a mature mineral economy in the early 1970s which the positive oil shocks restored to the youthful stage of the cycle. It most clearly illustrates the policies required for the adroit management of the transition into early and then late maturity. The following two sections focus upon the youthful stage of the mineral-driven cycle with reference to Botswana and PNG. Finally, the mature stage of the cycle is examined for an economy which has been strongly distorted with regard to Chile.

Successful Indonesian Transition to Late Maturity

The 1973 oil shock restored the dynamism of the youthful stage of the Indonesian mineral-led cycle and the 1979 oil shock amplified that change. Thereafter, however, oil revenues flagged from 1982 (early maturity) and the sharp decline in oil prices in 1986 called for a rapid adaptation to late maturity.

More specifically, the windfall from the first oil shock was around 16 per cent of non-oil GDP annually during the period 1974–8 (Gelb and Associates 1988) while the second shock was larger (but briefer) at 22 per cent of non-oil GDP annually during 1979–81. Thereafter, the oil price fall inflicted a negative shock that was equivalent to the loss of 15 per cent of GDP during 1986–8, having intensified from a level of 3 per cent of GDP in 1982–5 (Ahmed 1989). Yet, overall, the oil booms and downswing were associated with a sustained rapid growth in real per capita incomes (Table 6.4) and substantial welfare improvements (Table 7.1). Indonesia coped effectively with all three shocks, largely because of efficient but cautious macro-management.

Prudent rent deployment during the 1974–8 and 1979–81 oil booms

In the absence of a formal MRSF, Indonesia nevertheless managed to sterilize the oil rents through the booms. Gelb and Associates (1988) estimate that Indonesia saved one-third of its first windfall abroad (Table 7.2). The scale of its domestic absorption was also reduced during the first boom by the accumulation of a foreign debt of $10 billion by Pertamina. This debt required servicing and, as a result, slowed the rate of domestic absorption of the oil rent. This proved to be fortuitous because it delayed many heavy industry projects until the second boom. A high proportion of these projects were subsequently cancelled when oil prices softened, whereas the performance of most heavy industry projects that did proceed was disappointing (Auty 1990).

Around one-sixth of the windfall went into increased consumption during the first oil boom as public consumption rose by the equivalent of 1.5 per cent of non-oil output in real terms (Table 7.2) and offset a relative fall from the pre-shock trend in private consumption. But domestic windfall absorption was dominated by more productive investment, which accounted for the remaining 50 per cent. Much of the investment accrued to rural areas through higher expenditure on agriculture, subsidies for fertilizer (designed to achieve rice self-sufficiency), and rural infrastructure improvements (Gelb and Associates 1988). This diffused the benefits through the economy and helped to maintain the country's relatively equitable income distribution.

Overall, the 1974–8 oil boom resulted in a net increase in the rate of capital formation compared with the pre-shock rate of the equivalent of 4.5 per cent of non-oil GDP. But increased public investment led to some relative decline in private investment. Around one-quarter of all Indonesian development investment during the first

Table 7.1 Some welfare indicators: eight mineral economies, 1970–93

	Per capita GNP ($US)		Life expectancy (yrs)		Literacy	
	1970	1993	1970	1993	1970–2	1993
Botswana	120	2,790	51.9	65.3	41	74
Chile	830	3,170	62.4	74.0	89	93
Indonesia	80	750	47.9	63.2	57	77
Jamaica	720	1,400	67.7	73.7	96	88
Namibia	540	1,990	47.7	59.2	n/a	n/a
PNG	220	1,180	46.7	56.3	32	52
Peru	520	1,490	53.9	66.2	63	85
Trinidad and Tobago	960	3,830	65.4	71.8	92	96

Sources: World Bank (1995*a*); Hartman (1986) for Namibia, 1970.

Table 7.2 Oil windfall deployment, Indonesia and Trinidad and Tobago, 1974–8 and 1979–81 (% non-mining GDP)

	1974–8		1979–81	
	Indonesia	Trinidad and Tobago	Indonesia	Trinidad and Tobago
Domestic oil windfall	15.9	38.9	22.7	34.7
Real	1.6	2.3	–2.5	–7.4
Price effect	14.3	36.6	25.2	42.1
Absorption effects				
Trade and non-factor services	5.3	27.2	9.6	16.8
Current balance	4.8	26.7	6.1	19.2
Non-oil growth effects	–2.4	–7.8	–3.5	0.6
Real allocation and growth effects				
Private consumption	–1.5	19.4	7.7	27.2
Public consumption	1.5	n/a	3.0	n/a
Private investment	–3.4	–4.6	7.9	12.2
Public investment	7.9	5.5	n/a	n/a

Note: The table is based on a counterfactual of what would have occurred in the absence of the oil windfall. It makes four key assumptions: (1) relative price deflators constant at their average 1970–2 'base period' ratio; (2) a constant ratio of real mining output to non-mining GDP; (3) a constant ratio of total absorption to output; (4) consumption and investment change their share of absorption as per capita income rises in line with their normal shares derived from Chenery and Syrquin (1975).

The windfalls and their uses are then derived as deviations of actual supply and demand shares from the hypothetical projections and expressed relative to non-mining GDP to facilitate comparison. In this way it becomes possible to distinguish the contribution of volume changes and price changes in the parameters, and also to adjust for any acceleration or slowdown in the growth of non-mining GDP (assumed to be attributed to windfall absorption) compared with the base period. Further information is provided in Gelb and Associates (1988: 56–9).

Source: Gelb and Associates (1988).

oil boom went on infrastructure. A further two-fifths was also sensibly allocated, this time to the hydrocarbon sector to prolong oil production and to diversify into LNG through the successful construction of two large LNG terminals. Finally, industrial diversification accounted for the remaining third of development investment, which was evenly split between the metal and the non-metal sectors.

More than 40 per cent of the larger 1979–81 windfall was prudently sterilized by being saved abroad. But other aspects of the deployment were less effective because the Indonesian government found the euphoria engendered by the second oil boom difficult to resist and domestic absorption was overrapid (Auty 1990). Private consumption, public consumption, and investment all rose sharply so that domestic inflation accelerated. The benefits of an exchange rate devaluation in 1979, which had been designed to restore the flagging competitiveness of the non-mining tradeables, were quickly eliminated.

The hitherto efficient food grain sector was adversely affected by these trends and also by the expansion of subsidized consumption during the 1979–81 oil boom. Meanwhile, the competitiveness of manufacturing also weakened and industrialists successfully used the real exchange rate appreciation to secure an intensification of protection (and rent-seeking opportunities) against the Dutch disease effects. Hill (1995) reports that sectoral maturation rates were extremely lengthy for major manufacturing sectors such as steel, automobile assembly (where tariffs still ranged around 200 per cent in 1993, twenty years after targeting (Smith 1995)), as well as for the 'high-tech' activities. The latter provided scant evidence of the economy-wide externalities used by minister Habbibie to justify the subsidies.

Managing the post-boom transition to late maturity

Nevertheless, despite the Indonesian government's tolerance of such rent-seeking behaviour, the priority accorded to macro-orthodoxy led to timely shifts in order to correct the fiscal and current account imbalances when oil prices softened through the early 1980s. Sustained growth required a cut in public spending which the government promptly made and a broadening of the tax base. The net effect was to boost the non-oil tax share from 8.3 per cent of GDP to 13.2 per cent over the decade 1981–91. Although the external savings accumulated during the oil booms proved too small to cushion the economy to the downswing, the government was able to draw upon foreign loans because of its reputation for sound macro-management. But the loans pushed total debt above 50 per cent of GDP (Table 7.3) and the level of debt service rose to average 36 per cent of export earnings (Table 7.3). This underlined the urgency of the second key response to maturity, a rapid expansion of non-mineral exports.

The required rapid diversification of exports was achieved with the aid of two depreciations of the real exchange rate, in 1983 and 1986, backed up by a successful macroeconomic stabilization programme. The stabilization of prices helped to sustain the real depreciations which, when oil prices plummeted in 1986, took the exchange

Table 7.3 Current account, foreign debt, and debit service in eight mineral economies, 1971–93

	Botswana	Chile	Indonesia	Jamaica	Namibia	PNG	Peru	Trinidad and Tobago
Current account (% GDP)								
1970–3	−34.7	−2.4	−3.6	−11.1			−0.6	−10.9
1974–9	−11.4	−4.3	−1.2	−5.6		−9.6[a]	−4.7	7.7
1980–5	−13.9	−9.6	−2.5	−13.1	−0.9	−24.8	−4.0	−2.8
1986–9	11.2	−3.9	−2.9	−5.6	−10.5	−14.3	−5.4	−4.2
1990–3	−3.1	−2.6	−2.7	−7.4	−5.0	−4.4	−5.5	3.2
Foreign debt (% GDP)								
1971–3	54.0	32.7	47.3	64.0		54.7	39.3	12.0
1974–9	34.0	54.5	35.2	58.5		35.2	57.7	10.2
1980–5	22.5	88.5	33.5	131.8		66.5	54.2	17.0
1986–9	31.8	101.0	65.0	157.3		71.8	81.3	46.0
1990–3	18.0	54.0	65.8	134.3		80.3	65.8	50.2
Debt service (% exports)								
1971–3	1.4	23.7	17.9	38.3		40.7	53.0	4.0
1974–9	2.2	39.7	17.3	39.0		15.0	46.5	3.0
1980–5	3.1	56.8	19.5	39.7		26.8	40.8	7.7
1980–9	4.0	32.5	36.0	39.8		28.5	13.0	19.0
1990–3	4.2[a]	23.3	31.5	26.5		30.6	31.0	24.5

[a] 1990–1.

Source: World Bank (1995*a*).

rate down to 60 per cent of its 1983 value. A start was made on trade liberalization in 1986. Hill (1995) argues that the Indonesian trade and industry policy reforms of the late 1980s marked the collapse of the strategy of state-led industrialization financed by oil. The government share of investment fell by 1990 to 37 per cent of the total (from a peak of 48 per cent). Meanwhile, reform of the manufacturing sector was required to compensate not only for flagging oil revenues but also for a deceleration of agricultural growth (which had acted as a useful cushion until the mid-1980s) to 3 per cent. This decline reflected diminishing opportunities to extend irrigation or intensify rice yields (as opposed to estate crop output). The trade reforms elicited a surge in non-oil exports which by 1990 pushed hydrocarbon exports below 40 per cent of total exports and shrank the debt service ratio to a manageable 30 per cent of exports (Bhattacharya and Pangestu 1992).

The success of the Indonesian transition through the mature stage of the mineral-led cycle is reflected in the fact that through 1986–93 a recovery occurred in investment, investment efficiency, and GDP growth. Investment climbed to 30.4 per cent of GDP, the ICOR improved to 4.8 (compared with 7.8 over 1982–5), while GDP grew at more than 6 per cent annually (Table 6.4). Meanwhile, the attention to farming during the oil booms had helped to boost welfare among a predominantly rural population (Table 7.1) and bolster the social sustainability of the policy. Those below the poverty line fell from 39 per cent in 1976 to 15 per cent in 1990 and income distribution improved as the ratio of the income of the richest quintile to the poorest quintile fell from 6.2 to 4.9 between 1970 and 1990 (Woo *et al.* 1994; World Bank 1995*a*).

The successful Indonesian management of the country's abrupt transition through the mineral-driven cycle was facilitated by three favourable factors. First, Indonesia benefited from the consolidation of a benevolent autonomous (developmental state) government which ensured the continuity of a policy that was committed to the pursuit of orthodox fiscal and exchange rate policies. As noted above, the strong priority accorded to macro-performance led to prompt reversals of imprudent sectoral interventions, the cancellation of many state-owned heavy industry projects in 1983, and the trade reform in 1986 (Gillis 1984; Pinto 1987). In contrast, many mineral economies in Latin America and sub-Saharan Africa failed to take such decisive action and faced the transition to maturity with badly distorted economies.

A second favourable factor was the presence of sizeable and varied non-hydrocarbon resources, notably in the Outer islands. This resource advantage, in combination with a large domestic market, greatly facilitated the diversification of production away from mining compared with the smaller mineral economies that had deficient non-mineral resource endowments, as Chapters 8 and 9 show. A third important advantage arose from the fact that Indonesia's mean per capita income was still relatively low when the youthful stage ended (Table 7.1). This eased Indonesia's return to the successful growth path of labour-intensive industrialization. In contrast, the more typical mineral economy was required to make the transition to maturity with a mid-level per capita income whose relatively high labour costs hampered successful industrialization (Lal 1995).

These three specific advantages have two important implications for other mineral economies. First, the lessons from Indonesia for other countries is largely limited to its adherence to orthodox macro-policy. Second, countries lacking Indonesia's socio-economic preconditions may face greater difficulties in sustaining economic growth through the mature stage of the mineral-led cycle.

The Youthful Stage: Sustained Rapid Economic Growth in Botswana

Botswana was in the youthful stage of the mineral cycle through the period 1973–89 and, like Indonesia, managed that stage exceptionally well. Once more, a commitment to cautious orthodox macro-management played a crucial role. There were also some uniquely favourable characteristics, most notably the size and stability of the mineral rents.

The scale of the diamond rents

The scale of the rent stream which accrued to Botswana during the youthful stage of its mineral-led cycle, gave its economy more the character of an oil producer than that of a hard-mineral exporter. Figure 7.1 traces the growth of diamond production: output peaked in 1990 and dollar export revenues levelled off in 1989. The diamond rents comprised at least 50 per cent of export earnings according to estimates for the mid-1980s by Harvey and Lewis (1990) and to around 60 per cent in the early 1990s according to Auty (1996a). The government of Botswana adroitly negotiated with De Beers during the 1970s to capture much of the diamond rents: it quickly became the dominant shareholder in the diamond mining partnership and further boosted its retention of revenues via higher taxes. As a result, diamonds dominated the flow of government revenues from mining, whose contribution to total public revenues rose from barely 20 per cent 1976–7 to more than 50 per cent between 1985 and 1990. If the assumption that 60 per cent of diamond revenues were rents is correct for the entire period, then the rents averaged the equivalent of 14 per cent of GNP per year during 1976–82, and rose to 35.8 per cent 1983–9 before declining to average 24.7 per cent of GNP during 1990–3. These figures are similar in magnitude to those of the oil exporters, Indonesia and Trinidad and Tobago during the oil booms. But the rent stream had the added advantage of being more predictable and consistent than that experienced by the oil exporters (Gelb and Associates 1988).

Nevertheless, such a revenue stream can still be mismanaged: all too often governments cannot resist political pressure for the overrapid absorption of the mineral rents. But the Botswana electorate was dominated by pastoralists whose experience of drought and sudden loss of income, created a conservative consensus against the rapid dissipation of the mineral income. This helps to account for the readiness to

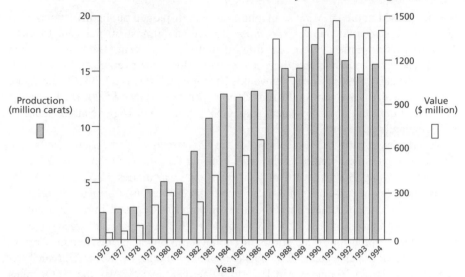

Figure 7.1 Botswana diamond production
Source: Bank of Botswana, Central Statistical Office.

save during the youthful stage of mineral-led growth and of a distaste for overambitious state intervention which has so often characterized resource-rich economies elsewhere (Lal 1995).

Successful rent deployment in the youthful stage, 1970–90

The Botswana government used special funds to accumulate sizeable financial reserves during the youthful stage of the mineral-led cycle. It established the Revenue Stabilization Fund and the Public Debt Service Fund in 1972, when the first mine was being constructed, in order to manage the projected mineral revenue flows. The financial reserves increased almost tenfold between 1984 and 1992 in nominal dollar terms to reach the equivalent of $3,000 per capita (Harvey and Jefferis 1995). By 1993, the accumulated financial *reserves* were $4.15 billion, equivalent to 125 per cent of the country's GDP (Bank of Botswana 1995).

The Botswana government prudently sterilized around two-fifths of the rents in offshore investments, mainly bonds, and by the mid-1990s the interest earned had begun to make a significant annual contribution to government revenues. It also dampened the domestic money supply, keeping inflation at an average rate of 11.5 per cent during 1975–94 (Bank of Botswana 1995; World Bank 1995).

The domestic absorption of more than three-fifths of the mineral rents underpinned an expansion of public expenditure at a rate which doubled every six years in real terms over the period 1976–93. Public *consumption* in the early 1990s was 30 per cent of GDP, almost double the early 1970s (Table 7.4). But as the flow of diamond

revenues eased in the late 1980s, an ambitious and ill-judged public investment programme boosted total public *expenditure* to average almost 50 per cent of GNP
1987–91 (World Bank 1995*a*), boosting inflation to 16 per cent (Bank of Botswana
1995). The level of public spending per capita in Botswana averaged 43 per cent of
GDP in the early 1990s (when Botswana's per capita GNP was $2,790 (Table 7.1)),
compared with 30 per cent in oil-rich Gabon (per capita GNP $5,000), 24 per cent
in resource-deficient Mauritius (per capita GNP $3,000), and 16 per cent in resource-
rich Thailand (per capita GNP $2,100).

Nevertheless, with the exception of the investments in the late 1980s, the
Botswana government deployed the rents sensibly during the youthful stage of the
mineral-led cycle. The expansion of state enterprises was modest in comparison with
many countries in sub-Saharan Africa. Public investment was principally directed
towards correcting for the country's infrastructure backlog and improving education and health provision. In other words, much of the mineral wealth was converted
from natural capital into other forms of capital, both physical and human. Current
public expenditure also focused on social spending which saw its share of such expenditure rise from 36 per cent in 1976 to 40 per cent in 1992. By the 1990s, rates
of infant mortality and literacy compared favourably with other countries at a similar level of per capita income (Jefferis 1996), despite the very low level from which
Botswana started at independence in 1966 (Table 7.1). But income inequality was
relatively high with an income ratio for the richest to the poorest quintile of 16.4
in 1986, some three times that of Indonesia (World Bank 1995).

Problems in adjusting to early maturity

Although the broad allocation of resources between domestic absorption and saving appears to have been sensible, the government appeared to be outstripping its
capacity to deploy funds effectively by the late 1980s. As noted, government efforts
to force the pace of economic growth in the late 1980s by boosting investment stoked
inflation, and investments proved disappointing. Further evidence of faltering public sector management is found in the non-financial parastatals which earned a rate
of return in 1994 that failed to beat inflation (Harvey 1993; Jefferis 1996). More
worryingly, some areas of public provision such as health and education services
displayed evidence of deteriorating quality.

The need to scale back public spending was underlined by the projection of budget deficits commencing in the mid-1990s and reaching 3.4 per cent of GDP by
2000–1 (Ministry of Finance and Planning 1994). GDP growth was expected to slow
to 4.3 per cent per annum over the 1990s compared with 10.1 per cent in the 1980s,
on a declining trend which would depress it below the rate of population increase
by the end of the decade, implying a fall in per capita income which is not consistent with sustainable development.

The slower economic growth associated with the shift to early maturity in the mineral-driven cycle, directed attention to the role of the country's large financial reserves in engineering the transition away from diamond-driven growth (Bank of Botswana 1995). A debate on this issue took place against a background in which the conservative character of the country's political economy was weakening because of the changes in social structure. The electorate, which was a relatively homogeneous rural peasantry at independence, provided a sizeable majority favouring cautious policies. But as the electorate became more urbanized, it became more heterogeneous. Moreover, many small farms became marginal during the 1980s, while urban poverty may become more intractable during a period of constrained public resources (Valentine 1993).

Further discussion of the transition to early maturity in Botswana is reserved for Chapter 9, which examines the legacy of the Dutch disease for ongoing structural change. It will suffice to note here that cautious macro-management helped Botswana successfully to transform a highly favourable stream of mineral rents into rapid economic growth and broader welfare enhancement during the youthful stage of its mineral cycle. But a successful youthful stage does not guarantee sustainable development as Chapters 8 and 9 show.[1]

The Youthful Stage: Managing an Uncertain Rent Stream in PNG

The youthful stage of the mineral cycle in PNG began at the same time as that of Botswana and, while it continued into the late 1990s, the relative size of the rents was much smaller and their flow was more erratic. Total mineral sector revenues in PNG (which include taxation on normal profits and therefore overstates the mineral rents) fluctuated between 0 per cent and 6 per cent of GNP during 1974–93 and averaged 3.3 per cent of GNP during 1974–9 (Daniel and Sims 1986) and 2.3 per cent of GNP over 1980–93 (Duncan *et al.* 1995). In addition, on three occasions (in the mid-1970s, the mid-1980s, and the late 1980s) confident forecasts of much larger mineral revenue flows proved premature (Mikesell 1975; Jackson 1984; World Bank 1988*b*).

Two world-scale copper mines were started in PNG (in the early 1970s and mid-1980s), to be followed in the 1990s by two major goldmines and a hydrocarbon project. The start-up of the first copper mine at Panguna (Bougainville) coincided with the 1973–4 copper boom and pushed the share of mining to 25 per cent of GDP, 50 per cent of exports, and 25 per cent of revenues (World Bank 1978). But the subsequent long-term copper price downswing (Figure 6.1) depressed the rents well below their projected levels and delayed the start-up of the second mine at Ok Tedi in the early 1980s. Finally, the abrupt closure of Panguna in 1989 undercut an optimistic World Bank (1988*b*) scenario which projected that a rapid expansion

---

[1] In fact, the Botswana government announced in 1996 that there would be a substantial expansion of one of the diamond mines, a move which provides some respite.

of goldmining would lift economic growth to 5.4 per cent annually from 1988 to 1995. The World Bank expected the share of mining in PNG exports to rise from 55 to 72 per cent, in GDP from 15 to 18 per cent, and in government revenues from 6 to 16 per cent.

Nevertheless, despite such forecasting disappointments, during the first sixteen years of independence (1974–90), PNG maintained a commitment to fiscal prudence and adjusted the exchange rate to changes in the terms of trade. These measures kept average inflation at 6.2 per cent and also sustained a modest rate of GDP growth in the face of a long-term deterioration in the country's export prices from 1974 to 1988. But thereafter, a commodity boom in the early 1990s was mismanaged, and cost the PNG government its reputation for fiscal prudence (Duncan *et al.* 1995).

Broadly successful macro-management, 1970–90

PNG was generously funded by Australian aid prior to its independence in 1974. The aid helped to bridge chronic trade (Table 7.3) and fiscal deficits, and was on a scale analogous to that of a sizeable rent stream (initially equivalent to almost one-fifth of GDP). Upon gaining independence, PNG needed to substitute an alternative revenue source, with mining offering the most obvious solution. Foreign aid declined in relative importance, falling from two-fifths of government revenues in 1975 to one-tenth in 1994 (Thac and Lim 1984; Duncan *et al.* 1995). But public expenditure increased its share of GDP, rising over the period 1971–5 from an initially high 33 per cent to almost 38 per cent, a level more than twice that of comparator countries (Table 7.4).

However, an MRSF was prudently established by statutes in 1974 and 1975 in order to smooth the absorption of the projected mineral revenues into the economy. Under the original agreements, the maximum that could be drawn down from the fund in any one year was the amount which would be sustainable, given the reserves within the fund, over each of the ensuing five years. However, an amendment in 1986 weakened the responsibility of the advisory board for assuring the drawdown could be sustained and this facilitated a rapid withdrawal of funds. As a result, the MRSF became less effective: data for 1980–94 suggest that the smoothing effect was limited. The coefficient of variation for outflows was 76 per cent whereas that for inflows was 83 per cent, providing net smoothing of barely 8 per cent (Duncan *et al.* 1995).

The MRSF required that foreign exchange revenues be deposited with the Central Bank which then credited the PNG government with the equivalent value in domestic currency. As long as the government did not radically expand its expenditure the mineral revenues were automatically stabilized and sterilized. If the funds were drawn down to purchase foreign items, the inflows remained sterilized even though the economy was not stabilized. But if the revenues were spent immediately by the government on domestic purchases, then neither stabilization nor sterilization was achieved.

Table 7.4 Composition of absorption, eight mineral economies, 1970–93

	Botswana	Chile	Indonesia	Jamaica	Namibia	PNG	Peru	Trinidad and Tobago
1970–3								
Private consumption	65.4	72.1	72.4	63.2		58.3	70.5	57.2
Public consumption	16.6	14.1	8.5	13.5		29.6	12.7	14.8
Investment	48.1	15.4	19.2	30.6		31.9	17.2	29.3
Total	130.1	101.6	100.1	107.3		119.8	100.4	101.3
1974–9								
Private consumption	61.6	66.4	62.7	65.6		51.2	70.3	47.3
Public consumption	19.3	14.8	9.3	19.6		27.9	11.7	12.7
Investment	38.9	19.5	23.5	19.1		20.6	21.9	26.6
Total	119.8	100.7	9.5	104.3		99.7	103.9	86.6
1980–5								
Private consumption	49.8	71.0	58.1	66.9	58.8	64.5	61.9	55.6
Public consumption	24.3	13.8	10.8	19.2	26.1	24.7	10.4	18.9
Investment	34.8	17.2	27.4	21.3	22.1	26.8	26.6	26.4
Total	108.9	102.0	96.3	107.4	107.0	116.0	98.9	100.9
1986–9								
Private consumption	31.4	62.4	60.6	64.1	54.9	63.3	70.8	59.5
Public consumption	24.4	11.6	9.7	15.0	29.8	22.7	8.5	20.4
Investment	23.0	23.4	31.6	23.8	15.6	22.7	21.6	17.7
Total	75.8	97.4	101.9	107.9	100.3	107.7	100.9	97.6
1990–3								
Private consumption	30.6[a]	62.2	59.4	61.6	56.4	56.9	78.9	63.3
Public consumption	30.0[b]	9.6	9.4	12.3	33.3	22.6	6.4	12.4
Investment	28.2	26.6	29.1	29.6	12.8	23.9	16.4	13.5
Total	88.8	98.4	97.9	103.5	102.5	103.4	101.7	89.2

[a] 1990–2.
[b] CSO.

Sources: World Bank tables (1995a).

The MRSF accumulated only modest reserves during the late 1970s due to low copper prices. Consequently, it could do little to mitigate the adverse effects of the second oil shock which triggered a serious balance of payments problem: the current account deficit ballooned to 20 per cent of GDP in 1982. The budget deficit also increased from 1.3 per cent of GDP to 6.2 per cent between 1977 and 1982. The PNG government responded by tightening fiscal policy and engineering a real depreciation of the exchange rate (Daniel 1985: 52). It financed the twin deficits by foreign commercial and concessional borrowing (Thac and Lim 1984). This caused the public debt/GDP ratio to almost triple between 1979 and 1983 and the external debt/GNP ratio continued to rise thereafter (Table 7.3). The debt service ratio reached an onerous 40 per cent of exports.

The start-up of the country's second large copper mine at Ok Tedi was expected to relieve this difficult situation. However, the start-up of the mine was postponed in the face of continued low copper prices, so the PNG government prudently halved the planned annual withdrawals from the MRSF for 1985–8 (FEER 1985). As a result, by 1988 the budget deficit was down to 0.5 per cent of GDP, the current account deficit fell below 5 per cent of GDP and the debt service ratio fell below one-fifth of export earnings (Table 7.3).

The MRSF did provide a vital breathing space in the late-1980s when the closure of Panguna abruptly terminated the improving economic outlook. The PNG government had planned to draw about $85 million (or 7 per cent of its revenue needs) from the MRSF, equivalent to just over half the revenue from Panguna in the year before it closed. The MRSF ended 1989 with $225 million because of the lagged inflow of those revenues. It could not sustain a similar level of drawdown until 1992, when taxes from the expanding Ok Tedi mine and the new goldmines were expected to ease the crisis. In 1990 PNG devalued its currency by 10 per cent, cut government spending by 8 per cent, restrained wage and credit rises, and requested IMF and World Bank assistance.

Mismanaged early 1990s' commodity boom

The MRSF, which had been weakened in 1986, failed to provide an adequate buffer between revenues and pressure for public spending during the commodity windfall of the early 1990s. Instead of sterilizing a fraction of the rents, the PNG government used them as collateral to increase the country's foreign borrowing. In both 1993 and 1994 the upsurge of commodity revenues was deployed immediately to finance a large expansion in public expenditure so that neither the stabilization function nor the sterilization goal of the MRSF was achieved. The government rashly raised public consumption, reduced taxation, and provided selected subsidies to non-mining activity. The overrapid expansion drove the economy at 10 per cent during 1991–4, but the fiscal gap widened to an unsustainable 5.4 per cent of GDP.

A more sustainable strategy would have earmarked a larger fraction of the resource rents for the expansion of human capital and produced capital (Duncan *et al.* 1995). Such a strategy would also recognize, however, that periods of revenue decline might call for some transfers in order to maintain ongoing education and infrastructure maintenance programmes. If the political will to undertake such a policy was absent, then an alternative would have been to disperse more of the windfalls to the private sector which reacted more wisely than government to the deteriorating domestic economic situation by increasing both its savings and its foreign holdings.

Duncan *et al.* (1995) consider several alternative sterilization mechanisms for PNG which include scrapping the MRSF in favour of the use of market instruments to hedge commodity price fluctuations, and the automatic transfer of rents to accumulate in offshore funds, with only the income from such funds available to be drawn down by the government. They conclude, however, that a third option, reform of the existing MRSF would be best, provided its drawdowns were biased towards caution. Duncan *et al.* (1995) propose that the revenues in a reformed MRSF should be held as foreign exchange assets and that *past* spending patterns should be used as a guide to the scale of the drawdown. This would require the restoration of the tighter drawdown rules of the type which had operated until 1986. They also recommend that if the MRSF resources increase, then a maximum rise of one-fifth in the drawdown should be allowed, whereas a decline in inflows would demand a reduction in the drawdown by a similar magnitude.

The problems which PNG encountered during the youthful stage of its mineral-driven cycle (which intensified in the 1990s) are rooted in overoptimism about mineral windfalls, which were invariably postponed, and led to neglect of the non-mining tradeables (discussed in Chapter 9). Nevertheless, PNG sustained a reputation for macro-prudence through the first fifteen years of independence despite a rent stream which, compared with Botswana, was smaller and more volatile; and also, despite a less favourable political economy (see Chapter 12). A critical element in the eventual policy failure was an easing of the MRSF drawdown rules in 1986 so that domestic absorption was excessive during the early 1990s commodity boom (*Financial Times* 1997).

Successful Adjustment to Maturity in a Distorted Economy: Chile

By the late 1980s, Chile had rekindled rapid economic growth and emerged as a model of 'best practice' for Latin American economies. It evoked favourable comparisons with the successful Asian countries on the Pacific Rim. But this accolade took more than a decade of reform during which the distortions which had accumulated over several decades of overly interventionist policies were removed. Prior to 1973, management of the country's mature mineral economy had mistakenly focused upon increasing domestic control of the mining sector through state ownership to enhance domestic revenue retention and deploying protectionism to safeguard the non-mining tradeables from the Dutch disease effects. The average tariff exceeded 100 per cent and both imports and exports faced extensive non-tariff barriers (Dornbusch and Edwards 1994). The Chilean economy exhibited the symptoms of a repressed economy: chronic inflation, a relatively low rate of economic growth, and frequent economic crises. There was also discontent over income inequality which led the 1970–3 Allende government to nationalize the mines, banks, and industry, and to undertake wholesale land reform while also sanctioning a sharp increase in real wages.

The populist boom which the Allende government triggered destabilized the Chilean economy (Sachs 1989) and led directly to the government's overthrow by the Chilean military. The new military government then reformed the economy along orthodox lines, persisting despite a severe setback in 1982. It insulated economic technocrats from political pressures and used first repression, and then the benefits from economic recovery, to gain grudging legitimacy. As a result, Chile provides an example of policy consistency after 1975, which is rare in most developing countries. These conditions increased the scope for bold (and, at times, overly dogmatic) orthodox policies.

Dogmatic Orthodoxy, 1974–82

The stabilization programme which Chile launched in 1974 might have been too ambitious for a non-authoritarian government. Few democratic regimes, facing re-election within five years, could have sustained such tight fiscal policies and swift economic restructuring as occurred in Chile. The poorest fifth of the population experienced a significant decline in income, health, nutrition, housing, and education. The decline reflected both labour market reforms, which weakened the trade unions, and wage indexation which failed to rise in line with the rapid rate of price increases for low-income goods. The country's income distribution worsened: the income ratio of the richest to the poorest quintile deteriorated from 12 in the late 1960s to 18 in the early 1990s (when, however, it was still below Colombia (21) and Peru (32) (World Bank 1995a)).

The military government faced an economy in deep recession in 1974 that was disrupted by civil disorder with inflation exceeding 100 per cent. By trial and error, it established the case for the phased reform of a distorted economy (rather than the 'big bang' reform favoured by the IMF), in which capital market liberalization followed trade liberalization. A stabilization programme shrank public spending from 45 per cent of GDP to 24 per ent during 1973–8 and cut the fiscal deficit from 25 per cent of GDP to 0.8 per cent over the same period (Ministry of Finance 1989). The spending curbs included a freeze on public sector wages, and the privatization of over 400 of the smaller state enterprises 1973–9 (Harvey 1980). Tax reforms complemented the expenditure cuts and included a 10 per cent tariff on most imports, a 20 per cent value-added tax, and a standard 49 per cent corporate tax.

Meanwhile, before inflation had been curbed, liberalization of trade commenced with the average tariff (which had exceeded 100 per cent in 1973) tapered off to 10 per cent by 1979. Tariff cuts were underpinned by a real depreciation of the exchange rate of two-thirds, followed by crawling peg (incremental) devaluations to compensate for domestic inflation in excess of global levels. Non-traditional exports and manufactures showed the fastest response to these measures as domestic recession squeezed home demand and pushed up the share of the Chilean global export market by one-third in 1974–6. Some import substitution also occurred despite the rapid trade liberalization (Balassa 1985). In response, the economy contracted by 13 per cent in 1975 (as the deflationary impact of stabilization was reinforced by slumping copper prices) but then grew at over 8 per cent annually from 1976 to 1979.

The recovery was not sustained, however, because wage indexation caused inflation to remain stubbornly high and the simultaneous pursuit of stabilization, trade liberalization, and capital market reform created policy conflict. An exchange rate appreciation was used to suppress the inflationary tendencies that were expected to accompany higher copper prices. It was achieved by periodic revaluations and depreciations (intended to break inflationary expectations) in which the devaluations tended to lag the revaluations (Moran 1987). The higher exchange rate triggered a substantial but volatile foreign capital inflow which, along with public saving, helped to compensate for a low rate of domestic private saving which was barely 3 per cent of GDP. Worse, imports surged as the wealthy used the rise in their asset values to purchase foreign goods whose real price had halved. Meanwhile, however, the higher exchange rate intensified external competition for the tradeables sectors. Exports flagged and the trade gap widened. This first checked the inflow of foreign funds and then reversed it, leading to the near-collapse of the domestic financial system.

Domestic interest rates rose sharply in response to capital flight, increasing the cost pressures on domestic firms that were already struggling to compete with liberalized imports. GDP fell by 14 per cent in 1982 and foreign debt reached 78 per cent of GDP and debt service approached two-thirds of export earnings (Table 7.3), causing the Chilean government to seek help from the IMF (World Bank 1987). Enders and Mattione (1984) estimate the 1979–82 trade and interest rate changes inflicted a negative shock equivalent to 4.6 per cent of GDP, with the interest rate hike being the more important. The size of the shock intensified in 1982 due to the simultaneous fall in copper prices and rise in interest rates. Corbo and de Melo (1987) estimate its impact at 12.2 per cent of GNP in 1982–3, with higher interest rates responsible for almost two-thirds.

Corbo and de Melo (1987) conclude that it was a mistake to liberalize trade before stabilization was complete and that countries with inflation in excess of 25 per cent should not proceed with liberalization because the economic contraction caused by stabilization, when combined with liberalization, hampers adjustment of hitherto protected sectors. The 1979–82 shock also underscored the need to boost domestic saving in order to reduce reliance on volatile external capital flows.

Pragmatic orthodoxy after 1982

The military government pursued a less doctrinaire policy after 1982 by stressing stabilization. It temporarily reversed the liberalization measures, and boosted the average tariff to 35 per cent during 1982–4. The IMF agreement brought an exchange rate devaluation, by two-thirds of its 1982 value, and sharp public expenditure cuts. Important institutional changes were belatedly made in order to mute the disruptive impact of mineral price shifts. The changes included greater autonomy for the Central Bank, a MRSF, and the adoption of a crawling band exchange rate (Williamson 1996). But, as with PNG, the MRSF took time to accumulate reserves. The 1983–4 IMF agreement assumed a copper price of 75c/lb, whereas the outturn was only 61c. The severity of the copper price downturn meant that, in the absence of MRSF reserves, foreign debt continued to grow until 1985 when it reached 140 per cent of GDP and debt service absorbed 48 per cent of export earnings. Chile had the highest per capita debt in Latin America and a government with less autonomy might well have abandoned the economic reforms.

An unexpected upswing in copper prices towards the end of 1987 yielded a large fiscal windfall which had the potential for economic destabilization. It was successfully managed by a combination of the MRSF, restrictions on short-term capital flows (which required a one-year residency for such funds), and use of a crawling band exchange rate. In contrast to the boomlet of 1980–2, the real exchange rate appreciated only modestly during the 1988–90 copper boom. The MRSF worked by setting a reference price for copper each year and separating the price differential into three steps: the first one required no deposit into the MRSF, the second required 50 per cent of the windfall, and the third called for 100 per cent. The funds that were deposited averaged 3.8 per cent of GDP per annum during 1988–9 and 1.2 per cent during 1990–2 (Marfan and Bosworth 1994).

With macroeconomic stabilization secure, attention returned to trade liberalization which benefited from the increased economic flexibility which flowed from the micro-reforms of the 1970s (labour market, price liberalization, and financial markets (Corbo and Fischer 1994)). In addition, import tariffs were cut to 15 per cent in 1988 and to a uniform 11 per cent by the early 1990s. This further cheapened imported inputs while exporters benefited from a rebate on value-added tax and special credit facilities (Stallings 1990). Unemployment declined from 25 per cent in 1982 to less than 10 per cent by 1987 and real incomes rose strongly as GDP expanded at 7.2 per cent per annum from 1984 to 1993 (World Bank 1995a). The rate of domestic saving recovered strongly from its low levels of the early 1980s to an average of 24 per cent over the period 1987–95 on a rising trend (Morande 1996). This owed much to the tightening of the fiscal stance (Holzmann 1996) and, along with a twelve-month deposit requirement on foreign capital, reduced the vulnerability of the economy to volatile short-term foreign capital flows. Stiglitz and Uy (1996) report from a broader study that income growth is a better predictor of savings growth than the reverse causal connection, underlining the importance for sustained growth of continuity in prudent macro-policy.

Of the eight countries in our sample, Chile is the clearest case of a country that has met the requirements for sustainable development. All sectors participated in the strong improvement of the Chilean economy through the late 1980s. The sustained rapid economic growth established a new political consensus in Chile that recognized the merits of the post-1982 orthodox policy with its emphasis on phased reforms, competitive growth, and the targeting of public subsidies on the neediest. The pre-1982 doctrinaire orthodoxy showed insufficient concern for the competitiveness of the non-mining tradeables sector and its vulnerability to Dutch disease effects. Such lost economic activity to Dutch disease effects is less easily compensated than is assumed by doctrinaire orthodoxy (Wheeler 1984; Krugman 1987; Faini and de Melo 1990). The policy error meant that Chilean adjustment took at least five years longer than it need have done. Inflation in the late-1970s would have been better controlled by monetary policy and, perhaps, brief application of an incomes policy (Corbo and Fischer 1994), rather than an exchange rate appreciation, especially under conditions where wage indexation maintains inflationary momentum.[2]

Conclusions

A common feature of the four more successful mineral economies is a commitment to orthodox macroeconomic policies, including prompt responses to changing external conditions. Such a policy stresses caution and helps to maintain high (and effective) investment beyond the youthful stage of the cycle. It is reinforced by a MRSF which buffers the adjustment to changes in foreign exchange flows, and in government revenues, and maintains the competitiveness of the non-mining tradeables. Although Varangis *et al.* (1995) may be correct to argue on theoretical grounds that an MRSF may yield a suboptimal employment of resources, the empirical evidence suggests that such a view underestimates the practical difficulty of forecasting revenue flows, of judging where exactly a country is within its mineral cycle, and of resisting political pressure for overrapid absorption during mineral booms. All four successful countries studied here operated MRSFs and the experience of PNG after 1988 illustrates the damage which the relaxation of MRSF discipline can cause.

A second important conclusion is that a bias in the mineral rent absorption policy towards caution is desirable because the economic damage arising from mistakenly assuming a favourable price shift is permanent when it is temporary, is greater than the damage arising if a permanent price shift is erroneously assumed to be temporary (Hill 1991). The lost output which occurs when the revenue expansion is overestimated, as in PNG in the 1990s, results from the dislocation caused by the need to withdraw resources in order to restore economic balance. This is consistent with

---

[2] But Marfan and Bosworth (1994) query the completeness of Chilean reform. They argue that the rapid economic growth of 1984–93 was due in large measure to recovery from the recession. This implies that sustained rapid growth requires higher domestic savings, higher investment and also higher total productivity growth (TFP) than the 1% annual rate achieved 1974–92 (a rate which, however, compares with 0.2% in the 1960s and 2.4% 1989–93 (Meller *et al.* 1996)). If higher TFP growth rate is not maintained, the lower-income groups, whose labour is in abundant supply, will find it difficult to maintain, let alone increase, their share of national income (Marcel and Solimano 1994). In the mid-1990s, Chile had still to establish productivity-driven growth. However, successful stabilization and liberalization, and the espousal of export-oriented growth, had provided a basis upon which to boost productivity and sustain economic expansion.

the findings of Gelb and Associates (1988) who report an important asymmetry in a mismanaged mineral boom whereby the gains during the high-rent phase do not compensate for the losses incurred in adjusting to the decline in rents.

A third conclusion is that local circumstances call for some moderation of theoretical policy advice. For example, the youthful stage of the mineral cycle was especially well managed by Botswana and Indonesia, less so by PNG. But Botswana was helped by three favourable factors, namely, the scale of the rents, the stability of the rent flows, and a political consensus within a conservative pastoral community that favoured cautious economic policy. Indonesia is more typical of mineral economies in that it experienced more erratic external conditions when the oil booms restored the youthful stage of the mineral-led cycle. Yet the lessons from Indonesian experience must be qualified also, and for three reasons. First, the Indonesian economy was less distorted than many mineral economies: on the eve of the 1973 oil shock Dutch disease effects were minimal and the economy was already quite diversified. Second, diversification into manufacturing was facilitated by a potentially large domestic market and significant non-mineral resources. Third, the country's relatively low level of per capita income also helped in diversification by easing the movement of the economy to the successful labour-intensive East Asian development path.

Consequently, Chile would seem to offer more practical lessons, especially for those which, like the four less successful mineral exporters in this study had attained mid-income levels with economies distorted by excessive intervention. Chilean experience reinforces the important role of cautiously orthodox macroeconomic management, but it also warns against a doctrinaire orthodoxy. Chile shows that the MRSF retains its usefulness during the mature stage, and may be reinforced by a crawling band exchange rate regime. Finally, Chile suggests that a distorted economy calls for the sequencing of reform in which stabilization precedes trade liberalization, followed by capital market liberalization. Nevertheless, macroeconomic reform may prove difficult for non-autonomous governments and require a different sequencing. In addition, diversification may be harder for small mineral economies which are deficient in both non-mineral resources and in their domestic markets for industrial goods, like Jamaica, Namibia, and Trinidad and Tobago. These countries, together with Peru, are the focus of Chapter 8.

8 Mismanaged Mature Stage of the Mineral-Led Cycle

This chapter focuses on the four less successful mineral economies in the sample (Peru, Trinidad and Tobago, Jamaica, and Namibia) which were all mature mid-income mineral economies that experienced difficulty in sustaining economic growth, once the youthful stage of the mineral-driven cycle had passed. Their rates of investment collapsed below 20 per cent of GDP with the exception of Jamaica where, however, the efficiency of investment was very low (Table 6.4). In all four countries excessive government intervention had severely distorted the economy, a condition associated with political pressure in resource-rich mid-income countries to force the rate of growth (Lal 1995). A further common feature was a reluctance to embrace orthodox economic reforms, which Mahon (1992) attributes to the inability of even autonomous governments to remain in power long enough to reap the rewards of such policies. Consequently, efforts to remove the economic distortions were unusually protracted, with sizeable losses in output and welfare.

After the collapse of its structuralist experiments in 1989 a new Peruvian government opted not for sequenced reform like that of Chile, but for a 'big bang'. The apparent success of that strategy raises an important question for the three smallest countries (Jamaica, Trinidad and Tobago, and Namibia) as to whether their tardy adjustment reflects policy error, or whether it arises out of the more limited options for economic diversification which result from the smaller countries' narrower non-mining resource bases and small domestic markets for manufactured goods. The answer is important not only for explanations of the differing performances of the resource-rich countries and therefore for the policy implications, but also for the resource curse thesis which was discussed in Chapter 2.

From Erratic Policy Shifts to Big-Bang Reform in Peru

In contrast to the broad consistency of policy of the autonomous post-Allende government of Chile, successive governments in the factional Peruvian State tacked between strongly structuralist and dogmatically orthodox policies. From the structuralist side of the policy controversy, Thorp (1987) has argued that by the early 1960s a more active role for the State was justified due to the fact that the scope for primary product export-led growth and also first-stage import substitution was becoming exhausted. Certainly, state intervention was stepped up following a military coup in 1968 which espoused redistributive policies in the face of high income inequality and associated social tension. Thorp (1991) continued to support

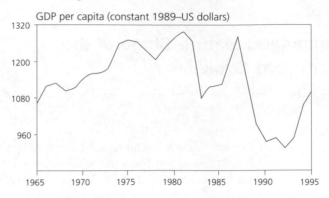

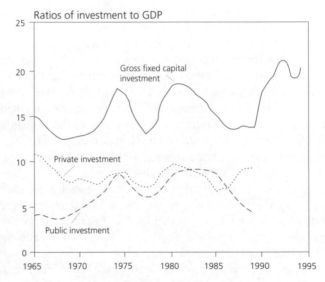

Figure 8.1 Trends in macroeconomic performance, Peru, 1960–95

Sources: Central Bank of Peru and Paredes and Sachs (1991).

such intervention in the early 1990s, arguing that the collapse of the structuralist policy experiment in the late 1980s was due to poor implementation rather than to basic flaws.

From an orthodox perspective, and consistent with Lal's theory of growth collapses in resource-rich countries, Webb (1991) sees the policy of the 1968–75 military government as a doomed effort to maintain a predatory State that had thrived by extracting rents from the populace at large, with insufficient regard for either the economic or the social consequences. Lago (1991) concurs and traces the roots of Peru's post-1975 economic collapse (Figure 8.1) directly to the interventionist policies of the military government. He argues that the adverse effects of these policies were initially masked by favourable external conditions in 1970–4 (Table 6.8).

Lago concludes that the actions of the military government intensified the inward orientation of the economy, curbed foreign investment, and set the scene for a long recession.

A severe economic crisis occurred in 1975 and economic stabilization was not achieved until the mid-1990s owing to the absence of either a national policy consensus of an autonomous government like that in Chile capable of sustaining initially unpopular policies. Peruvian macroeconomic policy was erratic. It swung towards orthodoxy after 1975 and, as in Chile, exhibited a strongly doctrinaire phase in 1978–80. This triggered a similar conflict of policy objectives to that which beset Chile at that time (see Chapter 7), but whereas in Chile the policy failure ushered in a more pragmatic orthodoxy, in Peru it triggered a decade-long period of intensifying government intervention. That policy in turn collapsed spectacularly during the 1985–9 APRA government and pushed per capita incomes below their levels of the early 1960s. The incoming Fujimori government turned to the IMF, but despite the lessons of Chile concerning the merits of incremental reform, it pursued orthodox policy in the form of a 'big bang'. Scepticism over the new policy persisted on the part of not only structuralists like Thorp (1991), but also orthodox economists like Sheahan (1994).

Policy error and rejection of orthodoxy

Faced with growing fiscal and current account deficits in 1975, the military government reduced its role in the economy and in 1978 signed an IMF agreement which required two fundamental policy corrections: a real depreciation of the exchange rate and a combination of public expenditure cuts and revenue-enhancing public sector price rises and large tax increases. The public expenditure on social services, infrastructure, and directly productive activities which had been favoured during 1969–75 were reduced (Thorp 1987). By early 1979, both the fiscal deficit and the current account deficit had closed. Some success was quickly achieved: exports almost doubled from their 1977 level to reach two-fifths of GDP, with the share of non-traditional products like manufacturing, rising sharply to one-fifth of exports.

But, inflation remained high and, as in the case of Chile, the Peruvian government seized upon a projected improvement in mineral export prices to engineer a real appreciation of the exchange rate in an attempt to curb inflation. Yet Schydlowsky (1986) argues that such a measure was unnecessary because the structure of the Peruvian mining sector would automatically mute the impact of a mineral boom. He points out that the bulk of any mineral windfall is sterilized because barely one-fifth accrues to small miners, the principal group with a high propensity to spend immediately on domestic goods. An additional one-quarter of a mineral windfall accrues to the dominant copper-mining MNC, which uses most of it to service its capital, and the rest goes to the government in the form of taxes. Overall, around two-thirds of a mineral windfall accrues to the Peruvian Treasury. However, Schydlowsky (1986) neglects the fact that in the absence of an MRSF, Peru lacked a formal sterilization mechanism.

The 1978 IMF stabilization programme was unpopular and this undermined the military government. An election in 1980 restored civilian rule and the orthodox policy was relaxed before stabilization was complete. The new government launched an ambitious public sector investment programme at a time when revenue from both internal and external sources was becoming more constrained. Public spending rose to almost 50 per cent of GDP during 1980–2, more than double that of a decade earlier (Paredes 1990a), and defence spending alone absorbed 6 per cent of GDP as growing internal violence brought military opposition to cuts (Scott 1990). The fiscal deficit ballooned to an unsustainable 8 per cent of GDP in 1982 (Paredes 1990a).

As in Chile, stabilization was not achieved: domestic inflation averaged 60–70 per cent during 1980–2 while the real exchange rate appreciated by 50 per cent. In these circumstances, the continuation of trade liberalization intensified the competitive pressure on the non-mining tradeables sector, reversing the favourable trends in exports of the late 1970s. Import tariff protection declined from an average of more than 100 per cent to barely 40 per cent and as the rate of effective protection in manufacturing fell, exports stagnated and imports surged. The decline in export revenues and foreign exchange constrained import capacity, with particularly adverse effects on Peru's slow-maturing, import-dependent manufacturing sector. Unemployment rose sharply as a consequence and real wages declined to three-fifths of their 1973 level (Scott 1990).

Such trends further weakened the resolve of the government to persist with an orthodox policy. But its room for manoeuvre was constrained by its need for IMF assistance. The government failed to meet IMF targets for public sector spending and excessive public sector deficits persisted. The real exchange rate was further devalued by 25 per cent and the trade liberalization measures were repealed as manufacturers successfully lobbied for increased protection. But in contrast to Chile, the repeal in tariff reduction was not temporary: import quotas were re-established in 1984 and a process commenced which left the Peruvian economy even more protectionist at the close of the 1980s than it had been when economic reform had begun fifteen years earlier (Paredes 1990b).

Although by 1985 the exchange rate was competitive so that the current account was in balance and GDP growth had recovered to 3.6 per cent, nevertheless, per capita incomes were below 1972 levels, half of all manufacturing capacity was idle, more than half the workforce was underemployed, and economic stabilization was still incomplete as inflation approached 200 per cent (*Economist* 1987). High inflation demanded public spending cuts and further austerity which, after a decade of orthodox prescriptions, the Peruvian electorate rejected in 1985 in favour of the structuralist policies of the centre-left APRA party.

The APRA government chose a heterodox economic policy. It opted to force the pace of growth by boosting domestic demand in the expectation that higher consumption would use up spare capacity and ease cost-push pressures so that the economy would grow out of inflation. Inflation was initially checked through price and wage controls as idle capacity was utilized. It was expected that the elimination of the inflation tax would transfer resources from the public to the private sector. Meanwhile, the resources with which to finance this expansionary policy were secured by ignoring the IMF and pegging foreign debt service to 10 per cent of export earnings. Politically, such a growth-based policy has strong appeal. Low-income groups expect to benefit because they suffer from unemployment under orthodox reforms. They also are least able to defend their incomes against inflation. The populist APRA government expressly targeted assistance to the peasant farmers on the Sierra and to the large urban informal sector (Lago 1991). Its strategy also carried a nationalist appeal because it rejected external demands for foreign debt service, an especially important consideration during a period of deteriorating external trading conditions (Scott 1990).

The 1986–9 APRA policy tracks very well the populist boom modelled by Sachs (1989). During the first two years of the populist cycle, economic growth proceeds rapidly, real wages rise sharply, and inflation slows. But the ratio of export volume to GDP shrinks, international reserves decline, and the real exchange rate appreciates. Finally, the exchange rate collapses while prices accelerate and real wages and growth fall sharply. In the case of Peru, the APRA government delivered a massive stimulus to the economy in 1986–7 by boosting both real wages and public spending. A price freeze was accompanied by cuts in indirect taxes and interest rates while subsidies were increased for agriculture and more credit was directed to the poor. The exchange rate was devalued and then repegged with a complex multiple rate system. Imports that competed with domestic producers were barred. These initial measures were intended to last for twelve months, the time it would take to activate spare productive capacity. Thereafter, growth would be export-led and investment-driven, using the funds made available by limiting foreign debt service.

The virtuous cycle of the APRA scenario did not materialize. Instead, the Peruvian boom followed a four-year sequence (Figure 8.1) common to populist cycles like that of Chile during 1971–3 and modelled by Sachs (1989). GDP grew by 17 per cent through 1986–7, but fell by 20 per cent in 1988–9, while inflation accelerated to four digits and the public sector deficit reached 13 per cent of GDP. The anti-export bias of the policy caused non-mining tradeables to became even less competitive while the mining sector was weakened so that private mining firms skimped on investment, including the search for new reserves and pollution-abating technology (see Chapter 11), while government attempts to offset the collapse in revenues down to only 5 per cent of GDP decapitalized the state-owned enterprises. Sadly, it was the poor, on whose behalf the populist policy was adopted, who bore the brunt of the economic collapse as real wages fell, social expenditure dried up, and nutrition and health standards deteriorated.

The APRA populist boom merely intensified the distortions in the economy and caused economic growth to collapse. Paredes and Sachs (1991) recommended that the new Fujimori government, elected in 1990, should pursue a phased reform programme of stabilization, trade liberalization, and capital reform. They argued, however, that such a policy could proceed quite rapidly because the imploded Peruvian economy had little inflationary potential within it in 1990. Instead, the Fujimori government opted for a 'big bang' reform (Sheahan 1994) on the grounds that this was required to demonstrate the credibility of the commitment of the government and avoid the risk of reform fatigue which had undermined the reform efforts through 1975–85. It was expected that public opinion would support the initial sacrifices after two decades of economic mismanagement.

The Fujimori government therefore boosted taxation and reined in public spending. The exchange rate was unified and allowed to float, while non-tariff barriers were removed and the average tariff was cut from 66 per cent in 1990 to 16 per cent by 1994. Finally, price controls were lifted and the capital market was also liberalized. Within five years, Peru achieved a primary fiscal surplus and inflation dropped to 10 per cent. The domestic savings rate rose by almost one-half from 1992, to 17.5 per cent of GDP and the rate of investment recovered from 16 per cent of GDP in 1990 to 25 per cent in 1995. The domestic saving rate was approaching the 22 per cent level, which Paredes and Sachs (1991) estimate is needed in order to sustain sufficient investment to lift GDP growth above 5.5 per cent, and remove the risk that capital flight would abort growth, as in Chile in 1982. This would pull the fraction of the workforce in full employment up from an estimated low point of 25 per cent in 1990 to a more tolerable 75 per cent. In fact, GDP growth rebounded to average 5.3 per cent during 1991–5, after faltering in 1990–2 (*Financial Times* 1996*a*). This initially satisfactory outcome from the big bang reform suggests that the more cautious Chilean approach was not required.

The big bang approach to reform like that adopted by the Fujimori government remains controversial and carries risks (Sheahan 1994). The tight fiscal policy and return of flight capital cause the floating real exchange rate to appreciate and discourage investment in export-competing activity. As Brewster (1994) wryly observes, the policy creates the Dutch disease symptoms whose legacy it is meant to cure. Poverty is intensified as the strong real exchange rate reduces export (and employment) potential and as falling import tariffs cause government revenues to fall. In the case of Peru, half the population remained in poverty in 1995 and one-sixth of those, mainly Andean peasant farmers, remained in absolute poverty. Meanwhile, the debt service ratio was expected to absorb one-fifth of export earnings in 1996, even after significant debt rescheduling.

The Peruvian central bank defends the big bang reform, however, by pointing out that in 1995 only 2 per cent of the current account deficit was financed by short-term funds, the remainder being bridged by privatization proceeds (2 per cent of GDP), the refinancing of interest payments (2 per cent), and coca proceeds (some 1 per cent of GDP). Meanwhile, the re-election of Fujimori in 1995 (albeit not without some controversial manipulation of the incumbent's political opponents) boosted confidence in the continuity of economic the reform. The central bank expected that a period of economic uncertainty from 1997 to 2000 would in fact be bridged, and that thereafter the gestation of long-term investments in mining, tourism, and irrigated agriculture would sustain economic growth while manufacturing would languish. If this comes to pass, Peru will be on the road to sustainable development and, like the Chilean recovery, the required diversification of the economy will be largely resource-based. This is an experience which may not be feasible for *small* mature mid-income mineral economies.

Misjudged Mineral Rent and Protracted Reform: Jamaica

Through the 1980s, the three small mineral economies of Jamaica, Trinidad and Tobago, and Namibia had difficulty in adjusting to the loss of dynamism in the mature stage of their mineral cycle (Table 6.4). There may be structural reasons for this arising out of their relatively narrow non-mineral resource endowments and the fact that they found manufacturing difficult to expand because of their small domestic markets and labour forces which, owing to their mid-income level, was expensive relative to its productivity. However, policy factors may also have been at work because all three small countries, like Peru in the 1980s, postponed economic reform.

Jamaican experience casts doubt on the merits of a strategy of cautious reform. Following a disastrous populist boom in 1973–6 which compounded distortions in the economy, stabilization proved elusive: trade liberalization was not pursued, however, until the mid-1980s, while efforts to liberalize the capital account were delayed to the early 1990s, when they reignited inflation. An initial reluctance to embrace reforms was partly die to overoptimistic hopes about a recovery in bauxite demand. Yet although reform speeded up after 1983, per capita GNP still stagnated and by 1993, real per capita GNP was 25 per cent below its level before the populist boom twenty years earlier (World Bank 1995*a*).

Abrupt loss of competitiveness

The post-1973 performance of the Jamaican economy is in sharp contrast to the previous decade. Jamaican bauxite production was still booming through the early 1970s, but output abruptly peaked at 15.3 million tonnes in 1974 and then declined to 6.2 million tonnes in 1985 before partially recovering. The reduced bauxite output abruptly propelled Jamaica into the mature stage of its mineral-driven cycle and was caused by three factors. First, the 1973 oil shock rendered the southern US aluminium smelters which Jamaica mainly served less competitive. Second, the more dynamic markets of Western Europe and the Far East were more effectively served by Australia and Guinea, and by new vertically integrated producers in Latin America and the Middle East. Finally, and most significantly, the Jamaican government unilaterally imposed a levy on its bauxite exports in 1974 which overestimated the mineral rent by at least one-third, causing the mining companies to source their aluminium smelters from elsewhere (Auty 1993).

The aluminium firms reacted to the imposition of the Jamaican levy by relegating their Jamaican mines and alumina refineries to the role of swing producers so that, during a prolonged period of excess global refining capacity, the four Jamaican refineries bore a disproportionately high share of production cutbacks. It was only towards the close of the 1980s, as excess global capacity was finally removed and Jamaica replaced the levy with a profit-sensitive tax system, that production began to recover, albeit to levels which remained below the 1974 peak. But by then, the Jamaican share of global bauxite output was 7 per cent compared to 20 per cent in the early 1970s.

The bauxite levy was to accumulate in a Capital Development Fund (CDF), which was sensibly intended to increase public ownership of the alumina refineries and promote economic diversification. The initial value of the Jamaican bauxite levy was 6 per cent of GDP and 22 per cent of public revenue in 1974–6. But the CDF was not tightly regulated and it failed to perform either of its intended functions: diversifying the economy or sterilizing and stabilizing mineral revenue flows. Most of the Jamaican mineral revenues were therefore quickly diverted into recurrent expenditure due to the deterioration of the economy that was associated with the 1973–6 populist boom. Between 1974 and 1982 the CDF received $1.5 billion of which 72 per cent leaked into recurrent expenditure, 11 per cent went into investment (mainly into housing construction and nationalization), and 17 per cent accrued to the central bank (Stone and Wellisz 1993).

The 1972 government pursued its redistributive goals through a populist boom which boosted urban consumption by a combination of high wage rises, food subsidies, and a 40 per cent real appreciation of the exchange rate which lowered the relative cost of imported goods. Real wages rose 30 per cent from 1972 to 1977, even as GDP declined by 11 per cent in real terms (Kincaid 1981). The boom pushed consumption to 90 per cent of GDP by 1976. The fiscal deficit grew to 19 per cent of GDP in 1976 and net foreign exchange reserves collapsed to minus 6.5 per cent of GDP from a positive 7 per cent of GDP at the start of the boom (Dipchand 1983). Investment over 1974–9 was one-third of the 1970–3 level and GDP growth turned negative (Table 7.4).

Protracted stabilization and economic recovery

Both the 1972 government and its more conservative successor were slow to agree IMF terms for stabilization and restructuring, partly because renewed growth in mining was expected which would avoid the need for harsher adjustments. The IMF targets for reducing the fiscal deficit and real wages set in 1977 and 1978 were not met and an inflow of private capital failed to materialize. By the time the government was replaced in 1980, GDP had declined 19 per cent in real terms during 1972–80, external debt had quadrupled to over 60 per cent of GDP (Table 7.3), and inflation and unemployment had both risen to 27 per cent (Bank of Jamaica 1982).

The new government responded by allowing the real exchange rate to appreciate by almost one-third over the years 1980–3 during a two-stage IMF recovery programme designed first to lift capacity use and then to restructure the economy. Although the rate of investment recovered to 21 per cent of GDP during 1980–5, GDP growth remained negative at −0.8 per cent annually (Table 6.4). The negative external shock which the Jamaican economy experienced over the period 1979–82 from the combined effects of commodity price shifts, volume effects, and interest rate rises was equivalent to the loss of 21 per cent of GDP annually. This was the second largest negative shock among thirty countries analysed by Balassa and McCarthy (1984). The fiscal and current account deficits were at unsustainable levels (Robinson and Schmitz 1989).

The IMF measures were intensified: further cuts were made in public spending even as taxation was eased. The bauxite levy was halved in 1987 to 3 per cent of the aluminium price and made a cost of production above which firms were eligible for corporation tax at 33 per cent. A start was made on trade liberalization as the real exchange rate was depreciated, most import controls were removed by 1985, and a commitment was made to streamline import tariffs to four bands ranging from 5 to 30 per cent. An export incentive package was also introduced. But even as reform accelerated a decade after the populist boom, foreign debt soared to 180 per cent of GDP and debt service more than doubled over the period 1980–7 to 49 per cent of export earnings, almost double the IMF's maximum sustainable level. Although the investment rate recovered to 26.7 per cent of GDP over 1986–93, GDP growth only averaged 2.5 per cent. The ICOR of 11 indicates the low efficiency of investment. Although Jamaica did secure favourable welfare conditions (Table 7.1) and a relatively modest level of income inequality (the income of the richest quintile was eight times that of the poorest (World Bank 1995*a*)), the average real per capita GNP was only one-third of what it would have been had GDP growth over the 1973–93 period been maintained at the rate of the final years of the youthful stage of the mineral-led cycle.

Evidence that the Jamaican failure to sustain economic growth into the mature stage of the mineral-led cycle is a result of policy error (tardy macro-adjustment) rather than structural constraints is provided by Mauritius. Jamaica shares with that country an historical dependence on sugar plantations whose expansion was checked by land shortages as a result of population growth; redistributive policies which exacerbated the squeeze on the plantation sector; and a small domestic market (Findlay and Wellisz 1993). Lal and Myint (1996) argue that the crucial difference is the fact that the bulk of the resource rents accrued to the public sector in mineral-driven Jamaica, but to the private sector in sugar-driven Mauritius. The 1972 Jamaican government promoted an unsustainable expansion of welfare services and public employment whereas more of the rents in Mauritius accrued to domestic sugar planters who invested in labour-intensive manufacturing in an export-processing zone, which provided a foundation for rapid economic growth after orthodox macro-policies were espoused in the 1980s. Jamaican economic reform failed to stabilize the economy so that when capital flows were deregulated in 1992, a sharp increase in inflation occurred which triggered high interest rates that encouraged speculative capital inflows but deterred long-term investment.

Protracted Adjustment to Maturity: Trinidad and Tobago

The case of Trinidad and Tobago is especially interesting because its adjustment to maturity was unsatisfactory, despite a bias towards cautious macroeconomic management and the accumulation of large financial reserves during the 1974–8 and 1979–81 oil booms. But the legacy of the windfall deployment was an over-expanded public sector and a highly protective trade regime. In contrast to Indonesia (see Chapter 7), there was no bold response to falling oil revenues in 1982 and 1986. Trinidad and Tobago shows how quickly macroeconomic deterioration can occur and how protracted a return to sustained economic growth can be. Some fifteen years after the second oil boom began to fade, it had yet to resume rapid economic growth.

The economic upswing, 1974–85

In the early 1970s the government of Trinidad and Tobago had been preparing the country to cope with declining oil rents. But the discovery of modest additional hydrocarbon reserves, and the positive oil shock of 1973, delayed that prospect. Table 7.2 shows the 1974–8 and 1979–81 windfalls were equivalent to an additional 39 and 35 per cent of non-oil GDP, respectively, twice as large as those of Indonesia, relative to GDP. The government opened a national debate on how the oil windfall should be used.

The government was initially prudent: it moved quickly to tax away five-sixths of the windfall. It established a special fund for long-term development and almost half the 1974–8 windfall was invested abroad and sterilized while a national debate established priorities for domestic investment. Some 70 per cent of the 1974–8 wind-fall was saved, whereas only 12 per cent was invested, and 18 per cent was con-sumed. Around two-thirds of the windfall invested domestically went into clearing up a backlog in socio-economic infrastructure, while a start was made in diversi-fying into gas-based industry like fertilizers and steel. But, less wisely, the invest-ment also went into nationalization of sugar production and oil refining, which were high-cost and needed rationalization. Meanwhile, the windfall spending on consumption raised subsidies on food, fuel, and utilities to 7 per cent of GDP by 1978.

As oil production began to decline in the late 1970s, the government of Trinidad and Tobago prudently drafted plans to reduce the country's hydrocarbon dependence, only to be blown off course, as in the early 1970s, by a combination of large nat-ural gas discoveries and an oil shock. The second oil shock boosted revenues by an extra 34 per cent of GDP in 1979–81 and by half that much in 1982–4. The absorption of the second oil windfall proceeded more rapidly than the first wind-fall, although almost one-half was saved abroad. The financial reserves, which had risen from $43 million to $1.8 billion during the first oil boom, reached $3.4 bil-lion in 1981, equivalent to almost 50 per cent of GDP.

The windfall revenues that were domestically absorbed were split roughly evenly between investment and consumption. One-quarter of the second windfall was, however, unwisely invested in loss-making resource-based industry, and in the inefficient nationalized oil refineries. The government also further boosted sub-sidies which proved unsustainable when oil prices weakened and quickly drained the financial reserve. The annual GDP growth rate, which had averaged 6.6 per cent in 1974–9, was barely positive in 1980–5 (Table 6.1).

Downswing adjustment, 1986–95

During the two booms the contribution of oil to tax revenues rose from one-fifth to three-fifths and the Trinidad and Tobago government's share in GDP reached 30 per cent, and its share in formal employment reached 50 per cent (World Bank 1996*d*). Instead of taking prompt measures to broaden the tax base and stimulate economic diversification, the Trinidad and Tobago government postponed reform and instead cushioned the adjustment to lower oil revenues by drawing down the reserves and accumulating foreign debt. Little progress was made in expanding non-oil revenues which contracted by one-third in real terms during the 1980s, thereby amplifying the compression exerted on the domestic economy by the oil revenue collapse. The financial reserves fell steadily by two-thirds between 1982 and 1985 and were exhausted by 1987. The country's external debt, which had doubled to $1.8 billion between 1980 and 1987, continued to rise and reached $2.3 billion in 1990, and averaged 50 per cent of GDP in 1990–3.

Meanwhile, instead of depreciating, the real exchange rate was allowed to appreciate sharply as oil prices weakened, and it reached 170 per cent of its 1970–2 level by 1985. A real depreciation of the exchange rate by 40 per cent was then achieved which, however, merely returned it to the level of 1980, at the height of the second oil boom. In 1989 the Trinidad and Tobago government was forced to turn to the IMF which demanded further reductions in public spending and an increase in the expenditure tax. A tight monetary policy strengthened the real exchange rate and, as in Jamaica and Peru, this intensified problems for exporters as non-tariff barriers were removed and tariff protection was lowered. In 1993 the exchange rate was allowed to float in the hope that this would bring a depreciation and permit some easing of the country's relatively high interest rates (IADB 1993). The economy contracted by 1.5 per cent annually from 1986 to 1993 and the debt service ratio rose to 34 per cent of exports in 1993.

Nevertheless, the tight financial policy kept the average annual rate of inflation at 9.3 per cent during 1986–93 and also restored the current account to balance (Table 7.3) so that a modest accumulation of reserves occurred (IADB 1993). But high interest rates and the relatively high exchange rate combined with earlier public expenditure curbs to halve the investment rate through the 1980s. The investment rate dropped back to 16 per cent during 1985–93 and was only 13 per cent of GDP in the early 1990s. Public sector savings plummeted from 18.5 per cent of GDP in 1981 to average 1 per cent through 1982–91 and remained below maintenance levels in the mid-1990s.

Although by 1994 the government had diversified its tax base so that it had halved its dependence on hydrocarbon taxes to 17 per cent of the total, public expenditure still accounted for 27 per cent of GDP, of which one-eighth (3.5 per cent of GDP) went towards debt service. The World Bank (1995*b*), in light of the slow pace of adjustment in Trinidad and Tobago, argued that the government still needed to make further reductions in current expenditure, to accumulate savings in an MRSF, to divest the loss-making state enterprises (which had been acquired during the oil boom years), and to encourage a more labour-intensive growth strategy. Such a strategy was required to help alleviate poverty in the light of the deterioration in social conditions since the oil booms. Per capita GDP fell back from $6,600 in 1982 to $3,700 in 1993 (below its 1973 level in real terms), and unemployment doubled to 20 per cent of the workforce (World Bank 1995b). Some 21 per cent of the population was classified as poor and half of these lived in absolute poverty. The level of income inequality was, however, moderate: the gini coefficient was 0.42 in 1992 and the expenditure ratio of the richest quintile to the poorest quintile was 12. But sustaining labour-intensive growth is more challenging for Trinidad and Tobago than for Jamaica or Namibia because its per capita income is twice theirs (and one-third higher than Botswana and three times that of PNG).

Tardy Adjustment to Maturity in a Divided Society: Namibia

Propelled mainly by its declining diamond mining sector, the growth rate of the Namibian economy decelerated from 10.6 per cent during 1946–57, to 6.1 per cent during 1958–70, and 1.7 per cent from 1970 to 1990 (Figure 8.2). By the time the country finally secured its independence from the Republic of South Africa (RSA) in 1990, the onshore diamond grades were 5.5 carats per 100 tonnes of rock compared with 9.9 in 1980 and 45 carats per 100 tonnes in 1950 (Anglo American Corporation 1989). The economic impact of the slowdown in diamond output was offset by an expansion of uranium mining in the 1970s, but when uranium sales stalled, per capita income fell by one-fifth during the 1980s (World Bank 1992). Consequently, some two decades after the end of the youthful stage of the mineral-driven cycle in the late 1960s (Hartman 1986), mining remained the mainstay of the Namibian economy and growth prospects were uncertain. Mining still generated in the 1980s some 76 per cent of Namibian exports, 38 per cent of tax revenues, 31 per cent of GDP, and almost one-fifth of its fixed investment (World Bank 1992).

   Meanwhile, the existence of apartheid meant that some two-thirds of the Namibian population remained neglected in the extreme northern region engaged in subsistence farming with inadequate agricultural resources. The failure of the Namibian economy to diversify and sustain rapid growth into the mature stage of the mineral-driven cycle was not a result of imprudent macro-management or overambitious state intervention, as in Trinidad and Tobago, Peru, and Jamaica. Rather, it arose largely from exogenous factors. The adverse effects of diamond depletion were compounded by trade sanctions against the colonial power (the RSA), by the war along the Angolan border, and by prolonged drought.

Tardy adjustment to maturity

Despite a reputation for fiscal prudence, the Namibian colonial government reacted to the relative decline in mining exports and tax revenues by postponing the required public expenditure cuts during the 1980s. Public expenditure was maintained

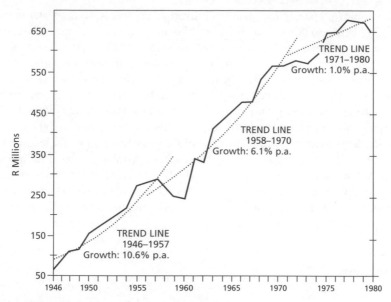

Figure 8.2 Post-war growth in the Namibian economy
Source: Hartman (1986).

at around 31 per cent of GDP over 1980–90 (Table 7.4) and the share of public consumption rose by 9.1 per cent of GDP between 1980 and 1989, an unsustainable trend. Public investment fell to 5.2 per cent of GDP and total investment dropped to barely 17 per cent of GDP.

The public finances continued to deteriorate after independence as fiscal deficits of up to 6 per cent of GDP were recorded, that were only partly financed with aid. Although the country had a relatively low ratio of external debt to GDP (13.5 per cent) the propensity for a rapid deterioration in the country's finances led the World Bank (1994c) to strongly advise against borrowing abroad. Despite constrained finances, the creation of an MRSF was warranted. This is because of the medium-term potential for some revival in mining through an expansion of offshore diamond production and higher uranium prices while, in the long-term, natural gas production could generate substantial revenues.

The Namibian government was constrained in its use of macro-policy instruments, however, because even after independence the exchange rate and monetary policies were linked to the RSA owing to the parity of the Namibian dollar and the rand. RSA macro-policy targeted inflation from the late 1980s so that the exchange rate remained fairly stable until early 1996. Meanwhile, the autarkic trade policy of the RSA had imparted a strong anti-export bias while the RSA had captured most of the region's import substitution manufacturing within its own borders. Some estimates suggested that by the mid-1990s, the Namibian exchange rate was overvalued by up to 20 per cent on a purchasing power parity basis. However, by then a combination of proposals for trade liberalization and pressure for faster economic growth had begun to depress the RSA (and Namibian) exchange rate (Auty 1996*b*).

The pressures generated in newly independent Namibia by stagnant incomes and a large and rising population in a low-rainfall area with negligible potential for irrigation extension, acutely illustrate the problems faced by mature mineral economies with a small domestic market and limited natural resources. Apartheid meant that even the most rudimentary skill training was neglected, not only during the mining boom of the 1950s and 1960s, but also over the next twenty years. The population doubled after the youthful stage of the mineral boom slackened in Namibia in the late 1960s. As the economy of the southern African region is reformed and reintegrated into the global economy, sustainable development in Namibia requires a dualistic development strategy which supports expanded investment in the modern sector while facilitating rapid labour-intensive growth in the lagging sector. Such a strategy is outlined in Chapter 12.

Conclusions

All four less successful mineral economies entered the mature stage of the mineral-driven cycle with relatively high per capita incomes and severely distorted economies. Such distortion resulted from overambitious government intervention to force the pace of economic growth and protect import substitution industry. Such measures were invariably counter-productive because they rendered diversification away from mining even more difficult to achieve. The problem was most acute for the three small countries whose limited domestic markets and narrow non-mining natural resource endowments imposed more constraints than were faced by more resource-rich Peru, let alone by large, low-income Indonesia, which was able to rapidly expand its manufacturing.

Conventional wisdom held in the late 1980s that the lesson of the Chilean reform was to avoid trade and capital market liberalization before stabilization was complete. That conclusion lends some support to the more cautious reform strategies of the governments of the smaller distorted mature mineral economies, Jamaica and Trinidad and Tobago. But the Peruvian reform casts doubt on the conventional wisdom: its government rejected Chilean sequencing in 1990 and opted for a big bang reform which, after two years of uncertainty, appeared to have successfully restored vigorous economic growth. An underlying rationale behind the Peruvian response was that a factional State must leave no doubt about the government's long-term commitment to reform.[1] Moreover, the more cautious reform strategies of Jamaica

---

[1] But doubts remained in 1997 about the medium-term prospects for the Peruvian economy because the relatively high interest rates and capital inflows associated with the reforms resulted in a relatively strong exchange rate. Similar difficulties also emerged in Chile owing largely to the capital inflows associated with a renewed rapid expansion of the mining sector: by 1995 the real exchange rate had appreciated by 20% compared with its 1986–9 level, despite the country's strenuous and 'eclectic' efforts to prevent it (Williamson 1996).

and of Trinidad and Tobago were associated with a prolonged decline in real income. Finally, Jamaica shares many structural features with Mauritius, a successful country which pursued vigorous reform.

The basic problem of the mid-income mature mineral economies is the need to reconcile their relatively high per capita incomes with a more labour-intensive growth strategy in order to sustain growth beyond the youthful stage. This problem is examined in more depth in Chapter 9 with regard to structural change and also in Chapter 12 which examines social sustainability.

9 Substituting for Depleting Mineral Assets: Economic Diversification

Macroeconomic analysis tends to treat sectoral developments like a black box and in doing so it misses important insights into the obstacles to structural change. This chapter explores at the sectoral level the problems of diversification away from mineral dependence during the mature stage of the mineral-driven cycle. Such diversification is required to sustain economic growth and thereby enhance the prospects for curbing environmental degradation and easing social tensions.

The second section examines the three larger mature economies (Indonesia, Chile, and Peru) which possessed greater scope for diversification than the smaller countries due to their larger domestic markets and more favourable non-mining natural resource endowments. The following section then examines the three small, resource-constrained, mature, mid-income mineral economies (Jamaica, Namibia, and Trinidad and Tobago) whose diversification away from mining has proved especially difficult. It notes the leap-frogging of the East Asian stage of labour-intensive industrialization and the adverse consequences for employment and social sustainability of high levels of unemployment. The final section then draws the lessons from all six mid-income countries for the two youthful mineral economies, PNG and Botswana.

Diversification in the Larger, Better-Endowed Countries

Indonesia: diversification in a large, low-income economy

Table 9.1 summarizes the degree of structural change in the three larger mineral economies between 1972 and 1990. It measures changes in the size of the key components in the non-mining sector and, after Gelb and Associates (1988), provides a counter-factual for comparison in the form of the economic structure of countries of a similar size and level of development based on data from the most recent study by Syrquin and Chenery (1989). The table confirms that on the eve of the first oil shock the production structure of the Indonesian economy had been only minimally distorted during the country's long experience as a mature mineral economy. The non-mining tradeables sector was similar in size to that of the Syrquin and Chenery average for the *large* primary-product-exporting countries (the comparator group for the other countries reviewed in this chapter, is that of the small primary-product exporters). In particular, the agricultural sector had proved very resilient, and this was a strong advantage during the oil booms.

Although the Indonesian mining sector still remained almost twice as large as the average for such countries over the 1972–90 period, the non-mining tradeables

Table 9.1 Structural change in three larger mineral economies, 1972–90

Country	Year	Index	Per capita GNP ($US 1980)	Non-mining GDP (%)				Mining (% GDP)
				Agriculture	Manufacturing	Construction and utilities	Services	
Indonesia	1972	Comparator	300	40.1	13.0	10.4	36.5	5.5
		Actual	260	43.0	12.1	4.0	40.8	10.8
	1990	Actual	660	24.9	23.0	7.1	45.1	13.4
		Comparator	650	32.5	17.2	12.4	37.9	7.4
Peru	1972	Comparator	1,000	25.3	16.2	13.4	45.0	8.5
		Actual	1,040	18.4	22.2	3.4	55.9	10.8
	1990	Actual	814	15.6	24.4	7.4	52.6	11.8
		Comparator	800	29.2	15.5	12.5	42.9	8.0
Chile	1972	Comparator	2,500	14.9	20.2	14.9	50.0	9.4
		Actual	2,460	8.3	23.4	14.4	53.8	6.2
	1990	Acutal	2,600	8.9	17.5	18.3	55.3	7.4
		Comparator	2,500	14.9	20.2	14.9	50.0	9.4

Sources: World Bank (1989 and 1995*a*); Syrquin and Chenery (1989).

sector was only slightly smaller in 1990 than in the comparator group (Table 9.1). The agricultural sector had shrunk slightly faster than the comparator group, but the divergence was far smaller than for the majority of the mid-income mineral economies discussed below. In addition, by 1990 the Indonesian manufacturing sector was larger than the comparator group and was also far more competitive than it had been a decade earlier when the government unwisely sought to promote state-led industrialization with an increasingly protective trade stance. The legacy of the state-led industrial policy was a dualistic manufacturing sector comprised of large, relatively efficient companies which earned sizeable rents (alongside small, high-cost private firms) (Flatters and Jenkins 1986) and a large, capital-intensive state-owned resource-based industrial (RBI) sector comprising mainly metals and petrochemicals (Auty 1990; Hill 1982).

The trade and industry policy reforms of the late 1980s were associated with a surge in non-oil exports which rose to average two-thirds of total exports in 1990–3 (Table 9.2). The major expansion was of manufactured exports which increased their share from 12 per cent in 1985 to 43.7 per cent in 1990–3 (Table 9.2) and out-stripped minerals. Within manufacturing, textiles overtook plywood to account for 12.5 per cent of total exports and became the most import manufactured export. RBI provided a third thrust in manufactured export diversification, but the economic benefit was undercut by the need for capital and input subsidies on the part of the predominantly state-owned firms (Hill 1990).

Industrial output tripled during the 1980s (Table 9.3) and went some way towards returning Indonesia to the East Asian development model. Some problems remained, however. Despite the expansion of textile exports, other key labour-intensive products like electronics, were underrepresented and Indonesian manu-facturing remained more capital-intensive than Taiwan and South Korea at a similar stage in their development (World Bank 1993a). This is a distinctive trait of resource-based development which creates tensions over employment growth (Lal 1995) that may corrode the social sustainability of economic and environmental policies, as is shown by the smaller mature mineral economies. A second problem with profound implications for sustainable development is the geographical con-centration of Indonesian manufacturing: one-third is adjacent to the principal market of Jakarta, and 80 per cent is within Java, which has just 6 per cent of the land area (Hill 1995). This spatial concentration may so exacerbate pollution as to curb industrial expansion unless decentralization policies are pursued (World Bank 1994d). Finally, the trade policy reforms still left ownership heavily concentrated in large firms, often built up by Chinese with close and potentially corrupting links to the presidential family (Smith 1995) which may also threaten social sustainability.

Resource-based diversification in Chile and Peru

In contrast to the rapid progress through maturity of the Indonesian economy, the more severely distorted economies of Peru and Chile (Table 9.1) struggled. Peru's agri-cultural sector was barely half the comparator country size and its manufacturing

Table 9.2 Composition of Exports: eight mineral economies, 1990–3 (%)

	Botswana	Chile	Indonesia	Jamaica	Namibia	PNC	Peru	Trinidad and Tobago
Minerals	87.0	49.5	38.4	57.5	57.9	64.2	49.5	66.7
Fuels	0.0	0.4	34.5	2.6	0.0	0.2	10.3	66.4
Other primary	3.5	34.8	17.9	11.2	20.4	20.4	32.5	2.3
Manufacturers	9.5	15.7	43.7	31.3	20.6	15.4	18.0	31.0
Textiles	2.8	1.4	3.1	9.8	n/a	0.1	3.8	1.8
Machinery	—	1.8	12.5	3.4	n/a	11.6	1.1	0.6

Sources: World Bank (1995*a*), except Botswana = CSO (1994); Jamaica = P1OJ (1994) data covers manufactures 1990–1 and includes sugar, coffee, and cocoa in manufactures category; Namibia = World Bank (1994*b*); PNG = 1990–2 only; Peru = 1990, 1991, and 1993 only.

Table 9.3 Industrial activity in eight mineral economies

	Per capita income 1990 ($)	Manufacturing value added per worker 1990 ($)	Manufacturing value added ($1990 m)	
			1980	1990
Botswana	2,583	5,923	0.062	0.144
Chile	2,293	29,274	4.209	5.359
Indonesia	581	4,265	6.923	21.115
Jamaica	1,793	12,787	0.619	0.824
Namibia	1,578	n/a	0.117	0.113
PNC	835	n/a	0.411	0.388
Peru	1,548	40,011	12.493	10.217
Trinidad and Tobago	4,139	13,456	0.492	0.471

Source: UNIDO (1995).

sector's apparent large size masked high levels of inefficiency that required strong protection by the late 1980s. Chile also had an agricultural sector which by 1972 had become much smaller than would be expected for a country of its size and resources. But by 1990 some modest revival of agriculture had occurred whereas the manufacturing sector had declined in relative terms by one-quarter (Table 9.1).

The shrinkage in the relative importance of Chilean manufacturing over the 1972–90 period (and also the slight expansion of agriculture) reflects the post-1975 trade reforms which opened up what had become a closed and highly protected non-mining trade-ables sector and realigned production with the country's comparative advantage in resource-based activity. The reforms reoriented agriculture away from protected food crop production and towards high-valued export crops such as fruit. Other resource-based sectors also contributed to export diversification, notably fish and forest products. But the relatively modest increase in the share of such activity in Chilean GDP underlines the critical importance of manufacturing to diversification.

The Chilean trade reforms removed the high levels of effective protection in the mid-1970s when domestic demand was flat and manufacturers had little alternative if they were to remain in production but to turn to export markets. Even so, production halved in the formerly highly protected sectors over the 1973–80 period, notably textiles, footwear, leather goods, and transport equipment. Smaller, but significant declines in output occurred in chemicals, rubber, electronics, electrical goods, and machinery (Gwynne 1985). These falls were somewhat offset by real output growth of 40 per cent or more in resource-based industries (metals, refined products, timber products, and construction goods). Moreover, there were substantial gains in productivity. Total factor productivity growth accelerated to average almost 5 per cent per annum by the late 1980s, according to Dornbusch and Edwards (1994).

---

[1] Dornbusch and Edwards (1994) cite 38%, their higher figure reflecting a broader definition of resource processing than that used by the World Bank (1995a).

The restructuring of the Peruvian economy in the early 1990s was also expected to favour primary products, including the rejuvenation of the run-down mining and fishing sectors (which together generated three-fifths of exports) and of export agriculture based upon the reversal of the 1968–75 military government's land reforms. Certainly, a sizeable share of Peruvian import-substitution manufacturing capacity shut down after the trade liberalization. Although manufactured goods, mostly textiles, averaged 18 per cent of total exports in 1990–3 (World Bank 1995*a*), that ratio was still only two-thirds the level which Peru had achieved by 1980 during the 1975–80 reform interval.

The reversal of trade policy during the 1980s discriminated against all export sectors, including mining. The state-owned mining firms like Centromin and Petroperu were decapitalized (Auty 1993) while private firms such as Southern Peru Copper Corporation (SPCC) deferred investment decisions with adverse consequences for pollution abatement (see Chapter 11). By 1989 the average level of total effective protection was 69 per cent compared with 48 per cent in 1980 (Rossini and Paredes 1991). Effective protection in 1989 was negative for primary product exports as well as pharmaceuticals and textiles, i.e. the main products in which Peru's comparative advantage lay.

The decidedly capital-intensive nature of Peruvian manufacturing (Table 9.3) limited employment opportunities. The perceived failure of the benefits of reform to trickle down to the poor fuelled apprehension over the sustainability of Peruvian economic growth through the late 1990s. Chile too had experienced a sharp increase in income inequality during its reforms which were only partially offset by targeting social spending on the poorest. In contrast, and despite the heavy investment in HCI, Indonesia maintained a more equitable income distribution. This reflected a slightly less capital-intensive manufacturing sector (Table 9.3) and also a persistent emphasis on rural investment.

Despite such concerns, the broader picture is one in which Peru, Chile, and Indonesia had potentially sizeable domestic markets and non-mineral natural resources with which to diversify their economies. The smaller mature mineral economies lacked these advantages and their problems of adjustment to maturity were compounded by past imprudent macro-policies and their associated Dutch disease effects, and a reluctance to reform.

Protracted Diversification: Small Mid-Income Mineral Economies

Dualistic development: Namibia

Of the three small *mid-income* mature mineral economies, Namibia illustrates most starkly the problem of providing employment for the poorest people whose skills, neglected under apartheid, were so mismatched with the cost of their labour. Although population in the lagging northern region of Namibia had long outstripped agricultural carrying capacity, farming still underpinned the regional economy. The lagging region contained two-thirds of the Namibian population but only produced between 3 and 6 per cent of GDP.

Table 9.4 shows that by the early 1990s, Namibian agriculture contributed barely one-third of its expected share of GDP and manufacturing scarcely one-half. Commercial agriculture was constrained by the scarcity of suitable land, the high costs of extending irrigation, and the difficulty of boosting productivity. Production needed to be reoriented away from cattle rearing and grain production, which enjoyed a rate of effective protection of between 75 and 140 per cent (Dewdney 1995), towards non-traditional export crops and wildlife management. Agriculture provided 15 per cent of exports in the early 1990s but it generated less than 9 per cent of Namibian GDP (Auty 1996*b*).

The most dynamic economic sectors at independence from the Republic of South Africa (RSA) in 1990, and the ones with the strongest medium-term growth prospects, were fishing and tourism. However, fish catches had declined from the 1960s owing to overfishing which occurred because the international community refused to recognize the 320-km territorial zone prior to independence. By the mid-1980s, the Namibian fishing sector employed only 1700 people and generated 2 per cent of GDP. The World Bank (1992) estimated that a sustainably managed fishery could boost Namibian GDP through the capture of rents equal to 25 per cent of total fish revenues. This could raise the sector's share of GDP from 7.4 per cent in 1994 to more than 10 per cent by the year 2000 and its share of exports, already 29 per cent in 1994, would also rise. Tourism also offered robust growth potential from a low initial base estimated at 6 per cent of GDP in 1992. Tourist numbers could double in the years 1992–2002 and increase further thereafter.

Manufacturing, however, was unlikely to take over as the leading sector for at least a decade. In the early 1990s, almost two decades into the mature phase of Namibia's mineral economy cycle, manufacturing generated barely 8 per cent of GDP, mainly in the form of resource processing such as food, beverages, furniture, and metalworking. The autarkic RSA trade policy, to which Namibia remained tied after independence, left a legacy of high and uneven levels of effective protection, which raised the price of manufactured goods well above world prices and imposed an anti-export bias (Maxwell Stamp 1994). A survey of firms representing two-thirds of Namibian output revealed an average effective protection rate of 52 per cent with rates in excess of 100 per cent for beverages, most food processing, garments, soaps, and paints. Rates above the average were also recorded for meat processing and leather goods. The least protected sectors were fish processing (7 per cent), machinery (14 per cent), and milling (29 per cent).

The best initial industrial opportunities for Namibia lay in expanded resource processing, whether of minerals, fish, livestock, or crops (Sodersten 1985). But the modest medium-term employment potential of such manufacturing, coupled with the need to reduce government employment, underlined the urgency of a labour-intensive development strategy for the lagging northern region. In the absence of such a strategy, the scale of out-migration to the cities in the modern sector could greatly exceed job creation, intensifying urban poverty and associated crime in a

Table 9.4 Structural change in two youthful mineral economies, 1972–90

Country	Year	Index	Per capita GNP ($US 1980)	Non-mining GDP (%)				Mining (% GDP)
				Agriculture	Manufacturing	Construction and utilities	Services	
Botswana	1972	Comparator	400	37.0	11.7	10.9	40.4	5.5
		Actual	420	36.9	6.6	12.4	44.1	10.8
	1990	Actual	2,308	10.3	8.2	14.4	67.2	46.4
		Comparator	2,300	20.1	15.7	14.7	49.7	9.1
PNG	1972	Comparator	750	29.6	15.2	12.5	42.6	7.8
		Actual	770	33.2	5.8	20.6	40.4	2.5
	1990	Actual	610	34.0	10.6	7.9	47.6	14.7
		Comparator	600	33.7	14.0	11.9	40.4	6.7

Sources: World Bank (1988*b* and 1995*a*); Syrquin and Chenery (1989).

way which could undermine investor confidence and slow the rate of economic growth in the modern sector. A labour-intensive growth strategy is discussed for Namibia in Chapter 12 and for Botswana, below.

Diversification constraints in Jamaica

In the early 1970s, the Jamaican agricultural sector was less than two-fifths the size of that of the comparator countries while manufacturing was also smaller (and heavily protected). Jamaican export agriculture declined further through the 1970s as a consequence of exchange rate overvaluation, nationalization of the sugar subsector, and declining agricultural practices. Like Peru, agricultural policy in Jamaica during the 1970s deliberately discriminated against exports and in favour of food production for the domestic market, contrary to the country's comparative advantage. The productivity of land turned over to domestic food production declined so that although food output expanded, it did so at high cost. Meanwhile, the nationalized sugar industry experienced mounting labour problems: output halved from its 1965 peak and by the late 1980s, costs were almost twice those of a competitive world producer and the sugar mills depended upon privileged access to the EU market.

Yet manufacturing did little to offset the country's poor agricultural performance because Jamaica pursued infant industry policies that created an uncompetitive sector. Industrial output fell by one-quarter in the years 1973–80 as macro-mismanagement caused domestic demand to slump. The average rate of effective protection was estimated at 58 per cent by 1980, but varied widely and was negative for wood products and textiles, subsectors in which Jamaica had a potential comparative advantage. Even with the change of government in 1980, investor confidence remained low. Nor did trade liberalization from 1983 stimulate an expansion like that of Mauritius which reformed its trade policy at the same level of per capita income as Jamaica (Wellisz and Saw 1993).

In contrast to Mauritius, the establishment of an export-processing zone (EPZ) in Jamaica brought little expansion in industrial output (Table 9.3). A brief production spurt in the mid-1980s by garments and food processing was not sustained. By the early 1990s the EPZ employed only 15,000 workers (barely one-sixth of the manufacturing workforce) and although it generated $450 million in exports, only one-tenth of the export value represented net foreign exchange (Planning Institute of Jamaica 1994). Table 9.2 overstates the scale of Jamaican manufacturing exports because it includes exports of alumina which, if they are reclassified as mineral exports, leave the mining sector with 66 per cent of exports in the early 1990s, crops a further 22 per cent, and textiles and garments 9 per cent. Other manufactured goods and primary product exports accounted for a mere 3 per cent.

Successive Jamaican governments failed to convince industrial investors that the country offered a solid base for manufactured exports. The failure raised doubts about the need of Jamaica to develop a manufacturing sector at all. But with tourism notoriously fickle and pressing against environmental absorptive capacity and little prospect for higher farm production, it is difficult to see which sectors will emerge to restore rapid sustainable economic growth in the absence of renewed expansion of mining.

Capital-intensive diversification: Trinidad and Tobago

The Trinidad and Tobago government decided to deploy the 1974 oil windfall to achieve economic diversification through gas-based RBI in the form of methanol, fertilizers, and direct-reduced steel production. It rejected a proposed LNG plant, which would have given the highest rent on the gas input because the plant would have absorbed the bulk of the gas. Diversification was urgently required because the country had experienced severe Dutch disease effects: the share of agriculture in GDP in the early 1970s was one-third of its value in the comparator countries and, although manufacturing was larger than expected, half the extra output came from oil refining and most of the rest from heavily protected import-substitution industry.

After a slow start on construction, the gas-based industry absorbed almost half of government capital expenditure during the second oil boom. But the scale of construction outstripped domestic implementation capacity, causing a sharp increase in costs with adverse effects on the efficiency of the capital invested (Auty and Gelb 1986). The real exchange rate strengthened sharply to 70 per cent above its pre-shock value by 1984. This intensified pressure on the inefficient agricultural and manufacturing sectors in both of which the State had acquired large firms during the booms. Capacity use fell, costs rose, and the resulting deficits were financed by the government. The inefficient state-owned sugar corporation alone, which had production costs by the early 1980s five times those of an efficient world producer, absorbed subsidies equivalent to 9 per cent of the oil revenues by 1983. The Dutch disease effects therefore intensified through the mid-1980s as manufacturing firms closed and agriculture languished: dependence on imported food increased to 90 per cent from a pre-boom 70 per cent.

The RBI diversification strategy was risky because it involved a small number of plants that were highly indebted and dependent upon volatile export markets whose accessibility could not be guaranteed. In addition, the execution of RBI strategies by other oil exporters had resulted in a glut in global capacity which depressed prices when demand fell short of projections. Although the petrochemical plants soon broke even, the steel plant failed to penetrate the US market and incurred losses that exceeded the initial $500 million investment before it was privatized (for a nominal sum). However, the recovery of RBI prices in the late 1980s led to an expansion of the gas-based industries, which pushed the country's share of methanol and fertilizers to sizeable fractions (over one-seventh) of global exports. Nevertheless, RBI represents a minimal diversification from dependence upon hydrocarbons, and provides few jobs (Table 9.3). Some $1.45 billion was invested in the Trinidad and Tobago RBI plants, excluding infrastructure, to create barely 2,100 direct jobs.

Industrial unemployment increased in the aftermath of the oil boom as falling real incomes shrank the domestic demand upon which much of the inefficient assembly industries depended. The non-hydrocarbon manufacturing sector generated negligible exports and was a large net consumer of foreign exchange. The costs of this inefficient sector were borne by consumers in terms of higher prices for goods of inferior quality. Food processing, the leading subsector, was hampered by high-cost domestic inputs, unreliable delivery, and variable quality. Yet a proposal to reform the large state sugar firm into a diversified agri-business was blocked by political sensitivities arising from its role as an important employer of the East Indian minority. After food processing, assembly industries ranked second in importance, but domestic linkages from the kit car industry and steel plant were disappointing. For example, a heavily subsidized tyre factory captured half the domestic market with the assistance of very high tariffs, but still lost money (World Bank 1988c).

Consequently, in the early 1990s oil still accounted for two-thirds of Trinidad and Tobago's exports (Table 9.2), followed by 31 per cent for manufactured goods (petrochemicals) and 6 per cent for food (World Bank 1995b). Webster (1993) argues that the industrial diversification of Trinidad and Tobago reflects the bidding up of wages by the oil sector, a process which has biased industrial diversification strongly towards capital-intensive goods. The country's capital-intensive exports used machinery to substitute for deficiencies in skilled and semi-skilled workers (Table 9.3). Such an outcome is at odds with the factor endowment of Trinidad and Tobago *vis-à-vis* its main trading partners (the USA, Britain, and Canada). Yet the dominance of capital-intensive industry was set to continue as the country turned to a $1 billion LNG scheme in the late 1990s to improve its economic prospects.

Unemployment in Trinidad and Tobago remained stubbornly high at 18 per cent in 1994 and was disproportionately concentrated on those with low educational qualifications (World Bank 1995b). The World Bank (ibid.) could only recommend further trade, financial, and labour market reforms as a basis for launching a labour-intensive growth strategy, which may also require a further real depreciation of the exchange rate. Fifteen years after the end of the oil boom, Trinidad and Tobago had still to restructure its economy to in order to secure sustainable economic growth.

Structural Change in the Youthful Mineral Economies

Table 9.5 contrasts the structural change which Botswana and PNG experienced during the youthful stage of their mineral-driven cycles. The rapid expansion of diamond production in Botswana quadrupled per capita GNP but the agricultural sector contracted rapidly to half the size of comparator countries with a similar per capita income and resource endowment, with no compensating manufacturing increase from its initial low 1972 base at barely half the expected size. The corollary was a service sector which was one-third larger than the comparator group with much of the extra output coming from a government sector whose growth, it may be recalled from Chapter 7, displayed decreasing efficiency.

PNG's disappointing economic performance during the 1970s and 1980s reflects a marked lack of dynamism in its non-mining tradeables sector rather than the Dutch disease effects. Table 9.5 shows that on the eve of the 1990s' boom, some relative

Table 9.5 Structural change in three maturing mineral economies, 1972–90

Country	Year	Index	Per capita GNP ($US 1980)	Non-mining GDP (%)					Mining (% GDP)
				Agriculture	Manufacturing	Construction and utilities	Services		
Trinidad and Tobago	1972	Comparator	1,800	18.2	18.7	14.5	48.7		10.6
		Actual	1,850	6.0	27.1	12.9	53.9		8.8
	1990	Actual	1,430	3.3	11.1	22.6	63.0		21.3
		Comparator	1,400	21.1	18.0	13.8	46.7		9.1
Jamaica	1972	Comparator	1,600	19.9	18.6	13.7	47.7		9.1
		Actual	1,630	7.4	16.8	10.1	55.5		10.1
	1990	Actual	1,280	6.4	19.2	15.0	49.8		9.5
		Comparator	1,300	22.0	18.0	13.5	46.5		8.9
Namibia	1980	Comparator	1,100	24.5	17.1	13.3	45.0		8.9
		Actual	1,100	12.4	4.6	3.1	40.5		39.4
	1990	Actual	800	10.4	8.1	3.3	58.6		19.6
		Comparator	800	29.2	15.5	12.5	42.9		8.0

Sources: World Bank (1989 and 1995*a*); Syrquin and Chenery (1989).

[a] Statistics not available prior to 1980.

expansion had occurred in the non-mining tradeables, mainly manufacturing. But two qualifications are required. First, the 1972 data reflect the huge expansion of construction activity associated with the start-up of the Panguna mine, without which the agricultural sector would have been bigger. Second, the non-mining tradeables have underperformed since the early 1970s, largely as a result of micro-policy errors. Both youthful mineral economies in this study, like the mature mid-income economies, were experiencing problems in generating adequate employment.

Retarded economic diversification in PNG

Although the youthful stage of the PNG mineral cycle expanded the infrastructure and more or less maintained the per capita incomes of most citizens, economic growth has been capital-intensive. One projection suggests that trends in the 1980s point to half the workforce being unemployed by the year 2000. When mining began in 1973, Panguna employed a mere 3,500 workers and the mining sector employed only 2.5 per cent of the workforce two decades later (AIDAB 1993). Subsistence farming employed more than two-thirds of PNG's workforce and accounted for just over one-fifth of GDP (World Bank 1978), a situation which had changed little by the 1990s (Duncan *et al.* 1995). In the modern sector, commercial farming provided 10 per cent of GDP, and the volatile mining sector between one-tenth and one-quarter. The remainder was split roughly evenly between the central government and manufacturing/services.

The disappointing growth of the non-mining tradeables reflects three constraints, namely a relatively high exchange rate, wages that are relatively high, and restrictions on foreign investment. In addition to prolonged exchange rate overvaluation, wage regulation hampered employment creation and discouraged investment. By the late 1970s, the minimum daily wage in PNG manufacturing was almost US$7, significantly higher than Malaysia and more than three times rates in Thailand or the Philippines (World Bank 1982). A decade later, wage indexation had pushed PNG wages 50 per cent above those of Korea, which had five times PNG's per capita GDP, and five times higher than those of Indonesia, a country with a similar per capita income. High wages helped to confine export agriculture to barely half its 5 per cent annual growth potential, despite favourable crop-growing conditions and proximity to the burgeoning export markets in East Asia.

The PNG government's regulation of new foreign investment in agriculture and forestry also constrained diversification and employment creation. For example, the World Bank (1988*b*) estimated that reduced agricultural regulation could boost the agricultural growth rate to 6.5 per cent and generate an additional 30,000 direct jobs over a decade. But instead, the potentially efficient commercial farming sector remained confined to 500–600 plantations, mainly expatriate-owned, employing 35,000 workers and exporting copra, coffee, and cocoa. The estates were kept to a suboptimal size for most major tree crops by restrictions on land trading and maintenance of communal ownership on 97 per cent of PNG land. Yet few peasant farmers had sufficient land, finance, and skills for viable cash-crop farming.

If agriculture was repressed, forestry was mismanaged. The sector employed only 4,000 workers in the late 1980s, fewer than mining, although forest covered 87 per cent of the country (40 million hectares). Policies to increase timber processing required foreign firms to make developmental investments in roads and processing facilities in return for export licences. But official forest production was curbed while large areas were illegally felled because the PNG government proved a poor administrator. The recorded annual forest product output was only one-quarter of PNG's estimated sustainable yield.

Manufacturing also languished as poor communications and low demand limited import substitution while remoteness from markets and high wages hampered exports. Recurrent government concern for unemployment encouraged the growth of tariff and quota protection which fostered an inefficient manufacturing sector. By the early 1990s high effective rates of protection (ERPs) supported some manufacturing, notably processed foods, with negative added-value while metals and wood products had zero or mildly negative ERPs and farm products experienced negative ERPs of 30 to 50 per cent (Duncan *et al.* 1995).

The economic crisis caused by the mismanagement of the early-1990s' boom finally triggered policy reform. In 1994 non-tariff protection was withdrawn and tariffs were stream-lined (with levels at 11 per cent, 40 per cent for infant industry, and 55 per cent for luxury goods). The minimum wage was abolished in 1992, but PNG needed to regain its reputation for macroeconomic stability in order to take advantage of the country's considerable opportunities for resource-based diversification. As noted in Chapter 12, this was not an easy task for a non-consensual factional government like that of PNG.

Policy lessons for Botswana's transition to early maturity

During the 1990s, Botswana began to shift into the mature stage of mineral-driven development, which a 20 per cent expansion in diamond output announced in 1997 is unlikely to reverse. Consequently, the optimum strategy for deploying the accumulated financial reserves (which totalled more than 125 per cent of GDP) in order to sustain development has become the subject of strong debate. Two alternatives for the deployment of the reserve may be termed 'super-cautious' and 'pragmatic'. Each strategy seeks to avoid yet a third strategy of rapid absorption (that is, a populist boom), which was believed to be favoured by opposition groups representing the urban poor.

The super-cautious strategy requires government expenditure to remain in step with recurrent revenue growth while deploying the reserves for long-term human and physical capital formation. Human capital formation would focus on upgrading the quality of primary education and easing skill shortages. The priority for physical capital would be to improve telecommunications and transport in order to reduce the disadvantage of Botswana's landlocked and isolated location in serving regional and global markets. Such a strategy has the theoretical appeal from the perspective of sustainable development of maintaining the total capital stock but it has three less attractive features. First, both types of investment have long gestation periods and do little to help with the immediate problem of maintaining economic growth during the transition from rent-driven to skill-driven growth. Second, the State is assigned a major role which it is not clear the State is efficient enough to carry out. It might therefore be better to reform the domestic private financial system in order to make part of the reserves available to the private sector. Third, the super-cautious strategy takes the maintenance of political stability for granted and assigns a low priority to the easing of social hardship (Chambers 1995). Yet this study shows in Chapter 12 that the neglect of the social sustainability of economic and environmental policies can quickly undermine such policies.

A 'pragmatic' fiscal strategy, on the other hand, would promote diversification and that would require a depreciation of the real exchange rate. Table 9.2 shows that minerals still accounted for 87 per cent of exports in 1991–3, with diamonds alone responsible for almost 80 per cent. The main alternative exports were animals (4 per cent of total exports) and textiles (2.6 per cent). Mining still generated over 40 per cent of GDP compared with only 5.2 per cent for farming and 4.3 per cent for manufacturing. Botswana displays strong Dutch disease effects, contrary to the views of Hill (1991), Harvey (1993), Norberg and Blomstrom (1993), and the Bank of Botswana (1994) who draw on the relatively stability of the country's real exchange rate to conclude that the country had largely avoided them.

Botswana would find a real exchange rate depreciation hard to achieve because of its large financial reserves, high import dependence on the Republic of South Africa (RSA), and the recent abandonment of food self-sufficiency (which means higher imported grain prices would hurt the poor). Yet without an exchange rate depreciation, the task of attracting inward investment in the non-mining tradeables, and of securing the skills which would accompany such investment, will be that much harder. This compounds the problems which the country faces as a small mid-income mineral economy with a narrow natural resource base.

Despite Botswana's large geographical area, agriculture is constrained by low, unreliable rainfall and sandy soils which favour extensive livestock farming and wildlife management (Sigwele 1993). The area suited to rain-fed crops is less than 5 per cent of the total and the opportunity cost of water in both urban uses and ranching is much higher than in irrigated cereal production (Sigwele 1996). Some expansion in agricultural value added became possible with the abandonment of the food self-sufficiency policy in the early 1990s. The production of crops better suited to local conditions can earn higher revenues per hectare and reduce the minimum viable size of farm. But already, the average farm of only 5.5 hectares, was several times too small to generate an adequate income with the low yields on traditional crops (Ministry of Finance and Development Planning 1991).

Livestock production will continue to be more important than crop production. But the low productivity of the smaller herds requires the replacement of the off-take tax (which discouraged sales) with a head tax, and also the return of grazing rights to the community. Larger herds benefit more from state intervention and encroach on the drier rangelands. Yet Namibian research shows that their owners may find it more profitable to diversify into wildlife management for meat and animal by-product sales as well as for tourism. Tourism generated barely 3 per cent of GDP in Botswana in the early 1990s (*Economist* 1993), and wildlife viewing could expand fourfold given estimates of carrying capacity based upon analyses of parks in Kenya (Barnes 1996).

If land-extensive activity offers Botswana limited prospects for economic diversification, manufacturing has difficulty in competing due to the small domestic market, landlocked location, and mismatch of skills and wages. The sector grew rapidly during the decade after independence based upon small-scale, competitive private firms, but from the late 1970s its growth (excluding meat packing) was driven by domestic demand and import substitution (Sharpley *et al.* 1990). The textile industry was severely depressed in the early 1990s when Zimbabwe devalued as part of a structural adjustment programme. Therefore, Botswana faced a similar position to that of Trinidad and Tobago after the 1979–81 oil boom, with large financial reserves, few diversification options, and potentially high unemployment.

Botswana therefore requires a dual industrial strategy to ease the transition to early maturity. This entails expanding a relatively small but globally competitive skill-driven formal sector, while improving access to inputs within the labour-intensive informal sector. The formal sector can build on the advantages which Botswana possesses as a focal point for the southern African market. These advantages include a soundly managed and relatively open economy; a reliable and effective infrastructure whose prices (excluding water) will converge on those of its partners as they remove price distortions and as regional networks emerge; a low and stable tax regime; an educational system capable of remedying skill shortages; and a social ambience which is distinctly less fraught than that in competing centres like Johannesburg and Durban.

Yet the shift to skill-driven growth calls for experience with marketing, management, and technology which few Botswana are likely to acquire in the near future. Like Singapore when it abruptly left the Malaysian Federation in 1965, Botswana needed to attract large-scale foreign investment to serve a larger regional market. Large 'flagship' firms can play a crucial role in establishing the locational advantages of Botswana and thereby act as a catalyst for other companies, both as suppliers and as new nucleus firms. Such a process has been successful in, for example, north-east England (Nissan) and south Wales (Sony). It typically has a lengthy gestation period as negotiations proceed (with some inevitable disappointments) and the initial plants are run in. The Botswana Development Corporation (BDC) considered prospects especially promising in components (electronic and automotive), pharmaceuticals, and textiles.

Botswana also plans to become a regional financial and service centre which one study estimates might generate 10,000 to 20,000 jobs. Such activity requires improved communications, not only by upgrading road links with Bulawayo and Johannesburg but also by improving air services for both freight and passengers. Air links require integrating the loss-making national airline into the network of a large international carrier seeking to build up a presence in the potentially dynamic southern African region. But business services and manufacturing in the formal sector both start from a small value-added base in Botswana and, being largely skill-intensive, they are likely to make only a modest contribution to direct employment.

Growth of formal sector manufacturing might generate 2,000 jobs annually and non-government services an additional 8,000 jobs. Yet, some 20,000 new jobs will be needed annually in order to reduce unemployment which is estimated at between 14 and 20 per cent. The informal sector is therefore expected to remain the major employer in Botswana into the next century. It lies largely outside the regulatory environment and offers relative ease of entry and exit and maximum flexibility for employment. As such it acts as a relatively low-cost incubator for new firms and, perhaps more importantly, provides a useful vehicle for the acquisition of a wide range of management and work skills. It has a vital role to play in sustaining the Botswana transition to the mature stage of the mineral cycle, acting as a bridge between the already overpopulated rural areas and the expanding skill-driven formal sector.

An improved institutional environment for the informal sector can maximize the multiplier effect from the formal sector, and also upgrade the quality of the labour force more cost-effectively than formal state training programmes. Easier access to investment could include the provision of market places and factory shells on a sites-and-services basis, along with security and credit for those firms willing to be registered and to meet basic minimum standards of public health. Some cost recovery might be possible through rental charges and the maintenance of positive real interest on the repayments of loans. Meanwhile, government awareness of the 'leading edge' of the informal sector would be improved and this might well stimulate additional measures such as business advice centres and new training programmes to target the skills needed to enhance performance and allow the more successful cases to graduate into the formal sector. Such a policy for the informal sector could accelerate the upgrading of skills which is made so pressing for Botswana and other mid-income countries whose mineral-driven growth has caused them to leap-frog the labour-intensive stage of the successful East Asian growth model.

Conclusion

Indonesia experienced a very modest distortion of its economy during its oil booms. The maintenance of rapid economic growth into the mature stage rested not only on effective macroeconomic management, but also upon a limited divergence between labour costs and productivity, a potentially large domestic market for industrial goods, and a relatively rich non-mineral resource endowment. Indonesia's modest per capita income also allowed the manufacturing sector to play an increasing role.

PNG's youthful stage had left that country with a per capita income that was, like Indonesia, still relatively low. Also like Indonesia, PNG had a potentially sizeable agricultural sector with which to pursue diversification and sustain growth, but in this case that sector was repressed. PNG's factional political State has been less successful in managing these advantages than Indonesia's autonomous benevolent State.

The remaining mineral economies had attained middle levels of per capita income and, in the process, they had leap-frogged the critical labour-intensive stage of the East Asian model. The capital-intensive nature of mineral-driven growth rendered unemployment an ever-present threat when growth in the mining sector slowed. The two largest mid-income economies, Chile and Peru, wrestled with significantly more distorted economies than that of Indonesia. Chile's reforms diversified the economy into non-copper resource-based activity while its manufacturing sector shrank in relative size, a pattern that Peru is emulating. But both possess non-mining resource endowments of a sufficient size with which to sustain diversified economic growth. But the ability of their resource-based growth to create sufficient employment was still not assured in the late 1990s.

The four smallest mid-income mineral economies must rely more heavily on manufacturing to sustain their economic growth. Yet they exhibit the strongest Dutch disease effects. All four small mid-income economies need to diversify in the face of limited non-mining resources and few options for manufacturing due to the wedge between the productivity of most workers and the cost of labour. In order to kindle manufacturing-led growth, a depreciation of the real exchange rate is required on a scale which seems difficult to achieve in small open economies (Brewster 1994). Meanwhile, all four governments faced political discontent associated with high urban unemployment and underemployment. Even Botswana's consensual democracy is threatened as growing urban poverty corrodes the country's social cohesion. Its financial reserves might therefore be deployed in a dual industrial strategy to foster skill-intensive services and industry for southern Africa while helping the informal sector to function as an incubator of labour-intensive business skills. The prospects for such a labour-intensive growth strategy are explored in more detail in Chapter 12 with reference to Namibia.

Part IV

Environmental and Socio-Political Sustainability

10 Substituting for the Depleting Assets: Environmental Accounting

Sustainable development calls for macroeconomic policies which maintain GDP growth beyond the youthful stage of the mineral cycle and promote economic diversification. The rate of investment is a critical component of this process. The more successful mineral economies are those which lifted their rate of investment above 25 per cent of GDP while also maintaining the efficiency of that investment, as shown by an ICOR of 5 or less. Among the most successful countries, investment remained high in the cases of Indonesia and Botswana and rose strongly through the 1980s in Chile to over 26 per cent of GDP. In contrast, investment faltered at a rate just below that level in PNG, the fourth most successful country in our sample, but it collapsed in three of the four least successful countries, Trinidad and Tobago, Peru, and Namibia. Jamaica is an interesting exception in this group because that country maintained a high rate of investment, but failed to translate it into sustained rapid economic growth, owing to investment inefficiency (Table 6.4).

As explained in Chapter 4, sustainable development requires that investment must not only occur at a relatively high rate and be efficiently applied, it must also stay positive after allowing for asset depletion, including the depletion of natural capital as well as produced (man-made) capital. An investment rate above 25 per cent of GDP implies, after deducting a 'rule-of-thumb' 10 per cent of GDP for the depreciation of produced capital, a net investment rate in excess of 15 per cent of GDP. But the depletion of natural capital must be deducted from that 15 per cent figure in order to estimate the true rate of capital accumulation. This means that if the net investment rate under conventional national accounting is low, say around 5 per cent of GDP, as in the case of the three low-investing countries in our sample, the deduction of mineral asset depletion may reveal that growth is occurring wholly at the expense of the consumption of the mineral assets, clearly an unsustainable situation.

This chapter measures mineral asset depletion and assesses the implications for investment and sustainability. It is structured as follows. The second and third sections deal with the potentially high-rent minerals, oil and diamonds. Among the oil-exporters, Indonesia yields data with which to analyse depletion trends over the entire mineral-driven life-cycle. The third section contrasts the two diamond producers, Botswana and Namibia, and explores the problems in measuring mineral asset depletion in more depth. The final two sections deal with base metals which tend to have lower rents and larger mineral reserves than oil and diamonds, characteristics which demand a clear decision about the most appropriate depletion coefficient to apply.

Mineral Asset Depletion in the High-Rent Oil Economies

Indonesian oil and gas

Repetto *et al.* (1989) and the World Bank (1994*c*) apply environmental accounting to Indonesia and conclude that the country's economic performance is less impressive as a result. Both these studies use the net price method to estimate mineral depletion, however, and this section shows that their findings are quite different from those based upon the user-cost method.

Repetto *et al.* (1989) adjust the Indonesian national accounts over the period 1971–84 for the depletion of the three principal natural assets, hydrocarbons, forests, and soils. They calculate that the inclusion of natural asset depletion reduces the Indonesian economic growth rate from 7.1 per cent per annum using the standard national accounting system, to a sustainable growth rate of only 4 per cent per annum. The bulk of the downward adjustment, around seven-tenths, reflects hydrocarbon depletion. Another one-quarter is the deduction for forest loss; and just one-thirtieth is due to soil loss. This means that the depletion of hydrocarbon reserves accounts for a reduction of around 2.1 per cent in the annual GDP growth rate. This figure would not be much higher if the depletion of other minerals, such as coal and copper, were also taken into account because they generate minimal rents. The other minerals are therefore considered no further here.

The findings of Repetto *et al.* (1989) suggest that more than one-third of Indonesian growth 1971–84 reflected the consumption of natural capital. Their case for moderately wasteful pattern of growth in Indonesia receives some support from Winter-Nelson (1995). The latter argues with reference to countries in sub-Saharan Africa that whereas the economic growth of the more-closed economies is overwhelmingly attributable to natural asset consumption, that of the more open economies (like Indonesia) relied to a much lesser extent on natural asset depletion for their economic growth.

The World Bank (1994*d*) builds on the work of Repetto *et al.* (1989) by extending the Indonesian data to 1990 and tracking the change in hydrocarbon reserves. It shows that, in volume terms, total Indonesian oil reserves at first expanded from 10 billion barrels to over 13 billion during 1970–4 and then began to decline, dropping back to just under 9 billion barrels in 1990. The average annual rate of decline in oil reserves from the mid-1970s is estimated to have been around 2 per cent. In contrast, natural gas reserves increased: they first doubled to 7.5 billion barrels of oil equivalent during the 1970s, then doubled again by 1986, and reached 18 billion barrels by 1990.

When the oil and gas reserve volumes are converted into monetary values the fluctuation becomes very substantial because of the sharp price changes associated with the 1973, 1979, and 1986 oil shocks. Using the net price method, the World Bank (1994*c*) calculates that the value of the oil reserves, in constant 1983 US dollars, quadrupled to $250 billion in 1974, peaked around $350 billion in 1981, and then fell back to just over $100 billion in 1986. The value of the gas reserves has

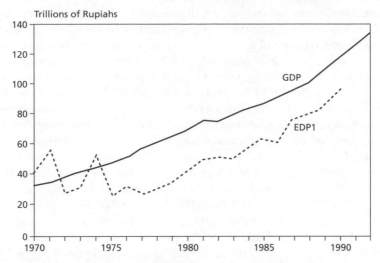

Figure 10.1 Growth in GDP and EDP1, Indonesia, 1970–90 (1983 prices)
Source: World Bank (1994*d*).

been less volatile than that of the oil reserves: it reached $200 billion in 1980, held that level until 1986, and then almost halved through the late 1980s. There are two reasons for the lower volatility of the gas reserves: first, as noted above, large new reserves were added, and second, gas sales are made under long-term contracts which moderate price fluctuations.

The World Bank (1994*d*) plots conventional GDP against environmental domestic product (EDP1), as shown in Figure 10.1. It may be recalled from Chapter 4 that EDP1 is GDP minus the depletion of both produced capital (giving net national product) and natural capital (in this case, timber, oil, and gas). The World Bank follows Repetto *et al.* (1989) in adjusting GDP growth for timber depletion as well as for oil and gas extraction but, as noted earlier, the adjustment is dominated by oil and gas. It should be noted that the changes in Figure 10.1 do not reflect the sharp 1986 fall in energy prices because the data are measured in constant 1983 prices.

Figure 10.1 shows that whereas total GDP increased more than threefold during 1970–90, EDP1 rose by barely two-thirds as much. More specifically, EDP1 is initially higher than GDP as the revival of the youthful stage of the Indonesian mineral cycle took off, owing to large net additions to the stock of oil in terms of both volume and value. But in the late 1970s EDP1 drops significantly below GDP because the combined depreciation of produced capital and natural capital exceeds the rate of investment. The gap then narrows through the late 1980s, however, as the diversification of the economy during late maturity brings a relative decline in the contribution of oil and gas to economic growth (see Chapter 9). In summary, Figure 10.1 suggests that the Indonesian economy was not growing sustainably through the 1970s, but that it moved steadily closer towards a sustainable path as oil revenues fell and economic diversification accelerated.

As noted in Chapter 4, however, the divergence between conventional accounting and environmental accounting is highly sensitive to the choice of the natural capital depletion measure. The net price measure used by both Repetto and the World Bank tends to heighten the divergence compared with the user-cost method. Other differences in estimating natural capital depletion can arise from variations in the volumetric estimates of the reserves, a fact which further underlines the subjective nature of the exercise. Moreover, both the net price and user-cost depletion indices overstate the divergence between EDP1 and GDP to the extent that they fail to take account of the use of natural capital receipts to accumulate human and social capital.

We recalculate the hydrocarbon depletion component for Indonesia by the user-cost method, based on the most recent time-series data for oil and gas which cover the period 1981–90 (Saleh *et al.* 1993). The dataset differs from that of the World Bank in recording an increase during the 1980s in Indonesian oil reserves as well as in natural gas reserves (Table 10.1). The gas reserves expanded almost 2.5 times to reach 19.8 billion barrels of oil equivalent (conversion figures from (BP 1994)) so that the output/reserves ratio rose from 38 to 48. The output/reserves ratio for oil is estimated to have risen from 15 to 21. It should be recalled, however, from Chapter 2 that the revised output/reserve ratios are almost certainly conservative, given the nature of the process of proving up recoverable reserves.

Rows one to four in Table 10.2 show the estimated rents accruing from oil and gas extraction during the period 1981–90. They show that, from a peak in 1981 of 18.3 per cent of GDP (which is 23.7 per cent of *non-oil GDP*, to assist comparison with the estimates of Gelb and Associates (1988) in Chapter 7), the rents averaged 13.2 per cent of GDP in 1982–5 and 7.9 per cent of GDP in 1986–90. Table 10.2 compares three mineral asset depletion measures in lines five to ten, namely (1) the net price; (2) the user cost with a low discount rate; and (3) the user cost with a 10 per cent discount rate. For the reasons given in Chapter 4, the size of the depletion coefficient under the user-cost method is sensitive to the longevity of the reserves and also to the discount rate used. Table 10.3 indicates that the depletion component is smaller the larger the reserves/output ratio and the higher the discount rate. The fraction of the rent which must be assigned to replace the depleting asset under the user-cost method assuming a social discount rate is applied, is no more than two-thirds of the oil rents and no more than one-half the gas rents (Table 10.3). But if a higher, private discount rate of say 10 per cent is adopted, then only 14 per cent of the oil rents and less than 10 per cent of the gas rents must be set aside to account for depletion.

The final three rows of Table 10.2 compare the conventional accounting rate of investment, expressed as a percentage of GDP, with the EDP1 rates, adjusted for mineral asset depletion under both the net price method and private discount user-cost method. The conventional measure is reduced by an average 11.5 per cent of GDP through 1981–90 under the net price measure and by only 1.5 per cent of GDP under the user-cost measure, a divergence of around eightfold between the two indices. The investment figures in Table 10.2 can be adjusted to approximate

Table 10.1 Oil and natural gas depletion, Indonesia, 1981–90

	1981	1982	1983	1984	1985	1986	1987	1988	1989	1990
Oil stocks (m. bls)										
Opening stock	7,850.0	8,011.1	8,301.2	7,913.3	8,223.4	8,192.9	7,470.8	10,298.7	11,054.5	10,899.1
Depletion	584.8	488.2	500.5	517.0	483.8	507.2	491.1	484.1	515.8	528.5
Oil costs ($US/bl)										
Cost	4.4	9.1	7.1	4.8	5.4	4.4	3.6	5.5	3.7	3.7
Price	35.2	34.7	31.0	29.4	27.2	13.8	17.3	17.5	17.4	22.0
Profit	30.8	25.6	23.9	24.6	21.8	9.4	13.7	12.0	13.7	18.3
Gas stocks (b blsoe)										
Opening stock	44.797	42.397	69.810	71.102	83.820	83.638	96.950	96.904	91.449	91.168
Depletion[a]	1.124	1.112	2.236	1.521	1.580	1.629	1.723	1.847	1.988	2.160
Gas costs ($US/bl)										
Cost	0.13	0.05	0.42	0.24	0.21	0.15	0.14	0.29	0.11	0.11
Price	3.59	3.77	3.33	2.45	2.53	2.66	2.11	2.06	1.97	2.49
Profit	3.46	3.72	2.91	2.21	2.32	2.51	1.97	1.77	1.86	2.38

[a] Depletion includes flare gas, internal use as well as sales.

Source: Saleh *et al.* (1993).

Table 10.2 Oil and natural gas depletion coefficients, Indonesia, 1981–90

	1981	1982	1983	1984	1985	1986	1987	1988	1989	1990
Oil rent										
Per barrel (85% profit)	26.2	21.8	20.3	20.9	18.5	8.0	11.6	10.2	11.6	15.6
Total ($bn)	15.32	10.64	10.16	10.81	8.95	4.06	5.70	4.11	5.98	8.24
Gas rent										
Per mcf (65%)	2.25	2.12	1.89	1.43	1.51	1.63	1.28	1.15	1.21	1.55
Total ($bn)[a]	1.40	1.36	1.35	1.47	1.62	2.17	1.52	1.51	1.69	2.38
Depletion cost ($USb)										
Net price	16.72	12.00	11.51	12.28	10.57	6.23	7.22	5.62	7.67	10.62
User cost at 2% discount	10.81	7.70	7.38	7.87	6.71	3.76	4.52	3.47	4.79	6.63
User cost at 10% discount	2.28	1.63	1.56	1.66	1.42	0.79	0.95	0.73	1.01	1.39
Depletion cost (% GDP)										
Net price	18.1	12.7	13.4	14.0	12.1	7.8	9.6	6.7	8.1	10.0
User cost at 2% discount	11.7	8.1	9.5	9.0	7.7	4.7	6.0	4.1	5.1	6.3
User cost at 10% discount	2.5	1.7	1.8	1.9	1.6	1.0	1.3	0.9	1.1	1.3
Investment (% GDP)[b]	33.7	27.9	29.0	29.7	29.8	27.3	32.9	34.0	37.5	32.1
Less net price	15.6	13.2	15.5	15.7	17.7	19.5	23.3	27.3	29.4	22.1
Less user cost at 10% discount	31.2	26.2	27.2	27.8	28.2	26.3	31.9	33.1	36.4	30.8

Sources: Saleh *et al.* (1993); [a] US Embassy (1994); [b] World Bank (1995*a*).

Table 10.3 True income as a percentage of net receipts

Life expectancy of ore reserve (yrs)	Discount rate (%)		
	2	5	10
2	6	14	25
5	11	25	44
10	20	42	65
20	34	64	85
50	64	92	99
100	86	99	100

Source: El Serafy (1989).

the true rate of investment by deducting the rule-of-thumb figure of 10 per cent for the depreciation of produced capital. The true investment rate for the net price method averaged only 6 per cent of GDP during 1981–5, but it rose to average 14 per cent during 1986–90.

Some caveats are in order. First, it should be noted that all of the figures understate the level of investment achieved, to the extent that they all three ignore additions to human and social capital which resulted from the effective Indonesian deployment of its oil windfalls. Second, the utility of the environmental accounting approach as a policy guide is weakened owing to the combination of a lack of consensus on which natural capital depletion to use, the divergence between the different depletion figures, and the neglect of associated changes in the human capital stock.

Trinidad and Tobago oil and gas

Time-series statistics with which to calculate the rents for the hydrocarbon sector in Trinidad and Tobago were not available to the authors. Consequently, recourse was made to industry estimates for the mid-1980s (World Bank 1986) and the mid-1990s (Barrow 1996). It may be recalled from Chapter 7 that the windfalls of Trinidad and Tobago were twice as large, relative to non-mining GDP, as those of Indonesia. When oil prices fell sharply in 1986, Trinidad and Tobago was hit hardest. This is partly because the production costs of both its oil and gas were higher than those of Indonesia, leaving a rent margin per barrel barely half that of Indonesia, and partly because the Caribbean country's oil production declined quite quickly, falling from 176,000 b.p.d. in 1985 to 135,000 b.p.d. in 1995 (IADB 1996) and, unlike Indonesia, its gas production did not expand on a sufficient scale to provide much compensation.

An estimate (Barrow 1996) of the potential rents from a new oilfield coming on stream in Trinidad and Tobago in the late 1990s with oil priced at around $21 per barrel, shows that the production costs of around $12 per barrel, including a 15 per cent return on capital, would absorb 57 per cent of total revenues (compared with 35 per cent for Indonesia based on 1986–90 figures when prices were 20 per cent lower). Taxation at 55 per cent would absorb a further 23 per cent of total revenues, leaving around one-fifth of the revenue as the rent component. If applied to the Trinidad and Tobago national production of around 130,000 b.p.d., this would yield an annual rent stream from oil extraction of $195 million.

A further $123 million in rent is estimated to emanate from the country's natural gas production of 592,000 mcfd which was mainly consumed by fertilizer plants (two-fifths) and electricity generation (one-quarter). The gas rent estimate is based upon 1986 data (World Bank 1986) when prices secured by the principal gas-based consuming industries were similar to those of the early 1990s. The rent estimate assumes an average extraction cost for gas of $0.63 per m.c.f. and an average selling price of $1.20 per m.c.f., based upon an actual price range of $0.93–1.50 per m.c.f.

The figures underline the sensitivity of the natural capital depletion charge to different assumptions concerning the oil and gas reserves. The country's oil reserves of 530 million barrels would last eleven years at prevailing extraction rates (IADB 1996), whereas the gas reserves were 10.6 trillion cubic feet, sufficient to sustain the output levels of the mid-1990s for thirty-eight years and more than three times the estimated life of the oil reserves (IADB 1996). The fraction of the rents to be treated as depletion under the user-cost method at 10 per cent interest would be around two-thirds in the case of oil (Table 10.3), but only 6 per cent for gas.

A significant reduction in the longevity of the gas reserves will occur, however, because of a decision made in 1996 to proceed with a $1 billion LNG plant, due on stream in 2000, together with further expansion of the gas-based industries. The projected expansion will halve the life of the gas reserves. The LNG plant alone will boost gas extraction by an extra 450 million c.f.d. over a twenty-year period (*Financial Times* 1996c). The net effect of the reduction in the longevity of the reserves under the user-cost measure would be to push the depletion share of the natural gas rent up from around 6 per cent to just over 15 per cent . These are still lower figures than either the user-cost depreciation charge for oil, or the net price measure for gas.

Without additional data, it is not possible to project for Trinidad and Tobago either the future rent stream or the gas depletion coefficient. However, earlier comparisons of the potential rents on alternative gas uses suggest that LNG offers potentially the highest rent (Auty and Gelb 1986). But, overall, the rents on natural gas tend to be considerably lower per unit of heat value than those on oil because of the higher costs of transporting gas to the market. These higher transport costs for gas stem from the need for significant processing of the gas prior to export (Auty 1990).

Turning to the implications of the estimates of the oil and gas depletion coefficients for the national accounts of Trinidad and Tobago in the mid-1990s, the combined hydrocarbon rent of $318 million is equivalent to 6.2 per cent of GDP. That figure is the hydrocarbon depletion coefficient under the net price method and compares with 2.6 per cent of GDP for the user-cost measure, with a 10 per cent interest rate. Given a total public investment rate in Trinidad and Tobago in the mid-1990s of less than 2 per cent of GDP, both the depletion figures underscore the fact that the rate of investment by the public sector was unsustainably low.

But another, more general, conclusion to be drawn from the estimates for Trinidad and Tobago is that there is a considerable discrepancy between the net price and user-cost natural capital depletion coefficients when the reserves exceed ten to twenty years of production. Yet such high reserve/production ratios are common in the case of hard minerals. Moreover, hindsight shows that this sometimes turns out to be the case in hydrocarbons. For example, Trinidad and Tobago has had sufficient oil reserves to last for a decade throughout the entire past twenty-five years.[1]

Diamond Rents in Botswana and Namibia

Botswana and Namibia illustrate how natural capital depletion may change through the different stages of the mineral cycle. In the early 1990s, Botswana was completing an especially vigorous youthful stage, whereas Namibia was in the final run-down of its onshore diamond mining. In addition, research by the Bank of Botswana (1994) facilitates a fuller discussion of the concept of net saving, and provides a method for including change in human capital. Finally, Botswana shows that sensible policies for the capture and deployment of the diamond rents may still result in disappointing trends in true saving and productivity growth.

Are the Botswana financial reserves inadequate or excessive?

The Bank of Botswana (1994) determines the true, or net, saving identity as follows:

$$NS = (NFKF + CA) - MR + HC$$

where NS = net saving; $NFKF$ = gross fixed investment minus depreciation; CA = current account balance (net foreign saving); MR = Mineral rent (government mineral revenues); HC = human capital (health and education spending).

The Bank of Botswana adjusts the figures for additions to human capital. It does so by using a rule-of-thumb which attributes to human capital formation some 30 per cent of the expenditure on education and health care. Table 10.4 shows that the long-term trend in Botswana's net saving has been anything but stable and rising: there have been two pulses in net saving since 1977.

The first pulse lifted net saving from 10 per cent of GDP in 1977 to a peak of 27 per cent in 1981 before falling sharply as mineral revenues levelled out, to become

---

[1] The explanation for this apparent imprecision is that it does not pay oil companies to prove up a larger reserve cushion. Both sets of differences, between the depletion coefficients and between the reserve estimates, seriously weaken the utility of the policy lessons to be drawn from the application of natural resource accounting to the mining sector.

Table 10.4 True saving, Botswana, 1977–1993 (Pula, million at 1985 prices)

Year	(1) Mineral revenue	(2) Net fixed capital formation	(3) Current account balance	(4) Net change in endowment expenditure	(5) Health and education recurrent expenditure	(6) Adjusted net change in endowment expenditure	Adjusted net change as % GDP
1977	50	55	29	35	50	85	9.2
1978	74	122	79	127	63	190	17.3
1979	103	174	72	143	68	211	17.5
1980	148	252	82	185	69	254	18.4
1981	164	296	201	332	86	418	27.7
1982	149	259	199	309	104	412	25.4
1983	201	173	42	13	107	121	6.4
1984	362	142	11	−208	120	−89	−4.2
1985	527	253	162	−111	119	8	0.4
1986	647	62	287	−298	120	−178	−7.4
1987	837	223	670	56	144	200	7.6
1988	923	405	724	206	155	362	11.9
1989	961	903	428	369	159	523	15.4
1990	1,007	1,747	202	942	191	1,133	31.2
1991	1,117	1,830	15	728	242	970	24.5
1992	1,015	1,489	151	626	286	912	21.7
1993	910	1,281	135	506	318	825	19.2

Note: (4) = (2) + (3) − (1).
(6) = (4) + (5).

Source: Bank of Botswana (1994: 41).

negative over the years 1983–6. The second cycle reflects the rapid expansion of diamond revenues in the late 1980s which pushed net saving to a new peak of 31 per cent of GDP in 1991 before falling away to 20 per cent. Averaging the cycles gives net saving of 11.1 per cent of GDP for 1977–86 and of 18.8 per cent of GDP for 1987–93. The Bank of Botswana (1994) concludes that the first cycle is well below the true saving rates achieved by, for example, the resource-deficient East Asian newly industrializing countries (NICs) at a similar level of per capita income (see Atkinson *et al.* 1997: 69–98). During the second cycle, true saving remained below the levels achieved by Singapore and South Korea, but not by Hong Kong and Taiwan.

The Bank of Botswana uses total factor productivity growth (TFP) trends for 1975–93 as a second index of sustainability.[2] Rapid productivity growth would indicate desirable upskilling and progress towards self-sustaining economic growth. Taking a three-year running average to smooth out the impact of short-run effects, the data reveal a solid growth rate in TFP of 3.2 per cent for 1978–86, but the rate is –0.4 per cent for 1987–93. This confirms that the sharply increased rent steam of the late 1980s was associated with a marked decline in investment efficiency, as noted in Chapter 7. The Bank of Botswana concludes that the country relied heavily on mineral rents to enhance its wealth and that the negative productivity change during a period of rapid accumulation of reserves is ominous.

Wright (1995) uses such evidence to support the 'cautious' strategy for deploying the $4.5 billion financial reserves which was discussed in Chapter 9: any expenditure from the reserves should be in line with the capacity of the economy (and the government) to effectively transform them into produced and human capital. He calls for government expenditure to remain in step with recurrent revenue growth while the reserves are deployed to human and physical formation. Such investments must meet two basic conditions: first, to generate an adequate threshold rate of return; and, second, to lie within the implementation capacity of the government.

The 'cautious' financial strategy has the theoretical appeal of maintaining total capital by transforming 'natural' capital into human and physical capital (Bank of Botswana 1994). But three criticisms of the cautious strategy were noted in Chapter 9: it ignores the weakening of the consensus in favour of caution (Valentine 1993; Chambers 1995; Denevad 1995), the investments have long gestation periods, and are likely to overburden the State. A fourth criticism is that the cautious strategy uses the net price method to estimate natural capital depletion.

Table 10.5 shows the stream of rents from Botswana diamonds. The rent stream is estimated on the assumption that the rents comprised 61 per cent of diamond exports, a figure calculated for the early 1990s based upon the annual accounts of Debswana (1994).[3] The true level of investment is also estimated by deducting a rule-of-thumb

---

[2] This is estimated as the constant term in the standard Cobb–Douglas production function with 1975 as the base year.

[3] This figure is broadly in line with an estimate for the early 1980s made by Harvey and Lewis (1990). Although it may be somewhat high for the late 1970s, prior to the start-up of the productive Jwaneng mine, the distortionary impact of any overestimation is reduced by the fact that the rents were only a modest fraction of GDP at that time.

10 per cent of GNP from the gross investment ratio (for the depletion of produced capital) and adding in the annual change in reserves. This allows a comparison to be made between the true investment figure and the adjusted figures after allowing for diamond depletion by both the net price and user-cost methods. The final two columns in Table 10.5 provide estimates of the user-cost depletion coefficients under social and private discount rates.

The diamond reserves are estimated by Debswana (personal communication) to exceed fifty years at the rate of production in the mid-1990s. Table 10.5 shows that, even if a social discount rate is used, the depletion component under the user-cost method is no more than one-third of the rents. The bulk of Botswana's mineral revenues could therefore be regarded as true income, and virtually all of it would be true income if the private discount rate is applied. Consequently, the rate of saving (estimated at 40 per cent of the rents in Chapter 7) appears to have been too high. However, the rate of saving in Botswana had more to do with domestic absorptive capacity than with accounting for the depleting asset (personal communication, C. Harvey).

It is difficult to accept such a low depletion component, a figure which is based on theory and neglects the real-world uncertainty. Gem diamond prices are set by a cartel and reflect fashion: they may not hold over the medium term and long term. Moreover, the difficulties experienced in the mature stage of the cycle by other small mineral economies with limited non-mineral resource endowments, and not least neighbouring Namibia, make a case for adjusting the user-cost depletion coefficient. This can be done, as noted in Chapter 4, by setting a ceiling of one generation on the life of the reserves. In the case of Botswana, this would lift the user-cost coefficient above 10 per cent of the rents with a private discount rate, still well below the country's actual rate of reserve accumulation. This perspective strengthens the 'pragmatic' approach to the use of the financial reserves which, as discussed in Chapter 9, would seek to strengthen the role of the hitherto neglected informal sector as an incubator of businesses and of business skills.

Diamond depletion in the Namibian economy

Namibia presents a very different situation from that of Botswana as onshore diamond mining nears the end of its commercial life. A transition must be made to offshore production, for which the mining technology has still to be fully established. Rents on the almost depleted Namibian onshore diamond reserves are small and well below those for Botswana. Calculations based on published figures (CDM 1994) suggest that the Namibian rents were no more than 5 per cent of revenues in the early 1990s, after allowing for a 15 per cent return on the total produced assets of the new joint-venture Namdeb, estimated to be around $500 million (Auty 1996*b*).

If that estimate is correct, the rents from onshore diamond mining would yield barely $17 million in 1990. Given the marginal nature of other mining activity in Namibia at that time (uranium and base metals), this implies that the total mineral rent, including non-diamond production, was no more than $25 million in the early

Table 10.5 Estimated diamond rent and asset depletion coefficient, Botswana, 1976–1993

Year	Estimated rent		Investment (% GNP)				Depletion component		
	(Pula bill)[a]	(% GNP)	Gross	Net[b]	Reserves[c]	True[d]	Net price	User	Cost
								2% discount	10% discount
1976	0.022	8.1	38.3	28.3	0.7	28.3	8.1	2.9	0.1
1977	0.028	8.6	28.1	18.1	6.7	24.8	8.6	2.9	0.1
1978	0.047	12.0	34.6	24.6	10.9	35.5	12.0	4.1	0.1
1979	0.110	21.2	34.9	24.9	18.5	43.4	21.2	7.2	0.2
1980	0.142	19.8	37.7	27.7	8.5	36.2	19.8	6.7	0.2
1981	0.082	9.5	40.6	30.6	−8.2	22.4	9.5	2.2	0.1
1982	0.151	16.9	43.6	33.6	4.1	37.7	16.9	5.7	0.2
1983	0.277	25.2	30.1	20.1	10.1	30.2	25.2	8.6	0.3
1984	0.390	28.7	26.3	16.3	7.0	23.3	28.7	9.8	0.3
1985	0.629	38.5	30.4	20.4	30.7	51.1	38.5	13.1	0.4
1986	0.736	35.1	16.2	6.2	36.3	42.5	35.1	11.9	0.4
1987	1.351	52.8	23.8[a]	13.8	61.2	75.0	52.8	18.0	0.5
1988	1.180	35.6	15.6	5.6	10.2	15.8	35.6	12.1	0.4
1989	1.717	35.1	19.1	9.1	23.7	32.8	35.1	11.9	0.4
1990	1.568	27.2	32.3	22.3	18.2	40.5	27.2	9.2	0.3
1991	1.765	26.2	32.0	22.0	10.9	32.9	26.2	8.9	0.3
1992	1.739	21.8	29.4	19.4	1.9	21.3	21.8	7.4	0.2
1993	2.003	23.9	26.6	16.6	8.2	24.8	23.9	8.1	0.2

[a] Estimated at 61% of export data in Jefferis (1996).
[b] Less 10% depreciation.
[c] World Bank (1995a) net annual charge.
[d] True investment = Gross invested − 10% GNP + reserves.

Source: World Bank (1995); Jefferis (1996).

1990s, or 1.2 per cent of GNP. Under the user-cost approach, assuming a ten-year figure for onshore diamond reserves in line with Namibian expectations, the depletion component on diamond mining would be 0.6 per cent of GNP with a *social* discount rate, and 0.3 per cent of GNP with a 10 per cent discount rate.

However, if offshore diamond mining is technically and environmentally feasible, the future mineral rents may be substantially higher. Assuming, after Miller (1995), that the cost of a vessel is $60 million, the annual extraction rate 125,000 carats at $325/carat, and the annual operating costs $11 million, then the rents would be around 24 per cent of total diamond revenues. However, if the user-cost method of natural asset depletion is adopted, the depletion coefficient shrinks because the offshore reserves are likely to be very substantial. Yet, here, as with Botswana, it would seem imprudent to treat the greater part of the diamond rents as true income. A compromise is justified between the inflexibility of the net price index and the profligacy sanctioned by the user-cost method in cases where the reserves/output ratio is high.

Accounting for Bauxite Depletion in Jamaica

Jamaica confirms the problems for environmental accounting that arise from the absence of a consensus on the depletion index and the uncertainty over the longevity of the reserves. It also illustrates another difficulty which arises from the fact that the rents are contested. The rents can accrue to governments in the form of taxes, to consumers through lower prices, to the workers through higher wages, and to the mining corporations as the return on the scarce corporate skills which make mining possible (Crowson 1994). As a result, it is useful to distinguish between the *potential* mineral rent and the *residual* mineral rent which accrues to the owner of the resource.

The *potential* rent is calculated by deducting the average cost of national production from the long-run global marginal cost of production, each set of costs including a risk-adjusted after-tax return on capital. The long-run marginal cost of global production is set by the price required for a new entrant to set up production. As noted in Chapter 2, where ownership of the mineral is vested in the State, adroit tax policies can capture the rent for the government. But even so leakage is likely to occur due to parties other than the mineral owner successfully contesting the rent, leaving the owner with the *residual* rent.

Mine workers have often captured a fraction of the potential rent in higher wages. This occurs because the typically small size of the mine labour force has an inherently modest role within the cost structure but wields the power to inflict heavy losses by halting production in a capital-intensive operation with high fixed costs. In the case of the Jamaican bauxite/alumina sector, wages and salaries in 1990 were $66 million (SIJ 1994) out of a sector revenue of over $580 million. The bauxite workers captured between $6 million to $22 million in rents, depending on whether their wages are assumed to be 10 or 50 per cent, respectively, above the shadow wage rate. But, as is shown in Chapter 11, that wage premium may also be conceptualized as a true cost to the industry which reflects the need to compensate workers for hazardous job conditions and/or for their isolation.

However, by far the most important beneficiary of bauxite rents since the 1960s has been the alumina consumer. This situation has arisen as a result of the installation of excess alumina capacity prior to the 1973 oil shock. The first oil shock sharply cut the growth of aluminium demand in the industrial countries and for the next two decades the surplus capacity depressed alumina prices. Producers expanded to reduce their average costs by capturing the scale economies and met additional demand by low-cost brown-field capacity expansion. Few greenfield alumina plants were built. As recently as 1990, a relatively good year for producers, the average alumina price for Jamaica was $222 per tonne (POIJ 1994) compared with the $320 per tonne price required to justify investment by an efficient new global producer (providing the marginal cost). Alcan estimates that the scope for low-cost brown-field expansion will not be exhausted before the year 2000.

The surplus alumina capacity meant that the residual rent on Jamaican bauxite and alumina in 1990 was barely one-third of the potential rent. The rent figure is derived by subtracting the average cost of production for the Jamaican alumina refineries (Table 10.6) from the long-run marginal cost of a new entrant. Assuming a conversion ratio of 2.5 tonnes bauxite per tonne alumina, the potential rent was $139 per tonne of alumina ($56 per tonne of bauxite). The actual realized price for Jamaican alumina in 1990 yields a unit rent of only $41 per tonne of alumina ($16 per tonne of bauxite). The total residual rent in 1990 was $181 million compared with $618 million of *potential* rent (Table 10.6).[4]

Table 10.7 uses the rent estimates to assess the sensitivity of the Jamaican national accounts to environmental accounting. It suggests that the correction required to the national accounts is a very modest one, even if the net price method is used. For example, the 2 per cent of GDP adjustment under the net price is well short of the adjustments made by Hamilton and O'Connor (1994) for a group of non-fuel primary product exporters. If the user-cost principle is applied, however, the longevity of the Jamaican bauxite reserves cuts the adjustment to negligible levels. This is because the estimated bauxite reserves are 2 billion tonnes, a figure which has not fallen since mining began in 1952, despite the depletion of 324.4 million tonnes in the intervening years (JBI 1992).

Yet another factor which makes the reserve life estimate somewhat subjective, is the choice of an appropriate extraction rate. For example, the annual bauxite extraction rate averaged 8.32 million tonnes and peaked at 15 million tonnes in the early 1970s. If it is assumed that output returned to its peak level and stabilized there,

---

[4] But, in fact, the Jamaican government received considerably less than this. It received $129.2 million in total which comprised just over $100 million in rent ($6.45 million royalties and $93.92 million for the bauxite levy), the remaining $29 million comprising corporation tax. The discrepancy between the government receipts and the estimated residual rents may reflect poor transparency in the reporting of tax breaks and government revenues for the sector.

Table 10.6 Estimated potential and actual rent on Jamaican bauxite, 1990

	Output (million tonnes)	Cost ($US/tonne)			Rent ($US/tonne)		Total rent ($m)	
		Operating	capital	total	Price $330	$222	Price $330	$222
Alumina refinery								
Alcan Ewarton } Alcan Kirkvine }	0.975	133	39	172	148	50		
Alcoa	0.706	126	39	165	155	57		
Alpart	1.188	160	39	199	121	23		
Sector	2.869	142	39	181	139	41	399	118
Kaiser bauxite mine	3.911	n/a	n/a	20	56	16	219	63
Total	10.921[a]				56	16	618	181

[a] tonnes bauxite.

Sources: IBA for output and production costs; Planning Institute of Jamaica (1994) for prices.

Table 10.7 Adjustment of Jamaican national accounts for bauxite depletion, 1990

	GDP	NDP[a]	EDP1 User cost	EDP1 Net price
Total economic output ($USbn)	4.242	3.945	n/a	n/a
Bauxite/alumina output ($USbn)	0.390	0.351[b]	0.326	0.176
Saving ($USbn)	1.164	0.867	0.842[c]	0.666[c]
Saving (% adjusted output)	27	20	20	16

[a] Less 7% GDP depletion of produced capital, as advised by SIJ.
[b] Less $39.52 million actual sector figure supplied by SIJ.
[c] Corrected for bauxite depletion only, based on Table 10.6.
Source: Statistical Institute of Jamaica (1994).

the remaining reserves would last 133 years. This adjustment lifts the fraction of the rent which is true income to more than 99 per cent at interest rates over 5 per cent, and it is 86 per cent if a social interest rate is selected. Even with the latter figure, the user-cost depletion coefficient is still barely one-seventh that calculated by the net price method. The gap between the net price and user-cost coefficients closes, however, if a lower (one generation) reserve figure is used.

Finally, environmental accounting sheds light on Jamaica's decision to impose a bauxite levy at the time of the first oil shock. The marginal cost of a new entrant into alumina refining in the early 1970s was $120 per tonne (Hashimoto 1982). The older Alcan refineries had production costs around $61 per tonne which yielded rents on the old amortized plants (Auty 1983). In contrast, the new Alpart refinery required a price around $72 per tonne, the average price of Jamaican alumina exports during 1970–3. But to be competitive at this price, the new Alpart refinery required accelerated depreciation and tax breaks on account of its higher capital service charges compared with the established plants. The tax breaks were granted on the expectation of compensating higher long-term government revenues. In the event, start-up problems pushed the costs of all three new refineries above their targets.

Table 10.8 suggests that alumina consumers already captured the bulk of the potential rents in the early 1970s, in terms of alumina priced below the costs of a new (marginal) entrant. This implies that incentives which Jamaica and other governments (including Britain) provided at that time to encourage aluminium expansion exacerbated a tendency to surplus capacity and low returns. The imposition by Jamaica of the bauxite levy resulted in sizeable losses by new entrants. The aluminium companies judged the $11 per tonne levy to be twice the residual rent on the country's bauxite. Under the net price method and with a rent of $5.5 per tonne of bauxite, environmental accounting would deflate 1973 GNP by 3.7 per cent. But the adjustment would be only 0.5 per cent of GNP with the user-cost method with a twenty-year reserves cap and either a social rate of discount or a 10 per cent discount rate.

Table 10.8 Estimated potential and actual rents on Jamaican bauxite, 1973

	Output (million tonnes)	Cost ($/tonne)	Unit rent ($US/tonne)		Total rent ($USm)	
			Price $120	$72	Price $120	$72
Refineries						
Alcan Ewarton	1.126	61.00	59.00	13.00		
Alcan Kirkvine	0.507	n/a	n/a	n/a		
Alcoa	0.507	n/a	n/a	n/a		
Alpart	0.979	100.00	20	−28.00		
Revere	0.167	n/a	n/a	n/a		
Subsector 1970–3	2.020	79.00	41.00	−10.60	82.82	−14.4
Export mining	7.490	20.00	16.40	−2.80	176.76	−20.97
Total	12.656	n/a	n/a		259.58	−35.11

Notes: 1973 GDP = $US1.892bn.
    Rent = $US0.070bn (at $US5.50/tonne on 12.656m tonnes).
    Net price asset depletion = 3.7% GDP.
    User-cost asset depletion = 0.5% GDP at 2% interest.

Sources: Harhimoto (1982); Karim (1968); JBI (1994).

Copper Asset Depletion

Copper mines vary widely in their competitiveness and therefore in the rents which they provide: data assembled by Pincock, Allen & Holt Inc. (1995) on a cash-cost basis, i.e. excluding capital charges, rank 217 mines in order of viability. A handful of mines outside the countries in this study operated with by-product credits that more than compensated for the costs of the copper mine. Most of the new SX/EW process mines had very low net costs of 20–36c per lb, but Grasberg (Indonesia) emerges as the largest low-cost mine, thanks to by-product credits of 44c per lb which pushed its net cost down to 12.9c per lb. The two large PNG mines were estimated to have net costs of 37–43c per lb and relied on sizeable by-product credits to offset relatively high mining and concentrate transport costs. Within Chile, a sharp contrast emerges between the state-of-the-art Escondida mine, with net costs estimated at 26c per lb and the mines of state-owned Codelco, whose costs ranged between 55c and 73c per lb.

    Cost data available for 1990 from the Bureau of Mines (1991) suggest that the copper price required to justify investment by an efficient new entrant was 99c per lb. This figure is taken as the marginal cost from which to estimate the rent. The estimate assumes an operating cost of 41c per lb and a capital charge which assumes an investment of $5,200 per tonne, depreciated over ten years, which earns a 15 per cent return on capital and is taxed at 33.3 per cent. On this basis, Codelco had average costs in 1990 of 72c per lb; the Peruvian state-owned Centromin had

Table 10.9 Mineral depletion: net price and user-cost comparison, PNG, 1985–90

	Net price method			User-cost method		
	Depletion ($m)	mining value added (%)	GDP (%)	Depletion ($m)	mining value added (%)	GDP (%)
1985	74.1	31.0	3.4	8.8	3.7	0.4
1986	130.6	38.4	5.5	16.7	4.9	0.6
1987	230.9	42.8	8.2	43.6	8.1	1.4
1988	123.6	17.4	3.7	28.3	4.0	0.8
1989	28.4	7.1	0.9	10.4	2.6	0.3
1990	189.6	47.8	6.5	37.5	7.5	1.2

Note: Annual fluctuations reflect prices changes and closure of Panguna in 1989.
Source: Bartelmus *et al.* (1992: 18 and 20).

costs of 80c per lb (World Bank 1994*b*); while the debt-burdened Ok Tedi mine in PNG was not expected to earn a taxable profit for a decade.

PNG has been the subject of two major economic studies on environmental accounting. Table 10.9 draws upon Bartelmus *et al.* (1992) who estimate the depletion coefficient by the net price method and also by the user-cost method using a 10 per cent discount. The net price method yields figures which range from 7.1 to 47.8 per cent of mining added-value, compared with only 2.6 to 9.5 per cent under the user-cost method. The net price method calls for a downward adjustment in GDP of between 0.9 and 8.2 per cent, depending on the year and prices, whereas downward adjustments of only 0.4 to 1.4 per cent are required by the user-cost method.

Duncan *et al.* (1995) estimate the impact of natural capital depletion for net savings in PNG for the period 1984–94 (Table 10.10). They combine minerals with forest resources and assume the depreciation of produced capital absorbs 10 per cent of GDP and that the forest resource is non-renewable. They recognize the problem of rent leakage, discussed earlier with reference to Jamaica, and conclude that they underestimate the depletion coefficient because they use government revenues as a measure of rent which neglects leakages to loggers and landowners. Table 10.10 shows the volatility of the natural capital depletion coefficients: they rose during the copper boom of the late 1980s, fell abruptly on the closure of Panguna, and then rose as gold and oil production expanded and timber prices increased.

Table 10.10 also shows a pronounced fall in true investment in the mid-1990s. Duncan *et al.* (1995) attribute this decline to the loss of investor confidence in macroeconomic management (see Chapter 7). That factor, combined with the depletion of produced capital and environmental capital, turns net investment in PNG negative in 1994. Table 10.10 therefore reveals a heightened dependence upon the consumption of natural capital during the early 1990s' commodity boom. The PNG reserves of copper, gold, and oil, all appear to be relatively small (but, as elsewhere, the reserve

Table 10.10 Adjustment of investment for capital depletion, PNG, 1984–94 (% GDP)

	1984	1985	1986	1987	1988	1989	1990	1991	1992	1993	1994
Gross investment	23.8	18.3	21.2	19.2	23.1	25.6	24.6	27.7	23.5	18.5	16.2
Consumption of											
produced capital	9.4	9.0	9.2	9.0	8.7	10.3	10.7	11.3	10.6	9.8	9.8
Depletion of mineral											
and forest	2.6	1.3	1.6	2.1	3.0	3.9	0.3	0.7	2.2	6.7	7.4
Net investment	11.8	8.0	10.4	8.1	11.4	11.4	13.6	15.7	10.7	2.0	–1.1

Source: Duncan *et al.* (1995).

Table 10.11 Adjustment of Chilean national accounts for copper depletion, 1990

	GDP	NDP	EDP1 user cost		EDP1 net price
			10% interest	2%	
Economy output ($bn)	30.17	28.06	28.02	27.49	26.77
Mining output ($bn)	2.20	1.82[a]	1.78[b]	1.25[c]	0.57[d]
Saving ($bn)	7.46	5.35	5.32	4.78	4.10
Saving (% GDP)	24.7	19.1	19.0	17.6	14.94

[a] Applies Codelio depreciation rate (11/lb) to industry as a whole.
[b] Depletion charge = 3% net revenue.
[c] Depletion charge = 36% net revenue.
[d] Depletion charge = 100% net revenue.
Source: ECLA (1994).

figures are not firm numbers). This implies high depletion coefficients for PNG even if the user-cost coefficient is adopted. This conclusion reinforces the case made in Chapters 7 and 9 for assigning the capital component of the PNG mineral rents to a strengthened MRSF.

The Chilean rents, in contrast to PNG, have been captured and sterilized in a MRSF since the mid-1980s. In 1990, the average cost of Codelco production implied a *potential* rent of 27c per lb but, when adjusted for the realized price of copper, the rent component rises to 36c per lb. That figure yielded total rents of $1.28 billion on the country's 1990 copper output of 1.58 million tonnes, implying a depletion component under the net price method equivalent to 4.2 per cent of GNP (Table 10.11). The user cost calculation, based upon a World Bank (1994*e*) estimate that Chilean copper reserves are sufficient for fifty-two years pushes true income above 97 per cent of the rents using the 10 per cent discount rate.[5] This yields a depletion coeffi-

[5] The reserves were estimated at 194 million tonnes and their longevity assumes production expands and then stabilizes at 3.7 million tonnes in 2,000.

cient of barely 0.1 per cent of GNP, although the coefficient rises to 0.6 per cent of GNP if a twenty-year cap on reserves is applied. But with a social discount rate, true income falls to 64 per cent of net revenue and the depletion coefficient rises to 1.5 per cent of GNP, while the adjusted saving rate drops to 14.9 per cent of GDP and is barely two-thirds of the conventional accounting measure.

Finally, in Peru, natural capital was wastefully exploited even as the man-made capital with which it was produced was allowed to run down. The Peruvian mining sector was very rundown in 1990 as a result of over two decades of macromismanagement (see Chapter 8). The largest state-owned firms, Petroperu and Centromin, had been decapitalized and the MNCs which had escaped state ownership like SPCC and Occidental had skimped on their investment. Exploration and development had been neglected, so that Peru reverted to the status of an oil importer and also lost market share in hard minerals. In the late 1980s, the Peruvian mining sector was on an unsustainable path but data deficiencies preclude meaningful measurement. The country's efforts to refurbish the mining sector are better-documented, however, and they are analysed in Chapter 11.

It should be noted that in the above analysis of mineral depletion, we have not dealt with the impact of the mineral industries on the quality of the environment (DQR) or with expenditures to restore or prevent deterioration of the environment (PR). These aspects were identified in Chapter 4 as being deducted from GDP in order to determine EDP2, an estimate of the net domestic product fully corrected for natural resource and environmental depletion. The calculation of EDP2 requires more data than we have available, although some costs of environmental damage abatement are estimated in Chapter 11. It should be noted, however, that if DQR and PR are taken into account, EDP2 is lower than EDP1, mineral rent is lower, and the amount of saving and investment required to compensate for the loss of both natural resource and environmental capital is higher in order to assure sustainable EDP2.

Conclusions

The net price method of accounting for mineral asset depletion requires substantial adjustments to the conventional accounts when applied to high-rent minerals such as oil and diamonds. The pattern in the adjusted accounts over the mineral-led cycle from renewed youth to late maturity, is illustrated by Indonesia, the country with the most complete mineral rent figures. After an initial large divergence of EDP1 from conventional GDP during the renewal of the youthful stage (first reflecting the revaluation of the mineral asset and then asset depletion), effective deployment of the rents to diversify the economy through the mature stage of the mineral cycle narrows the gap.

But the user-cost approach yields a much smaller gap between GNP and EDP1, especially if a private discount rate is applied and the reserves/output ratio is high. This divergence weakens the utility of environmental accounting as a policy guide in the absence of a consensus on which is the more appropriate measure, the net price or user-cost. An additional problem arises for the user-cost measure from the fact that the reserve estimates are imprecise. This problem is most acute for the hard-mineral economies which often have large reserves. Basically, the user-cost method of mineral asset depletion requires very limited saving where a 10 per cent discount rate is used and reserves exceed forty years' supply.

It seems appropriate, however, to apply a rule which caps the reserve figure at twenty years, given the uncertainty which a long time-horizon necessarily implies about technological trends and future supply and demand. But such a rule introduces yet another discretionary element into environmental accounting, along with those relating to reserve estimates, the difference between potential and residual rents, and the incorporation of human capital accumulation. This weakens the policy value of environmental accounting. Nevertheless, failure to take account of mineral depletion could lead to policy decisions based on an understatement of the amount of investment required for sustainable development. We therefore conclude that the user-cost approach, adjusted through a cap on reserves and interest rates, as discussed in Chapter 4, is the preferred measure.

11 Internalizing Environmental Degradation Costs

This chapter reviews the environmental impacts of the larger private and state mines and monitors their progress in internalizing the costs of environmental damage. After an initial discussion of the principal factors at work in encouraging pollution abatement, the chapter discusses the three major pollution problems in turn: land rehabilitation, water pollution abatement, and the control of air-borne emissions.

As was noted in Chapter 5, the costs of environmental damage from mining must be covered by increased investment if the economy is to be fully sustainable, since environmental damage is, like mineral depletion, a reduction of capital unless the damage is restored or offset by other capital investment. But no attempt is made to adjust the national accounts by deducting the costs of environmental degradation from the EDP1 figures calculated in Chapter 10. The reason for this is that the costing of environmental damage poses greater problems than is the case with asset depletion. This is because even less progress has been made with standardizing the costing of environmental damage (Hamilton 1996). In addition, data deficiencies preclude the provision of uniform coverage of all the mining operations in each country studied.

It may be recalled from Chapter 5 that the position adopted here is that the costs of abating the environmental degradation arising from mining should be internalized by the firm, but only up to the point at which the rising marginal social costs of abatement equal the marginal social benefits. The degree of abatement is therefore linked to the environmental absorptive capacity which is a function of regional ecology and population density. But concern for the protection of less densely settled areas increased through the 1980s, largely in response to activism over rainforest destruction. The environmental damage from mining impacts the supply of environmental services; biologically based livelihoods and health; the maintenance of cultural and recreational resources; and the resilience of the global pollution sinks. The global issue is excluded from the present discussion, however, because it is more appropriately addressed at the international level rather than at the national level which is the focus here.

The emphasis in this chapter is upon the nature of the environmental impacts: the identification of the order of magnitude of the costs of environmental damage; the degree to which those costs have been internalized; and the implications for sustainable mining. Afsah *et al.* (1996) argue that differences between countries in the level of pollution abatement arise from the interaction between national governments, local communities, and companies. Three principal conclusions are emerging about pollution abatement in the developing countries, namely that:

- it is more likely to be accorded priority, the more soundly managed the economy and the higher the per capita income (World Bank 1992*b*);
- formal government intervention to abate pollution is likely to be preceded by community pressure for damage abatement (Pargal and Wheeler 1996); and
- multinational companies (MNCs) lead other firms in pollution abatement, often under pressure from local communities and international capital (Warhurst 1994*a*).

The evidence presented in this study contributes to the testing and refinement of these emerging conclusions.

Bernstam (1991) demonstrates that as per capita incomes rise in market economies, the intensity with which they use energy and materials, and also the rate at which the emit pollutants, at first increases and then declines. This 'inverted U-shape' or Kuznets curve reflects the changing structure of the economy (as countries first build up the infrastructure of a modern economy and then spend an increasing fraction of their income on services), technological change and a growing preference for a cleaner environment (Dasgupta *et al*. 1995). Reductions in the pollution-intensity of GDP have historically preceded an increase in government concern for the environment, so that the subsequent adoption of policies to correct market failure has served to accelerate this process (World Bank 1992*b*). Grossman (1995) records the historical downturn of the U-shape for a range of pollutants. The downturn in suspended particulates and sulphur dioxide emissions, for example, occurs around a per capita income level of $5,000 (measured in $US purchasing power parity). This is the per capita income in the early 1990s of Chile, the wealthiest country in our sample.

The initial reaction of the developing country governments to pollution problems tended to favour command-and-control measures. Many adopted emission standards in the 1970s which were modelled on developed-country practice but they invariably lacked the administrative capacity and political will to enforce them. More recently, the World Bank (1994*d*) has shown that targeting large point sources with presumptive emission charges can achieve a sizeable abatement with a minimum of administrative input. As large polluters, mines and refineries attracted increasing attention through the late 1980s as the second wave of global environmental concern gained momentum. But, as noted in Chapter 5, global capital markets also exerted pressure on large mining firms to abate pollution by making sound environmental practice a condition for loan dispersement. Some companies had already reacted to government policy failure by negotiating with local communities over pollution. In doing so, they often applied their own corporate emission standards without being required to, mainly in anticipation of tighter standards and possible litigation over clean-ups (Warhurst 1994*a*).

In contrast to the MNCs, many SOEs and smaller domestic private firms tended to delay best practice. Although cleaner technology can cut emissions very substantially and new plants can often abate pollution at low cost (Jaffe *et al*. 1995), it is costly to back-fit technology to older mines and refineries when investment has been neglected (Warhurst 1994*a*). For example, a one-third cut in sulphur gas emissions requires a $50 million investment in an acid plant, but to achieve global best practice (over 97 per cent reduction) costs several times as much because the refinery must be replaced (World Bank 1994*b*). Consequently, if environmental regulation is imposed too quickly, long-established mines and refineries may shut and leave no one with liability for cleaning up. Governments must therefore recognize that the type of mining enterprise affects the speed of abatement and be flexible in applying emission curbs.

Mine-Site Rehabilitation

The principal mining regions in this study range through the arid areas of coastal Peru and the Andean plateaux, the semi-arid Central Valley of Chile, the moist limestone plateaux of Jamaica, and the high-rainfall tropical highlands of New Guinea (and some high-rainfall tropical lowlands in Borneo and the Amazon basin). The importance attached to land rehabilitation is strongly linked to population pressure which largely reflects precipitation and topography, and ranges from over 227 per km^2 in tiny Jamaica, through 64 per km^2 in southern Borneo, and 9 per km^2 in mountainous PNG, to the virtually uninhabited desert regions of South America.

Densely settled Jamaica

Land scarcity and the juxtaposition of mines and farms in Jamaica focused government attention early on land reclamation and legal requirements were set for rehabilitation from the start-up of bauxite mining. The Mining Regulation Act of 1947 explicitly required reclamation and restoration of productive activity 'as soon as may be practical after mining operations are concluded' (IBA 1992). In practice this required the companies to secure certificates both for mine reclamation and for the restoration of land use. The sanctions were relatively weak, however, so that corporate pride and self-interest were more important spurs to compliance (IBA 1992). For example, the fine imposed for non-compliance was only $75 until 1988 when it was raised to $4,500 plus mandatory expenditure on reclamation (JBI 1992).

Prior to 1974, the mining companies had either bought or leased land and they had acquired around 81,000 ha, about 8 per cent of the country's land area (Weir 1982). But in that year the government purchased all the company land at book value except for the 3,600 ha on which the plant and equipment was sited. The government then renegotiated the mining leases so that each company had sufficient land for thirty to forty years of operation (IBA 1992). The reserves for a typical 4 million tonne per annum mine like Kaiser Jamaica Bauxite (KJBC), extended over almost 130 km^2. During twenty-five years of mining KJBC mined 428 ha and disturbed a total of 985 ha.

Jamaican bauxite occurs on the country's central plateau (Figure 11.1). It is situated in pockets of limestone near the surface which contain from 25,000 tonnes up to 1 million tonnes (Figure 11.2). There is relatively little overburden to remove

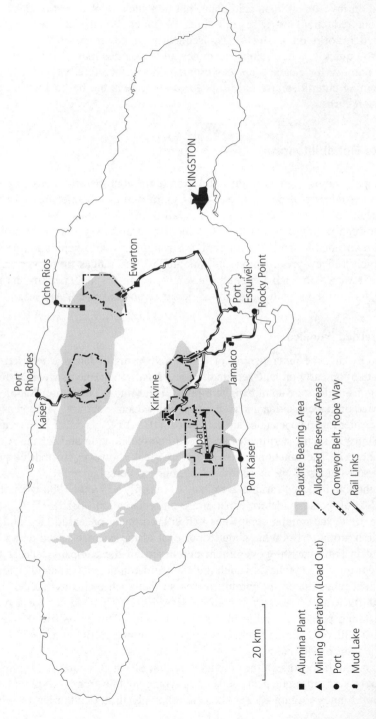

Figure 11.1 Distribution of mining activity in Jamaica

KINGSTON

Ewarton

Ocho Rios

Port Esquivel

Rocky Point

Port Rhoades

Kaiser

Kirkvine

Jamalco

Alpart

Port Kaiser

20 km

■ Alumina Plant

▲ Mining Operation (Load Out)

● Port

⬤ Mud Lake

Bauxite Bearing Area

Allocated Reserves Areas

Conveyor Belt, Rope Way

Rail Links

Figure 11.2 Pattern of bauxite occurrence in Jamaica

and most of the material displaced by mining can easily be restored. The high moisture content of the ore and the lack of toxic chemical elements help to reduce, but do not eliminate, dust problems. The bauxite soils are relatively infertile with a low humus content and high risk of erosion where slopes exceed 5° (Wellington 1986). Crop yields are inherently low, but they can be improved with careful attention and scientific farming practices.

Early reclamation of mined land rarely left yields as high as previously. Studies suggest that pH levels are higher on reclaimed land (7.7 compared with 6.1) while organic content is lower (1.1 per cent compared with 3.5 per cent) and water-retention capacity is reduced (World Bank 1993*b*). Data for 1982–5 indicate that even pastoral activity is sensitive to mining, with productivity likely to be lower on reclaimed land. Comparisons of mined and unmined land revealed that cattle-stocking rates were one-third lower on reclaimed land; that milk yields were 25 per cent lower; but that beef yields were only 5 per cent less (Wellington 1986). Restoration to pasture tended to be preferred even over crops with shallow roots, let alone deep-rooted citrus trees. This was especially true in the drier northern areas where grazing was the norm in the absence of irrigation.

Low productivity may not indicate significant loss of output compared to pre-mine conditions, however, because the bulk of the land acquired by the mining companies was under pasture on large estates which used the land extensively, unlike the resettled peasant farmers (Salmon 1987). Moreover, the companies improved the reclamation techniques for mined-out bauxite land in the 1980s in response to local community complaints (Neufville 1993). Previous measures involved storing the top soil during mining and replacing it to a depth of 15 to 30 cm only. In addition, the soil had been restored only to the bottom of the mined-out pit and vegetation was left to recover on its own so that rain erosion prior to vegetative regeneration could remove up to half the restored top soil (ibid.). This restricted subsequent land use because a soil depth of 15 cm will only support pasture whereas 45 cm are required for cropping and 60 cm for fruit trees (Weir 1982). Under the new practices, at least 30 cm of topsoil were restored and in order to improve the organic structure, grasses were planted during the first two years and both chemical and organic nutrients (such as chicken manure) were added. Slopes were also graded to smooth out the sides of the mined-out hollows where this could be done.

Restoration practice within Jamaica reflects differences in local population pressure. The newer mines in the south (Figure 11.1) displace mostly peasant farmers who need to squeeze as much as possible from their smallholdings, so that crop restoration rather than pasture is required. Most peasant farms are mixed comprising livestock, cash crops, and citrus trees. Yields on reclaimed land can exceed pre-mining levels if the companies provide extension services (JBI 1992). Evidence of the success of improved reclamation comes from displaced farmers who, even on the dry pasture of the northern coast, request resettlement on mined-out land, rather than on undisturbed land provided by the companies.

The costs of land rehabilitation are low in relation to total production costs. Alcoa estimates the cost at around $25,000 per ha. This figure is based on charges for earth-moving equipment (which comprise around two-thirds of the cost assuming a usage rate of 50 hours per ha) and the costs of crop restoration. Although this figure may be 30–40 per cent below the 'full cost' due to the exclusion of any overhead charge, the addition of a 30 per cent overhead charge leaves the reclamation cost still modest at 16c per tonne bauxite (which is around 37c per tonne of alumina and less than $1 per tonne of aluminium). The 16c per tonne figure compares with the royalty of 59c per tonne of bauxite which the MNCs pay to the government (IBA 1992).

An industry-wide annual charge can be calculated from these estimates. The Jamaican bauxite sector restores 200 ha of mined-out land annually at a cost of $5 million (less than 0.25 per cent of GDP) compared with total mining revenues which normally exceed $500 million (PIOJ 1994). Data supplied by the Jamaican Ministry of Production Mining and Commerce (1994) indicate that between 1952 and 1993, some 5,359 ha had been disturbed for bauxite mining, of which around one-half had been restored and certified and some 850 ha were being rehabilitated. This land restoration represents a cumulative expenditure of $75 million expressed in present-day money, a sum easily absorbed by the industry and likely to be amply justified nationally by the benefits arising from post-mining crop production as well as from other rural activity made possible by the improved graded and straightened roads which the companies leave.

New Guinea humid tropical regions

The ratio of solid waste material to mineral ore is much higher in the case of copper mining than bauxite, with ratios in excess of 100 for copper, compared with 4–5 for bauxite. The rock waste and ore tailings removed during copper mining would ideally be stored temporarily adjacent to the mines, to be used for infilling at the end of the mine's life. But such storage requires assurances that the material will be stable and that cannot be guaranteed in an environment like that of New Guinea which is characterized by heavy rainfall, steep slopes, seismic activity, landslips, and rocks which are both chemically and physically unstable. These conditions initially encouraged the companies to revert to riverine disposal, given the fact that New Guinea rivers already carry high levels of silt and that their waters are characterized by high heavy metal content (reflecting the nature of the parent rock).

Riverine disposal proceeds via dumps which are positioned to allow undercutting by the river and associated slumping. In large river systems, the discharge may be carried away via bed-load and suspension to be deposited in the estuarine area. The sediments transported to the ocean reside in the delta for up to a century. The delta therefore has a buffering effect and subsequent dispersal is diluted, thereby ameliorating harmful marine effects (Economic Insights 1994). But in smaller systems the river bed aggrades just downstream from the dump and the material is deposited across a widening area of the valley. Such material is likely to have a relatively high metal content and to remain potentially unstable. Erosion and associated slumping will accelerate once mine deposition ceases.

The Panguna mine in PNG (Figure 11.3) had developed plans for rehabilitation prior to its abrupt closure in 1989. The plans entailed leaving the 400–600 ha pit to fill with water (and provide local hydro potential). The 300–500 ha of waste rock would be capped with weathered material in order to foster revegetation. Further downstream, some 3,000 ha of onshore tailings would be stabilized and revegetated while parts of the stabilized delta would also be revegetated. The funding of these measures was made in the corporate plan. Elsewhere in New Guinea, the Freeport company in Irian Jaya took measures in the early 1990s to improve the rehabilitation of rock waste by taking advantage of the relatively high limestone content in the rock (30 per cent) to help neutralize natural oxidation. Topsoil was conserved and hydro-mulching techniques were developed in order to improve and accelerate the process of revegetation. Natural greenbelts were fostered adjacent to the mines in order to improve prospects for natural recolonization. The cost was easily absorbed by one of the world's most competitive copper mines (see Chapter 10).

Mine restoration in sparsely settled arid environments

The cost of rehabilitating mines in arid regions such as the Andean plateaux is minimal compared with either Jamaica or New Guinea. This reflects the low opportunity cost of the site in such a remote and barren location, which forms part of a vast region that functions very much as a barrier to be crossed in order to reach the

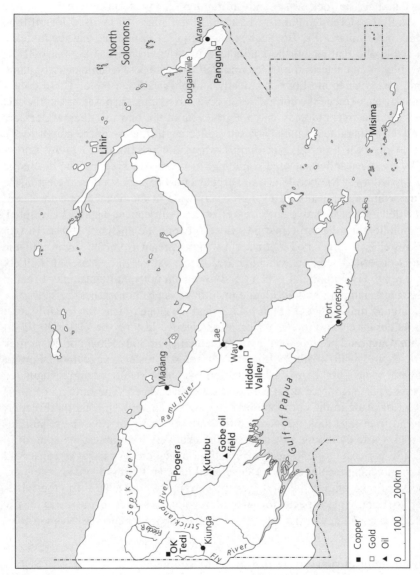

Figure 11.3 Mining operations in Papua New Guinea

Source: Aidab (1994).

high Andes and beyond. For example, the disposal of overburden did not compete for land at the state-owned Chuquicamata mine, which lies in the Atacama desert at 2,700 m. But the size and age of the mine, meant that the haulage distances from the mine to the waste dump had risen steadily so that disposal costs had become relatively expensive. By the early 1990s, the oldest mine at Chuquicamata was 600 m deep and 4.2 km wide. The cost of waste disposal reduced the capital expenditure available to the cash-strapped SOE to abate refinery pollution (Munoz 1994) so that it is fortunate that any rehabilitation costs will be minimal.

But in the Namibian desert region, high rehabilitation costs are being borne by the Rossing uranium mine due to the need to decommission the site. In 1995, decommissioning was expected to occur within twenty years at an estimated cost of $US57 million (in 1992 prices). In line with best practice, the mining MNC, a subsidiary of RTZ, set funds aside annually which had cumulated to $16 million by 1995 in order to achieve its target. The $57 million will permit the firm to dismantle the plant, stabilize the waste and tailings dumps, decontaminate any eroded material, and protect water resources around the mine. The infilling of the mine is not justified because of the low opportunity cost of the land. Instead a fenced-off pit will be left which will be 3 km long by 1 km wide and 2/3 of a km deep. As in Jamaica, the cost of mine rehabilitation is absorbed by the MNC and is less than 1 per cent of annual revenues.

Mining and Water Pollution

Concern over air and water pollution in the developing countries increased sharply through the 1980s, culminating in efforts in the early 1990s to legislate effective controls. Previous emission standards, where they existed, were either lax or else overambitious and poorly enforced, so that the companies had discretion over the degree of abatement. Standards therefore varied according to the form of ownership and the effectiveness of local community pressure. But in mismanaged economies, firms skimped on all investment and environmental abatement lagged.

Water contamination in rural Jamaica

In contrast to mine rehabilitation in Jamaica, government measures to deal effectively with air-borne and water-borne emissions (including tailings) lagged so that *ad hoc* agreements were negotiated between local communities and mining companies. The Jamaican alumina refineries discard around 50–60 per cent of the bauxite in the form of red mud which has high caustic soda content. The health danger from seepage into the water table is increased by high sodium levels which are particularly troublesome in Jamaica, where the genetic make-up of the population renders it susceptible to hypertension which can be aggravated by high sodium levels (World Bank 1993*b*).

The prevention of seepage requires that the tailings pond is sealed with clay and the surroundings monitored for leakage into the water-table as well as for air-borne emissions. The initial ponds for red mud disposal were set in mined-out ore pockets blocked by dykes: each typically occupied 40–50 ha and had a capacity of 5–7 years (Fields 1987). This system gave a high risk of seepage and newer tailings ponds are lined with 30–40 cm of clay. Although the oldest red mud lakes were not consciously sealed, they do appear to have done little damage to the water-table. Some of them have filled in and become difficult to locate because of vegetation regeneration.

As with land reclamation, so with tailings disposal, there are regional differences in the ease with which abatement can be achieved. In this case, Alcoa has had the least problem and Alpart the greatest difficulty, with the Alcan plants in between (Figure 11.1). The Alcoa plant is sited in a region of alluvial aquifers which consist of sand and stones that are less prone to contamination. In contrast, the other plants are near limestone aquifers which hold water in pore spaces and so are especially vulnerable to pollution (Bell 1986). Alpart experienced seepage from three red mud ponds which doubled sodium levels in wells adjacent to the plant and tripled them in wells more distant. The Alcan Ewarton plant is believed to have damaged a stream at Moneague near the north coast and an aquifer near the interior town of Linstead to the south (Coke *et al.* 1987). Alcan responded by tightening its targets for discharges to 20 p.p.m. maximum sodium carbonate content for potable water, and 100 p.p.m. for non-potable applications.

The high cost of caustic soda which Jamaican refineries use in large amounts has provided an incentive to recycle water. By the early 1990s, Alcoa recycled around 50 per cent of its process water, justifying the costs by the reuse of expensive caustic soda. New red mud disposal methods can also facilitate recycling: for example, Alcan invested $50 million in a system which sprayed red mud solids around the edge of the tailings pond, allowing the liquid to accumulate by gravity in the centre of the pond so that it can be drained off for clarification and reuse. The reclaimed caustic soda should amply cover the costs of the new process. An alternative disposal method thickens the red mud mix from 18 per cent solids to 25 per cent. The red mud can then be stacked in a deep tank to produce a slurry with 25 per cent or more solids. The greater weight of this slurry consolidates the particles while liquid suited to recycling can be piped from the top of the tank. Such mud hardens faster than in traditional broad tanks and reduces leakage. It is also easier to capture and recycle caustic soda from stacked dry mud than from ponds. If a commercial use is found for the red mud, the process will also be self-funding.

Tailings and irrigation water in arid environments

The much greater volume of tailings waste which copper processing produces compared with alumina has caused problems in semi-arid farming regions like the central valley of Chile (Figure 11.4). At first the problem of water-table contamination was largely ignored: evidence collected during the mid-1970s suggests that

Figure 11.4 Copper mining operations in Chile and Peru

the national water quality standards set under Decree 1,333 were breached by mine pollution on the Mapucho, Elqui, Aconcagua, and Copiapo rivers (Lagos and Velesco 1993). For example, tailings from Andina mine in the Rio Blanco pushed molybdenum to levels which were unsafe for irrigation. But that river was not in a farming area and by the time its water reached the Ancagua, which irrigated the Central Valley, it did comply (Munoz 1994).

The most serious incidence of river pollution in Chile occurred in the Salado River which, after the first tailings dam was filled up in 1938, resorted to marine deposition at Chanarel Bay. When an alternative disposal site was required in the mid-1970s, a period of recovery from economic crisis, local views were ignored by the SOE, Codelco, and a canal was constructed in 1975 to divert the river water and tailings to Caleta Palitos where a similar infilling of the bay occurred and more marine life was destroyed. All told, some 330,000 tonnes of tailings were discharged into the sea before the Supreme Court ruled in 1990 that a suitable tailings dam must be constructed.

Nevertheless, the overall loss of land productivity that is attributable to mine water pollution in central Chile appears to be minimal. In fact, it can be argued that the provision of recycled water by the mining companies to local farmers for irrigation has the potential to *enhance* the productivity of otherwise arid and unproductive land. Research at Disputada and El Teniente (Figure 11.4) suggests that there is no evidence that farm productivity in surrounding areas is depressed by high metal content. The research reveals differences among plants in the take-up of toxic materials. The green leaves of plants tend to absorb undesirably high levels of toxic substances whereas fruit is safe. Consequently, although recycled tailings water is not suited to growing fodder for animal feed, it can be used to produce acceptable crops of corn, pulses, and fruit.

In response to the increasing effectiveness of local farming community pressure from the mid-1980s, Codelco experimented with tailings water for irrigation in connection with the construction of an 87-km tailings pipe and a tailings dam for the El Teniente mine. Mine tailings were transported by an open concrete channel to Caren which had 80 years of storage capacity at current production. Alternative disposal solutions were rejected because of cost (Aljaro Uribe 1994): they included an extension of the tailings pipe to the ocean for an extra 25 per cent ($50 million) and the construction of a plant at Caren to remove the sulphates from the water. Although the water at Caren was highly alkaline and had levels of molybdenum and sulphate which exceeded Decree 1,333 levels (requiring special government dispensation) it was used to grow crops and to rear animals on a 10-ha farm owned by the mining company (Codelco 1991*b*). The crops included: wheat, maize, asparagus, grapes, beans, tomatoes, melons, citruses, peaches, while the animals reared include sheep, cattle, and rabbits. Tests indicate that water quality throughout the Caren pond resembles that at a nearby reservoir. But when the effluent passing into a nearby stream exceeded permissible levels, the firm compensated farmers by buying the surface water rights and substituting underground water supplies (Munoz 1994).

Mining companies can more easily absorb abatement costs if they can expand capacity because the scale economies justify the cost of newer, more efficient processing equipment. The MNC-owned Disputada mine built a new tailings dam north of Santiago (Figure 11.4) as part of an expansion programme. The new site lies in a 10,000-ha basin surrounded on all but one side by hills and underlain by 60 m of clayey soils lying on top of bedrock. Not only can it cope with the expanded tailings output, it can also absorb 76 million tonnes of *accumulated* tailings from past mining which many believe to be insecurely impounded 2,000 m higher up in the Andean foothills. The accumulated tailings will be pumped over a twenty-year period some 60 km to the new dam. Even so, half the land at the tailings facility will still be free for irrigated agriculture using recycled water. Disputada has proved the feasibility on company farmland and will make the water available to adjacent farmers (Smith 1993). As in Jamaica, mine activity can boost, rather than depress farm productivity.

In the desert regions of northern Chile, the problem is one of water shortage rather than of water contamination. The water used by the two largest Atacama mines, Chuquicamata and Escondida, is drawn from Andean aquifers that contain high levels of arsenic as a result of volcanic activity. The water is further polluted because its high temperature causes chemical reactions with the rocks over which it passes *en route* to the surface. Chuquicamata built an arsenic treatment plant and recycles around 80 per cent of the water used. But tailings deposited at the Talabre tailings dam have infiltrated adjacent lagoons, leaking into the water-table and lowering the quality of water in the Loa River.

The new and highly profitable Escondida mine draws water from 25 aquifers which are some 25 km distant from the mine (Ojeda 1994). Water consumption is 1.1 m^3 per tonne of ore processed and about 40 per cent is drawn from recharge water sources and the rest from the water-table. Water from Punta Negra, which contains 3,000–4,000 p.p.m. salt and also some arsenic, is used to transport the concentrates in slurry some 180 km to Coloso on the coast where it is reclaimed and decontaminated (albeit, not to standards of potable quality). The company reports that the marine discharge exhibits minimal impact compared with pre-operating 'background' data, a claim which is verified by the local authorities.

Water deposition in humid New Guinea

Where environmental instability renders the construction of a tailings dam risky, as in humid and geomorphologically unstable New Guinea, deep marine disposal is preferable to riverine disposal. This is because as long as the material is mixed with cold water when it is discharged into the ocean its higher density will carry it down below the photic zone where little life exists to be adversely affected. Natural sedimentation processes fix the heavy metals in the deep sea. Even if circulation does occur, the rate of movement is so slow that thousands of years would pass (in which dilution would occur) before up-welling took place.

In New Guinea, three large copper mines span the range of sites from close prox-
imity to the ocean (Panguna is 30 km away), through 100 km distant (Freeport) to
1,000 km distant (Ok Tedi). The river waters in New Guinea already have a high
heavy metals background which rises in the vicinity of the mine dumps (where the
human population is small) but falls sharply in the lower reaches (where the population may be higher). The commercial use of the river waters is impaired by
their high turbidity, even before riverine dumping, on account of the high natural
sediment load. In fact, investigation of river water revealed pollution by human
faeces to be a more serious problem than metal contamination.

The local impact of the Panguna mine is enhanced by the Jaba River's relatively
short journey to the sea (Figure 11.3) and its steep gradient. Tailings from Panguna
raised the Jaba river bed by 30 m and spread sediment across the valley to a width
of 1 km. Meanwhile, the finest sediments were carried down to the ocean and
built a delta out into Empress Augusta Bay that extended over some 900 ha by 1988.
Yet, water contamination by mine operations at Panguna was within required limits
and the main environmental threat arose from inadequate rural sanitation. Apart from
the physical transformation of the Jaba River and its estuary (for which compensation was agreed with local communities), environmental impacts were modest.
Mining MNCs have historically internalized environmental costs by compensating local people for land that was leased, for lower crop yields, and for disturbance
arising out of mine operations. But, as analysed in more detail in Chapter 12, local
people may incorrectly ascribe problems to mine operations and to exaggerate impacts
in order to maximize compensation. In the case of Panguna, crop disease was often
ascribed to the impact of mining, although there was no evidence that this was the
cause. An independent survey by Applied Geology Associates Ltd (1989) could
recommend only modest adjustments to the negotiated agreements. Nevertheless,
the owners of the mine, RTZ, opted to build a marine tailings pipeline which was
almost complete when the mine was abruptly closed in 1989.

Pipeline disposal would be more expensive for the Ok Tedi mine, some 1,000
km distant from the river mouth, which tipped 240,000 tonnes of rock and tailings
daily into the Ok Tedi River. The mine operations augmented the natural sediment
load of the adjacent Ok Tedi system sevenfold, doubled the load further downstream,
at the confluence with the Fly River, and raised it by 50 per cent lower down still
in the Strickland River (Figure 11.3). Around half the material deposited remained
within the river valleys and raised their beds (Economic Insights 1994). Some 40
million tonnes of mine sediments passed annually into the Fly River. Most of this
sediment reached the delta where it joined a mobile layer that covered two-thirds
of the tidal delta by the early 1990s and had a predicted residence time of around
a century.

The Ok Tedi River bed is expected to be raised at Kuambit by 2.2 m when
mining ceases in 2008. Such an increase has been shown to be rather less than the
increases caused by recorded natural land-slips and the Ok Tedi will revert to
its original gradient within fifteen to twenty years after the cessation of mining
(Table 11.1). Vegetation recovery following sedimentation damage appears to be

Table 11.1 Reserves and waste disposal of the principal mines PNG

	Copper			Gold			Oil	
	Panguma	Ok Tedi	Freeport	Misuma	Porgera	Lihir	Kutubu	Hides
Construction	1969	1981	1969	1988	1990	1995	1991	n/a
Production	1972	1984	1972	1959	1990	1996	1993	n/a
Initial reserves (mt)	675	410	1,100	62	54	170	n/a	n/a
(bls)	n/a	n/a	n/a	n/a	n/a	n/a	170	n/a
(mcf)	n/a	n/a	n/a	n/a	n/a	n/a	n/a	15.1
Grade								
Gold (g/t)	0.45	0.30	0.30	1.4	5.7	3.2	n/a	n/a
Copper (%)	0.40	0.70	1.27	—	—	—	n/a	n/a
Silver (g/t)	—	—	—	20	10	—	n/a	n/a
Investment ($USm)	357	1,536	146	226	838	770	730	n/a
Initial mine life (yrs)	26	21	25	10	20	>25	>10	
Expected remaining life (yrs)		>30	27	75	n/a	>25	>7	
Rock waste								
Disposal	Dumps	Riverine	Dump	Old pits	Riverine	Submarine		
Tonnes/day	15,000	159,000	385,000	18,000	80,000	30,000		
System affected	Minesite	Minesite	Minesite	Old pits	Fly River	2km off shore 125m deep		
Tailings								
Disposal	Riverine	Riverine	Riverine	Marine and Pits	Riverine	Submarine		
Tonnes/day	135,000	80,000	111,000	18,000	<5,500	8,500		
Systems affected	Jaba Rᵃ	Ok Teil River	Ajkwa River	Sea and Pits	Fly River	2km off shore 125m deep		

ᵃ planned switch to direct ocean discharge almost complete when closed 1989.

Source: Economic Insights (1994).

rapid. Copper levels from tailings in the river occasionally exceed the standards adopted, even in the Ok Tedi, but contrary to the effects on marine life in the river in the first years of Ok Tedi's operations, in recent years discharges from the mine have not had an adverse effect on fish (although the willingness of the mine to increase compensation to landowners raises some doubts on this score). Further downstream, within the Fly River system, the mine impact is considered to be minimal.

Even so, by the early 1990s growing international concern for the environment was imposing more costly environmental defence strategies on the mining companies, albeit ones which they could comfortably finance. In the mid-1990s, legal action by local landowners at Ok Tedi led the company to raise proposed compensation payments. The settlement required expenditures of $5.6 million annually over the remaining fifteen years of the mine. In addition to the $2.5 million annually which Ok Tedi expended on environmental monitoring at twenty-six stations, plans were drafted to expend a further $18.5 million annually over the life of the mine to dredge 300 million tonnes of sediment from the Ok Tedi system and store it in a layer some 20 m thick over an area of 18 km². This solution was preferred to the alternative of investing $330 million to build in the Star Mountains a new tailings dam whose security could not be guaranteed. The company placed a $385 million ceiling on environmental expenditures, above which its viability would be compromised. Although Ok Tedi had not declared profits since mining commenced (due to the heavy debt burden incurred at its start-up), the costs imposed by the mid-1990s agreement can be offset from the efficiency gains arising out of expanded output.

A more radical solution to tailings disposal was attempted by the third large New Guinea copper mine in Irian Jaya. From 1977, the Indonesian government developed stronger environmental legislation for mining (Teter *et al.* 1995). In 1993 the Bureau of Environment and Technology was set up to streamline the rules for new mining projects. The new environmental procedures called for four sets of documentation for new projects, namely terms of reference (an initial screening), an environmental impact assessment (which established the base-line parameters), an environmental management plan (which focused on the mitigation of environmental impacts), and an environmental monitoring plan. In this context of tightening legislation, the Freeport mine invested $25 million from 1994 to build embankments along the course of the Ajkwa River in order both to control sedimentation and to facilitate revegetation (Figure 11.5). The embankments reach a height of 2–3 m, but in places of highest deposition the height can reach 10–12 m. In the latter area some 130 km² of tailings is expected to accumulate and be revegetated. An extra benefit from the embankments is the prevention of tailings and natural sediment from the Ajkwa from being deposited in the Kopi and Minajerwa rivers. This ensures that the Mawati system and the Lorentz Nature Reserve will not be affected.

The embankment system has annual operating costs of $12.5 million in a total annual environmental expenditure of $41 million. That $41 million represented 3.3 per cent of total annual revenues in the mid-1990s, a sum which was comfortably absorbed by a copper mine whose net cash costs were only three-quarters those

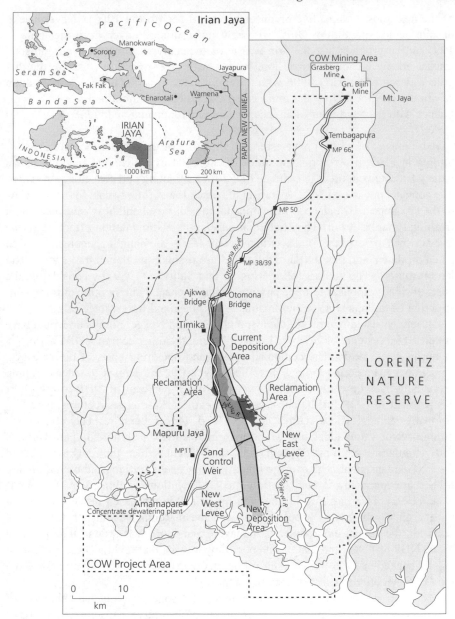

Figure 11.5 Reserve deposition controls, Grasberg

of the next most competitive producer (Freeport-McMoRan 1995).[1] Nevertheless, despite such expenditure, OPIC withdrew its insurance cover from the mine in 1995 on the grounds that the firm was not adequately tackling the environmental impact arising out of its expansion. In line with emerging best practice, the dispute was settled in early 1996 with a commitment to accumulate a $100 million rehabilitation fund before the mine is closed. OPIC will monitor Freeport's compliance with the conditions of an independent environmental audit (*Financial Times* 1996d).

Bartelmus *et al*. (1992) have estimated the costs of the environmental impact of mining in PNG, providing some index of the scale of adjustment required to the national accounts in order to estimate EDP2 for the mining and concentration stages. The authors draw upon PNG Department of Minerals and Energy data for an overview of the key impacts which arise from mine tailings disposal and heavy metals in both fresh and marine water. They note that substantial sedimentation effects, like the floods which affected the Fly River in the early 1990s, are natural phenomena in such an environment and that the damage to land use is small in relation to the total PNG land resources. The authors follow Hughes and Sullivan (1989) by considering the costs of three responses to mine environmental impacts, namely mine closure, construction of tailings storage and treatment facilities, and unrestricted dumping.

Closure is costed in terms of the lost output to the PNG economy and would have entailed 14.3 per cent of GDP for 1985–90, rising to 23 per cent of GDP for 1991–5 (Duncan *et al*. 1995). The combined capital and operating costs of building systems either to impound tailings or to detoxify waste and haul it to safer dumping grounds, ranges upwards from a low figure of 1.3 per cent of NDP to a high of 3.8 per cent of NDP for the construction of earthquake-proof structures, based on company studies. These figures are 15.5 and 44 per cent, respectively, of net mining-sector value added and would marginalize even a highly competitive mine and, as an additional cost of production, they would reduce the rents available to the PNG government. The damage limitation costs actually incurred by the mining MNCs are much lower than the intermediate solutions examined by Bartelmus *et al*. (1992). They are also in line with the principle discussed in Chapter 5, that the marginal social costs should not exceed the marginal benefits. In the case of Ok Tedi, the annual environmental damage expenditure was around 0.62 per cent of the NDP of PNG (and that of Freeport almost twice that level). These costs were legally backed in 1996 from a court ruling on a test case for Ok Tedi and also from the OPIC negotiations in the case of Freeport.

The cases studied suggest that for mining and concentration, first, the cost of pollution abatement in line with environmental absorptive capacity can be comfortably internalized by most mining firms; and, second, the adjustment to the environmental accounts (to calculate EDP2) is relatively small. This is not the case for air-borne emissions from copper refineries, however.

---

[1] The ore reserves of 1.1 billion tonnes have 1.3% copper content (14 million tonnes of copper) together with by-products of gold (50 million ounces) at 1.47 g per tonne and silver at 4.04 g per tonne (US Embassy 1994).

Mining and Air Pollution in the Copper Industry[2]

The abatement of air pollution from copper mining imposes much higher costs than the mining and concentrating stages. The costs are more difficult for the established producers to meet because, historically, they have lagged best practice. The laggards include most state-owned enterprises and also MNCs in mismanaged economies. By the 1990s, many lagging plants in the developing countries captured only 50 per cent or less of the sulphur in the effluent gas, whereas industrial country smelters used flash smelting technology to capture 97–9 per cent of such gases (World Bank 1994*e*). Although the level of gas capture can be boosted to 70 per cent by large investments in sulphuric acid plants, best practice requires an expensive conversion of the production process from the traditional reverberatory furnace technology. However, new entrants can incorporate best-practice pollution abatement technology in their basic plant design and thereby operate at much lower cost (Warhurst 1994*a*). This situation calls for a flexible response by developing-country governments if they are to avoid plant closures that could mean not only the loss of jobs and taxes, but also the need to shoulder costly clean-up charges at public expense.

Air pollution abatement in Chile

Some fifteen years after the introduction of economic reforms, a rapid expansion of private investment in copper mining began in Chile which pushed the share in production of the erstwhile dominant state-owned firm, Codelco, down to less than half by the mid-1990s. The MNC mines tended to be more competitive and for the most part, they did not need to contend with burdensome environmental add-ons, unlike the state-owned mines whose costs of production rose significantly in the late-1980s. By the mid-1990s, Codelco's production costs, including capital charges, were estimated at 69c per 1b compared with 55–60c per lb for the MNCs.

If Chile had acceded to the intensifying pressure to adopt North American environmental standards, Codelco would have been most severely affected. US copper producers accused Chilean firms of environmental dumping because they failed to meet North American environmental standards. In addition, US producers of farm goods cited mining pollution as grounds for banning Chilean produce, causing Chilean farmers to lobby for tighter domestic mine emission standards. But the courts dismissed both charges on the grounds that the low population densities in Chile make EPA standards excessively stringent. Moreover, some believe the EPA standards are needlessly strict even in a North American context.

The northern refineries in Chile are located in remote arid regions (Figure 11.4) where the climate reduces the incidence of acid rain, and where the prevailing southwesterly winds abate air pollution by 'natural' ventilation. Even so, the air around the Chuquicamata complex in the early 1990s was classified as 'saturated' because

[2] For a discussion of alumina-refining air pollution and its abatement costs, see Auty (1997*a*).

it exceeded permissible levels for both particulates and SO_2, while dust was above permissible limits for 30 per cent of working days. The main negative impact of mining in such an area is therefore upon the health of the workforce and its families. There are reports, for example, of a high incidence of birth defects and lung cancers in the city of Calama, 10 km from Chuquicamata, where more than 100,000 people live, but there were no scientific studies in the early 1990s (Lagos and Velesco 1993). Yet it can be argued, on the basis of hedonistic pricing, that the costs of impaired health are being internalized by Codelco in terms of the higher wages it pays. In 1990 the pay of mine workers at Chuquicamata averaged $1,000 per month compared with $275 for coalminers in the south (*Financial Times* 1990). Such reasoning does not, of course, imply that it is not preferable for investment to take place in the installation of process hoods to capture flue gases and of electrostatic precipitators to capture dust (Munoz 1994).

The tardy response of the state-owned complexes meant that as late as 1989, Chilean copper smelters produced 93 per cent of the country's SO_2 emissions or some 922,000 tonnes of sulphur. At that time Chile was the world's fourth largest emitter of sulphur from point sources—after the USA, China, and Russia. But by 1991 Chilean emissions had already dropped by 15 per cent and projected improvements should cut them by a further two-thirds (to 250,000 tonnes) by the year 2000. This advance will require around $1 billion in investment together with additional sums to reduce arsenic emissions (Lagos and Velesco 1993). Air pollution abatement costs in copper are dominated by capital outlays. The rule-of-thumb ratio between environmental investment and total investment is one-fifth, based on data from Ventanas and Disputada (ibid.). Matters are not so simple, however: many environmental investments to reduce gas emissions (as opposed to water disposal) incorporate improvements in productivity which lower production costs.

As already noted, expanded production makes the cost of reducing pollution easier to absorb because it captures the scale economies and enhances competitiveness. For example, the Exxon Disputada smelter (Figure 11.4) was relatively high cost in the 1980s and in order to adopt new less polluting technology it expanded capacity threefold. The expansion cut its production costs to the middle of the international range. In line with emerging expectations about MNC standards, Disputada was the first to comply with government regulations, even before its expansion. Disputada shares with the SOE-owned Ventanas refinery, one of the least favourable locations on account of its low environmental absorptive capacity. It is situated adjacent to a town and surrounded by fertile farmland. Disputada was shut down for 1.5 months during 1993 in order to comply with emission standards. The closure caused the loss of one-eighth of output and revenue, an amount which the suboptimally sized smelter could ill afford, underlining the paradoxical need for expanded production in order to curb pollution and abatement costs.

Large-scale investments in expansion and environmental upgrading of smelters have been harder to justify in the state sector because they compete for public funds with other social projects that have strongly positive returns. Despite the advantages of a higher absorptive capacity conferred by its arid and remote location, Chuquicamata

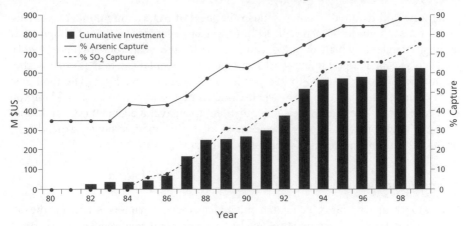

Figure 11.6 Cumulative environmental investment and emission levels, Chuquicamata, 1980–99

Source: Codelco (1991*b*).

had to expend a large part of its limited cash flow on the construction of acid plants to absorb sulphur which doubled the cost of refining and added 11 per cent (8c per 1b) to the subsidiary's production costs. This increase was, however, partly offset by linked productivity improvements and also by-product sales to an acid-leaching operation on old tailings near the complex's southern mine (Munoz 1994).

The burden of environmental problems on the older complexes is intensified by keen competition from new private mines like Escondida which use state-of-the-art technology (Figure 11.4). The richer ore of the Escondida mine produced concentrates with 43 per cent copper content and higher (compared with 30–2 per cent world norms) which were initially shipped mostly to Japan for blending before smelting (Fluckiger 1994). Escondida's production costs were estimated at two-thirds those of Codelco, and the project recouped its initial capital investment within three years of starting up in 1990. Its competitiveness was further improved through expansion and the working of oxide reserves costing only 20c per 1b to produce. The competitive squeeze on Codelco tightened in the late 1990s when Escondida began constructing a state-of-the-art smelter. A further threat to the state-owned firms emanated from the adoption by private firms of a new process of solvent extraction, electro-winning technology (SX-EW), which is a less environmentally sensitive way to produce copper than traditional smelting. By the year 2000, Chile could secure one-quarter of its total production of 3.5 million tonnes (50 per cent more copper than in 1993) from the new SX-EW techniques (*Financial Times* 1994).

The intensifying cost pressure on the state-owned mines requires negotiated abatement compliance if the State is not to end up footing the clean-up bills of a closed plant. Chuquicamata invested $564 million on environmental equipment during the period 1980–94, of which more than 80 per cent went on three acid plants. By the early 1990s, some 40 per cent of the sulphur and 70 per cent of the arsenic were fixed at Chuquicamata (Figure 11.6). But additional investments on a similar scale were still required in order to push the level of SO_2 capture up to 75 per cent and for arsenic up to 90 per cent. Chuquicamata negotiated a phased adoption of ambient standards which required compliance by the year 2000 (Munoz 1994). Codelco's second largest refinery, El Teniente, faced similar catch-up problems after its production costs doubled to 75c per lb between 1986 and 1992. The total cost of decontaminating all the state-owned Codelco plants was estimated at $1 billion over nine years. These estimates are equivalent to an average annual cost of 4.4 per cent of Codelco revenues, or 1.5 per cent of total Chilean government expenditure, or 0.5 per cent of the country's GDP (World Bank 1994*f*).

Air pollution abatement in Peru

Following a generation of economic mismanagement (Chapters 8 and 9), the reforming Peruvian government introduced tighter environmental regulations in 1993, partly in order to eliminate uncertainty for potential MNC investors returning to the country after twenty-five years in response to a privatization programme. The regulations were negotiated at the sectoral level but they have been criticized because, like Chile, they favour regulation and assign the market a minimal role (Pasco-Font 1996). The government decided to accept liability for past pollution and retained one state firm, Mineroperu, in order to manage residual mining properties and supervise the new contracts (Moran 1996). The new regulations required an environmental assessment programme (EVAP) to identify the scale of the problems. This information was used in conjunction with an economic profile to negotiate remedial measures (a PAMA) that commenced on 1 January 1997. The firms had five years to comply with mine regulations, and ten years to improve processing facilities. The standards set are modelled upon US levels, but they are slightly less strict.

The substantial clean-up costs faced by Peru's state-owned mines deter private investors. The large state mining firm, Centromin, was unable to attract a buyer and so the government reluctantly accepted a piecemeal disposal of its assets. As a condition of privatization, investment commitments were secured. For example, the Antamina project was disposed of for $20 million but with investment commitments for $2.5 billion. However, the remaining state-owned refinery, La Oroya, poses the greatest challenge. The government estimated the clean-up costs for La Oroya at $80–240 million, depending upon whether the problematic zinc plant was shut (thereby halving SO_2 emissions), or the copper refinery was closed, or the entire plant was replaced. RTZ estimated the costs at $800 million, but that figure may have included large provisions in case of legal action (Tarnawiecki 1996). Compliance with environmental standards demands an 83 per cent reduction in emissions over eight years, and pushes the ageing refinery to the economic margin.

SPCC provides an example of an MNC mining firm which neglected environmental expenditures. It responded to the years of Peruvian economic mismanagement by deferring investment. Its domestic mines are in remote interior locations, so that the company's major problem is refurbishment of the Ilo refinery which it purchased from the government for $67 million in 1992. Refineries have ten years in which to comply (in effect shadowing Chile which will require reduction by the year 2000 and legal norm by 2005). The Ilo smelter was reported to emit 2,000 tonnes of SO_2 daily, some ten to fifteen times the permitted US level and SPCC faced a series of lawsuits. The lawsuits included one within Peru from the mayor of Tacna for $100 million in damages to health and crops for the alleged harmful deposition of tailings, slag, and smelter emissions and a second within the US judicial system from 700 Peruvians (SPCC 1995). Both court cases were dismissed, but they combined with accusations of environmental dumping, to prompt SPCC to accelerate its investments.

SPCC's renovation programme requires expanded production which will raise output by 70 per cent over ten years, to around 500,000 tonnes. The company lifted its estimate of proven and probable reserves by two-thirds to 1.3 billion tonnes of ore of 0.7 per cent copper content (*Financial Times* 1996e). The total investment will exceed $1 billion of which the mine expansion will cost $245 million in 1997–9 which includes a $41 million tailings dam so that the dumping of some 30 million tonnes annually of untreated tailings offshore near Ilo can cease (*New York Times* 1995). But $787 million will be invested in refurbishing the Ilo refinery to boost sulphur recovery to 69 per cent by 2005 and to international standards of 95 per cent by 2008. Environmental expenditure absorbed 30 per cent of the SPCC investment budget in 1996 when the main projects were a sulphuric acid conversion plant to supply a new SX-EW leachate process. However, SPCC made no provision for site-clearance when mining ceases in fifty years.

Conclusions

In the absence of practical environmental standards for air and water emissions, there is little evidence of a Kuznets pollution curve from the countries studied. Rather, the degree of pollution abatement cost internalization varies according to the soundness of economic management (lagging in mismanaged economies), local environmental absorptive capacity (more advanced where population density and community pressure are both high), and firm ownership (MNCs lead SOEs, in well-managed economies).

Mine rehabilitation costs are small in relation to total mine revenues, even in a densely settled region like Jamaica, where the opportunity cost of land is high. In barren arid regions, like the deserts of central western South America and Namibia, the opportunity costs of despoiled land are so low as to render the costs of a re-habilitation programme minimal. Even so, when required, rehabilitation funds can be set aside as an annual charge during the life of the mine. Mine rehabilitation has a higher priority in less stable humid regions like New Guinea, where disposal and storage of mine waste is problematic.

Water contamination also imposes modest costs which have been dealt with historically, by negotiating local compensation where economic conditions were favourable. Although water from copper mining may restrict the crops that can be grown, there appears to be little effect on farm productivity. Moreover, the provision of recycled process water for irrigation may actually enhance yields at lower cost than would otherwise be the case. The most difficult water-pollution problems arise in upland mines in the geomorphologically unstable regions of the humid tropics like New Guinea. Here, a trade-off is required, based upon marginal social costs and benefits, between dam construction which can marginalize the most efficient mine and controlled (and compensated) riverine disposal. Estimated pollution abatement costs are likely to be less than 1 per cent of GDP.

The costs of pollution abatement from refining are much more onerous, however. In anticipation of formal centralized rules, MNCs in well-managed economies have adopted best-practice technology and internalized the cost with little effect on competitiveness. Established firms (mostly SOEs, but not exclusively so) in mismanaged and reforming economies have underinvested and lag in the adoption of pollution-abating technology. These older plants must aim at a moving target as new producers emerge with more favourable combinations of emissions and production costs. The costs of curbing air-borne emissions are more easily absorbed where they form part of an investment package designed to expand output. Yet, overall, the evidence presented in this chapter suggests that the mining sector is moving swiftly to absorb the costs of environmental damage and that, given a flexible timetable for compliance, most firms will be able to absorb the costs and operate in a sustainable manner.

12 Achieving Social Sustainability

Social sustainability is a relatively new concept which has arisen out of criticism of policy implementation aimed at both the macroeconomic and the micro- (project) levels. The macro-criticism arose in large measure out of the disappointing results of the structural adjustment programmes that were executed with increasing frequency following the first oil shock (Reed 1996). The microeconomic criticism stems from allegations that grass-roots opinion has been neglected in project design and execution, at the cost of both (O'Brien 1997). The effectiveness of macroeconomic, micro and environmental policies for sustainable mineral-driven development will be seriously impaired if the socio-political constraints upon their implementation are neglected.

Social sustainability is therefore concerned with the ability of the different tiers of government (and the economy in general) to pursue the policies which are considered essential for sustainable development, including, in the case of this study eliminating economic distortions; coping with external shocks; maintaining adequate true investment levels beyond the youthful stage of the mineral-driven cycle (which substitute for the income stream from the depleting mineral asset); and internalizing the cost of environmental damage in order to curb such damage. Social sustainability requires that these objectives be achieved without engendering socio-political responses which impair the ability of the government to implement the necessary policies. Social sustainability may be enhanced by education and a variety of social measures such as the equalization of opportunity, the diffusion of democratic processes, and environmental management. But the contribution of these factors to sustainability will vary among countries according to their historical background, the racial and ethnic composition of their population, and the stage of development, among others.

Progress with the operationalization of social sustainability has been slower than in the case of environmental sustainability. Koo and Perkins (1995) note the diversity of approaches towards 'social capability', a term which they prefer and which is adopted here. In editing a collection of essays on social capability and long-term economic growth, they record a lack of agreement on the relative importance of the factors which might determine the outcome. For example, Lal and Myint (1996) assign education a weaker role in economic success than other researchers, such as Wood (1994) and the World Bank (1995c).

At the most basic level, it is accepted that social capability relies on group knowledge and trust, backed up by sanctions, to provide information and security, thereby reducing risk and uncertainty and facilitating economic activity. At the local level 'civic associations' promote efficient market outcomes by sharing information, aligning individual incentives, and by improving collective decision-making' (World Bank 1997: 81). Importantly, the civic associations appear to be more successful where income distribution, and therefore, power, is relatively evenly shared (Knack and Keefer 1997).

More specific definitions of social capability range from the narrowest conceptualization, which sees it as the density of social networks that influence the productivity of a community (Putnam *et al.* 1993); through more complex social structures with vertical and horizontal forms that facilitate individual or corporate activity; to the broader consideration of social and political factors which mediate socio-economic activity. The broadest definition therefore encompasses national as well as local institutions, and embraces formalized structures such as the legal system, ethical norms, and the political regime. This level of definition is favoured by Bardhan (1995) because of the benefits that he sees arising from its greater comprehensiveness. The broader definition also recognizes that social institutions may in some cases work to impede welfare improvement. For example, national government failure can occur and local social networks can be captured by overlords.

Killick attempts to be more specific about social capability. He focuses on the 'flexible economy', which he defines as one in which, 'individuals, organizations and institutions efficiently adjust their goals and resources to changing constraints and opportunities' (Killick 1995: 18). He identifies the principal determinants of *national* economic flexibility as market efficiency, economic openness, and political autonomy. But he is also concerned with the local agents of change, both individuals and institutions. At the local level, Killick sees the main agents for flexibility as education, technological capability, and social factors (such as values, reward systems, and leadership quality).

Killick (1995) also usefully speculates about the evolution of social capability. He suggests that the positive impact of institutional capability is likely first to wax and then wane as development proceeds. This is because, at low income levels, countries lack the institutions required to use capital efficiently. The rectification of this situation therefore requires the creation of new forms of social capability. But at high-income levels, social institutions appear to become so elaborate and powerful as to damage resource use efficiency. Such damage may occur, for example, through the action of lobbying groups, whose single-minded objectives may be secured at the expense of the more diffuse and broader social interest. In addition, as a national population ages, so the ratio of workers to dependants deteriorates and the population also becomes more resistant to change. Social capability may also decline as per capita incomes rise because the opportunity cost of the time input required to maintain social groups also rises. However, social capability can regress at lower-income levels also. This may result from profound socio-economic shocks such as those which hit many countries in Latin America and sub-Saharan Africa in the 1980s, causing sizeable numbers of individuals to withdraw from civil society. Colombia presents stark examples of this which are discussed in Chapter 14.

It is possible to recognize the potentially positive returns from fostering social capability, even if early attempts at measurement have proved problematic. These benefits occur at the macro-level (in terms of effective financial, legal, and economic policy measures) and at the micro-level (through, for example, the promotion of trust-enhancing institutions). Many NGOs seek to build social capability. They choose to operate mainly at the micro-level, performing a 'mediating role' between the liberalizing world economy and weaker groups within society.

An alternative approach to social sustainability seeks to identify and measure social capital. Efforts in this direction are spurred by the fact that conventional accounting models are unable to explain a significant component of growth with reference to capital and labour inputs alone. For example, barely one-third of the difference between the economic growth of the East Asian countries and that of other regions is explained by such accounting (World Bank 1993*a*), although Young (1995) and Mankiw (1995) have more recently demonstrated how the explanatory power of conventional accounting can be improved by taking note of the improvements in the *quality* of the two basic inputs.

The maintenance and improvement of human capital is regarded as an important component of sustainable development (Wood 1994) and its measurement has so far proved easier than the measurement of social capital. The World Bank (1997) has made an initial attempt to assess the relative contribution of this factor to wealth. Human capital can be measured on the basis of years of schooling, or on the estimated value of the future earning (income) stream. These two measures of human capital correlate quite well, with an R^2 of 0.75. But the wealth measure selected by the World Bank (1997) is the residual value after, first, subtracting from GNP the agricultural GNP multiplied by 45 per cent (to reflect the 'return to labour') and, second, adding non-agricultural GNP (minus the rents from subsoil assets which are included in natural capital). The resulting income stream over the average number of productive years of the population is then calculated with a 4 per cent discount rate. The total value of *produced* capital is estimated from a perpetual inventory model, drawing upon conventional accounting data and discounting at 4 per cent per annum. The measurement of *natural* capital is based upon the raw materials entering world trade together with land. It therefore excludes other important environmental services, notably for residuals disposal. Natural capital is quantified as the stream of rents from the resources.[1]

Table 12.1 summarizes the World Bank results for a set of regions and for the countries in the present study. The findings suggest that traditional national accounting may overstate the role of produced capital, while neglecting not only natural capital but also human capital. In analysing the contribution of the different forms of capital to wealth, the World Bank (1997) concludes that, such is the overwhelming importance of human capital, a fourth category of capital (along with produced, natural, and human capital) should be identified within it, namely 'social infrastructure'. The latter subsumes the 'institutional and cultural bases required for a society to

[1] The rent from land is calculated as 30–50% of its gross value in grain, and arable land under other land uses is assigned a value 80% that of land under grain. The rent from pastureland is assigned as 45% of the gross value of output.

Table 12.1 Per capita wealth, global regions, and nine countries

	Total wealth ($/capita)	Wealth composition (%)		
		Natural	Human	Produced
Regions				
Western Europe	236,348	2	74	23
Middle East	180,048	54	31	15
South America	95,264	10	73	17
East Asia	46,326	8	76	16
East and S. Africa	30,102	11	65	24
Countries				
Botswana	89,605	6	77	17
Chile	149,041	11	78	12
Colombia	84,545	8	79	14
Indonesia	59,623	13	74	13
Jamaica	46,655	9	48	43
Namibia	74,794	9	78	13
PNG	38,935	20	63	17
Peru	59,974	8	67	25
Trinidad and Tobago	121,960	13	56	32

Source: World Bank (1997).

function', but the World Bank has not yet been able to isolate and quantify it. A paper by Knack and Keefer (1997), however, reports initial efforts to measure trust and civic associations and to compare their effect on economic growth for a number of countries. Trust appears to be much more significant than civic associations.

Recognizing the preliminary nature of investigation into social capital and social sustainability, this study has used a typology of political states to capture significant aspects of social capability at the national level, as discussed in Chapter 6 and applied in subsequent chapters. The present chapter therefore concentrates on the local level. It first examines the relationship between local communities and the firms which manage major projects, in this case mines, showing the interactions with national aspects of social capability. The second portion of the chapter addresses efforts to upgrade social capital among mature mineral economies which exhibit a mismatch of wages and skills that presents for them, as noted in Chapters 8 and 9, an especially severe challenge to sustainable development.

Local Social Capability: Corporate–Community Relations

This section traces the evolving relationship between mining companies and local communities as the companies respond to local and external pressures by shifting the emphasis of their local spending from a preoccupation with the build-up of produced capital (economic and social infrastructure) within the mining region to the expansion of human capital, especially through the transmission of business skills. It does so with reference to contrasting conditions in PNG and the Irian Jaya province of Indonesia. But first, an overview of the local impacts of mines is presented.

Corporate–community relations in Mining

At the micro-level, mine–community relations harbour latent social discontent which stems from a combination of the often modest local economic linkages, the comparatively extravagant living conditions of the mine employees, and the social and environmental upheaval associated with the depletion of a natural asset. Economic Insights (1994) argues that the socio-economic impact of a large mine, like Ok Tedi in PNG, resembles that of an aurora with strong positive effects in the immediate vicinity of the mine operations and a shadow area of neglect just beyond. The main impacts tend to be concentrated and they entail the displacement of a limited number of landholders at the mine site and its associated installations, the creation of a modern settlement, and the provision of effective infrastructure links to the outside world. The limited number of people usually displaced by mining implies that the reasonable costs of compensation are modest compared with total mine revenues.

In this context, the second environmental revolution of the late 1980s provided a new lever with which local communities could seek not only legitimate compensation for damage to their health and lifestyles, but also to maximize their share of the mining rents. Greater worldwide concern for environmental issues, has sharply increased the scale of compensation which local communities demand. It has also forced the mining companies to provide a clearer rationale for their conduct and to investigate more carefully the alternative methods for abating pollution and also of building local social capability.

The fact that the mining company can often pay more than it does to the local community is a source of tension. When a new mine starts up local people tend to view the company as a new resource which they can exploit to enhance their welfare. But this attitude runs the risk of intensifying the dependence of the community on a depleting asset with a finite life. Moreover, increased communal remuneration may cause social discontent to persist, if only because any rise in compensation tends to be outstripped by the rising aspirations of the recipients. Yet the mining company risks being regarded as greedy by local groups for not paying more.

Mining companies must therefore tread a fine line between what they could expend to secure immediate goodwill and what is prudent for the long-term interest of the community. In these circumstances, transparency over revenue flows is an important antidote to mistrust. It can lay a foundation upon which to build the local trust that is needed to avoid mutually damaging conflict of the type which befell Panguna. Increasingly, recourse is being made to an independent audit which can check not only compliance with environmental standards, but also the fairness of compensatory payments to the community. Consequently, in addition to economic and environmental auditing, the social audit now has a role to play. The agency which performs such a social audit might be an NGO, a consultancy firm, or a division of one of the international financial institutions. A social audit has great potential to build the social capital which sustainable development requires.

Community rent allocation in a factional State: PNG

New Guinea provides examples of some of the sharpest conflicts between mining companies and local communities. It may be recalled from Chapter 6 that PNG achieved independence as a parliamentary democracy which lacked the advantage of cultural homogeneity. A variety of regionally isolated groups look to the political system to provide local largesse, much in line with the clientelistic model of Kurer (1996). The social fragmentation of the electoral districts means that members of parliament are often elected by a only a handful of their constituents. Such MPs act as single-term agents who, as 'big men', are expected to maximize the flow of revenue from central government sources to a small fraction of the local electorate.

In the 1980s, the riverine disposal of mine tailings in a humid mountainous area emerged as a major social issue with considerable potential to enhance local welfare, but also with increasingly adverse political ramifications. When mining began at Panguna in the early 1970s, however, environmental concern was well down the list of priorities. This is why the Panguna mine opted to dispose of its tailings along the 35-km course of the Jaba River into Empress Augusta Bay. Riverine disposal of mine tailings was also adopted by the smaller Freeport copper mine in Irian Jaya when it began operations in the 1970s. Even a decade later, when Ok Tedi started up, disposal into the Fly River was still accepted as a second-best solution after technical problems and cost overruns caused the abandonment of a planned tailings dam (see Chapter 11).

In the case of Panguna, attitudes towards the opening of the mine were equivocal within the area affected which was initially populated by 500 people near the mine and a further 2,000 within the 13,000 ha lease area (Applied Geology Associates 1989). The local benefits flowing from the mine were perceived as being unevenly distributed. Some villagers were relocated to superior accommodation near an all-weather road and given significantly improved health and education facilities. But not all villages had electricity, while water supplies and sanitation were often deficient. Moreover, despite the expenditure of $1.97 million, the resettled villages were considerably less well equipped than the company towns.

By the late 1980s, some 610 million tonnes of ore had been removed from Panguna but a further 510 million tonnes of mineable ore remained. A new waste-disposal system was nearing completion which met stringent environmental controls. It would pipe the tailings directly into the sea and reduce the environmental impact on the Jaba River Valley and allow for some immediate rehabilitation (Economic Insights 1994). Nevertheless, local landowners at Panguna began a campaign of sabotage in

1989 in support of claims for $12 billion compensation for damage inflicted over the life of the mine (*Financial Times* 1989). A central government proposal to compensate both the provincial government and local landowners from its 19 per cent equity stake in the mine was rejected and the mine was closed in May 1989. Panguna had provided 17 per cent of the domestic revenues of the PNG government so that its closure inflicted a significant negative macroeconomic shock (see Chapter 7).

The abrupt closure of Panguna carried implications for Ok Tedi which also relied on riverine tailings disposal. The mine had been projected to generate $10 billion in revenues over its lifetime, of which 39 per cent was expected to accrue to the different tiers of government and local landowners. The original mining agreement provided for barely one-sixth of 1 per cent of the projected $4 billion revenue stream to go to the local landowners and 3 per cent to the provincial government, leaving 96.8 per cent for the central government (Jackson 1993). Local landowners were compensated for leased land which included an occupation fee, a physical disturbance fee, and a bush clearance fee. The 400 inhabitants of the four communities which were most disturbed by the mine received annual payments of $188,000 in 1990, some $650 per head, a sum around three-quarters of the per capita income of PNG. In addition, 15 per cent of the $1.5 billion invested in Ok Tedi went into local communications, urban infrastructure, community health, and education. The mine provided directly and indirectly the main means of support for almost half the Western Provinces' 110,000 population.

PNG mining agreements were restructured in 1991. The share of the royalties going to the landowners was increased from 5 to 30 per cent. In the case of the Western Province government, its share of total provincial revenues jumped from 2.9 per cent in 1984 to 7.7 per cent by 1991, compared with its 3.1 per cent share of the national population. In per capita terms, provincial spending reached almost three times the national average of $87. But the Western Province had been split into northern and southern sections in 1987, and the south resented the smaller spend which it subsequently received without any diminution in the damage to the local environment. To counter this, a levy equivalent to 1 per cent of mine revenues was imposed in 1991 and earmarked for projects in the lease areas along the river system. Nevertheless, as noted in Chapter 11, those living in the southern region some 100 km below the mine, where a 30 km^2 area was affected by flooding, brought a lawsuit for $2.7 billion against Ok Tedi in 1994. The case was settled in June 1996, with the company paying the landowners' legal costs and proceeding with the $87 million disbursement over the remaining fifteen-year life of the mine. Some $31 million was made available to residents on the Lower Ok Tedi for training, business development, damage compensation, and village relocation (*Financial Times* 1996*f*).

The emerging pattern within PNG is for the benefits of mining to heighten divisions. The loss of revenue by the national government has impaired its ability to provide adequate services so that either mining companies like Ok Tedi fill the gap or the services began to deteriorate. When local landowners increase their receipts, they exacerbate divisions within local regions, as in the case of the Western

Province. The welfare of inhabitants of areas which lack large resource-based projects therefore fall increasingly behind those areas which do have such projects. Worse, the higher revenues that are transferred from the central government to the resource-rich provinces do not appear to be deployed in a sustainable manner. The country's clientelistic political system requires the recipients of the rents to disperse them rapidly throughout the community. Banks (1997) estimates that in excess of 85 per cent of such revenue is likely to be dissipated on immediate consumption as opposed to the long-term accumulation of skills and produced capital required for sustainability.

This unsatisfactory situation provides scope for agencies like the NGOs to establish institutions to enhance communication between the different parties involved in sharing the mineral rents. It is necessary to trace the distribution of revenues, the productivity of their deployment, and also the consequences of any redistribution. Such a system has emerged in neighbouring Irian Jaya in the form of a social audit.

Conflicts in an autonomous State: Irian Jaya

Mine-related problems of social discontent, secessionist threats, and environmental damage were handled very differently in Irian Jaya by the autonomous authoritarian bureaucratic government of Indonesia. The national government regarded the Grasberg copper mine as an agent for strengthening its political grasp on a distant province. The mine also made an important contribution to both the regional and national economies. It employed 15,000 workers directly in Indonesia in 1995, and an additional 75,000 in indirect employment. Direct annual benefits to the Indonesian economy were estimated at $275 million from wages, taxation, royalties, and local purchases. An expansion called for a new 200,000-tonne smelter at Gresik, near Surabaya, to absorb 600,000 tonnes of copper concentrate, or two-fifths of the expanded production (Freeport McMoRan 1995). There were also important precedents because a second MNC (Freemont) planned to open a mine of similar size in northern Irian Jaya.

The Grasberg mine profoundly affected settlement within the region. The local population in the vicinity of the mine, estimated at fewer than 100 when it started up in the early 1970s, rapidly expanded as many migrated in over long distances. New ore discoveries encouraged the company to double production between 1987 and 1993, when a further expansion was planned. By the mid-1990s, some 50,000 people lived in the area surrounding the mine, including more than 15,000 from elsewhere in Indonesia many of whom settled under transmigration schemes in the lowland areas south of the mine.

The greater autonomy of the Indonesian government allowed it to give more weight than the PNG government to long-term national development over local and regional interests. The Soeharto government moved quickly and fiercely to quash local groups seeking to impede mine operations. It gave rapid approval for mine expansion, but it also required measures to increase control over the greatly expanded tailings emissions and also an intensification of environmental auditing. The measures which

Freeport adopted to reduce tailings damage, described in Chapter 11, imposed modest costs compared with the total revenues of the mine. The expansion in output provided a strong incentive to the company not only to make the additional environmental outlays, but also to increase its social spending in an effort to allay local discontent (Dames and Moore 1996). In 1994, social spending by the Grasberg mine was $18.6 million, of which one-third went to health care, one-third to education and training, and the remaining one-third to community relations, trusts, and subsidies for incubator industries.

The MNC commissioned an independent social audit in 1996. The gist of the findings of the social audit report was that a misunderstanding existed between contrasting cultures concerning the status of local people, the speed and directness with which decisions of concern to the wider community could be taken and implemented by the company, and the cultural (as opposed to economic) value of land. The interim conclusion of the social audit was that the problems of the mining region could be remedied by greater consultation and a greater sharing of decision-making between the company, the central government, and local communities. It noted the unhelpful nature of inaccurate reporting by local interest groups and the media which served to inflame issues that were already difficult enough to resolve. The report called upon the MNC to devolve the implementation of its social programmes to NGOs. It also advised the Indonesian government to assume much more responsibility for ensuring the development of the Irian Jaya region.

The social audit echoed the concerns of Grasberg, Ok Tedi, and other mining MNCs: a large mining company may be willing and able to play a leading role in building social capability, but it is reluctant to shoulder the full responsibility for change, especially in a politically sensitive region. The Freeport company responded to the audit by dedicating at least 1 per cent of its revenues over each of the ensuing ten years to community development projects whose expenditure would be coordinated by the local community and the provincial government. It also agreed to double the number of local people in its workforce by 2000, and to double that number again by 2005.

Reducing social dependency

The developments in New Guinea described above reflect trends under way in many countries. In densely settled Jamaica, for example, the aluminium companies have long regarded outlays on community relations as an essential part of their operations. The companies provide assistance with community centres, clinics, schools, and basic services such as electricity and water when they move into a new area. But the companies are also anxious to avoid the establishment of a paternalistic relationship with surrounding communities. With this in mind, Alcoa for example, helps locals to acquire skills such as sewing and furniture-making to generate extra income. In an interesting experiment in the early 1990s, Kaiser Bauxite offered those experiencing noise nuisance from mining the option of participation in a broiler farm in lieu of direct payment for noise compensation. Kaiser estimated that those who joined its scheme would earn an extra $227 annually above their compensation payments (at least double the compensation) in a project which would last long after mining moved on, thereby reducing the risk of enhanced dependence on the company for an income.

In Chile, the new Escondida mine restrained its social spending in order to discourage excessive dependence on the firm by the local community, notably in the port of Antofagasta. The Escondida mine employed many fewer workers than the older state-owned mine at Chuquicamata. No mining town, like that at Colama adjacent to Chuquicamata, is planned. The workforce in 1995 (1,100 direct workers) was barely one-ninth that of Chuquicamata and spent relatively short periods (four days) at a mine camp, being principally resident in Antofagasta. Assuming a labour multiplier of between 2.5 and 4 indirect jobs, the total population dependent upon Escondida is probably one-fifth that of the older Chuquicamata mine, which supports a city of more than 100,000. The company contributes to the communal life of Antofagasta but seeks to promote the region's economic diversification.

Finally, in Namibia, Rossing Uranium has long pursued the sustainability objective of diversifying local skills through the establishment of a foundation. The trust has assets exceeding $25 million which have accumulated through the annual allocation of 3 per cent of Rossing's profits (with matching contributions from other agencies) to a fund for the training of local people in education and crafts.

The schemes described in this section for building social and human capital, as well as produced capital, as a basis for sustainable development focus on the local community. As the tensions in PNG show, the benefits of mining must be spread more widely. A critical problem identified in Chapters 8 and 9 is a lack of employment for the least skilled members of the workforce in mature mid-income mineral economies. Such high unemployment may tempt governments into overambitious interventions that damage economic growth through efforts to force the pace of economic growth by, for example, launching populist booms (Lal 1995). An alternative approach is reviewed in the next section with reference to Namibia. That country is in the mature stage of its mineral cycle and may have an opportunity through a revival of uranium mining and offshore diamond mining to remedy the historical neglect by the pre-independence oligopolistic political State of social capital accumulation during the youthful stage of the cycle (Auty 1996*b*).

Building Social Capital: A Labour-Intensive Growth Strategy

The legacy of social neglect

Chapters 8 and 9 show that economic diversification during the transition to maturity has presented especial difficulties for the smaller mineral economies with limited non-mining resources and small domestic markets for manufacturing. Unemployment tends to be high and a sizeable fraction of the workforce exhibits levels of productivity which are low in relation to the cost of labour. For example, after fifteen years during which real incomes have halved, Trinidad and Tobago has yet to price a sizeable fraction of its labour force into competitive activity. Elsewhere, manufacturing has performed disappointingly in Jamaica and concern has been growing in Botswana concerning the expanding urban poor. Nowhere are such problems more acute, however, than in Namibia where the legacy of apartheid has been the almost total neglect of two-thirds of the workforce on the 'communal lands', mostly along the Angolan border (Figure 12.1).

Despite the arid conditions throughout Namibia, agriculture supports directly and indirectly, around 70 per cent of the population but it generates less than 9 per cent of GDP. It underpins the economy of the lagging northern region where almost two-thirds of the country's population live but they produce only 3 to 6 per cent of GDP. Within the northern region, 120,000 smallholdings provide partial employment for between 220,000 and 370,000 people (the bulk of the workforce). These workers in turn support a total of 800,000 people. The other communal areas in Namibia support perhaps one-tenth of that number. In the early 1990s the communal areas as a whole produced barely 15 per cent of measured farm production which generated 1.7 per cent of GDP (World Bank 1992*a*). Worse, the per capita land ratio of 3 ha. was at the sustainable limit so that population pressure threatened to damage the environment.

Relatively small public transfers (around 3 per cent of GDP) from the modern sector to the lagging region could raise per capita incomes in the lagging regions by 50 per cent. It could be justified by the fact that the north, with over half the population, currently receives barely one-tenth of government spending (some 3 per cent of GDP). But such an increase in the scale of transfers does not upgrade work skills as sustainable development requires, and it resembles the discredited public employment programmes favoured by Trinidad and Tobago during its oil booms (Gelb and Associates 1988). Many northern households already rely heavily on transfers from the Namibian government and relatives (often government employees) for a significant fraction of their income. The typical northern household of seven individuals secures one-quarter of its income from pensions and remittances from relatives, one-quarter from formal sector employment, one-quarter from informal employment, and barely one-quarter from farming. It is preferable to raise incomes by expanding productive employment rather than building a dependence on government entitlements.

The combination of modest medium-term employment potential of manufacturing in Namibia, a need to reduce public employment, and the lack of new resource-based development options, implies that a labour-intensive development strategy is required for the lagging northern region. In the absence of vigorous growth in jobs, there is a risk that the scale of out-migration to the cities in the modern sector will outstrip job-creation there. This would intensify urban poverty and associated crime in a way that could undermine investor confidence and slow economic growth even further in the modern sector. A dualism already exists *within* the Namibian modern sector: a relatively high-paying formal sector coexists with a lower-paying informal sector and high levels of urban unemployment, estimated at 26 per cent compared with 16 per cent for rural unemployment (Gaomab 1994).

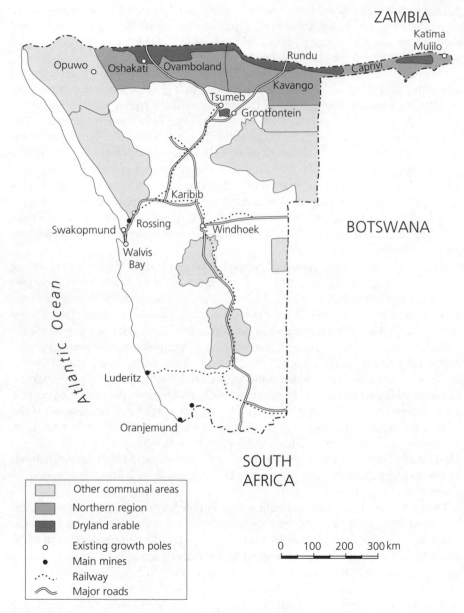

Figure 12.1 Location of economic activity in Namibia

A labour-intensive growth strategy

If northern unemployment and poverty are not to overburden the job-deficient modern sector, a labour-intensive growth strategy must be developed for the lagging region. Not only is this where the majority of Namibians live, it is also where water is most plentiful and where, because of the greater efficiency of servicing areas of dense population, infrastructure can be most cheaply upgraded. The basic objective of a labour-intensive growth strategy should be to lift the regional economic growth rate to 10 per cent (twice the modern sector), implying per capita income growth of 7 per cent (three times the modern sector). Such rates would raise northern GRP sixteenfold in a generation and boost per capita incomes at least eightfold. This would still leave a wide income gap between the modern and lagging regions in the year 2020 because, under the above assumptions, per capita income in the modern sector would be seven times that of the north (compared with almost thirty-fold in the early 1990s).

Briefly, the first stage of a labour-intensive growth strategy would entail some redistribution of resources in favour of smaller farmers in the lagging region. The second stage would kick-start the local economy by a combination of simple farm innovations and increased employment in the labour-intensive construction of basic infrastructure. Stage three would be driven increasingly by the local multiplier from the spending of higher incomes and entail the proliferation of local services and basic manufacturing, much of it likely to occur within the informal sector. The fourth stage would be driven by interregional trade, mainly in labour-intensive manufacturing and services, first with adjacent regions such as the Namibian modern sector and southern Angola, and then with more distant regions.

More specifically, stage one is a preconditioning stage which involves institutional developments that are geared towards increasing the availability of resources. It involves four basic measures. First, ranches on fenced rangelands adjacent to the densely settled Ovamboland area would be annexed (with compensation at market value) in order to augment the land available to small grazers and ease pressure on existing communal grazing areas (Ashley 1995). Second, an expansion of irrigation would occur beside the northern rivers. Third, the agricultural extension service would be strengthened. Finally, title to land would be given to individuals in the neo-urban areas of the north (where growth will be rapid) in order to encourage investment.

The second stage involves a substantial expansion of labour-intensive employment which boosts local income by drawing on surplus labour and encouraging further job specialization. The employment expansion is achieved by expanding irrigated horticulture; modestly boosting farm productivity (past neglect affords ample scope) by giving smallholders inputs with which to double grain yields to 750 kg per ha; and increasing off-farm paid employment through upgrading local infrastructure (secondary rural roads, schools, and clinics) through 'sites and services' funding and building major infrastructure projects such as a new highway and water pipeline.

Non-farm activities will become dominant as the population increases still further and land resources come under still greater pressure. Consequently, in the third stage of the labour-intensive strategy, the local multiplier to non-farm businesses becomes critical. The proliferation of informal sector businesses accelerates in response to the higher spending associated with increased farm production and off-farm wages. For example, local grog shops can diversify their merchandise to include basic farm inputs and the sale of both fresh local produce and other goods which super-markets cannot effectively supply to more dispersed rural populations. Such informal activity has played a critical role in stabilizing Peruvian society during and after the period of economic mismanagement (De Soto 1989). It may be required to play a key role in the transition of Botswana towards the mature stage of its mineral cycle, as discussed in the penultimate section of Chapter 9. Tourism will also grow in northern Namibia, both in connection with the further extension into the north of wildlife tourism as well as the growth of lower-cost tourism run by communal groups (Ashley and Garland 1994).

These income-augmenting activities will boost the local multiplier in stage three and, although a sizeable fraction of that multiplier will leak out of the region to purchase both manufactured goods from South Africa and higher-order services from Windhoek, the growth in regional purchasing power will still create many opportun-ities for local firms. Such opportunities include the provision of building materials, house fixtures and furnishings, beverages and clothing as well as the farm inputs required for irrigation and ploughing. The third stage therefore plays a vital role in building local business experience and entrepreneurial skills, i.e. by building social capability with markets, rather than the government, as the principal agent.

The fourth and final stage of the model is characterized by expanding export potential for labour-intensive goods and services, initially to adjacent regions in south-ern Angola and the modern sector of Namibia, but increasingly to more distant regions. A *labour-intensive* EPZ could exploit the north's location on a major transport corridor linking the central African countries to ports on the Atlantic coast. Mean-while, as the northern workforce becomes more specialized and urbanized and population growth decelerates, pressure on the land will ease, so that farm size can increase and help to raise farm incomes.

More research is required into the viability of such a strategy for directing min-eral rents into building social capability through interaction between the formal and informal sectors, and also into its application to improve the employment prospects of lagging groups in other mineral economies. A still better strategy, however, is for emerging mineral economies to seek to deploy the mining rents during boom times in an attempt to minimize the social exclusion of a significant fraction of the population.

Conclusions

This book identifies the policies required for the sustainable development of min-eral economies, stressing the need to mitigate the effects of external shocks, to invest in the replacement of the income stream from the depleting mineral asset, and to

encourage the abatement of environmental damage. The prescription of such policies is one thing, however, and their effective implementation is quite another. As
the third section has demonstrated, national governments, especially those in non-
consensual factional States, face many conflicting pressures which render difficult
the pursuit of a coherent set of policies to maximize long-term welfare. Meanwhile,
at the local level, communities do not always pursue objectives *vis-à-vis* mineral
revenue streams that foster sustainability. For these reasons, building social sustainability into policies is a critical requirement which has only recently begun to
receive the attention which it warrants.

The focus of this chapter has been the local level, at which social tensions often
involve conflicts over mineral rents and, more recently, over the uneven distribution of the burden of the costs of environmental degradation. The rise of environmental concerns in the 1980s has at times been deployed by local agents to extract
a higher share of the rents, sometimes in the form of extravagant claims which lack
a rationally costed basis. Acceding to such demands works against sustainability
because it counter-productively heightens community dependence on a depleting asset
and transfers resources away from those communities which lack a local resource
to exploit.

Probably the most productive legacy the mine could provide a community is
education and training, particularly directed towards industries that might be in
operation after the mine is gone. The mining companies can play a positive role in
building social capability within the local community, by giving greater emphasis
on expenditure to encourage skill accumulation and business diversification, as opposed
to their traditional support for infrastructure provision. NGOs have a constructive
role to play in this task, by mediating between local communities and both MNC
mining firms and higher tiers of government. Social audits undertaken by responsible agencies can play a vital role in building trust among the stakeholders in the
mining sector by documenting the mineral revenue flow at the national and local
levels, the efficiency of its deployment, and the consequences of redistribution. An
increase in the transparency of both the flow of mineral rents and the effectiveness
of their deployment can diffuse tensions. MNCs began to deploy social audits in
the 1990s as they sought to anticipate and defuse social tensions which threaten
sustainability. The participation of NGOs is potentially useful: however, some
NGOs seem, at times, to employ staff with only a limited knowledge of, and/or
outright hostility towards, the orthodox economic policies which this study has shown
to be essential for sustainable mineral-driven development.

The failure of excluded groups within society to acquire the skills during the youthful stage of the mineral cycle with which to secure employment through the mature
stage has been identified as a major obstacle to sustainable development, especially
for the smaller mineral economies. Social sustainability requires that when economic
reforms are instituted which severely impair the welfare of low-income or even large
middle-income groups, measures should be taken to mitigate these effects, even at
the expense of retarding somewhat the desired overall adjustments. It also requires
that rapid increases in rents from mineral exploitation should benefit all income groups

and stimulate growth in the regions where minerals are not produced. Governments should not simply assume that what is good for one industry, and for those who benefit directly from it, is good for the country. What is good for the country involves maximizing the difference between social benefits and costs, at national, regional, and local levels. Since most mineral-exporting developing countries continue to have a largely rural population, it is especially important that rents are directed towards rural development. Namibia provides a stark warning of the problems which the prolonged neglect of such communities can generate.

Part V

Policy Implications for Mineral-Led Development

13 Policies for the Sustainable Development of Mineral Economies

Introduction

This chapter summarizes the principal findings and draws on the evidence presented throughout this study to derive lessons for other mineral economies at each stage of the mineral-led cycle. Such lessons are intended to help improve the generally disappointing economic performance of the mineral economies compared with other developing countries with different natural resource endowments. Their implications for the Central Asian mineral economies in transition such as Kazakstan, Turkmenistan, and Mongolia are still in the process of being assessed (Auty 1997c, 1997d).

The second section examines the macroeconomic requirements for sustainable development. Foremost among these requirements is the removal of structural obstacles to sustainable growth that were created by government intervention in most mineral-exporting countries during the 1960s and 1970s. The third section summarizes the conclusions of this study on the macroeconomic policies needed for dealing with fluctuations in export income during the principal stages of the mineral cycle. Policies are required for avoiding the symptoms of the Dutch disease and for stabilizing both foreign and domestic expenditures by means of a mineral revenue stabilization fund. The fourth section reviews natural capital depletion and the utility of environmental accounting as a policy instrument. The fifth section explores the internalization of the cost of environmental damage, and the following section considers the socio-political conditions for sustainable mineral-driven development. The seventh section summarizes the conclusions on mineral management, including promotion of exploration and development, taxation of mineral rents, and the establishment of mineral management institutions. Throughout these sections the policies appropriate for different stages in the mineral cycle are noted, together with their application to economies with different degrees of diversification and size.

Prerequisites for Sustainability

Mineral economies as a group have tended to underperform since the 1960s, especially in comparison with resource-deficient developing countries. The variations in the economic performance of the mineral economies show, however, that underperformance is by no means inevitable. These variations reflect differences in the evolution of the politico-economic structure over time, the type of mineral and the market for it, and, most importantly, the capacity of the State to adopt appropriate policies for dealing with economic shocks.

The initial politico-economic structures of the mineral-exporting countries covered by this study differ substantially and the countries have displayed significantly different development trajectories over the 1960–96 period. During the 1960–80 period, many of these countries nationalized their foreign-owned mining and petroleum companies, discouraged private foreign and domestic investment in exploration and development, adopted import-substituting manufacturing programmes by means of trade controls and subsidies, and pursued non-competitive domestic policies involving price, credit, and investment controls. These economic structures, which were adopted by Peru (1968–75), by Chile (1970–3), and Jamaica (1973–6), among others, not only limited the growth and productivity of the mineral industries, but generated price distortions which led to the repression of agriculture and those manufacturing sectors in which the countries have a comparative advantage in world trade. These structural conditions were often accompanied by populist-generated efforts to redistribute income in favour of certain socio-politico groups, which had the effect of reducing incentives for production and for private and foreign investment in the economy. Over the past two decades, most of the countries studied have undertaken structural reforms in various degrees. These reforms have included partial denationalization of the mineral industries, increased incentives for foreign and domestic exploration and development of the mineral industries, trade liberalization, monetary and fiscal policies for controlling inflation, the establishment of competitive domestic markets, and the adoption of realistic exchange rates compatible with balance of payments equilibrium. More recently, a number of countries have privatized or eliminated inefficient and loss-producing state firms in the non-mineral sector. A fundamental conclusion of this study is that these structural and policy reforms provide the essential conditions for achieving sustainable development of mineral-exporting economies.

Economic structure and macroeconomic policy

Sound macro-management underlies the successful transition of Indonesia through the mineral-driven cycle, the maintenance of rapid diamond-driven growth in Botswana, the recovery of Chile to best practice in Latin America, and the relative stability of PNG through the external and internal stresses of its first sixteen years of independence. The ability and willingness of a government to use macro-policies for achieving goals essential to sustainability is an important element of economic structure, which is not always present. The structural elements have to do with the independence of the central bank and the flexibility of the government to adjust its tax structure and fiscal expenditures without political compromise. The government should also be in a position to adjust tariffs and other forms of import restriction, to adjust exchange rates, and to control external indebtedness. Adopting the correct macro-policies requires competent staffs as well as independence from political pressures. Few governments exhibit all of these conditions, but some that do may not follow the correct policies or their policies may be resented by a large segment of the population.

Sustainable development in mineral-exporting countries is promoted by low inflation, trade liberalization, and free capital markets. However, the exercise of monetary and fiscal policy for reducing inflation and the freeing of foreign trade and external capital markets requires appropriate timing to avoid unemployment, price distortions, and economic recession. There are basic differences among economists regarding both the degree of monetary and fiscal tightening and their timing in relation to trade and capital-market liberalization. For example, a 'big bang' approach is often advocated by the IMF, while a more gradual reform process was adopted by Chile after its 1982 recession (Corbo and Fischer 1994). The Chilean experience recommends a three-step sequence, which initially targets stabilization until inflation falls below 20–5 per cent, followed by trade reform. Trade reform in turn requires raising taxes to offset revenue losses as tariffs are reduced. Fiscal reform also calls for reduced subsidies and broadening of revenue sources, such as a value-added tax. However, value-added taxes are potentially inflationary and politically unpopular. The third stage of the reform sequence is capital-market liberalization, a step which may lead to large capital imports or exports, both of which may have disturbing impacts.

Economic reforms are often seen as harming those with low incomes, thus compounding the political difficulty of implementation. They pose special difficulties for factional political States because their governments are likely to respond to the short- and medium-term hardships of adjustment in a way that diminishes the long-term benefits (Mahon 1992). Opposition to economic reform may result in the election of a new government which abandons the reform. Therefore, the reform policies may require the government to boost demand in order to mitigate unemployment and reduced growth.

The economic stability resulting from economic reforms has sometimes triggered large capital inflows and produced Dutch disease effects by pushing up the real exchange rate and hampering the diversification of the non-mining tradeables sector (Williamson 1996). This phenomenon dogged post-reform Jamaica and Trinidad and Tobago, and was also evident in Peru during the mid-1990s. The consequences of strong capital inflows are more difficult to manage by mid-income countries and by smaller countries lacking economic diversification. In particular, employment creation is too weak in the mid-income countries, in contrast to the situation in low-income Indonesia.

Chile may offer more practical lessons than Indonesia for the more typical mineral exporter which reaches mid-income levels before the mature stage sets in. Chilean experience reinforces the important role of cautiously orthodox macroeconomic management, but it also warns against a doctrinaire approach. The country's sustained recovery from the deep recession of 1982 was assisted by the adoption of an MRSF, the temporary raising of import protection, and greater autonomy for the central bank. Chile also holds lessons for badly distorted economies. But the lessons from a specific country need qualifying in light of the specific socio-political conditions. Chile benefited from the evolution of the authoritarian Pinochet regime into a developmental State and subsequently into a consensual democracy, and it also enjoyed a diversified non-mining resource base.

The risk of rapid sequence reform is illustrated by the decision of the Fujimori government in Peru to adopt a bold 'big bang' reform programme upon gaining office in 1990. Although the Peruvian government had not been elected to pursue such policies and had in fact attacked the reformist policies of its chief opponent, it promptly adopted similar policies once in office. The sequencing of reform was compressed and resulted in almost three years of economic stagnation before a robust recovery was actually under way. The stagnation might have been avoided by a combination of more gradual fiscal and monetary tightening and slower trade liberalization plus government spending and investment incentives that would have their principal impact on the lower-income classes.

But there is also the risk of overstimulating the economy. The clearest instances of populist booms among the countries studied here occurred in Chile 1970–3, Jamaica 1973–6, and Peru 1985–8. In addition, government policies permitted overstimulation during the commodity booms. This occurred during the 1979–81 oil boom in the case of Trinidad and Tobago, and to a lesser extent Indonesia; and in PNG during the early 1990s. There was also overstimulation in Botswana during the late 1980s. All these episodes proved counter-productive and while they were quite quickly rectified in the developmental States like Indonesia and Botswana, where the economies had been only very moderately distorted, that was not the case for the two small economies, Jamaica and Trinidad and Tobago.

Macroeconomic Policies for Dealing with Export Fluctuations

The major function of macro-policy in dealing with sharp fluctuations in export revenue is to prevent the symptoms of the Dutch disease, which include real exchange rate appreciation and unstable government expenditures. Real exchange appreciation can be avoided by sterilizing export revenue accruing directly to the government or from the proceeds of taxes on mineral rents. Central banks can also operate in exchange markets to prevent real exchange rate appreciation. Government expenditures should be controlled to limit consumer expenditures and to direct a substantial portion of increased government revenues into productive capital projects. Sharp reductions in government expenditures that impact low-income groups as well as requiring suspension of essential capital projects, should also be avoided. The adoption and implementation of an MRSF is an important instrument for carrying out macro-policies for achieving these objectives.

Youthful stage: role of a mineral revenue stabilization fund (MRSF)

The case for an MRSF rests partly upon the *un*predictability of the revenue stream over both the long-run and the short-run, and partly upon the *predictable* inflationary effects of an overrapid absorption of the mineral rents. An MRSF can help to sterilize the revenue flows during boom periods, such as the youthful stage of the mineral cycle, and also smooth the adjustment of public spending to the boom-bust cycle. The use of an MRSF to control the deployment of revenues from natural capital depletion provides a rationale for distinguishing between the capital component and the true income component of the mineral revenue stream. Although, macro-theorists argue that an MRSF may yield a suboptimal employment of resources (Varangis *et al.* 1995), the empirical evidence suggests that the difficulty of forecasting revenue flows and of resisting political pressure for overrapid absorption during booms justifies a more cautious approach. All four of the more successful countries studied operated MRSFs.

One function of the MRSF is to sterilize the capital inflow and moderate fluctuations in the real exchange rate. Macro-theorists tend to assume that shifts in the real exchange rate will be clearly signalled so that the relative size of the non-tradeables and non-mining tradeables sectors will automatically adjust (Davis 1995). During an upswing the former will expand at the expense of the latter, only to reverse as the mineral boom tapers off. However, the adjustment is rarely as smooth and unidirectional; capacity in the tradeables sector which is lost during an upswing is not so quickly replaced during a downswing. The legacy of Dutch disease effects in the form of a prematurely shrunken agricultural sector and a highly protected manufacturing sector is evident in most of the mineral economies studied.

Roemer (1994) identifies the two most critical aspects of the Dutch disease legacy in mineral-endowed countries as the emergence of a severe foreign exchange constraint (as mineral revenues decline relative to GDP) and the loss of the 'learning by doing' effect associated with a dynamic non-mining tradeables sector. A tradeables sector which is inadequately diversified and insufficiently competitive to drive the economy, lies at the root of the problems of the smaller mid-income mature mineral economies. Some appreciation of the real exchange rate seems unavoidable during a mineral boom, however, especially during the sustained expansion in mineral production, which is often associated with the youthful stage of the mineral cycle. This real appreciation is likely to increase pressure for protection from the non-mining tradeables like agriculture and manufacturing. Such pressure may be conceded on a temporary basis, where the upswing is expected to be brief, or where some time-constrained adjustment to sharply changed circumstances seems appropriate (as even Chile permitted after the 1982 recession). But the ever-present risk of policy capture means the subsequent repeal of such assistance may prove politically challenging.

A second important function of an MRSF is to smooth the effect of the boom-bust cycle on government revenues. An MRSF biases the mineral rent absorption policy towards caution, and helps to discourage governments from acting upon the basis of overoptimistic forecasts (Duncan *et al.* 1995). In line with Gelb and Associates (1988) and Hill (1991), such caution is preferable because the economic damage arising from a permanent favourable price shift that is assumed to be temporary is less than that arising if a temporary price improvement is assumed to be permanent. This is because of the dislocation, which arises when the revenue expansion is overestimated and resources must be withdrawn from the economy to restore economic balance. For example, in Trinidad and Tobago a relatively cautious government found itself committed to unsustainable levels of public expenditure and unable to move quickly enough to balance its finances, even with an accumulated financial reserve that was almost 50 per cent of GDP. A third function for the MRSF is to track the use made of the revenue stream emanating from the depleting capital asset, an issue discussed in the following section.

Among the countries studied here, the youthful stage of the mineral cycle was especially well managed by Botswana and Indonesia, but less so by PNG. However, Botswana was helped by three favourable factors, two of which were linked to the characteristics of the mineral, diamonds. These favourable factors were the scale of the rents, the stability of the rent flows, and a political consensus within a conservative pastoral community that favoured cautious economic policy. As an oil exporter, Indonesia experienced more erratic external conditions than Botswana but it prudently responded by saving 30–40 per cent of the windfall abroad during the booms. It also carefully deployed the mineral rents, with the exception of its inefficient state-led industrial policy. But the country's readiness to dismantle the state-led industrial policy when oil prices fell in the mid-1980s clearly shows the primacy accorded to macro-management.

Maintaining growth in the mature stage

The Dutch disease effects during mineral booms, especially during the youthful stage if it is particularly dynamic, may reverse economic diversification and leave the economy in a weak position should mineral revenues decline steeply (as occurred in the case of Jamaica after 1976 and of Trinidad and Tobago after 1981). The onset of the mature stage of the mineral-driven cycle brings a relative decline in the importance of the foreign exchange, taxation, and economic multiplier from the mining sector. In those cases where a sizeable financial reserve has been accumulated through the MRSF, as in the case of Botswana by the early 1990s or Trinidad and Tobago a decade earlier, one option is to draw down the reserve to cushion the adjustment.

Drawing on the MRSF can buy time with which to adjust government finances and the production structure of the economy to a sustainable path. This requires tax reforms to readjust the fiscal burden away from trade (that is, from export taxes and royalties on primary products and import duties on manufactured goods) and towards sales taxes and value-added taxes. It may also require the resetting of priorities for government spending in order to concentrate resources on where they achieve the highest return, a move which will usually require a shift away from middle-income groups in order to target the poorest in society. Such a shift in the tax burden is likely to be accompanied by cutbacks in public investment (which are politically easier to make than cutbacks in current expenditure in times of fiscal austerity), and it may also bring a decline in private savings. Consequently, economic growth prospects receive a double blow because the slower growth in mining is accompanied by an overall fall in domestic savings and investment. In addition, a relative or absolute decline in foreign exchange income compresses imports. Under these circumstances, it is important to attract additional foreign investment outside the mining sector to ease both the foreign exchange and the investment constraints, and also to accelerate the restructuring of the economy.

The Indonesian government was able to achieve each of these objectives in a relatively short time through the late 1980s, but it did so at the cost of a sharp increase in foreign debt and in its debt service ratio, with the latter briefly approaching 40 per cent of exports and threatening to become unmanageable. However, the effectiveness of the Indonesian fiscal and trade reforms was associated with a doubling in the level of investment relative to GDP through the 1980s so that, despite a disappointingly high ICOR (Roemer 1994), economic growth was successfully sustained. Yet the lessons of Indonesia's experience for other mineral economies must be qualified. First, the Indonesian economy was less distorted than many mineral economies, both before and after its mineral boom. Second, the diversification of the economy when maturity was restored, was facilitated by the country's potentially large domestic market (as a platform for manufacturing), and significant non-mineral and other natural resources in its sparsely settled outer islands which attracted significant foreign investment. Finally, Indonesia's relatively low level of per capita income also helped in diversification by easing the reversion of the economy to a successful 'East Asian' labour-intensive development path.

Such vigorous growth in manufacturing is less likely to be experienced by the larger mineral economies (such as Chile and Peru) that mature at higher per capita income levels and whose diversification therefore relies more on other primary products. But the small, maturing mid-income mineral economies may lack comparative advantage in either manufactured exports or non-mineral resources, and therefore experience a lag before resuming rapid economic growth. That lag will persist longer, the more distorted the economy and the more reluctant the reform effort, but Botswana and Namibia show that even cautiously managed economies may experience a growth pause which is sufficiently long to strain the patience of even a hitherto well-functioning political consensus. Overall, the transition through the mineral-driven cycle appears easier the more autonomous and benevolent the political State, the less distorted the economy, the lower the per capita income at which the transition takes place, and the larger (and more diversified) the non-mining natural resource base. This implies that the transition is especially difficult for a small economy with a factional or predatory autonomous government whose mineral revenue stream requires it to make the transition to maturity at a mid-income level.

This unfortunate outcome for the smaller, resource-deficient mid-income mineral economies suggests two additional policy lessons. First, mineral economies with such a narrow resource endowment have a greater need to minimize the Dutch disease effects during mining booms than do the better-endowed mineral economies. Second, a sizeable real depreciation of the exchange rate may be required to create a comparative advantage in the non-mining tradeables and stimulate vigorous non-mineral-led growth. Yet, as both a rapidly-reforming country like Peru and a slowly-reforming one like Jamaica illustrate, the inflows of foreign capital associated with structural adjustment reforms impede the required real exchange rate correction.

Replacing Depleting Natural Resources

Sustainable development requires that the income stream generated by a nation's depleted natural resources be replaced by an equivalent income stream. This is in accordance with the principle that revenue in the form of capital depletion cannot be sustained. Although natural resource assets should be regarded as natural capital, economists are not in general agreement on how resource depletion should be defined and measured. Measuring depletion is important for two reasons. First, it is necessary to deduct annual depletion when estimating the environmental domestic product (EDP) as used in environmental resource accounting (EARA). Failure to deduct natural resource depletion results in an overstatement of a nation's economic performance and may lead to the adoption of policies incompatible with sustainability. And second, an accurate measure of depletion is required to determine how much a nation needs to save out of the total revenue generated by a natural resource asset in order to provide for replacing the net output lost by depletion.

The two principal measures of natural capital depletion are the net price and the user-cost methods, but these measures yield substantially different estimates when applied to the same country, with the difference depending upon the importance of minerals in the country's total output. The differences in these estimates of depletion are reflected in the degree to which EDP1 differs from the conventional measure of net national product (NNP). The net price measure usually yields a lower EDP1 relative to NNP than the user-cost method. This is especially the case for high-rent, oil-rich, and diamond-rich mineral economies. For example, the application of the net price approach to Indonesia reveals a sizeable divergence between that country's NDP and its EDP1 in the youthful stage. Thereafter, during the mature stage the gap narrows as the relative importance of mining declines, a process which was especially rapid in Indonesia due not only to the sharp fall in oil rents but also to the effective deployment of the rents to diversify into manufacturing.

The user-cost method tends to produce a much smaller divergence between NNP and EDP1 because it conforms with the conventional definition of sustainable income of requiring that the natural capital asset be replaced only to the extent needed to maintain the income stream indefinitely. This implies that the net price method may overstate the investment component associated with the depletion of finite resources. But the user-cost method is open to criticism for *understating* depletion, especially where the mineral reserves are large in relation to production. For example, where reserves exceed fifty years' supply, a not unusual situation in the case of hard minerals, the application of the private discount rate calls for less than 1 per cent of the rents to be accumulated to replace the income stream (Table 10.3).

But the possibility of changes in demand and of technological substitution reinforce the lesson of macro-management, which is to err on the cautious side. As a
result, this study concludes that it is sensible to set a twenty years' cap on the life
of the mineral reserve. Such a limit would still only require one-sixth of the rent
to be allocated to depletion if a 10 per cent discount rate is used, so that caution
might also warrant the adoption of a lower discount rate.

That portion of the revenue generated by the mineral industry after deducting
the costs of extraction, which does not represent depletion, may be used for public
consumption expenditures, but the portion representing depletion should be used
for productive investment, which will generate a net income stream equivalent to
that generated by the depleted resource. That portion of mineral rents accruing to
the government that represents mineral depletion may be invested in infrastructure
projects provided they yield an adequate rate of return, but the programmes should
be sufficiently flexible so they can be accelerated or slowed down depending upon
the revenue stream available for that purpose. Mineral depletion funds can also be
invested abroad where they earn a return replacing the income generated by the depleted
minerals, until such time as expanded domestic absorptive capacity promises superior returns on those assets.

However, to the extent that public consumption includes health and education,
such public spending might also be considered as capital formation. The Central
Bank of Botswana (1994) uses as a rule-of-thumb assumption that 30 per cent of
such spending represents human capital accumulation. Alternatively, some of the
income component may be applied to boost private consumption by a lowering of
taxation. But this strategy, while politically appealing, runs the risk of establishing
patterns of consumption whose momentum requires the fiscal gap to be bridged by
the government even if the revenue stream declines unexpectedly.

An alternative deployment strategy for mineral rents, which would avoid relying
upon public sector spending, would be to disperse it to private citizens, thereby decen-
tralizing the decision-making process. Such a distribution system has the political
appeal of allowing the citizens to make the decisions about the appropriate balance
between consumption and investment. It appears to have advantages where, for example, the rents emanate from booming crop prices and farmers are permitted to retain
a larger share of the windfall. Varangis *et al.* (1995) report sensible adjustments to
the coffee boom of the late 1970s by Kenyan farmers who saved an estimated 60
per cent of the windfall. Or again, in Thailand rice farmers appear to adjust to higher
prices in ways other than by the counter-productive strategy of overplanting.

However, in the case of minerals, the separation of the vast majority of rent
recipients from the direct source of those rents may blunt the bias towards caution
exhibited by farmers in receipt of crop rents. Moreover, the likelihood of unexpected
and severely prolonged downswings in mineral revenue streams creates difficult
adjustment problems, as the experience of Alaska shows. Alaska allocated part of
the mineral lease rents and royalties to the Permanent Fund from which a 'dividend' was paid to each resident each year from 1982. The Permanent Fund totalled
$15.6 billion in 1993, or $26,000 per resident, and the annual dividend was $950.

But declining revenue was forcing cut-backs and/or higher taxation in the mid-1990s. Yet if the State had not distributed annual dividends and had also kept a tighter rein on public expenditure, the fund would have cumulated to $75 billion, yielding annual revenue of $3.9 billion, a sum sufficient to sustain public spending levels indefinitely without raising taxes.

Internalizing the Costs of Environmental Damage

Three requirements for mine rehabilitation are the implementation of environmental baseline studies of the area likely to be impacted by mining, the execution and submission of an environmental impact assessment, and the accumulation of funds over the (conservatively estimated) life of the mine to ensure an adequate clean-up upon closure. Mine rehabilitation costs appear small in relation to total mine revenues, even in densely settled regions like Jamaica where the opportunity cost of land is high. Rehabilitation costs are minimal in barren regions like the deserts of Atacama and Namibia. Nevertheless, rehabilitation costs are still likely to be sufficiently onerous to encourage best practice for waste management during the operating life of the mine. But upland mines in humid geologically unstable regions such as New Guinea face major problems in the disposal and storage of mine waste.

Most MNCs are moving towards establishing funds to rehabilitate their mines, but state-owned mines lag best practice either because they have been badly run in mismanaged economies (where MNCs may also have eked out their investment and fallen behind best practice) or because they cannot compete for scarce public expenditure against social projects. Small mines tend to lag even further behind and to pose even greater problems for governments in securing compliance with emerging systems of environmental standards.

Minimizing water contamination

Where waste-disposal costs can only be kept under control by recourse to riverine deposition, substantial social and environmental disruption may nevertheless occur, even in relatively underpopulated areas such as New Guinea. Water contamination has been dealt with historically by the mining companies negotiating compensation with local communities. The agreements have subsequently been reinforced by the constraints imposed on waste disposal by shareholders and international banks. Consequently, this study has reported historical evidence of environmental abuse with respect to tailings disposal, but it has found relatively few current adverse effects of mine-related water emissions on farm productivity.

In the countries studied, water contaminated by mining may restrict the crops that can be grown, but it appears to depress farm productivity only minimally and yields may even be enhanced where low-cost recycled process water is made available for irrigation. Chile shows that the provision of recycled process water for irrigation may enhance farm yields at a lower cost than would be the case in the absence of the mines and their process water. Damage from mine drainage in populous areas has long been dealt with by negotiating local compensation, but in anticipation of formal rules, the larger private firms have adopted best-practice technology and internalized environmental costs with little effect on competitiveness. But older firms, especially state-owned ones, lag in the adoption of pollution-abating technology which is more cheaply absorbed as part of an investment designed to expand output and productivity.

There have, however, been recent episodes of groundwater contamination in the Jamaican bauxite sector. These episodes have been associated with the older and more neglected refineries, a finding which is consistent with the general conclusion from this study that even MNCs may diverge from best practice in mismanaged economies where uncertain long-term economic prospects encourage owners to eke out their investment and thereby miss opportunities to upgrade their technology. Even so, leading MNCs like Alcan have searched for alternative methods of disposing of the red mud effluent from their refineries. For example, the Alcan Ewarton alumina refinery pioneered dry mud-stacking techniques. In contrast, the joint-venture Alpart refinery in western Jamaica continued to lag best practice, citing the marginal nature of its relatively high-cost operation as a reason for postponing action. A change of ownership at Alpart which lifted the stake, and therefore the profile, of Norsk Hydro may herald improvements.

The most difficult water-pollution problems are associated with the upland mines in the geomorphologically unstable regions of the humid tropics like New Guinea. Here, a choice must be made between constructing an expensive tailings dam or marine pipeline, which can marginalize even an efficient mine, and controlled (and compensated) medium-term damage through riverine disposal. In defence of riverine deposition it is argued that the volumes of rock involved are not outside those occurring as natural events; they will be largely self-adjusting when mining ceases; such river systems had limited use as fisheries prior to mining because of the nature of the flow and the rock which they erode; and greater pollution damage is associated with faeces following the build-up of population which mine-related transport systems attract. Nevertheless, compromises have been adopted which entail moderate investment and include pipelines that permit ocean deposition and embankments which control the area over which deposition occurs.

Atmospheric pollution

The problems of land rehabilitation and water treatment are readily solved by modest allocations of capital, unlike the pollution abatement in smelters. The older plants chase a moving target set by new producers with ever-lower production costs and emissions. This problem is especially acute where refineries in mismanaged economies have neglected investment and are orders of magnitude away from best practice. Compliance in such cases requires the adoption of a wholly new technology and investments of several hundred million dollars. In order to be feasible, such costs require a sizeable expansion in production (doubling or trebling) in order to capture the economies of scale and thereby defray the higher capital charges of a renovated facility. Such an expansion of capacity is a paradoxical outcome of efforts to reduce the environmental impact of refining.

The potentially high cost of curbing air-borne emissions is more easily absorbed where it is designed into the initial investment than where such technology requires back-fitting. The costs of building-in pollution-abating technology from the outset do not appear to comprise a large part of the total capital cost, perhaps between 1 and 3 per cent. Even so, developing-country governments have tended to incur unnecessary costs which depress social welfare because they have adopted international standards for basic emissions in an effort to reduce the risk of accusations of environmental dumping. There is some recognition that the North American standards which are widely modelled may be excessively stringent. In addition, variations in environmental absorptive capacity provide scope for varying emission standards.

But developing-country governments face greater environmental problems from artisinal mining due to the difficulty with the enforcement of standards. Given the local importance of such small firms for employment, the Colombian Ministry of Mines proposes to encourage such mines to adopt the role of contractors to larger mines who would then take on the responsibility for curbing the environmental damage inflicted by their partners. In line with the weak sustainability stance towards environmental issues, such problems are most easily resolved under conditions of rapid economic growth, a fact which serves to underline the primacy of prudent, market-sensitive macroeconomic management in the achievement of sustainable mineral-driven development.

Achieving Social Sustainability

The concept of the *social* sustainability of mining activity emerged rapidly during the mid-1990s, when this research was undertaken. The broader definition of social capability is preferred here, extending from the national level down to the local community. At a national level, further light is shed on the differing ability of countries to pursue sound policies by a typology of developing-country States. Within this typology the autonomous authoritarian bureaucracies (Indonesia and Chile 1975–90) and the consensual democracy of Botswana are associated with sustained economic growth.

But a more common form of political State in the resource-rich countries, like the mineral economies, is the factional State. The diversion of scarce economic resources by such States into efforts to maintain their power focuses upon the capture and/or creation of rents. This leads to a distorted economy and slower and more erratic economic growth. In turn, the diminished economic prospects and uncertainty of low-growth economies cause producers to eke out their investment and to fall behind best-practice (pollution-abating) technology.

At a local level, social tensions often involve conflicts over mineral rents and the uneven distribution of the burden of the costs of environmental degradation. Mounting international concern for environmental degradation has given local communities a powerful issue with which to harness external interests to their cause. In some instances this behaviour has degenerated into crude rent-seeking in which the losers are not the companies, but rather less vocal (and often needier) communities far from the mining region. MNCs have tended to respond to such situations positively and pragmatically, aware of the risk of heightening community dependence on a depleting asset.

Compensation payments have been negotiated from the outset of mining, irrespective of government regulations, and these have been renegotiated where necessary. The more progressive firms, such as Rossing in Namibia, have set aside funds to encourage both non-mine-related skill accumulation and business diversification. Under such circumstances, central governments have been tempted to devolve responsibility for infrastructure provision (including education in some instances) to mining firms which may then find themselves in dispute with less advantaged groups which lie outside the principal mine-affected areas.

Recent conflicts in New Guinea illustrate the potential social risks involved in mining, but they also suggest some lessons. The risks include the mine exposing the relative material poverty of local communities (which may supply only a few workers to the adjacent well-paid mining towns), MNCs being embroiled in power conflicts between local communities and the central government, and MNCs becoming a target for the enmity of liberals in the developed countries who may be attracted by notions of the 'unquantifiable' existence value of 'unspoilt' wilderness and non-Western culture. *In extremis*, as in Colombia (see Chapter 14), MNCs have found themselves caught up in violent conflicts between local communities and distant national governments.

One means of reducing such conflict is for the MNC to request that an external agency perform a social audit, including evaluating the adequacy of compensation payments. A second, and closely related, solution is to increase the transparency of the distribution of the mineral rents. This calls for the measurement of the mineral rents so that not only is their distribution among firms, mine workers, and the various tiers of government clearly monitored, but also the effectiveness with which the rents are deployed is evaluated. For example, such an audit procedure, if applied to the 1995–6 dispute between Ok Tedi and local landowners, might have revealed that any increased transfer of resources to the landowners would occur, not at the expense of the MNC, but rather at the expense of poorer regions elsewhere in PNG. The audit might also have drawn attention to the 'leakage' to special interest groups in the deployment of mineral rents and also to the high rate of spending by 'top men' on immediate consumption rather than investment. In dealing with these issues it is important that MNCs continue to stress the need to avoid boosting the dependence of communities on the depleting mineral resource.

A second means of ameliorating potential conflicts is to improve the conversion of the mineral revenue stream into sustainable and equitable long-term economic growth. This reinforces the role of institutions such as an MRSF which enhance the transparency of the development process and restrict the extent to which politicians can divert mineral revenues to short-term political and personal gain. Encouragement should also be given to institutionalizing the targeting of welfare spending at lagging regions and poverty alleviation. In this context the informal sector of the economy may warrant more state assistance because its potential role as an incubator of human and social capital may render it more effective at poverty alleviation than more direct attempts by governments to upgarde workforce skills. But if the nature of the political State renders it impervious to such institutional changes, then MNCs mines will need to reinforce the enclave character of their operations and pursue strategies such as those of SPCC in Peru during the 1980s which eke out investment in the expectation of political change bringing better prospects.

Mineral Industry Management

Sustainability is promoted by the efficient management of a nation's natural resources, which includes optimum exploration and production of mineral products, maximizing rents from resources, and the allocation of rents for maximizing long-run economic growth with due regard to social welfare and environmental protection. This requires the provision of incentives for exploration and mineral development by private domestic and foreign investors, which includes a favourable financial, legal, and regulating environment. Mineral-exporting countries that maintain obstacles to mineral investment prevent the mineral industry from making the maximum sustainable contribution to economic growth.

Efficient mineral management also requires a tax system which will promote the realization of maximum resource rents and allocate the mineral revenue between government and private investors in a manner consistent with realizing the full potential of the nation's mineral reserves. An efficient mineral industry management also enforces environmental regulations that will protect the nation's natural resource endowment, while making sure that marginal social costs of protection do not exceed marginal social benefits. Finally, sustainability requires a mineral programme that is responsive to the welfare of the workers in the industry and internalizes environmental impacts on the community at large. To accomplish these objectives requires mineral management institutions that are independent of special economic and political interests, and are adequately financed and competently staffed.

14   Policy Applications: Colombia

This chapter applies the lessons from this study to Colombia which was embarking on the youthful stage of the mineral-driven cycle during the 1990s. More exactly, Colombia in the mid-1990s was a nascent mineral economy which exhibited some of the opportunities and also some of the problems associated with the youthful stage of the mineral-driven cycle. Although mining is unlikely to dominate the Colombian economy, it is sufficiently large to prompt careful evaluation of possible impacts (Planecion y Desarrollo 1994).

The chapter is structured as follows. The next section briefly traces the build-up of Colombian mineral production, focusing upon oil and coal. The third section reviews the preconditions in Colombia. The following section examines the Colombian macro-policy stance with particular regard to the key sustainability conditions: removal of distortions, sterilization of the rents, and maintenance of saving, investment, and economic diversification. The final section analyses Colombian progress towards environmental and social sustainability with regard to measures for deploying the rents, internalizing the environmental costs, and achieving social sustainability.

The Scale of the Colombian Mineral Expansion

The oil shocks of 1973 and 1979 revived interest in mineral exploration in Colombia. As a result, the decline in the economic importance of minerals which had occurred from the 1950s was reversed (Table 14.1). The revival began with the expansion of coal exports from the early 1980s, followed by oil from the mid-1980s (first the Cano Limon field and then Cusiana).

Coal production is projected to reach 50 million tonnes by 2,000, a figure which will still leave the reserve/output ratio between 90 and 320 since the reserves are estimated to be between 4.5 billion tonnes and 16 billion tonnes. Despite its rapid expansion, however, coal's added value has been disappointing because of the fall in energy prices. Four-fifths of coal production is for export, yet international coal prices have fallen well below expectations. The realized prices of $30–40 per tonne are half the levels projected and they barely cover the combined costs of operating the mines at $20 per tonne (which includes a $3 per tonne royalty), and depreciation of $8 per tonne, let alone an adequate return on capital. For example, Exxon earned only 5 per cent on the equity in its joint-venture mine at El Cerrejon with state-owned Carbocol.

Coal is not expected to generate a sizeable rent stream, but oil will. Initial oil exploration was undertaken by Occidental and BP mainly in the Llanos towards the

Table 14.1 Export composition by value, Columbia, 1910–90 (%)

	1910	1919[a]	1930	1940	1950	1960	1970	1980	1990
Coffee	31	69	54	44	78	71	64	60	21
Hides	10	11	3	1	—	—	—	—	—
Tobacco	2	2	—	—	—	—	—	—	—
Bananas	9	3	8	3	2	3	3	2	5
Flowers	—	—	—	—	—	—	—	3	3
Textiles	—	—	—	—	—	—	—	—	3
Oil	—	—	23	24	16	17	8	—	23
Coal	—	—	—	—	—	—	—	—	8
Jewels	19	1	8	25	—	—	—	2	2

[a] 1920 not available.

Sources: 1910–60 Thorp (1991); 1970–90 ECLA (1994).

Venezuelan border (Figure 14.1). Cano Limon was discovered in the early 1980s by Occidental and it doubled the country's proved reserves to 1.3 billion barrels. BP then made a larger discovery at La Cusiana which added a further 2 billion barrels. The total reserves in the mid-1990s were estimated at 3.5 billion barrels of oil with 5.2 billion m³ of natural gas. The hydrocarbon reserves may increase still further, but that will require that the country's harsh fiscal regime be reformed in order to encourage the development of new reserves north of Cusiana where technical obstacles and lawlessness are more severe (Heffner 1996). The northern reserves are 6 km deep, twice the existing level, and the wells are six times more expensive to drill. In addition, law and order is fragile as private militias, allegedly linked to the military, terrorize local residents in prospective exploration areas. In such difficult circumstances, the Colombian government needs at the very least to reduce its share of petroleum revenue from a punitive 83 per cent down to around 65–75 per cent, in line with countries such as Indonesia and Peru (Petroconsultants 1996).

The expansion in Colombian oil production since 1980 along with a projection of production to the year 2010 are shown in Figure 14.2. Total national oil output is expected to stabilize by the year 2000 at 900,000 barrels per day (b.p.d.), while an additional 150,000 b.p.d. of oil equivalent will be derived from natural gas. The expansion in production will allow oil *exports* to peak at 600,000 b.p.d. in 2000, but exports will then halve during the next decade as domestic consumption expands. At an f.o.b. price of $20 per barrel, the peak production level would generate almost $4.5 billion annually in exports. This is equivalent to 45 per cent of total Colombian exports in the mid-1990s.

Figure 14.3 summarizes the estimated production costs for the new Cusiana oilfield. It projects a rent of $3.80 per barrel, or around one-fifth of the expected price (compared with three-fifths for Botswana diamonds). The projected Colombian rent stream is similar in scale to that from the Cano Limon field over the years 1985–93 (Booz *et al.* 1995, see Table 14.2). Two revenue scenarios can be derived from the

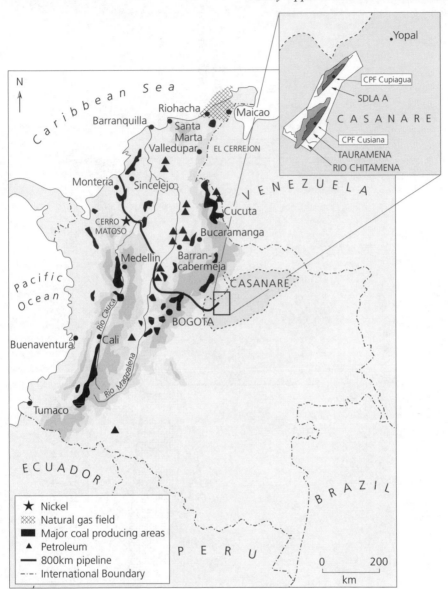

Figure 14.1 Location of economic activity in Colombia

assumptions behind the calculations in Figure 14.3. The low output projection of 600,000 b.p.d. would generate rents for the government of $832 million per year. By comparison, the rents from 50 million tonnes of coal would yield only $120 million for the State. Returning to oil, total government revenue would be further boosted by taxation of $657 million and the return on the State's equity of $1.91

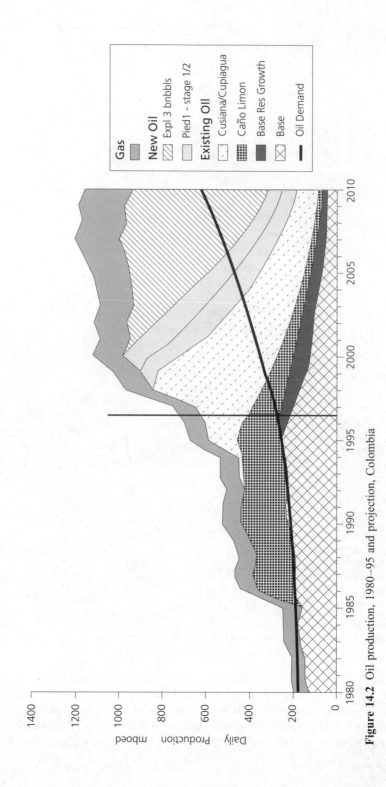

Figure 14.2 Oil production, 1980–95 and projection, Colombia

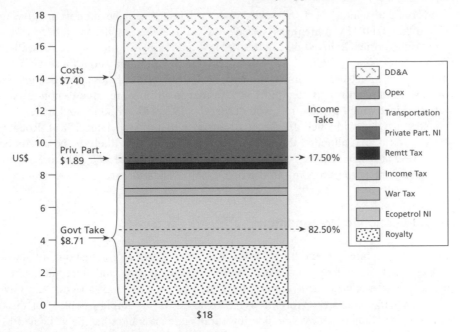

Figure 14.3 Estimated rents on Cusiana Oil

Table 14.2 Estimated Revenue stream from Cano Limon, 1985–93

	$USbn	% Total
Total revenue	9.680	100.0
Investment recovery	2.133	22.0
Operating cost	0.986	10.2
Net revenue	6.560	67.8
Net revenue	6.560	67.8
Net income of private firms	1.330	13.7
Corporation tax of private firms (40%)	0.887	9.2
Net income and tax of ecopetrol	2.217	22.9
Rents	2.126	22.0
Total government take	5.230	54.0

Source: Booz *et al.* (1995).

billion. The low oil production scenario would therefore increase government revenue by 16 per cent, equivalent to an extra 2.8 per cent of GDP in 1994. But BP's high-output scenario (Figure 14.2) would raise the contribution of oil to 24 per cent of government revenue, or around 4.2 per cent of the 1994 GDP.

Such figures imply that the scale of the oil sector will be modest relative to Colombian GDP. Even the 'high' revenue stream is much smaller than those which most oil exporters enjoyed during the 1974–8 and 1979–81 oil booms. As well as being more modest, the flow of mineral revenue to Colombia should also be more predictable, given the less militant stance of OPEC. Nevertheless, the Colombian oil revenue stream is expected to be of a similar magnitude, relative to non-mining GDP, to that which Mexico received during the 1979–81 oil boom and which that country handled with such disastrous results (Gelb and Associates 1988). Roemer (1994) warns that although the Colombian economy is less likely to be swamped by oil revenues than, say, the economy of Indonesia was after the 1973 oil shock, 'there is much more of the economy to damage should Dutch disease not be contained'.

Socio-Economic Preconditions

Colombia exhibited several highly favourable characteristics for sustainable development, notably a long-established consensual democracy and a reputation for prudent macro-management running back at least into the 1930s (when the government made extensive efforts to avoid reneging on its foreign debt). But these strengths are threatened by smouldering rural violence which has been fanned by drug-related capital flows.

Colombia's consensual democracy reflects the efforts of the two leading political parties to contain the social tensions that erupted into rural violence and guerrilla activity after World War II and threatened the country with political fragmentation. The pursuit of compromise by the Liberal and Conservative parties prompted successive Colombian governments to avoid macro-policy extremes, notably the populist booms which overexpanded the public sector in many Latin American countries.

Yet, despite the country's reputation for prudent macro-management, Colombian trade policy has been inward-oriented for many decades, with adverse long-term consequences for the competitiveness of both the agricultural and manufacturing sectors. The resulting legacy of weakness in both these sectors renders Colombia more vulnerable to the negative effects of a mineral boom. The origins of Colombian inward-orientation go back to the 1930s' depression when the government opted to promote import-substitution industry in an attempt to reduce the economy's heavy dependence on coffee. But the desired export diversification, especially into manufacturing, was slow to occur in spite of cautious macro-management which made timely corrections of trade and fiscal deficits, and also deployed investment relatively efficiently (Berry 1995).

Three efforts were subsequently made at trade reform, commencing in 1967, 1978, and 1984, the first two of which faltered in the face of external shocks. The third trade reform of 1984 was reinforced in 1991. It coincided with the expansion of Occidental's Cano Limon oilfield, whose build-up made timely contributions to taxation, economic output, and the trade balance. The oilfield is estimated to have paid some 80 per cent of its net revenues to the State, some 2.5 per cent of total government revenues 1985–93. It also contributed an average net positive trade balance of $1 billion during 1987–92. The multiplier from oil was estimated at 2.4 by Booz *et al.* (1995), who argue that without Cano Limon, Colombian GDP growth would have averaged only 2 per cent through 1986–93, as opposed to the actual rate of 3.5 per cent. But, despite the timely arrival of Cano Limon oil revenues for the pursuit of politically unpopular trade reforms, much of the manufacturing sector remained weak. Although Table 14.3 suggests that the manufacturing sector was one-tenth larger than would be expected for a country of Colombia's size and per capita income according to the Chenery and Syrquin comparator country norm, that figure flatters the sector because of the high levels of protection which the sector still received. Nor did agriculture compensate: in 1990 its size relative to GDP was barely two-thirds that of the comparator group, down from six-sevenths in the early 1970s.

In fact, Colombian agriculture has fallen far short of its very considerable potential, despite a relatively rapid growth rate during 1965–80. Its impact on the non-agricultural sector has been unusually low (Berry 1995). This unsatisfactory outcome reflects a mismatch of land use to land quality. The grassland area more than doubled between 1950 and 1986, to 26.7 million ha as a result of large-scale pasture expansion. However, pasture is a misallocation of resources because it often occupies flat, low-lying areas which are better suited to cultivation. The appeal of pasture lies not in the economic return which it gives, but in a reduced risk of violence compared with crop farming. Crop farming requires the physical presence of landowners and thereby renders them vulnerable to attack by workers and guerrillas (Heath and Binswanger 1996). Not surprisingly under such circumstances, the cropped area increased by only two-thirds to 4.3 million ha between 1950 and 1986, a meagre growth which included the encroachment of land-scarce small farmers upon the steeper Andean slopes where they grew crops that denuded the vegetation and caused soil erosion that harmed irrigation water downstream.

The productivity of farming was further depressed by policies which subsidized land-extensive animal-rearing and capital-intensive grain production. The net result of these policies and security constraints is that cropland, which is employment-intensive, occupies barely one-quarter of the potentially suitable land, whereas extensive pasture occupies twice the land believed to be favourable to it. The onset of these unfavourable developments can be traced back to the mid-1950s. Prior to that, between 1925 and 1955, the decline in primary sector employment was in line with Syrquin and Chenery (1989) expectations. But thereafter its share fell more steeply to only two-thirds its expected level (Heath and Binswanger 1995). This more recent trend implies nor only a loss of rural income but also a loss of demand for domestic manufactured goods.

The disappointingly low income- and employment-generation in agriculture might have been offset by a dynamic, labour-intensive *export*-oriented manufacturing sector. But Lieberman and Hanna (1992) show that Colombian manufacturing is characterized by outmoded management and ageing technology, with the notable exceptions of steel mini-mills and petrochemicals. In 1986, for example, the average

Table 14.3 Structural change in Colombia and Indonesia, 1972–90

Country	Year	Index	Per capita GNP ($US 1980)	Non-mining GDP (%)				Minging (% GDP)
				Agriculture	Manufacturing	Construction and utilities	Services	
Colombia	1972	Comparator	100	28.4	19.0	13.1	39.5	8.4
		Actual	970	24.5	21.8	7.2	47.9	1.7[a]
	1990	Actual	1,310	17.9	21.9	8.3	51.8	9.3[a]
		Comparator	1,300	25.7	20.0	13.6	40.7	7.9
Indonesia	1972	Comparator	300	40.1	13.0	10.4	36.3	5.5
		Actual	260	43.0	12.1	4.0	40.8	10.8
	1990	Actual	660	24.9	23.0	7.1	45.1	13.4
		Comparator	650	32.5	17.2	12.4	37.9	7.4

[a] ECLA (1994).

Sources: World Bank (1989 and 1995a); Syrquin and Chenery (1989).

effective rate of protection was 71 per cent for manufacturing as a whole compared with levels of −8 per cent for mining and agriculture (Hallberg and Takacs 1992). Export incentives came nowhere near to compensating for this anti-export bias and would have needed to be five times larger (and one-fifth of the fiscal budget) to compensate effectively.

The capital-intensive nature of Colombian manufacturing, a characteristic of most resource-rich countries (Roemer 1994), is shown in Table 14.4. This is in stark contrast to the initially more labour-intensive growth that typifies resource-deficient countries like those of East Asia (World Bank 1993*a*). Moreover, manufacturing growth tended to be strongly productivity-driven in the resource-deficient East Asian economies, once the initial rapid expansion had eliminated the labour surplus (a condition favourable to the maintenance of income equality). Colombia's rather high ICOR of 4.8 also compares unfavourably with a figure of 3.5 for South Korea as well as the ICOR of 3.5 which Chile achieved 1986–93, following its successful reforms. A World Bank (1989) analysis of the contribution of capital, labour, and total factor productivity (TFP) to economic growth in Colombia shows that, for the period 1950–86 when manufacturing output increased by 4.8 per cent annually, capital inputs grew at 4.3 per cent, labour inputs at 2.9 per cent, and TFP by merely 1.3 per cent.

In short, despite a reputation for sound macro-management which did help to avoid the debt crisis that afflicted much of the rest of Latin America in the 1980s, tardy reform of an inward-oriented trade policy combined with micro-policy distortions and simmering rural violence to misallocate land use and build a capital-intensive and inefficient manufacturing sector. Consequently, neither manufacturing nor agriculture had achieved its potential for growth and employment as oil expanded.

Sustainability of Colombia's Macro-Policy

In preparation for a modest oil boom of moderate duration, Colombian macroeconomic policy in the 1990s needed to achieve four principal objectives for sustainable development, namely:

* remove economic distortions,
* sterilize the rents,
* maintain investment rates and investment efficiency,
* minimize the loss of non-mining tradeables activity,

Removing economic distortions

Initially favourable policy developments were adversely affected by a change in government in 1994, which resulted to an overrapid expansion in public expenditure. On the favourable side, the trade reform of 1984 was intensified in 1991, as production from the Cano Limon oilfield peaked. Although the effective rate of protection

Table 14.4 Comparative manufacturing performance, 1980–93

Country	Per capita GDP (1990 $)		Value added/ Worker ($)		Manufacturing/ GDP (%)		Degree of specialization	
	1980	1993	1980	1993	1980	1993	1980	1993
Botswana	1,433	2,694	7,445	9,675	4.0	4.4	33.7	27.1
Chile	2,086	2,730	24,050	31,428	14.7	18.7[a]	16.0	10.7
Colombia	1,086	1,323[b]	13,809	19,726	23.3	17.8	14.6	13.1
Indonesia	408	669	3,497	4,949	13.0	22.4	17.6	14.7
Jamaica	1,579	1,809	9,734	10,666	16.1	17.4	18.8	19.2
Namibia								
PNG								
Peru	2,162	1,554	18,238	50,213	20.2	23.9	12.7	13.8
Trinidad and Tobago	5,960	3,987	11,099	15,042	5.2	9.3	28.3	19.3
Malaysia	1,744	2,822	8,198	14,400	21.2	26.5[b]	15.7	16.4
South Korea	2,732	6,911	9,545	43,961	29.6	26.1	9.1	10.2

[a] 1990.
[b] GDP estimate.
Source: UNIDO (1995).

was initially raised for consumer goods, partly as an interim measure while import quotas were replaced by an average effective tariff of 33.7 per cent and partly as an incentive to investment, the higher tariff was subsequently cut to 12 per cent by the end of 1995 and streamlined from a nine-level tariff structure to four levels of 5 per cent, 10 per cent, 15 per cent, and 50 per cent for cars (Hallberg and Takacs 1992; Hommen 1992). The competitiveness of exporters was also initially boosted by an 8 per cent real depreciation of the exchange rate (Hallberg and Takacs 1992).

The trade policy reforms were accompanied by financial reform which made the central bank independent with a mandate for economic stabilization and removed the central bank's monopoly of foreign capital transactions (Carrasquilla 1996). Other financial reforms included the elimination of forced investment, privatization of five banks which had been nationalized in the early 1980s, and an easing of restrictions on direct foreign investment including the financial sector. An attempt was also made to increase the flexibility of labour markets which had hitherto tended to overvalue wages within the modern sector.

Sterilization and deployment of mineral rents

Colombia has two areas of inflexibility with regard to the capture and sterilization of the mineral rents. First, Colombian mining royalties are less sensitive to profitability than is desirable so that exploration and development are discouraged and long-term mineral production may be depressed as a consequence. For example, the royalties range from 3 per cent for emeralds, through 5 per cent for copper and coal (under 3 million tonnes), to 10 per cent for larger coal mines, 12 per cent for nickel, and 20 per cent for oil. The royalty level is certainly too high in the case of oil (Figure 14.3), and also for coal, given for example the low capital return of El Cerrejon. In addition, corporate returns within mining are further squeezed by the war tax which, in the case of the oil sector, was levied at a rate of $1 per barrel (Penate 1996). Some mining companies in remote locations were also believed to make additional payments to placate the guerrillas and narco-traffickers (*Financial Times* 1995).

The second source of inflexibility for revenue sterilization arises out of the rules governing rent deployment which are too rigid to achieve effective sterilization in the way advocated, for example, by the National Planning Agency (Departmento Nacional de Planeacion 1994). This came about as a result of measures in 1992 which devolved social expenditure to local governments, effectively bypassing any sterilizing mechanisms operated by the central bank. The new measures for dispersal require that the central bank must distribute half the oil royalty to the regions and towns where the oil is produced, and the remainder to the non-producing local governments. The net result is that the central government received no more than one-sixth of the oil royalties. Also excluded from the sterilization mechanism is the corporation tax paid by both Ecopetrol and the MNCs which accrues directly to the Colombian Exchequer. However, the *equity* earnings of Ecopetrol (see Figure 14.3) are sterilized by the central bank in an offshore fund to help limit Dutch disease.

The constitutional requirements governing the disbursement of the oil royalty leave much responsibility for the level of domestic absorption with local governments which, as shown below, have tended to sanction increased spending. The inadequate sterilization of the rents has meant that the capital flows for the expansion of Cusiana, along with those attracted by economic reform and also those associated with the drug trade, have contributed to a sizeable real appreciation of the exchange rate through the 1990s.

Fiscal policy and investment levels

The adverse consequences of the inadequate sterilization of the windfall revenues could be offset if the central government were to reduce its spending. Instead, the leftward-leaning president, elected in 1994, pledged to expand government expenditure. Although the level of government spending in 1994, at 17 per cent of GDP, was still low compared even with Chile, for example, it had already risen sharply by two-fifths during the previous decade (World Bank 1996e), with a sharp jump of 17 per cent in real terms in 1991–4 (*Financial Times* 1995). The underlying rapid growth in public spending partly reflected the rising costs of combating civil disorder as drug revenues fuelled activity by both gangsters and guerrillas.

The new government proposed to raise public spending by a further 7.4 per cent of GDP over its four-year term. It planned to finance this increase by boosting the value-added tax from 14 to 18 per cent. Extra state spending included agricultural subsidies to compensate for Dutch disease effects as well as added outlays for internal security. Quite apart from the dubious economic merit of farm subsidies, given the likely duration of the oil boom, the increase in public spending exacerbated the fiscal deficit and pushed interest rates (and therefore the real exchange rate) higher still. Opposition to the increased public spending and, in particular, to the expansion of subsidies, emerged from the central bank. The central bank correctly argued that, far from boosting public expenditure, the State needed to adopt a much tighter fiscal stance, aiming for a surplus on the budget. Such tighter measures were necessary in order to more effectively sterilize the oil windfall. In the absence of appropriate fiscal adjustments, the central bank sharply boosted real interest rates. This elicited calls from some within the government for a reduction in the autonomy of the central bank, the exact opposite of what historical experience suggests is needed.

Meanwhile, levels of domestic saving also displayed a worrying trend. Although the Colombian rate of *investment* had finally risen in the late 1980s, after having stagnated around 18 per cent of GDP for several decade, the rise was due largely to higher foreign capital inflows. In fact domestic *saving*, having remained fairly constant at around 19 per cent of GDP through 1970–90, actually drifted down to barely 15 per cent by 1994, whereas a rise to 25 per cent of GDP is associated with the high-performing developing economies. This decline in domestic saving reflected a halving in *private* saving due to a combination of higher taxes and a sharp rise in asset prices which created a wealth effect not unlike that experienced

Table 14.5 Export composition, Indonesia and Colombia, 1990–3 (%)

	Indonesia	Columbia[a]
Fuels	34.5	31.5
Other minerals	3.9	0.8
Other primary	17.9	37.1
Manufactures	43.7	30.6
Textiles	3.1	10.6
Machinery	12.5	6.5

[a] 1990–2.

Source: World Bank (1995*a*).

in Chile one decade earlier (World Bank 1996*e*). The rise in asset prices was driven by the capital inflows which were engendered by the expansion of oil sector investment and the 1991 trade reforms (Williamson 1996).

Maintaining the competitiveness of the non-mining tradeables

Higher public spending, higher interest rates, and the exchange rate appreciation, stifled the benefits of the trade reforms as the oil boom accelerated. The inflow of capital triggered a real exchange rate appreciation of 25 per cent during 1991–5. This exposed the still backward manufacturing sector to global competition under difficult circumstances (Sanchez 1996). Not surprisingly, the upsurge in manufacturing investment which had occurred between 1992 and 1994 was not sustained. The high exchange rate and high interest rates of the mid-1990s therefore made it harder to secure the required improvements in manufacturing productivity and competitiveness (ibid.).

The share of total exports in GDP remained at only 15 per cent in 1994, the same as two decades earlier (World Bank 1996*e*). Fuels already provided almost one-third of Colombia's exports by the early 1990s (Table 14.5). Meanwhile, the share of manufacturing in total exports had fallen back to just over 30 per cent (of which textiles comprised one-third). Other primary products, notably coffee, bananas, and cut flowers (ECLA 1994) accounted for 37 per cent of total exports. The trade balance was in deficit at 0.6 per cent of GDP while the current account deficit was 4.5 per cent of GDP.

The coffee sector faced especial hardship in coping with the real exchange rate appreciation because it was cultivated on steep hillsides which made mechanization difficult. Since labour accounted for 75 per cent of direct production costs, it was difficult to contain costs by substituting machinery for labour (*Financial Times* 1995). Worse, diminished prosperity in the coffee-growing districts threatened to bring violence to areas that had hitherto been largely free of it. In addition, faltering coffee incomes created added opportunities for drug traffickers to launder money through the acquisition of cheap coffee land.

Nevertheless, the level of foreign capital investment continued at around 4 per cent of GDP (some four to eight times earlier levels) and the financial reserves accumulated. The best that could be expected of macro-policy was to avoid a further real appreciation of the exchange rate while seeking to speed up productivity growth to improve the long-run competitiveness of manufacturing. But this would require lower public spending and stronger sterilization measures.

Colombian Environmental and Social Sustainability

Natural capital deployment

Turning to the distribution of rents between consumption and investment, the limited size of the proven oil reserves in Colombia (and therefore, the relatively short duration of the oil revenue stream) requires that the bulk of the rent should be allocated to saving or investment. Calculations of the depletion coefficient by either the user-cost or net revenue method would yield similar advice. The situation is reversed for coal whose reserves are sufficient for more than ninety years of production but, as noted earlier, the rent is much smaller on coal than on oil.

Even with the lack of central control over oil royalty expenditure, overrapid windfall absorption is not inevitable in Colombia. This is because, under the existing dispersement mechanism, the royalties may be either invested in infrastructure or allowed to accumulate as an investment fund. Nevertheless, regional governments like that in Aucauna where the Cano Limon oilfield is located, have chosen to spend and they have become too dependent on royalty flows. There is a risk that they will not be able even to maintain the infrastructure constructed during the years of largesse as the revenues wane (Booz *et al.* 1995). Elsewhere, far from saving the inflow, the pattern of revenue absorption around Cusiana is already inflicting local Dutch disease effects (CRECE 1995). Despite such problems, reform of the inflexible royalty deployment system is unlikely to occur because the regional dispersal of the revenue is helping to reduce regional income differences in a politically fragmented country.

Internalizing costs of environmental damage

Colombia, like most developing countries, has been slow in setting up practical environmental regulations. In the 1990s, it attempted to regulate environmental improvements through a centralized ministry, in contrast to Peru and Chile which both opted to strengthen controls by consultation between sectoral ministries and business. The regulations proposed in 1993 for the Colombian mining sector were too restrictive and required reform. The regulations will extend the duration of mine leases, but they require an environmental impact plan and also a management plan within the first five years of a lease being taken up. Taxes fall due within two to three years on any part of the concession not released in order to discourage hoarding. Corporate taxes are levied at the national rate (35 per cent) on top of the mineral-specific royalties described earlier. In addition, the larger mining firms are expressly obliged to contribute to the expansion of both local skills and infrastructure.

The larger companies have had little difficulty in absorbing the costs of abating the environmental impact of mining. For example, the costs to the coal sector of complying with the environmental standards are estimated to be less than $1 per tonne (barely 3 per cent of total costs). The costs entail the use of water to contain dust emissions and the accumulation of a reserve fund (5 per cent of total investment) to rehabilitate the mine (Quijarno 1996). In the case of oil, the operator of the Cusiana field, BP, expended $60 million annually in the mid-1990s on environmental measures. Of the $60 million expended, some 10 per cent was absorbed by administration and the remainder went to capital outlays, mainly to reduce emissions from oil wells through water treatment and the disposal of waste (Heffner 1996). The oil firms are also required to replant 5 ha of forest for every hectare cut down, as with the construction of the 800-km pipeline from Cusiana to the ocean (*Financial Times* 1995). The total cost of environmental measures is around 40c. per barrel, barely 2.5 per cent of the unit cost, even after deducting the rent.

The smaller mining firms experience much more difficulty in internalizing the environmental costs and they present a challenge to the government in securing their compliance. Consequently, a National Mining Development Plan proposed to assist small and medium firms with finance as well as with technical assistance. The smaller firms are also to be encouraged to evolve from independent miners into contractors to the larger firms because the latter can absorb environmental costs more easily, be regulated more effectively, and also be responsible for the environmental impact of their small-firm contractors (Chaparro 1996).

The struggle for social sustainability

The Colombian mineral boom is expected to favour urban and middle-class groups over rural and poor groups in the absence of policy changes. Even in Indonesia, income inequality rose sharply through the 1970s despite efforts to disperse oil spending. Outside Java, real incomes stagnated during 1969–87 in those rural areas where the green revolution had a minimal effect. Moreover, Colombia lacks the Indonesian advantage of starting with a relatively equitable income distribution on the eve of its oil boom (Berry and Knaul 1994). The hardest hit areas of rural Colombia would be the non-coffee-growing regions of the Pacific and Atlantic coasts as well as parts of the Llanos. The fragile coalition of regions which makes up the country of Colombia (Atlantico, Central, Este, Pacifio, and Territorio Nacional) prompts the Colombian government to foster *regional* convergence in per capita income levels. The income gap between the richest and poorest departments narrowed from 10 : 1 in 1950 to 3 : 1 in 1989 (Cardenas and Ponton 1995).

The income gap between social classes is much higher, however, and is likely to remain so until the labour force is more fully employed. The prospects of heightened income inequality and growing urban unemployment in Colombia make it especially important to target social spending on those least likely to benefit from economic growth. This could be achieved by improving the socio-economic infrastructure of both rural areas and low-income urban zones and also by boosting skills. Even with a higher level of investment and faster employment creation, the Colombian economy will have difficulty in absorbing surplus labour. This is partly because Colombia has a fairly high rate of population growth (Berry and Knaul 1994), partly because, as in many mid-income resource-rich countries, labour costs are not adequately offset by higher productivity, and partly because of the capital-intensive nature of Colombian industrialization. Higher mineral revenues, if inadequately sterilized have the potential to intensify the Dutch disease effects and thereby exacerbate the severe social stress which Colombia exhibited in the mid-1990s. A coherent strategy for helping marginal groups is therefore required.

The adjustment to increased mineral rents is complicated for Colombia by the drug trade. Drug-related activity may have some positive effects on the rural economy, however. Whynes (1992) estimates that drug trafficking brings between $1 and $7 billion in revenues into the country. It provides between 3 and 5 per cent of Colombian employment, mostly in the cultivation of over 40,000 ha of coca and 20,000 ha of poppy plants (*Economist* 1995*b*). Whereas these contributions ease the foreign exchange constraint and boost employment, they are more than offset by negative impacts. Such negative economic impacts include fuelling inflation (Kamas 1986) and feeding rural violence so that agricultural production is warped towards extensive ranching.

The drug trade also corrodes the social capital of the country at both the national and local levels, the reverse of what is required for mineral-driven development to be socially sustainable. Its illicit nature evades legitimate government taxes, undermines law and order through the bribery of poorly paid civil servants, and funds guerrilla activity. Lawlessness boosts the costs of legitimate businesses and retards foreign investment. By mid-1996, an estimated one-third of the country was in revolt against the destruction of drug-related crops. Ransom payments on kidnap victims were believed to total $100 million annually (*Economist* 1996). Illegal activity appeared to some Colombians at least, to offer better material prospects than the legal economy.

Within the mining sector, the oil companies reported more than 200 attacks on their installations during a twelve-month period in the mid-1990s and, as a result, they were forced to rely upon the army to protect their operations. This led to accusations that BP supplied video information to the army relating to dissidents at its meetings with the local community, and also that right-wing militia groups, thought to be linked to the army, were systematically clearing local people away from prospective drilling sites (*Financial Times* 1996*g*). The oil companies also remained open to accusations that they had strengthened their relations with the distant central government and failed to establish satisfactory links with the local community. For example, BP was accused of building infrastructure to connect its heavily fortified installations, at the expense of improved provision of health and education services to the local community. Demonstrations and strikes in the drilling areas led to clashes with the police and the military and one of the first Cusiana oil rigs was burnt down.

BP responded by transferring some executives from Bogotá to the local capital of Yopal and giving greater publicity to its regional expenditure programme. BP was caught in an extremely delicate position between the government-backed troops which it required to protect its installations, and the local community into which lawless elements could blend.

Conclusions

Colombia's long-term commitment to prudent macro-management is threatened by lower private saving and increased social spending at a time when the large capital inflows associated with economic reform and the build-up of oil production are strengthening the real exchange rate. Central bank countermeasures push interest rates to very high levels so that manufacturing investment and economic growth both slow just as trade reforms expose farmers and manufacturers to international competition. This in turn, threatens to slow, or even reverse, economic diversification.

The projected low ratio of oil reserves to output implies a need to capture the bulk of the oil rents and transform them into alternative forms of capital (notably into manufacturing skills and rural infrastructure), as a critical condition for sustainable development. But the insensitivity of the oil royalty regime threatens to depress exploration and development while the devolved royalty spending limits central government control over the allocation of the rents and the rate of domestic absorption. Meanwhile, sustained rapid economic growth is required to defuse social tensions which are greatly exacerbated for Colombia by drugs money which sustains violence by guerrillas, gangsters, and kidnappers. Peasant farmers in remote regions demonstrate against government efforts to destroy their coca and poppy fields while right-wing militias engage in counter-terror activities. Increased expenditure on security raises the costs to foreign investment, distorts agricultural production, compromises central government sterilization efforts, and breeds a climate of fear and suspicion.

The unfortunate synergy of imprudent public spending, higher interest rates, Dutch disease effects, and acute social stress makes Colombian prospect for sustainable mineral-driven development unpromising. Political uncertainty linked to the alleged funding of President Samper's 1994 election campaign by the drug barons has compounded such problems, and helped to depress GDP growth by around 2 per cent per annum during 1995–7. Changed public spending priorities by the central government plus greater control of domestic windfall absorption and its targeting on the more disadvantaged groups were all urgently required in order to improve the prospects for socially sustainable development as the oil boom gathered momentum.

References

Afsah, S., Laplante, B., and Wheeler, D. (1996), 'Controlling industrial pollution: A new paradigm', *Policy Research Working Paper* 1672, Policy Research Dept., World Bank, Washington, DC.

Ahmed, S. (1989), 'Indonesia: External shocks, policy response and adjustment performance', *World Bank Discussion Paper*, World Bank, Washington, DC.

AIDAB (1993), *The Papua New Guinea Economy*, Australian International Development Assistance Bureau, Canberra.

Ambursley, F. (1983), 'Jamaica, from Michael Manley to Edward Seaga', in F. Ambursley and R. Cohen (eds.), *Crisis in the Caribbean*, Heinemann, London, 72–104.

Aljaro Uribe, M. (1994), Interview, Codelco, Santiago.

Alesina, A., and Perotti, R. (1994), 'The political economy of growth: A critical survey of recent literature', *World Bank Economic Review*, 8: 351–71.

Anglo-American Corporation (1989), *Diamond Mining in Namibia: Yesterday and Today*, Anglo-American Corporation, Johannesburg.

Applied Geology Associates (1989), *Environmental, Socio-Economic and Public Health Review: Panguna*, Applied Geology Associates Ltd, New Zealand.

Arrow, K. J. (1966), 'Discounting and Public Investment Criteria', in A. V. Kneese and S. M. Smith (eds.), *Water Resources Research*, Johns Hopkins University Press, Baltimore.

Ashley, C. (1995), 'Population dynamics, the environment and demand for water and energy in Namibia', *DEA Research Discussion Paper* 7, Directorate of Environmental Affairs, Windhoek.

—— and Garland, E. (1994), 'Promoting community-based tourism development', *Research Discussion Paper* 4, Directorate of Environmental Affairs, Windhoek.

Atkinson, G., Dubourg, R., Hamilton, K., Munasinghe, M., Pearce, D., and Young, C. (1997), *Measuring Sustainable Development: Macroeconomics and the Environment*, Edward Elgar, Aldershot.

Auty, R. M. (1983), 'MNC strategy and bauxite in the Caribbean', in J. B. Ooi (ed.), *Natural Resources in Tropical Countries*, Singapore University Press, Singapore: 73–116.

—— (1990), *Resource-Based Industrialisation: Sowing the Oil in Eight Developing Countries*, Clarendon Press, Oxford.

—— (1993), *Sustaining Development in Mineral Economies: The Resource Curse Thesis*, Routledge, London.

—— (1995a), *Patterns of Development*, Edward Arnold, London.

—— (1995b), Policy capture in Taiwan and South Korea, *Development Policy Review*, 13: 195–217.

—— (1996a), 'Sustainable development in a mature mineral economy: Botswana in the 1990s', Working Paper 96/01, Lancaster University.

—— (1996b), *Namibia: Achieving Sustainable Development*, Southern Africa Department, World Bank, Washington, DC.

—— (1997a), 'Sustaining mineral-driven development: Chile and Jamaica', in R. M. Auty and K. Brown (eds.), *Approaches to Sustainable Development*, Pinter, London: 197–219.

Auty, R. M. (1997*b*), 'Natural resource endowment, the state and development strategy', *Journal of International Development*, 9: 651–63.

—— (1997*c*), 'Does Kazakstan oil wealth help or hinder the transition?' *HIID Development Discussion Paper* 610, Harvard Institute for International Development, Cambridge, Mass.

—— (1997*d*), 'Sustainable mineral-driven development in Turkmenistan', *HIID Environment Discussion Paper* 36, Harvard Institute for International Development, Cambridge, Mass.

—— and Gelb, A. H. (1986), 'Oil windfalls in a small parliamentary democracy: Their impact on Trinidad and Tobago', *World Development*, 14: 1161–75.

Balassa, B. (1964), *Trade Prospects for Developing Countries*, Irwin, New York.

—— (1985), 'Adjusting to external shocks: The newly industrializing developing economies in 1974–76 and 1979–81', *Weltwirtschaftliches*, 121: 116–41.

—— and McCarthy, F. D. (1984), 'Adjustment policies in developing countries 1979–83: an update', *World Bank Staff Working Paper 675*, World Bank, Washington, DC.

Bank of Botswana (1994), *Annual Report 1993*, Bank of Botswana, Gaborone.

—— (1995), *Annual Report 1994*, Bank of Botswana, Gaborone.

Bank of Jamaica (1982), *Annual Report*, mimeo, Kingston, Jamaica.

Banks, G. A. (1997), 'Mountain of Desire: Mining Company and Indigenous Community at the Porgera Gold Mine', Papua New Guinea, Unpublished Ph.D. diss., Australian National University, Canberra.

Bardhan, P. (1995), 'Research on poverty and development twenty years after "Redistribution with Growth"', *Annual Bank Conference on Development Economics 1995*, World Bank, Washington, DC: 59–72.

Barnes, J. I. (1996), 'Economic characteristics of demand for wildlife viewing tourism in Botswana', *Development in Southern Africa*, 13: 1–30.

Barnett, L. J., and Morse, C. (1963), *The Economics of Natural Resource Availability*, Johns Hopkins University Press for Resources for the Future, Baltimore.

Barrow (1996), *Barrow's World Petroleum Arrangements*, Barrow, Washington, DC.

Bartelmus, P., and van Tongeren, J. (1994), *Environmental Accounting: An Operational Perspective*, Working Paper Series 1, Dept. for Economic and Social Information and Policy Analysis, United Nations, New York.

Bartelmus, P., Lutz, E., and Schweinfest, S. (1992), 'Integrated environmental and economic accounting: a case study for Papua New Guinea', *Environmental Working Paper* 54, World Bank, Washington, DC.

Bates, R. H. (1988), *Toward a Political Economy of Development: A Rational Choice Perspective*, University of California Press, Berkeley and Los Angeles Calif.

—— and Krueger, A. O. (1993), *Political and Economic Interactions in Economic Policy Reform*, Blackwell, Oxford.

Baumol, W. J. (1968), On the Social Rate of Discount, *American Economic Review*, 68: 788–802.

Beals, R. E. (1980), *Tax and Investment Policies for Hard Minerals: Public and Multinational Enterprises in Indonesia*, Ballinger, Cambridge, Mass.

Bell, J. (1986), 'Caustic waste menaces Jamaica', *New Scientist*, 3 April: 33–7.

Bernstam, M. (1991), 'The wealth of nations and the environment, *IEA Occasional Paper* 85, Institute for International Affairs, London.

Berry, R. A. (1995), 'The contribution of agriculture to growth: Colombia', in J. W. Mellor (ed.), *Agriculture on the Road to industrialization*, Johns Hopkins University Press, London: 263–306.

—— and Knaul, F. M. (1994), 'Employment, income distribution and the social sectors: Lessons for Colombia from Indonesia's oil boom experience', *Planeacion y Desarrollo* 25: 139–78.

Bhattacharya, A., and Pangestu, M. (1992) *Indonesia: Development Transformation and Public Policy*, World Bank, Washington, DC.

Bird, R. M. (1989), 'Taxation in Papua New Guinea: Backwards to the Future?' *World Development*, 17: 1145–57.

Booz, Allen, and Hamilton (1995), *Impacto Economic de Cano Limon*, mimeo, Bogotá.

Borensztein, E., Khan, M. S., Reinhart C. M., and Wickham, P. (1994), 'The behaviour of non-oil commodity prices', *IMF Occasional Paper 112*, IMF, Washington, DC.

BP (1994), *Statistical Review of World Energy 1994*, BP, London.

Brewster, H. (1994), 'Dutch disease in the age of adjustment', Paper presented to the UNCTAD Conference on Development, Environment and Mining, World Bank, Washington, DC.

Bureau of Mines (1991), *Copper*, Bureau of Mines, Washington, DC.

Cairncross, A. K. (1962), *Factors in Economic Development*, Allen & Unwin, London.

Cardenas, M., and Ponton, A. (1995), 'Growth and convergence in Colombia: 1950–89', *Journal of Development Economics*, 47: 5–37.

Carrasquilla, A. (1996), 'The changing role of the public sector: The Colombian case', *Quarterly Review of Economics and Finance*, 36 (2): 167–181.

CDM (1994), *CDM Review 1992–93*, CDM, Windhoek.

Central Statistical Office (1994), *Statistical Bulletin, Republic of Botswana*, Government of Botswana, Gaborone.

Chambers, F. (1995), Letter to Matthew Wright at the Bank of Botswana Research Dept., 23 November.

Chenery, H. B. (1961), 'Comparative advantage and development policy', *American Economic Review*, 61, March: 18–51.

—— and Strout, A. M. (1956), *Foreign Assistance and Economic Development*, AID Discussion Paper 7, Office of Programme Coordination, US Dept. of State, Washington, DC.

Chenery, H. B. and Syrquin, M. (1975), *Patterns of Development 1950–70*, Oxford University Press, Oxford.

Codelco (1991*a*), *Codelco Memoria Annual 1990*, Codelco, Santiago.

—— (1991*b*), *Codelco: Making a Future*, Codelco, Rancagua.

Coke, L. B., Weir, C. C., and Hill, V. G. (1987), 'Environmental impact of bauxite mining and processing in Jamaica', *Social and Economic Studies*, 36: 289–333.

Collier, P., and Gunning, A. W. (1996), *Policy toward Commodity Shocks in Developing Countries*, IMF Working Paper, International Monetary Fund, Washington, DC.

Coppock, J. D. (1962), *International Economic Instability*, New York McGraw Hill, New York.

Corbo, V., and de Melo, J. (1987), 'Lessons from the southern cone policy reforms', *World Bank Research Observer*, 2: 111–42.

—— and Fischer, S. (1994), 'Lessons from the Chilean stabilization and recovery', in B. P. Bosworth, R. Dornbusch, and R. Laban (eds.), *The Chilean Economy*, Brookings Institution, Washington, DC: 29–80.

Corden, M., and Neary, J. P. (1982), 'Booming sector and Dutch disease economics: a survey, *Economic Journal*, 92: 826–44.

CRECE (1995), *Construcion de un Sistema de Cuentas Economicas y Sociales para Casanare*, Centro Regional de Estudios Cafeteros y Empresariales, Manizales.

Crowson, P. C. F. (1994), 'Mineral rents, taxation and sustainability', Paper presented to the UNCTAD International Conference on Development, Environment and Mining, Washington, DC, June.

Dames and Moore (1996), *PTFI Environmental Audit Report*, mimeo, Jakarta.

Daniel, P. (1985), 'Minerals in independent Papua New Guinea: Policy and performance in the large-scale mining sector', Working Paper 85/10, National Centre for Development Studies, ANU, Canberra.

—— and Sims, R. (1986), *Foreign Investment in Papua New Guinea*, ANU, Canberra.

Dasgupta, S., Mody, A., Roy, S., and Wheeler, D. (1995), 'Environmental regulation and policy development', *Policy Research Working Paper* 1448, Washington, DC.

Davis, G. (1995), 'Learning to love the Dutch Disease: Evidence from the mineral economies', *World Development* 23 (10): 1765–79.

Debswana (1994), *Annual Report 1993*, Debswana, Gaborone.

Denevad, A. (1995), 'Responsiveness in Botswana politics: Do elections matter?' *Journal of Modern African Studies*, 33: 381–402.

Departmento Nacional de Planeacion (1994), *Fondo de Estabilizacion Petrolera*, CONEPES 2728-MINHA-DNP:UMACRO, Bogotá.

De Soto, H. (1989), *The Other Path: The Invisible revolution in the Third World*, I. B. Taurus & Co., London.

Dewdney, R. (1995), *Desertification Policy Framework: Analysis and Recommendations for Reform*, September draft, NAPCOD, Windhoek.

Dipchand, C. R. (1983), 'Flow of funds in Jamaica', *CSO Research Papers* 12: 14–33.

Domar, E. D. (1946), 'Capital expansion, rate of growth and employment', *Econometrica*, 14: 137–47.

Dornbusch, R., and Edwards, S. (1994), 'Exchange rate policy and trade strategy', in B. P. Bosworth, R. Dornbusch, and R. Laban (eds.), *The Chilean Economy*, Brookings Institution, Washington, DC: 81–115.

Douglas, P. H. (1934), *The Theory of Wages* Macmillan, New York.

Duncan, R. C., Warner, R., and Temu, I. (1995), *The Papua New Guinea Economy: Improving the Investment Climate*, Australian International Development Assistance Bureau International Development Issues 38, Commonwealth of Australia, Canberra.

ECLA (1993), *Statistical Yearbook for Latin America and the Caribbean*, ECLA, Santiago.

Economic Insights (1994), *PNG: The Role of Government in Economic Development*, International Development Issues 33, Australian International Development Assistance Bureau, Canberra.

Economist (1987), 'Peruvian economy: the other path', *The Economist*, 19 Dec.: 64–5.

—— (1993), 'Natural gems', *The Economist*, 27 Nov.: 73.

—— (1995*a*), 'Peru: The dark side of the boom', *The Economist*, 5 Aug.: 21–3.

—— (1995*b*), 'Standing guard for Uncle Sam', *The Economist*, 14 Jan.: 58.

—— (1996), 'Backlash in Latin America', *The Economist*, 30 Nov.: 25–9.

Edwards, S. (1986), 'Commodity export prices and the real exchange rate in developing countries: coffee in Colombia', in S. Edwards and L. Ahamed (eds.), *Economic Adjustment and Exchange Rates in Developing Countries*, University of Chicago Press, Chicago: ch. 7.

—— (1989), *Real Exchange Rates, Devaluation, and Adjustment*, MIT Press, Cambridge, Mass.

Eggert, R. (1994), *Mining and the Environment: International Perspectives on Public Policy*, Resources for the Future, Washington, DC.

El Serafy, S. (1989), 'The proper calculation of income from depletable natural resources', in Y. J. Ahmad, S. El-Serafy, and E. Lutz (eds.), *Environmental Accounting for Sustainable Development*, World Bank, Washington, DC: 10–18.

Enders, T. O., and Mattione, R. P. (1984), *Latin America: The Crisis of Debt and Growth*, Brookings Institution, Washington, DC.

Faini, R., and de Melo, J. (1990), 'Adjustment, investment and the real exchange rate in developing countries, *Working Paper Series* 473, Country Economics Dept., World Bank, Washington, DC.

Fajnzylber, F. (1995), 'Latin American development: From the "Black Box" to the "Empty Box"', in B. H. Koo and D. H. Perkins (eds.), *Social Capability and Long-Term Economic Growth*, Macmillan, Basingstoke: 242–65.

Far Eastern Economic Review (1985), 'Almost-ready OK Tedi', *Far Eastern Economic Review*, 15 Aug.: 104–7.

Fields, R. M. (1987), 'Jamaica: Country Environmental Profile', R. M. Fields & Associates, Kingston, Jamaica.

Financial Times (1989), 'PNG mine disrupted by renewed sabotage attacks', *Financial Times*, 18 Apr.

—— (1990), 'Chilean miners have to dig in stony ground', *Financial Times*, 10 Aug.

—— (1992), 'Cusiana biggest BP field since 1970s', *Financial Times*, 20 Oct.

—— (1994), 'Copper price seen holding gains', *Financial Times*, 28 June.

—— (1995), 'Colombia: A Survey', *Financial Times*, 9 Oct.

—— (1996*a*), 'Peru: A Survey, *Financial Times*, 7 Mar.

—— (1996*b*), 'Strikes undermine Jamaican bauxite expansion', *Financial Times*, 1 Mar.: 27.

—— (1996*c*), 'LNG project puts Trinidad and Tobago on the map', *Financial Times*, 5 Sept.: 33.

—— (1996*d*), 'Indonesia: A Survey', *Financial Times*, 25 June.

—— (1996*e*), 'Latin American Mining Survey', 22. Ap.

—— (1996*f*), 'Ok Tedi copper mine damage claim settled', *Financial Times*, 17 June: 33.

—— (1996*g*), 'Oil giant in troubled waters', *Financial Times*, 8 Nov.: 17.

—— (1997), 'PNG voters ask: Why are we no richer?' *Financial Times*, 26 June.

Findlay, R. (1990), 'The new political economy: Its explanatory power for LDCs', *Economics and Politics* 2: 193–221.

—— (1995), *Factor Proportions, Trade and Growth*, MIT Press, Cambridge, Mass.

—— and Wellisz, S. (1993), *Five Small Open Economies: The Political Economy of Poverty, Equity and Growth*, Oxford University Press, New York.

Fisher, Irving (1907), *The Rate of Interest*, New York, Macmillan.

Flatters, F., and Jenkins, G. (1986) 'Trade policy in Indonesia, mimeo, HIID, Cambridge, Mass.

Fluckiger, M. (1994), 'Interview', Comision del Cobre Chilena, Santiago.

Freeman, A. M. (1993), 'The Measurement of Environmental and Resource Values: Theory and Methods', Resources for the Future, Washington, DC.

Freeport-McMoRan (1995), *Freeport-McMoRan Annual Report 1994*, New Orleans.

Friedeberg, A. S. (1969), *United Nations Conference on Trade and Development of 1964*, Rotterdam University Press, Rotterdam.

Gaomab, M. (1994), 'Fiscal policy and employment in Namibia', *NEPRU Working Paper* 43, Namibian Economic Policy Research Bureau, Windhoek.

Garnaut, R., and Clunies-Ross, A. (1983), *Taxation of Mineral Rents*, Clarendon Press, Oxford.

Gavin, M., Hausman, R., Perotti, R., and Talvi, E. (1996), *Managing Fiscal Policy in Latin America and the Caribbean*, Working Paper Inter-American Development Bank, Washington, DC.

Gelb, A. H. and associates (1988), *Oil Windfalls: Blessing or Curse?*, Oxford University Press, New York.

Gelb, A. H., Knight, J., and Sabot, R. (1991), 'Public sector employment, rent-seeking and economic growth', *Journal of Economic Literature* 101: 1186–99.

Gillis, M. (1984), 'Episodes in Indonesian economic growth', in A. C. Harberger (ed.), *World Economic Growth*, ICS Press, San Francisco, Calif.: 231–64.

Grossman, G. (1995), 'Pollution and growth: What do we know?' in I. Goldin and L. A. Winters (eds.), *The Economics of Sustainable Development*, Cambridge University Press, Cambridge: 19–46.

Gwynne, R. N. (1985), *Industrialization and Urbanization in Latin America*, Croom-Helm, London.

Hallberg, K., and Takacs, W. (1992), 'Trade reform in Colombia: 1990–94', in A. Cohen and F. R. Gunter (eds.), *The Colombian Economy: Issues of Trade and Development*, Westview Press, Boulder, Colo.: 259–99.

Hamilton, K. (1996), 'Greening the national accounts: Valuation issues and policy uses', mimeo, Paper prepared for the International Symposium on Integrated Environmental and Economic Accounting in Theory and Practice, Tokyo, 5–8 March.

Hamilton, K., and O'Connor, J. (1994), 'Genuine saving and the financing of investment', Working Paper, Environment Division, World Bank, Washington, DC.

Harberger, A. C. (1986), 'Economic adjustment and the real exchange rate', in S. Edwards and L. Ahamed (eds.), *Economic Adjustments and Exchange Rates in Developing Countries*, University of Chicago Press, Chicago: ch. 11.

Harrison, A. (1992), 'Natural assets and national income', Working Paper 1992–34, Environment Department, World Bank, Washington, DC.

Harrod, R. F. (1939), 'An essay in dynamic theory', *Economic Journal*, 44: 14–33.

Hartman, P. (1986), 'The Role of Diamond Mining in the Economy of SW Africa/Namibia 1950–85', Unpublished M.Sc. diss., Dept. of Economics, University of Stellenbosch.

Hartwick, J. (1977), 'Intergenerational equity and the investing of rents from exhaustible resources', *American Economic Review*, 66: 972–4.

—— (1978), 'Substitution among exhaustible resources and inter-generational equity', *Review of Economic Studies*, 45: 347–54.

—— and Hageman, A. P. (1991), 'Economic depletion of mineral stocks and the contribution of El Serafy, Working Paper 1991/27, Environment Dept., World Bank, Washington, DC.

—— (1993), 'Economic depreciation of mineral stocks and the contribution of El Serafy', in E. Lutz (ed.), *Toward Improved Accounting for the Environment*, World Bank, Washington, DC.

Harvey, C. (1993), 'The role of government in the finance of business in Botswana', *IDS Discussion Paper* 337, IDS, Sussex.

—— and Jefferis, K. (1995), 'Botswana's exchange controls: Abolition or liberalization?' *IDS Discussion Paper* 348, IDS, Sussex.

—— and Lewis, S. (1990), *Policy Choice and Development Performance in Botswana*, Macmillan, Basingstoke.

Harvey, R. (1980), 'Chile's counter-revolution: A survey', *The Economist*, Centre Supplement, 2 Febr.

Hashimoto, H. (1982), 'Bauxite processing in developing countries', Commodities and Export Projects Division Working Paper 1982/2, World Bank, Washington, DC.

Heath, J., and Binswanger, H. (1996), 'Natural resource degradation effects of poverty and population growth are largely policy-induced: The case of Colombia', *Environment and Development Economics* 1: 65–83.

Heffner, M. T. (1996), Interview, Health, Safety and Environment Dept., BP Exploration, Bogotá, 4 Sept.

Hicks, J. R. (1946), *Value and Capital* (2nd edn.), Oxford University Press, Oxford.

Hill, C. B. (1991), 'Managing commodity booms in Botswana', *World Development* 19: 1185–96.

Hill, H. (1982), 'State enterprises in competitive industry: An Indonesian case study', *World Development* 10: 1015–23.

—— (1990), 'Manufacturing industry', in A. Booth (ed.), *The Oil Boom and After: Indonesian Economic Policy and Performance in the Soeharto Era*, Oxford University Press, Singapore: 204–57.

—— (1995), 'Indonesia: from "chronic dropout" to "miracle"?' *Journal of International Development* 7: 775–89.

Hirschman, Albert O. (1958), *The Strategy of Economic Development*, Yale University Press, New Haven.

Holzmann, R. (1996), 'Pension reform, financial market development and economic growth: Preliminary evidence from Chile', *IMF Working Paper* 96/94, IMF, Washington, DC.

Hommes, R. (1992), 'Challenge to the private sector in the nineties: Colombian economic policies and perspectives', in A. Cohen and F. R. Gunter (eds.), *The Colombian Economy: Issues of Trade and Development*, Westview Press, Boulder, Colo.: 87–92.

Hotelling, Harold (1931), 'The economics of exhaustible resources', *Journal of Political Economy*: 137–75.

Hughes, H. (1988), *Achieving Industrialization in East Asia*, Cambridge University Press, Cambridge.

Hughes, P., and Sullivan, M. (1989), 'Environmental impacts assessment in Papua New Guinea: Lessons for the wider region', *Pacific Viewpoint* 30: 34–55.

IADB (1993), *Economic and Social progress in Latin America*, Inter-American Development Bank, Washington, DC.

—— (1996), *Trinidad and Tobago Country Paper*, Inter-American Development Bank, Washington, DC.

IBA (1992), 'Bauxite mining and environment management at Kirkvine', IBA/EB/LIII/07/92, Kingston, Jamaicu.

International Finance Corporation (1992, 1995), *Annual Report of the IFC*, IFC, Washington, DC.

International Monetary Fund (1994), *The Behaviour of Non-Oil Commodity Prices*, IMF, Washington, DC.

—— (1996), *Macroeconomics and the Environment: Proceedings of a Seminar*, IMF, Washington, DC.

Jackson, P. T. (1993), *Cracked Pot or Copper-Bottomed Investment? Ok Tedi 1982–91*, Melanesian Studies Centre, James Cook University, Queensland.

Jackson, R. T. (1984), 'OK Tedi: Lessons hardly learnt', in C. C. Kissling *et al.* (ed.), *Regional Impacts of Resource Development*, Croom-Helm, London: 117–33.

Jaffe, A., Peterson, S. R., Portney, P. R., and Stavins, R. N. (1995), 'Environmental regulation and the competitiveness of US manufacturing: What does the evidence tell us?' *Journal of Economic Literature*, 33: 132–53.

JBI (1992), *The Bauxite/Alumina Industry and the Environment*, Jamaica Bauxite Institute, Kingston, Jamaica.

Jefferis, K. R. (1996), 'Botswana's public expenditure', mimeo, Gaborone.

Kamas, L. (1986), 'Dutch disease economics and the Colombian export boom', *World Development*, 14: 1177–98.

Karim, A. (1968), 'Economics and directional growth in the aluminium industry', mimeo, Kaiser, Oakland, Calif.

Kaufman, R. R. (1990), 'How societies change development models or keep them: Reflections on the Latin American experience in the 1930s and the postwar period', in G. Gereffi and D. Wyman (eds.), *Manufacturing Miracles*, Princeton University Press, Princeton: 110–38.

Kenen, P. B. (1994), *Ways to Reform Exchange Rate Arrangements*, International Finance Section, Princeton University, Princeton.

Keynes, J. M. (1936), *The General Theory of Employment, Interest, and Money*, Macmillan, London.

KJBC (1993), Kaiser Jamaica Bauxite Company Supplement, Co-op Printers, Kingston, Jamaica.

Killick, T. (1995), *The Flexible Economy: Causes and Consequences of the Adaptability of National Economies*, Routledge, London.

Kincaid, O. R. (1981), 'Conditionality and the use of fund resources', *Finance and Development*, 18(2), June, 26–9.

Kindleberger, C. P. (1956), *The Terms of Trade: A European Case Study*, MIT Press, Cambridge, Mass.

Kissling, C. C. *et al.* (1984), *Regional Impacts of Resource Development*, Croom-Helm, London: 117–33.

Knack, S., and Keefer, P. (1997), 'Does social capital have an economic pay-off? A cross-country comparison, *Quarterly Journal of Economics*, 112: 1250–88.

Knight, F. H. (1931), 'Professor Fisher's interest theory: A case in point', *Journal of Political Economy*, 39.

Koo, B. H., and Perkins, D. H. (1995), *Social Capability and Long-Term Economic Growth*, Macmillan, Basingstoke: 288–309.

Kopp, R. J., and Smith, V. K. (1993), *Valuing Natural Assets: The Economics of Natural Resource Damage Assessment*, Resources for the Future, Washington, DC.

Krueger, A. O. (1993), *Political Economy of Policy Reform in Developing Countries*, MIT, Cambridge, Mass.

Krugman, P. R. (1987), 'The narrow band, the Dutch disease and the competitive consequences of Mrs Thatcher', *Journal of Development Economics*, 27: 41–55.

—— (1991), *Currencies in Crises*, MIT Press, Cambridge, Mass.

Krutilla, J. V., and Fisher, A. C. (1975), *The Economics of Natural Environments: Studies in Valuation of Commodity and Amenities Resources*, Johns Hopkins University Press for Resources for the Future, Baltimore.

Kurer, O. (1996), 'The political foundations of economic development policies', *Journal of Development Studies*, 32: 645–68.

Lago, R. (1991), 'The illusion of pursuing redistribution through macropolicy: Peru's heterodox experience 1985–90', in R. Dornbusch and S. Edwards (eds.), *The Macroeconomic of Populism in Latin America*, University of Chicago Press, London: 263–330.

Lagos, G. E. (1994), 'Developing national policies in Chile', in R. Eggert (ed.), *Mining and the Environment: International Perspectives on Public Policy*, Resources for the Future, Washington, DC.

—— and Velasco, P. (1992), 'Mining and environment: the Chilean case', Working Paper, CESCO, Santiago.

—— —— (1993), 'Environmental Policies and Priorities of Selected Mining Companies in Chile: A Case Study', mimeo, CESCO, Santiago.

Lal, D. (1995), 'Why growth rates differ: the political economy of social change in 21 developing countries', in B. H. Koo and D. H. Perkins (eds.), *Social Capability and Long-Term Economic Growth*, Macmillan, London: 288–309.

—— and Myint, H. (1996), *The Political Economy of Poverty, Equity and Growth: A Comparative Study*, Clarendon Press, Oxford.

Larrain, F., Sachs J. D., and Palomino, M. (1991), 'Exchange rate and monetary policy', in C. E. Paredes and J. D. Sachs (eds.), *Peru's Path to Recovery: A Plan for Economic Stabilization and Growth*, Brookings Institution, Washington, DC: 253–74.

Leamer, E. E. (1987), 'Paths of Development in the Three-Factor, n-Good General Equilibrium Model', *Journal of Political Economy*, 95 (5): 962–3.

—— (1995), 'The Heckscher-Ohlin Model in Theory and Practice', Princeton Studies in International Finance, 77.

Leftwich, A. (1995), 'Bringing politics back in: Towards a model of the developmental state', *Journal of Development Studies*, 31: 400–27.

Leibenstein, H. (1957), *Economic Backwardness and Economic Growth*, Wiley, New York.

Lieberman, I. W., and Hanna, J. C. (1992), 'Colombia: Industrial restructuring and modernisation', in A. Cohen and F. R. Gunter (eds.), *The Colombian Economy: Issues of Trade and Development*, Westview Press, Boulder, Colo.: 119–55.

Lewis, W. A. (1952), 'Economic Development with Unlimited Supplies of Labor', *Manchester School of Economics and Social Studies*, 20.

Macbean, A. I. (1966), *Export Instability and Economic Development*, Harvard University Press, Cambridge, Mass.

McMoRan Copper and Gold (1994), *Annual Report 1993*, McMoRan Copper and Gold, New Orleans.

Mahon, J. E. (1992), 'Was Latin America too rich to prosper? Structural and political obstacles to export-led growth', *Journal of Development Studies*, 28: 241–63.

Maizels, Alfred (1968), *Exports and Economic Growth of Developing Countries*, Cambridge University Press, Cambridge.

Mankiw, N. G. (1995), 'The growth of nations', *Brookings Papers on Economic Activity*, 2: 275–326.

Marcel, M., and Solimano, A. (1994), 'The distribution of income and economic adjustment', in B. P. Bosworth, R. Dornbusch, and R. Laban (eds.), *The Chilean Economy*, Brookings Institution, Washington, DC: 217–55.

Marfan, M., and Bosworth, B. P. (1994), 'Saving, investment and economic growth', in B. P. Bosworth, R. Dornbusch, and R. Laban (eds.), *The Chilean Economy*, Brookings Institution, Washington, DC, 165–215.

Martyn, P. (1992), *Bauxite Mine Rehabilitation Survey*, International Primary Aluminium Institute, London.

Matsuyama, K. (1992), 'Intercultural productivity, comparative advantage, and economic growth, *Journal of Economic Theory*, 58: 317–34.

Maxwell Stamp PLC (1994), *Namibia, Trade Policy Reform Study: Phase I Report, 3*, Maxwell Stamp PLC, London.

Meadows, D. H., Meadows, D., Randers, J., and Behrens, W. (1972) *The Limits to Growth*, University Books, New York.

Meller, P., O'Ryan, R., and Solimano, A. (1996), 'Growth, equity and the environment in Chile: issues and evidence', *World Development* 24: 255–72.

Michaely, M. (1962), *Concentration in International Trade*, North Holland, Amsterdam.

Mikesell, R. F. (1968), *The Economics of Foreign Aid*, Aldine Press, Chicago.

—— (1975), *Foreign Investment in Copper Mining*, RFF, Washington, DC.

—— (1977), *The Rate of Discount for Evaluating Public Projects*, American Enterprise Institute for Public Policy Research, Washington, DC.

Mikesell, R. F. (1979), *The World Copper Industry*, Johns Hopkins University Press for Resources for the Future, Baltimore.

—— (1987), *Foreign Dependence and National Security*, University of Michigan Press, Ann Arbor.

—— and Williams, L. (1992), *The International Banks and the Environment, From Growth to Sustainability: An Unfinished Agenda*, Sierra Books, San Francisco.

Miller, P. (1995), *Diamonds*, Yorkton Securities, London.

Milliman, S. R., and Prince, R. (1989), 'Firm incentives to promote technological change in pollution control', *Journal of Environmental Economics and Management*, 17: 247.

Ministry of Finance (1989), Gastos, Ingresos y Deficit Fiscal 1970–88, Budget Office, Ministry of Finance, Santiago.

Ministry of Finance and Development Planning (1991), *National Development Plan 7: 1991–1997*, Government Printer, Gaborone.

—— (1994), *Mid-Term Review of NDP 7*, Government Printer, Gaborone.

Ministry of Production Mining and Commerce (1994), Commissioner of Lands Office, Kingston, Jamaica.

Moran, C. (1987) 'Economic stabilization and structural transformation: Lessons from the Chilean experience 1973–87, *World Development*, 17: 491–502.

Moran, L. (1996), Interview, Vice-President, CEPRI, Centromin, Lima.

Morande, F. G. (1996), 'Savings in Chile: What went right?' *Development Policy*, IADB, Washington, DC.

Morgan, T. (1959), 'The long-run terms of trade between agriculture and manufacturing', *Economic Development and Cultural Change*, 7, Oct.

Munoz, G. (1994), Interview, Codelco, Chile.

Neary, P. J., and S. N. van Wijnbergen (1986), *Natural Resources and the Macro Economy*, MIT Press, Cambridge, Mass.

Nelson, R. R. (1956), 'A theory of the low-level equilibrium trap in underdeveloped countries', *American Economic Review*, 46: 894–908.

Neufville, L. N. (1993), 'The impact of mining on occupational safety and health and the environment', Paper presented at Mining-Tech 1993, Lulea, Sweden.

New York Times (1995), 'In Peru, a fight for fresh air', 9 Sept.

Norberg, H., and Blomstrom, M. (1993), 'Dutch disease and management of windfall gains in Botswana', in M. Blomstrom and M. Lundahl (eds.), *Economic Crisis in Africa: Perspectives on Policy Responses*, Routledge, London: 162–78.

Nordhaus, W. D. (1992), 'Is growth sustainable? Reflections on the concept of sustainable growth', mimeo, Paper prepared for the International Economic Association, Varenna.

Norgaard, R. (1994), *Development Betrayed: The End of Progress and a Co-Evolutionary Revisioning of the Future*, Routledge, London.

North, D. C. (1963), 'Aspects of economic growth in the United States, 1815–1860', in B. E. Supple (ed.), *Experiences of Economic Growth*, Random House, New York.

Nurkse, R. (1957), *Problems of Capital Formation in Underdeveloped Countries*, Oxford University Press, New York.

O'Brien, P. J. (1997), 'Global processes and the politics of sustainable development in Colombia and Costa Rica', in R. M. Auty and K. Brown (eds.), *Approaches to Sustainable Development*, Pinter, London: 169–94.

Ohlin, D. (1967), *International and Interregional Trade*, Harvard Economic Studies, Cambridge, Mass.

Ojeda, J. M. (1994), Interview, La Escondida, Antofagasta.

Partowidagdo, W. (1993), 'Petroleum resource accounting and energy policy in Indonesia', *Jurnal Ekonomi Lingkungan*, Jan.: 41–52.

Paredes, C. E. (1990*a*), 'The behaviour of the public sector in Peru 1970–85: A macroeconomic approach', mimeo, Brookings Institution, Washington, DC.

—— (1990*b*), 'Trade policy and industrialization in Peru', mimeo, Brookings Institution, Washington, DC.

—— and Sachs, J. D. (1991), *Peru's Path to Recovery*, Brookings Institution, Washington, DC.

Pargal, P. and Wheeler, D. (1996), 'Informal regulation of industrial pollution in developing countries: Evidence from Indonesia', *Journal of Political Economy* 104: 1314–27.

Pasco-Font, A. (1996), Interview, Administrative Director, GRADE, Lima.

Pearce, D., Hamilton, K., and Atkinson, G. (1996), 'Measuring sustainable development: progress on indicators, *Environment and Development Economics*, 1: 85–101.

Penate, A. (1996), Interview, Government Liaison Department, BP Exploration, Bogotá, 4 Sept.

Petroconsultants (1996), *Review of Petroleum Fiscal Regimes*, Petroconsultants (UK) Ltd, London.

Pincock, Allen & Holt Inc. (1995), *1995 Copper Supply Cost Summary*, Pincock, Allen & Holt Inc., New York.

Pinto, B. (1987), 'Nigeria during and after the oil boom: A comparison with Indonesia', *World Bank Economic Review*, 1: 419–25.

Planecion y Desarrollo (1994), Lecciones de Indonesia, *Planeacion y Desarrollo*, May special edition, 25: 13–208.

Planning Institute of Jamaica (1994), *Economic and Social Survey Jamaica 1993*, Government of Jamaica, Kingston, Jamaica.

Prebisch, R. (1964), *Towards a New Trade Policy for Development*, Proceedings of the United Nations Conference on Trade and Development, I-VIII, United Nations, New York.

Putnam, R., with Leonardi, R., and Nanetti, R. F. (1993), *Making Democracy Work*, Princeton University Press, Princeton.

Quijarno, R. (1996) Interview, Environmental Unit, Ministry of Mines, Bogotá, 3 Sept.

Radetzki, M. (1990), *A Guide to Primary Commodities in the World Economy*, Basil Blackwell, Cambridge.

—— (1992) 'Economic development and the timing of mineral exploitation', in J. E. Tilton (ed.), *Mineral Wealth and Economic Development*, Resources for the Future, Washington, DC.

Ranis, G., and Mahmood, S. (1992), *The Political Economy of Development Policy Change*, Blackwell, Oxford.

Reed, D. (1996), *Structural Adjustment, the Environment, and Sustainable Development*, Earthscan, London.

Repetto, W. (1992), 'Accounting for environmental assets', *Scientific American*, 266 (6): 64–70.

—— Magrath, W. Wells, M, Beer, C., and Rossini, F. (1989), *Wasting Assets, Natural Resources in the National Income Accounts*, World Resources Institute, Washington, DC.

Robinson, R. J., and Schmitz, L. (1989), 'Jamaica: Navigating through a troubled decade', *Finance and Development*, 26 (4): 30–3.

Roemer, M. (1994), 'Dutch disease and economic growth: legacy of Indonesia', *Planeacion y Desarrollo* 25: 67–79.

—— (1996), 'Could Asian Policies Propel African Growth?' Development Discussion Paper 543, Harvard Institute for International Development, Cambridge MA.

Romer, P. A. (1986), 'Increasing returns and long-run growth', *Journal of Political Economy*, 94: 1102–39.

Rosenstein-Rodan, P. (1943), 'Problems of Industrialization of Eastern and South-Eastern Europe', *Economic Journal*, 53: 202–11.

Rossini, R. and Paredes, C. E. (1991), 'Foreign trade policy', in C. E. Paredes and J. D. Sachs (eds.), *Peru's Path to Recovery: A Plan for Economic Stabilization and Growth*, Brookings Institution, Washington, DC: 275–98.

Rostow, W. W. (1956), 'The take-off into self-sustained growth', *Economic Journal*, 66: 25–48.

Rugoff, K. (1996), 'The purchasing power parity puzzle', *Mineral Economics Literature*, June: 647–68.

Sachs, J. D. (1985), 'External debt and macroeconomic performance in Latin America and East Asia', *Brookings Papers on Economic Activity*, 2: 529–73.

—— (1989), 'Social conflict and populist policies in Latin America', *NBER Working Paper* 2897, National Bureau of Economic Research, Cambridge, Mass.

—— and Warner, A. M. (1995a), Economic Convergence and Economic Policy, *NBER Working Paper No. 5039*, NBER, Cambridge, Mass.

—— —— (1995b), 'Natural resources and economic growth', mimeo, HIID, Cambridge, Mass.

Saleh, K., Sugiarto, Safuddin, L., Purwadi, B., and Sudartono (1993), 'Oil and natural gas resources', in S. T. Djajadiningrat, Suparmoko, M. and Ratranngsih, M. (eds.) *Natural Resource Accounting for Sustainable Development*, Central Bureau of Statistics, Jakarta.

Salmon, M. (1987), 'Land utilization within Jamaica's bauxite land economy', *Social and Economic Studies*, 36: 57–92.

Samuelson, P. (1948), 'International trade and equalization of factor prices', *Economic Journal*, 58: 111–31.

Sanchez, F. J. (1996), Interview, Macroeconomic Analysis Unit, Departmento de Nacional Planeacion, Bogotá, 6 Sept.

Schydlowsky, D. M. (1986), 'The tragedy of lost opportunity in Peru', in J. Hartlyn and S. A. Morley (eds.), *Latin American Political Economy; Financial Crisis and Political Change*, Westview Press, Boulder, Colo.: 217–42.

Scott, C. D. (1990), 'Cycles, crisis and classes: The state and capital accumulation in Peru 1963–84, in C. Anglade and C. Fortin (eds.), *The State and Capital Accumulation in Latin America*, Macmillan, London: 106–48.

Sharpley, J., Lewis, S., and Harvey, C. (1990), 'Botswana', in R. C. Riddell (ed.), *Manufacturing Africa*, ODI, London: 73–108.

Sigwele, H. K. (1993), 'Food self-sufficiency versus food security: Which way forward?' Paper presented to the Botswana Society, mimeo, Ministry of Agriculture, Gaborone.

—— (1996), 'Strategic economic facts about Botswana's precious resource', mimeo, Ministry of Agriculture, Gaborone.

SIJ (1994), *National Income and Product 1992*, Statistical Institute of Jamaica, Kingston.

Smith, W. S. (1993), 'Chile and copper', *The Lamp*, 75 (2); 1–9.

Sheahan, J. (1994), 'Peru returns towards an open economy', *World Development*, 22: 911–23.

Smith, H. (1995), 'Industry policy in East Asia', *Asia-Pacific Economic Literature* 9 (1): 17–39.

Sodersten, B. (1985), 'Mineral-led development: The political economy of Namibia', in M. Lundahl (ed.), *The Primary Sector in Economic Development*, Croom-Helm, Beckenham: 206–17.

Solow, R. M. (1974), 'Intergenerational Equity and Exhaustible Resources', *Review of Economic Studies*, 41: 29–45.

SPCC (1996), Southern Peru Copper Corporation, *Annual Report 1995*, SPCC, Lima.

Stallings, B. (1990), 'Politics and economic crisis: A comparative study of Chile, Peru and Colombia', in J. Nelson (ed.), *Economic Crisis and Policy Choice*, Princeton University Press, Princeton: 13–67.

Stern, D. I. (1994), 'Is mining income sustainable income in developing countries?' Working Paper, Dept. of Environmental Economics and Environmental Management, University of York, York.

Stiglitz, J. E. (1979), 'A neoclassical analysis of the economics of natural resources', in V. K. Smith (ed.), *Scarcity in Growth Reconsidered*, JHUP for RFF Baltimore.

—— and Uy, M. (1996), 'Financial markets, public policy and the East Asian miracle', *World Bank Research Observer*, 11: 249–76.

Stone, C., and Wellisz, S. (1993), 'Jamaica', in R. Findlay and S. Wellisz (eds.), *Five Small Open Economies: The Political Economy of Poverty, Equity and Growth*, Oxford University Press, New York: 140–218.

Suparmoko, M., and Ratnaningsih, M. (eds.), *Natural Resource Accounting for Sustainable Development*, Central Bureau of Statistics, Jakarta: 51–60.

Syrquin, M., and Chenery, H. B. (1989), 'Patterns of Development 1950 to 1983', *World Bank Discussion Paper* 41, World Bank, Washington, DC.

Tarnawiecki, A. (1996), Interview, Privatization Consultant, COPRT, Petroperu, Lima.

Teter, D., Vincent, J., and Wiryanto, K. (1995), 'Coal mining in Indonesia: Environmental impacts, sustainability and economic development', *Environment Discussion Paper* 2, HIID, Cambridge, Mass.

Thac, C. D., and Lim, D. (1984), 'Papua New Guinea's tax performance 1965–77', *World Development*, 12: 451–9.

Thorp, R. (1987), 'Trends and cycles in the Peruvian economy', *Journal of Development Economics* 27: 355–74.

—— (1991), *Economic Management and Economic Development in Peru and Colombia*, Macmillan, London.

Tilton, J. (1994), 'Mining wastes and the polluter pays principle in the U.S.', in R. Eggert (ed.), *Mining and the Environment: International Perspectives on Public Policy*, Washington, DC.

—— Millett, J., and Ward, R. (1986), *Mineral and Mining Policy in Papua New Guinea*, Institute of National Affairs, Port Moresby, PNG.

UNIDO (1995), *Industrial Development: Global Report 1995*, Oxford University Press, Oxford.

US Department of Commerce (1994), *Natural Resource Accounting*, Department of Commerce, Washington, DC.

US Embassy (1994), *Minerals Report 1994*, US Embassy, Jakarta.

Valentine, T. R. (1993), 'Drought, Transfer entitlements, and income distribution: The Botswana experience', *World Development*, 21: 109–26.

Valenzuela, L. F. (1994), Interview, Compania Minera Disputada de las Condes, Santiago.

Van Tongeren, J. *et al.* (1991), 'Integrated environmental and economic accounting: A case study for Mexico, *Environment Working Paper* 50, World Bank, Washington, DC.

Varangis, P., Akiyama, T., and Mitchell, D. (1995), *Managing Commodity Booms and Busts*, World Bank, Washington, DC.

Vincent, J., Panayoutou, T., and Hartwick, J. (1995), *Resource Depletion and Sustainability in Small Open Economies*, Environmental Discussion Paper 8, Harvard Institute for International Development, Cambridge, Mass.

Warhurst, A. (1994*a*), 'The limitations of environmental regulation in mining', in R. G. Eggert (ed.), *Mining and The Environment: International Perspectives on Public Policy*, Resources for the Future, Washington, DC. 133–72.

—— (1994*b*), *Environmental Degradation from Mining and Mineral Processing in Developing Countries: Corporate Responses and National Policy*, OECD, Paris.

Webb, R. (1991), 'Prologue', in C. F. Paredes and J. D. Sachs (eds.), *Peru's Path to Recovery: A Plan for Economic Stabilization and Growth*, Brookings Institution, Washington, DC: 1–12.

Webster, A. (1993), 'Comparative advantage and the long-run Dutch disease effects: The international trade of Trinidad and Tobago', *Development Policy Review* 11: 153–65.

Weir (1982), 'Impact of bauxite alumina industries on the Jamaican environment', Weir Consulting Services Ltd, Kingston.

Wellington, K. E. (1986), 'Utilization of bauxite lands for agriculture', *Journal of the Geological Society of Jamaica*, 53, 49–54.

Wellisz, S., and Saw, P. L. S. (1993), 'Mauritius', in R. Findlay and S. Wellisz (eds.), *The Political Economy of Poverty, Equity and Growth: Five Small Open Economies*, Oxford University Press, New York: 219–55.

Westley, G. (1995), 'Economic volatility from natural resource endowments', *Development Policy*, Inter-American Development Bank, Washington, DC.

Wheeler, D. (1984), 'Sources of stagnation in sub-Saharan Africa', *World Development* 12: 1–23.

Whynes, D. K. (1992), 'The Colombian cocaine trade and the war on drugs', in A. Cohen and F. R. Gunter (eds.), *The Colombian Economy: Issues of Trade and Development*, Westview Press, Boulder, Colo.: 329–52.

Williamson, J. (1996), *The Crawling Band as an Exchange Rate Regime*, Institute for International Economics, Washington, DC.

Winter-Nelson, A. (1995), 'Natural resources, national income and economic growth in Africa', *World Development* 22: 1507–19.

Woo, W. T., Glassburner, B., and Nasution, A. (1994), *Macroeconomic Crises and Long-Term growth in Indonesia 1965–90*, World Bank, Washington, DC.

Wood, A. (1994), *North-South Trade, Employment and Inequality*, Clarendon Press, Oxford.

World Bank (1978), *Papua New Guinea: Its Economic Situation and Prospects for Development*, World Bank, Washington, DC.

—— (1982), *Papua New Guinea: Selected Development Issues*, World Bank, Washington, DC.

—— (1986), *Trinidad and Tobago: Issues and Options in The Energy Sector*, Report 5930-TR, World Bank, Washington, DC.

—— (1987), *Chile: Adjustment and Recovery*, Report 6726-CH, World Bank, Washington, DC.

—— (1988*a*) *Environmental Guidelines*, World Bank, Washington, DC.

—— (1988*b*), *Papua New Guinea: Policies and Prospects For Sustained and Broad-Based Growth*, vols. 1 and 2, World Bank, Washington, DC.

—— (1988*c*), *Trinidad and Tobago: A Program for Policy Reform and Renewed Growth*, World Bank, Washington, DC.

—— (1989), *Colombia: Industrial Sector Report*, No. 7921-CO, World Bank, Washington, DC.

—— (1992*a*), *Namibia: Poverty Alleviation with Sustainable Growth*, World Bank, Washington, DC.

—— (1992*b*) *World Development Report 1992*, Oxford University Press, New York.

—— (1993*a*), *The East Asian Miracle: Economic Growth and Public Policy*, World Bank, Washington, DC.

—— (1993*b*), *Jamaica: Economic Issues and Environmental Management*, World Bank, Washington, DC.

—— (1994*a*), *World Development Report 1994*, Oxford University Press, New York.

—— (1994*b*), *Public Expenditure Review: Namibia*, Southern Africa Dept., World Bank, Washington, DC.

—— (1994*a*), *Indonesia: Stability, Growth and Equity in Repelita IV*, Report 12857-IND, World Bank, Washington, DC.

—— (1994*b*), *Market Outlook for Major Energy Products, Metals and Mineral*, World Bank, Washington, DC.

—— (1994*c*), *Chile, Managing Environmental problems: Economic Analysis of Selected Issues*, Report 13061-CH, World Bank, Washington, DC.

—— (1994*d*), *Indonesia Environment and Development: Challenges for the Future*, Report 12083-IND, World Bank, Washington, DC.

—— (1994*e*), *Market Outlook for Major Energy Products, Metals and Minerals*, World Bank, Washington, DC.

—— (1994*f*), *Chile, Managing Environmental Problems: Economic Analysis of Selected Issues*, World Bank, Washington, DC.

—— (1995*a*), *World Tables 1995*, World Bank, Washington, DC.

—— (1995*b*), *Trinidad and Tobago: Poverty and Unemployment in an Oil-Based Economy*, World Bank, Washington, DC.

—— (1995*c*), *Monitoring Environmental Progress: A Report on Work in Progress*, Environmentally Sustainable Development, World Bank, Washington, DC.

—— (1996*a*), *A Mining Strategy for Latin America and the Caribbean*, Technical Paper 345, World Bank, Washington, DC.

—— (1996*b*), *Annaul Report 1996*, World Bank, Washington, DC.

—— (1996*c*), *Environment Matters*, World Bank, Washington, DC.

—— (1996*d*), *Trinidad and Tobago: Macroeconomic Assessment and Review of Public Sector Reform and Expenditures, The Changing Role of the State*, World Bank, Washington, DC.

—— (1996*e*), *World Development Report 1996*, World Bank, Washington, DC.

—— (1997), *Monitoring Environmental Progress: Expanding the Measure of Wealth*, Environment Department, World Bank, Washington, DC.

WRI (1992), *World Resources 1992–93*, Oxford University Press, Oxford.

—— (1994), *World Resources 1994–95*, Oxford University Press, Oxford.

Wright, M. (1995), 'The reservation principle in sustainable budgeting: The case of Botswana', *Bank of Botswana Research Bulletin*, 13 (1): 1–21.

Young, A. (1995), 'The tyranny of numbers: Confronting the statistical realities of the East Asian miracle', *Quarterly Journal of Economics*, 110: 641–80.

Young, A. N. (1916), *The Single Tax Movement in the United States*, Princeton University Press, Princeton.

Young, C. E., and da Motta, R. S. (1995), 'Measuring sustainable income from mineral extraction in Brazil', *Resources Policy*, 21: 113–25.

Index